CW01509062

Auto/Biography and Auto/Eth

Praxis of Research Method

BOLD VISIONS IN EDUCATIONAL RESEARCH
Volume 2

series editors

Kenneth Tobin and Joe Kincheloe - *The Graduate Center, City University of New York, USA*

editorial board

Heinz Sunker, *Universität Wuppertal, Germany*

Peter McLaren, *University of California at Los Angeles, USA*

Kiwan Sung, *Woosong University, South Korea*

Angela Calabrese Barton, *Teachers College, New York, USA*

Margery Osborne, *Centre for Research on Pedagogy and Practice, Nanyang Technical University, Singapore*

W.-M. Roth, *University of Victoria, Canada*

scope

Bold Visions in Educational Research is international in scope and includes books from two areas: *teaching and learning to teach* and *research methods in education*. Each area contains multi-authored handbooks of approximately 200,000 words and monographs (authored and edited collections) of approximately 130,000 words. All books are scholarly, written to engage specified readers and catalyze changes in policies and practices.

Defining characteristics of books in the series are their explicit uses of theory and associated methodologies to address important problems. We invite books from across a theoretical and methodological spectrum from scholars employing quantitative, statistical, experimental, ethnographic, semiotic, hermeneutic, historical, ethnomethodological, phenomenological, case studies, action, cultural studies, content analysis, rhetorical, deconstructive, critical, literary, aesthetic and other research methods.

Books on *teaching and learning to teach* focus on any of the curriculum areas (e.g., literacy, science, mathematics, social science), in and out of school settings, and points along the age continuum (pre K to adult). The purpose of books on *research methods in education* is **not** to present generalized and abstract procedures but to show how research is undertaken, highlighting the particulars that pertain to a study. Each book brings to the foreground those details that must be considered at every step on the way to doing a good study. The goal is **not** to show how generalizable methods are but to present rich descriptions to show how research is enacted. The books focus on methodology, within a context of substantive results so that methods, theory, and the processes leading to empirical analyses and outcomes are juxtaposed. In this way method is not reified, but is explored within well-described contexts and the emergent research outcomes. Three illustrative examples of books are those that allow proponents of particular perspectives to interact and debate, comprehensive handbooks where leading scholars explore particular genres of inquiry in detail, and introductory texts to particular educational research methods/issues of interest to novice researchers.

BOLD VISIONS IN EDUCATIONAL RESEARCH

Auto/Biography and Auto/Ethnography
Praxis of Research Method

W.-M. Roth

Applied Cognitive Science, University of Victoria, Canada

SENSE PUBLISHERS
ROTTERDAM / TAIPEI

A C.I.P. record for this book is available from the Library of Congress.

ISBN 90-77874-04-6

Published by:
Sense Publishers,
P.O. Box 21858,
3001 AW Rotterdam,
The Netherlands

Printed on acid-free paper

All Rights Reserved
© 2005 Sense Publishers

No part of this work may be reproduced, stored in a retrieval system, or transmitted in any form or by any means, electronic, mechanical, photocopying, microfilming, recording or otherwise, without written permission from the Publisher, with the exception of any material supplied specifically for the purpose of being entered and executed on a computer system, for exclusive use by the purchaser of the work.

Printed in the UK.

Contents

Contributors

Christiane Kraft Alsop teaches in the intercultural relations program at Lesley University, Cambridge, Massachusetts, and works as a freelance writer. Her current research interests focus on methodology and auto/ethnography. She is writing an auto/ethnographic novel *The Ideology of Love*.

Angela Calabrese Barton is an associate professor of science education at Teachers College Columbia University in New York City. Her research focuses on urban science education from feminist and critical perspectives.

Franz Breuer is a professor of psychology at the University of Münster, Germany. His main research fields are qualitative research methodology and methods, socialization, and organizational development from an interdisciplinary perspective.

Margaret Eisenhart is the University Distinguished Professor in the School of Education at the University of Colorado-Boulder. She also holds the Bob and Judy Charles Endowed Chair in Education. Her research focuses on anthropology and education, ethnographic research methods, and women in science.

Carolyn Ellis is a professor of communication and sociology in the Department of Communication at the University of South Florida. Her research focuses on emotions, relationships, loss, and grief from a qualitative and auto/ethnographic perspective.

David R. Geelan is an associate professor of science education in the Department of Secondary Education at the University of Alberta. He has research interests in teacher expertise and explanatory frameworks in science education, web-based and other computer-mediated forms of learning, epistemology and the philosophy of science, and has used auto/ethnographic fictionalized narratives to explore teaching and learning.

Joe L. Kincheloe is professor of education at the City University of New York Graduate Center. His research focuses on the ways in which pedagogy, social theory, research, power, curriculum, and cognition intersect. His major publications address these intersections in relation to knowledge production and its political dimensions.

Stuart Lee is currently working as a science and technology policy analyst for the Canadian federal government in Ottawa. His work includes issues of the so-called "ethical" development of emerging technologies, science knowledge communication, and building and maintaining networks to foster knowledge and create new hybrid understandings.

Judith Anne McGonigal is a fifth grade teacher in the Haddonfield Public School District in New Jersey, an adjunct instructor in the professional development program at the University of Pennsylvania, and a lecturer in the teacher preparation program at Rutgers-Camden University. As a reflective practitioner, her focus has been on documenting how communities of teachers, students, and parents, functioning as colearners, coteachers, and coresearchers, construct their own best practices for science and literacy learning.

Sharon E. Nichols is an associate professor of science education at the University of Alabama. Her research has focused on epistemological and cultural aspects of elementary science teacher education drawing on feminist, sociocultural, and narrative methodologies as a basis for research collaboration and re-presentation.

Chaim Noy is teaching in the Department of Communication at the Hebrew University of Jerusalem. His research interests include narrative, performance, identity, gender, social construction, sociolinguistics, ethnography, experimental and creative writing, tourism, and Israeli society.

Margery Osborne is an associate professor at the Centre for Research on Pedagogy and Practice, Nanyang Techological University, Singapore and at the University of Illinois at Urbana-Champaign. Her research focuses on pedagogical issues in science education and science education reform contextualized within emergent local needs shaped by a global economy.

Les Pereira is a lecturer in education at Edith Cowan University in Western Australia. His doctoral thesis was a reflexive self-study informed by integral philosophy. Les' research engages studies of transformative education, ethical practice, arts-based research, consciousness, and the nexus between the individual and the collective.

Wolff-Michael Roth is Lansdowne Professor of Applied Cognitive Science at the University of Victoria. His research focuses on knowing and learning in science and mathematics across the lifespan taking an interdisciplinary approach and drawing on a broad range of methods from the disciplines of applied cognitive science, anthropology, linguistics, social psychology, and sociology.

Elisabeth Settelmaier is a lecturer in curriculum studies in the Department of Education at Curtin University of Technology in Perth, Western Australia. Her research interests lie in the areas of the cultural contexts of curriculum, multicultural education, and teaching and learning of ethics and values in science education. Elisabeth's research is primarily interpretive and draws from a variety of methodologies such as auto/ethnography, auto/biography, and phenomenology.

Peter Taylor is an associate professor of transformative education at Curtin University of Technology. His research focuses on the professional development of teachers of science and mathematics and the contextualization of science and mathematics education in transitional cultures. Of particular interest to him is the use of life-writing and auto/ethnography to explore alternative knowledge systems.

Deborah J. Tippins is a professor of science education at the University of Georgia. Her research utilizes narrative and de-colonizing methodologies to explore questions related to teacher knowledge and belief, community-based science education, and culturally relevant science teaching and learning.

Kenneth Tobin is Presidential Professor of Urban Education at The Graduate Center of The City University of New York. His research is concerned with understanding teaching and learning to teach in urban schools.

I

Introduction

1   Auto/Biography and Auto/Ethnography: Finding the Generalized Other in the Self

Wolff-Michael Roth

Auto/biography and auto/ethnography already have had histories as research strategies and tool kits in other domains, but have yet to be explored as such in education. I provide the sketch of an argument where the use of auto/biography, paired with radical doubt, is legitimated as a strategy to arrive at intersubjectivity thereby avoiding false claims to objectivity and failure-prone inner (hyper) subjectivity. This argument is used to contextualize the contributions to this thematic issue on auto/biography and auto/ethnography in respect to education and educational research.

Seeing the title of this book, readers might have wondered why there is a slash that separates auto, on the one hand, and biography and ethnography, on the other. Whereas I am not certain what the reasons are for others, I use the slash in writing auto/biography and auto/ethnography because of my dialectical training and experience. Thus, the individual and its society—which is the seat of the social and the cultural—mutually presuppose one another. They stand in a dialectical relationship. Without the individual, there is no society; yet without society, each individual would have to fend for itself, scrounging for food, fending off predators, either inherit knowledge genetically or learn entirely on its own, and so forth. The specifically human form of existence is possible only because of society. Auto/biography therefore always also is biography, a pattern of life history not only of an other but also of a generalized other; auto/ethnography therefore always also is ethnography, the exploration of culture in general, whether it is someone else's or, because of transference and countertransference in the research process, one's own (on this latter point, see Breuer [Chapter 5]).

We can also approach the issue from an action perspective. What an individual does is always a concrete realization of cultural-historical possibilities. Because actions are the heart of identifying and identification processes, writing an auto/biography always realizes the possibilities in the biographical genre and the biographical plot. Every auto/biography always also realizes the cultural-historical patterns of biography. This symmetrical relation of biography and auto/biography becomes very clear in and through the intersubjectivity of the biographical interview, where biographical questions and autobiographical responses together constitute the realized interview protocol (Roth, Hwang, Lee, & Goulart, 2005). Similarly, auto/ethnography reveals concretely realized patterns in one's own actions rather than the actions of others, a form of research we have come to know as ethnography. All auto/ethnography, because it inquiries the concretely realized action possibilities that exist at the collective level is a concretely realized form of ethnography viewed generally.

Coming to Auto/Biography and Auto/Ethnography

Auto/biography as a critical method to write research has already had a considerable history in other fields such as anthropology (Reed-Danahay, 1999; Watson & Watson-Franke, 1985), feminist writing (Gilmore, 1994), and interpretive research more generally (Denzin, 1989). Auto/ethnography has also been used to deal with a variety of issues in a variety of disciplines (e.g., Bochner & Ellis, 2002). In these fields, auto/ethnography and auto/biography are genres that blend ethnographic interests with life writing and tell about a culture at the same time it tells about a life; at the same time, auto/ethnography and auto/biography have become important means of critiquing other forms of representing the generalized other, individuals and their culture. In education, however, a similar development has yet to happen, though there are some scholars in our field who have explored self and other using this medium (Neumann, 1998; Roth & Harama, 2000). The contributors to this book explore, by means of examples, different possible uses of auto/biography and auto/ethnography as means for critical analysis and as toolkits for educators as teachers and researchers. The important contribution auto/biography and auto/ethnography made to my own work slowly entered my consciousness over the past twenty years of working as a teacher and researcher.

First, having had to repeat fifth grade myself, I always have been aware as a teacher that the children in my care might be in a situation where I had been years before: I acted toward and talked about entities in the world as I saw them, and yet received (especially in that fifth-grade year but also later) feedback that suggested I was wrong. My auto/biographical recollections of school failure always helped me in being a better teacher, especially for students who normally are suffocated in the maelstrom of schooling. Somehow, my way of seeing and understanding problems, essay assignments, tasks and so on was not appropriate. These experiences later influenced both my teaching and research. As a teacher, when students did not understand, I often thought back about my own difficulties and, rather than faulting the children and invoking low motivation, lack of intelligence, or cognitive deficits (as it often happens in teaching and research practice), I attempted to engage the children to find out more about how the world looked to them (e.g., Roth, 2005). As a researcher, finding out what the children experienced, saw, acted towards the things that made their worlds became a major preoccupation in my research. That is, I increasingly focused on children's view of the curricular maze rather than that of the all-knowing observer who watches children run the maze.

Second, over the past decade and a half, I conducted several collaborative research projects with my fellow teacher and later graduate student Mi-

Auto/biography and Auto/ethnography as Tools for Learning about Learning

Day 1. As I am cycling along, I am aware of my surroundings (trees, flowers, and so forth) without really focusing on anything in particular. Although I am aware at the moment, here at home, I remember few things in particular, few stretches of the trip. But those things I do remember are associated with a particular type of experience. There are things, like a particular house or a road sign ("Landwehr") that are pulling my gaze to take a closer look. As I focus, sometimes with considerable delay, a memory surfaces—the house looks like the one I had lived in forty years earlier, "Landwehr" was the name of a professor and of a street in the city where I went to university.

Day 2. As I am riding along taking the same route as yesterday, there are features in the environment that I have not remembered yesterday at home after the trip, but which I nevertheless re-cognize the moment I approach them. As I come around the Y-fork, I re-member that I have seen from here the child on the bike and with the dog ahead of me. They then turn into the farm some 200 meters further on. I re-member the field with the freshly sprouting grain plants though I had not remembered them at home. Thus there are things that despite the complexity of the experience, I re-cognize even before I reach the place, that I start to anticipate when I get within reach. But then there were other farms, other signs, other features that I seem to see for the first time.

Day 5. I notice for the first time the little plates, inscribed with numbers that increase by 0.1 about every 100 meters. I infer that these are distance indicators with

chael Bowen. Our research concerned graphing and other practices in ecology. As we interacted intensively trying to make sense of videotapes and artifacts produced by our student and scientist participants, it was evident that he and I looked at the world differently and came to different understandings based on what appeared to be the same data—I now understand that only the material base, the ink

reference to some starting point. (I subsequently find the starting point during an explicitly planned trip.)

Day 7 taking the same trip. I notice for the first time the upper parts of two gigantic towers that are visible above the treetops.

From then on, I not only saw the towers each time I came by this place, but I was expecting them to show up even before I got to the place.

and sound patterns were the same, not how we saw them. Rather than making these differences disappear, we made them the focus of further analysis. As we progressed in our analyses and using stories from our lives as students and professionals, I began to understand our interpretive horizons as culturally (his reflection biology, mine physics culture) and historically constituted so that, to understand our respective interpretations, we needed to understand aspects of our respective biographies. Autobiographical evidence provided us with strong clues to understanding the interpretations of any other.

Third, the importance of using auto/biography and auto/ethnography as a critical tool became evident in a recently completed project on coteaching—a way of teaching in which two or more individuals collectively realize the responsibility for the lesson. I cotaught a four-month unit on water and water ecology with Nadely Boyd, a preservice teacher who was completing her two-year post-baccalaureate training with a four-month practicum. One day, I had moved into the background, I observed Nadely explode at a student and then sending him out of the classroom although from my (and his own) perspective, he had not done anything wrong. As my indignation was welling up, another image began to emerge. Images reappeared in my mind's eye of an incident early in my career (and admittedly, under very difficult circumstances) when I had slapped a student who pressed a candy wrapper into my hand that he had just pulled out of his mouth. I came to understand that the indignation was but a prejudgment, which I was able to grabble with through my own lived experience. Here, my own auto/biography became a tool to critically deal with my own pre-judgments at a later point in my life.

Auto/biography and auto/ethnography are legitimate ways of establishing intersubjectivity that escapes the false dichotomy opposing objectivism and subjectivism. Auto/biography, auto/ethnography, and other first-person methods enacted together with radical doubt are important aspects in making rigorous any disciplinary method. One of the major questions of any discipline that aspires academic legitimacy is: "How do you make its knowledge claims justifiable?" (on this point see Geelan [Chapter 11]).

The problem of the justification of knowledge claims arises from the separation of knowing from that which is known. For a long period of time, at least from Descartes to the early twentieth century, the natural sciences have been based on the assumption that observer-independent knowledge of the world is possible. Descartes, in his (in)famous analysis claimed that there were two independent substances *res extensa* (matter) and *res cogitans* (mind). Within the Cartesian paradigm body and mind became separated, and therefore also the connection between knowledge, a subject of the mind, and our being in and of this material world. While this ap-

proach has provided the sciences with (its presupposition of) objectivity, the separation of mind and matter has led to a fundamental problem in epistemology: How is knowledge grounded in the world? That is, by thinking knowledge as independent from the world we observe, we have the problem of explaining how the objects of thought, the tokens or signs that we manipulate (representations) relate to the world that we observe.

Figure 1.1. The observer is observing the observer. Out of view, however, is the technology that mediates observation.

Observer and Observed

The idea of an independence of the observer (and therefore his/her knowledge) and the world observed has been seriously questioned both in the natural and the social sciences. In the natural sciences, relativity theory and quantum mechanics both suggest that the status of the observer codetermines what and how it is observed. Relativity theory provides a mathematical formalism that translates the observations of one observer

When observation now turns in upon itself and directs its attention to the Notion existing as free Notion, it finds, to begin with, the *Laws of Thought*. . . . But *observing* is not *knowing* itself, and is ignorant of it; it converts its own nature into the form of *being*, i.e., it grasps its negativity only as *laws* of knowing. It is sufficient here to have pointed out the invalidity of the so-called Laws of Thought from the general nature of the case. (Hegel, 1977, pp. 180, 181)

into those of another; it can therefore survive relatively unscathed the critique of an observer dependence because simple calculations translate one observation into another. More serious is the critique that is associated with the Copenhagen interpretation of quantum theory. Here, the knowing observer is implicated in every observation without recourse; observer and observed are coupled and need to be accounted for in the mathematics which contains both a pan for the developing but inaccessible system, and a part that accounts for the act of observation; observation is not passive but an active operation which determines both observational categories and the range of possible observables.

Critiques of an observer-independent world also have been constructed in European phenomenology and existential and hermeneutic philosophy from Søren Kierkegaard through Edmund Husserl, Martin Heidegger, Hans-Georg Gadamer, Maurice Merleau-Ponty, Paul Ricœur, and Pierre Bourdieu. From a phenomenological perspective, the very condition of having experiences at all is that as body among bodies. Both Merleau-Ponty and Bourdieu insist that without our material bodies, no cognition would be possible. Having a body that moves about in the world is a precondition of all perception. Recent research in the cognitive neurosciences confirms that such conditions need to exist. First, perception of movement requires the same neuronal groups that are needed to execute the movements themselves. Second, we know objects and events not in abstract terms but in terms of a collection of perspectives. Third, it is movement in the world that brings about axon sprouting and brain connectivity.

The observer and the observed cannot be separated, and if what and how the observer perceives is determined by the current state of the observing organism that has its history. If we want to understand (that is, where it comes from and what its groundings are) the what and how of the knowledge claims of another, we need to understand his/her history. In human terms, this requires us a better understanding of the auto/biography of the individual observer. Therefore and ultimately, practical understanding testifies to our being as belonging to a praxis that precedes all objectification, all opposition between subject and object. It is only after the fact that we begin to articulate our experience, explicate it, and ultimately theorize it in a variety of ways.

Science and Phenomenology

Phenomenological thought begins with the assumption that we are always already part of the social and material world, as bodies among bodies, shot through with meaning. From a phenomenological perspective, the aspect of the world which individuals perceive and towards which they orient their actions, is always and already transparent (understood). Any hope of coherence between the (scientific) knowledge of ourselves and our idiosyncratic experiences in the world requires that both sides, science, the external (inter!) subjectivity and personal experience (inner subjectivity) are pushed. Scientists of all brands— including the Princeton physicist Piet Hut and the neurophysiologist Francisco Varela—have begun to suggest that we can overcome the epistemological problems raised by the observer/observed and mind–body dichotomies by drawing on first-person methodologies (see special issue of the *Journal of Consciousness Studies*, 1999, Volume 6(2). Among these first-person methodologies auto/biography and auto/ethnography can furnish descriptions of experiences that phenomenological methods attempt to investigate in terms of deeper structures.

In the quest of finding an answer to the question "What is actual?" the ultimate goal of scientific knowledge has to be able to model my personal experience of looking at a sun set of the Pacific, or the rush (flow) I experience cycling the mountains of Colorado. On the other hand, the study of personal experience requires a radical suspension of judgment and submission to systematic method of dealing with one's own prejudices and prejudgments—lest auto/biography and auto/ethnography are to lead to ideology, delusion, and conceptual blindness. The authors in this volume deal in different ways with this problem, some favoring an entirely first-person perspective whereas others play first- and third-person perspectives against one another (a method and genre I personally prefer). The two ways of knowing, one grounded in science the other in rigorous first-person accounts, can be usefully employed in constraining the theorizing of the other; "disciplined first-person accounts should be an integral element of the validation of a neurobiological proposal, and not merely coincidental or heuristic information" (Varela, 1996, p. 343). Auto/biography and auto/ethnography, when they are conducted in a disciplined manner, can therefore contribute tremendously to the study of cultural practices concretely realized in our patterned behaviors acquired in and through socially mediated participation in societal affairs.

There are, in fact, not even two methods, scientific explanation and first-person understanding, for strictly speaking, only the former is methodical (Ricœur, 1991). The two methods are but two sides of the *same* coin. Practical understanding is the non-methodical moment that makes all explanation possible. That is, understanding precedes, accompanies, concludes, and therefore envelops explanation; in turn, explanation develops understanding in analytic ways. Auto/biography and auto/ethnography are but two ways in which educators can expose their pre-judgments (prejudices) that they bring to the understanding of issues in teaching and learning.

Epoché, Radical Doubt, and Suspicion of Ideology

Auto/biography and auto/ethnography could easily lead us into the mires of fuzzy thinking, will-o'-the-wisp inspiration, and self-congratulatory, feel-good accounts of worldly events. Fluffy stuff, however, is not what the authors in this collection have in mind when they draw in different ways on auto/biography and auto/ethnography to explore relevant or pressing issues. By advocating auto/biography and auto/ethnography as a means of generating understanding in education, we do not intend to support self-indulgence, ideology, and prejudice.

The irremediable functional dependence between the individual, its knowledge, and its world requires—if we want to have any hope of establishing an educational science that self-reflexively includes knowing the conditions of knowing—a radical questioning and suspension of beliefs. This requirement has come to be known as the phenomenological *epoché* (Gr. έποχή, suspension of judgment), the process of setting aside cultural-historical presuppositions and factual knowledge, or phenomenological reduction, radical doubt, and suspicion of ideology. These are systematic methods of stepping out of the work to step more fully into it; it is a method that is analogous to laboratory work in science, where the complexity of the world is controlled in small environments. Because the pre-constructed is everywhere, which we notice when we question our habitual ways of thinking about and doing things, we need to subject our pre-understandings themselves to a radical questioning.

Figure 1.2. Auto/portraits teach us that in auto/ethnography and auto/biography there always remains something hidden. They usually all leave out the structural determinations from the outside of our lifeworlds, here, for example, the ideology embodied in photography as a form of representation and the machinery of the representational tool itself.

The dialectical model, which combines an explanation-seeking, theoretical and historically embedded (disciplinary) method and individual understandings that have evolved through our own histories (auto/biographies, auto/ethnographies), appears to me a useful way of pursuing the quest for deeper, more elaborate understandings of teaching and learning. Especially, a rigorous study of how we cope and learn in difficult situations should allow us to evolve better understandings of the difficulties students face when it comes to teaching or learning some subject matter or of being and becoming a researcher and scholar in education. This dialectic approach allows us to move from the individual and idiosyncratic understandings that characterize each umwelt to the world (environment, "Welt") that we share with others, that is, which is inter-individual subjectivity.

Auto/Biography (Ethnography) is Otobiography (Ethnography)

More than anyone else, Jacques Derrida may have laid the groundwork for auto/biography and auto/ethnography as central issue of postmodernism. First, he helped us understand that all auto/biography (ethnography) is also otobiography or otoethnography (Gr. ὤτο- combining form for ear, *oto-*), that is, a biography (ethnography) that comes to life only through the countersignature of the reader or hearer (Derrida, 1985). *Oto*, that which pertains to the ear, plays an important role because it is for the other that we write and speak; for the other, through the other, in terms of the other's language. So in Derrida's writing, as in Ricœur's hermeneutic phenomenology, or Bourdieu's sociological phenomenology, both the specific other whom we face in situations and the anonymous generalized other (who constitutes society of which we are a member) play most crucial roles in the ultimate meaning of the text. Both auto/biography (auto/ethnography) and biography (ethnography) are for the readers, the generalized other, who in both genres recognize ways of doing auto/biographical work. At the very moment that the author of an auto/biography (ethnography) articulates something for another, he or she presupposes the intelligibility of his or her account and the way of accounting. But the required intersubjectivity can be presupposed only because of our experience of intersubjectivity. Thus, my subjectivity always is a form of concretely realizing intersubjectivity. Similarly, auto/ethnography and auto/ethnography are genres written for a generalized other who, in the descriptions of the authors, recognize descriptions of cultural-historical and sociocultural practices that they might have given themselves. Any auto/biography or auto/ethnography is therefore never quite owned by the person who signs through assuming authorship, and who is the principal figure of the account. Rather, because any meaning of the text arises from the interaction of text and reader, the reader also owns it. This also provides a basis for countering those critics that fault authors for writing heroic stories and myths. Auto/biography as otobiography and auto/ethnography as otoethnography place as much responsibility for meaning on the reader as these genres place on their authors. Because readers always counter-sign a text, critical (deconstructionist) readers must take explicit responsibility for the meanings they de/construct.

Second, Derrida further problematized the ownership of words and texts in suggesting that they are never just one's own, they always also belong to someone else (Derrida, 1998). This someone else, the generalized other, listens with one ear, monolingually, which provides an inherent interpretive and ontological flexibility and ambiguity to any text. If language is of the other, even the "I" that I utter is of the other, and so there is a fundamental alienation that in the very moment I want to point to myself, I have to do so by using language which also belongs to culture and therefore the other. Auto/biography as written text is therefore also associated with alienation, for we always have to use the words which are not entirely our own, but always already belong to the Other.

Finally, Derrida (1995) pointed out that auto/biography is a process of creating an archive of Self. He focuses on the historical constitution of our Selves, which always participates in future constructions of Selves in an evidently recursive process. Thus, "[t]he technical structure of the archiving archive also determines the

Although, as consciousness, [self-consciousness] does indeed come *out of itself*, yet, though out of itself, it is at the same time kept back within itself, is *for itself*, and the self outside it, is for *it*. It is aware that it at once is, and is not, another consciousness, and equally that this other is *for itself* only when it supersedes itself as being for itself, and is for itself only in the being-for-self of the other. Each is for the other the middle term, through which each mediates itself with itself and unites with itself; and each is for itself, and for the other, an immediate being on its own account, which at the same time is such only through this mediation. They *recognize* themselves as *mutually recognizing* one another. (Hegel, 1977, p. 112)

structure of the archivable content even in its very coming into existence and in its relationship to the future. The archivization produces as much as it records the event" (p. 17). The Self as auto/biographical and auto/ethnographical text therefore augments itself, engrosses itself, and gains in authority. In the process, the (auto/oto-biographical and auto/oto-ethnographical) texts which define each Self remain spectral (i.e., have multiple meanings) which is perhaps a general structure of every archive. But in the same stroke auto/biography also loses any absolute and meta-textual authority it might claim to have.

Writing and W/ri(gh)ting

Postmodern, feminist, and constructivist critiques took, among others, aim at the way in which the world of our experience came to be represented in language, diagrams, mathematical forms, and so on. Representations and especially academic representations came to be criticized because, in and through the context where they appeared, they laid claims to truth. In the wake of this critique, representations were recognized to be context-dependent, always embodying interests, politics, and power. Yet much of the postmodern, feminist, and constructivist literature continued to employ genres characteristic of modernism. That is, the critiques, lacking self-reflexivity, merely wrote new truths. This problem, however, was squarely addressed in the sociology of science, particularly in the *The Reflexive Thesis: Wrighting the Sociology of Scientific Knowledge* (Ashmore, 1989) and *Knowledge and Reflexivity: New Frontiers in the Sociology of Knowledge* (Woolgar, 1988).

How do you write social research (education, sociology) without committing the same errors that are characteristic of modern scholarship, which rested on the notion of absolute truth? How to right

[VOICE OVER:] It/Id happens . . . by means of ruptures and disruptions of the code in one's manner of writing, teaching, practicing, or trafficking in language or the instruments of logic and rhetoric, as by means of what are called actions intervening in or through the most recognizable form of the [literary] apparatuses. (Derrida, 1995b, p. 57)

the wrongs of previous writings? These considerations led Malcolm Ashmore to reflexivity and the *wrighting* of research, which led me a few years later to attempts of *w/ri(gh)ting* research (Roth & McRobbie, 1999). These attempts used a variety of means to break the voice of the dominant narrative to the point that the different voices intersect, overlap, resist, and contrast one another. It is a form of writing that resists language, all the while making use of it.

The contributors to this volume employ a variety of ways of writing within the genre of auto/biography and auto/ethnography. These different forms of writing are especially important when there are multiple voices within the same text, which, in the very form that they are presented, change the background against which the authors write. Above all, the assert the presence of the "I," the knower alongside the known in a dialectical knower|known relation, the knower and the known presupposing one another.

Looking Ahead

Because we are the products of the world that we attempt to describe, our auto/-biographies and our scholarly works are deeply integrated. Recent authors in ethnography and anthropology reject the notion that we can somehow write in-nocent descriptions of others (e.g., Marcus & Fischer, 1986). Ethnography is better considered as encounters of actors that are differently embedded with-in particular social/cultural milieus. On this view, our knowledge of the other is always relational. Rather than describing attributes of a population from some neutral position outside the field of view, accounts of cultural meanings and practices are inevitably created from particular standpoints that set up the lines of comparison and contrast between the speaker/writer and the persons and prac-tices described. The stories ethnographers create are as much a reflection of their own cultural positioning as they are descriptions of the positioning of others. Making these historically constituted positions clear to the reader, that is, writ-ing auto/biography and auto/ethnography, is one way of understanding and in-corporating our prejudices into our practices and into what we produce. Making sense and use of representations of some Other involves our own positioning in relation to what we are seeing as much as any meaning inherent in the images themselves; auto/biography is one of the central means of making this position-ing salient.

The chapters in this collection attempt, each in its own way, to elaborate and render salient the position of the author or, alternatively, use auto/biography and auto/ethnography as methods to have others explore important issues related to education. All too often, students and teachers in educational research appear to be disembodied and to have no life other than voices of talking heads, com-puting and cognizing heads, and so forth. More so, researchers most often dis-appeared making their accounts impersonal, objectivity-exacting pretentious claims for an illusive objectivity in which observer and observed are clearly separated. On the other hand, the accounts provided by all authors to this vol-ume show how our lives are entangled with our projects, whether these are teaching, working in shelters, or learning in schools and elsewhere.

I have divided the book into sections, each being opened by a brief editorial commentary on its underlying ideas and the chapters that constitute it. The con-tributions to Section II highlight the possibilities and pitfalls that the genres and methods of auto/biography and auto/ethnography offer to educators who want to better understand themselves, their culture, and their context. In Section III, the authors use auto/biography to explore teaching and teacher education and thereby show how we can elaborate and explicate our experiences to arrive at better understandings. The contributions to Section IV exemplify how auto/biography and auto/ethnography can be employed as a form of institutional critic and, in this, are forms of doing critical, that is, positional scholarship. Sec-tion V focuses on explorations of activities that constitute everyday life, reading and writing reflexive sociology, tending graves, doing dissertation research and writing dissertations, or dealing with emigration|immigration. In the epilogue, Franz Breuer and I take a look over this volume to find answers to the question what educational researchers can gain by adopting auto/biography and auto/-ethnography into their methodological repertoires. The authors generally do not simply write *about* auto/biography and auto/ethnography, but *practice* the methods they are (implicitly) arguing for to set the stage for a reflection on how the method provides them with an understanding of cultural-historical practices more generally.

In its entirety, the volume assembled here shows how auto/biography and auto/ethnography can be used to construct knowing and an understanding of this knowing. Rather than seeing auto/biography and auto/ethnography as ways of retreating into personal, inner subjectivity, we should adopt them as means to establish and stabilize intersubjectivity. As bodies among bodies, we cannot achieve removed and disembodied knowledge; all our knowledge is singular and embodied but also representative of the collective in that it constitutes a concrete realization of cultural-historical and sociocultural possibilities. Rather than pretending to create objective observer-independent knowledge or retreating into an inner subjectivity, we can use critical methods together with inner subjectivity to bring about a maximum of intersubjectivity, that is, understanding the Self to understand the Other.

Here at the end of this introduction, I want to alert readers of the potential dangers of auto/biographical and auto/ethnographical methods that both Alberto Rodriguez and I present in the first section—auto/biography and auto/ethnography bring with them the danger of illusion, grandiose myths, and delusion. More so, they can—it is very evident in totalitarian systems-support ideology and prejudice. Critical literary methods can be used to deconstruct such accounts. However, with deconstruction also come dangers our advice to contribute intentionalities does not sufficiently address. Because every auto/biography is otobiography and every auto/ethnography is otoethnography, the meaning of a text arising from the countersigning, overzealous and self-righteous critics may do great injustice to a text. Take for example the story of the American cyclist Lance Armstrong who, despite what doctors had called a fatal cancer, won the most prestigious road bicycle race, the Tour de France. One can take his own accounts and deconstruct them as heroic myths of the "everyone can do it" type; but we can also read it as an inspiration, not to win the Tour de France, not to admire the hero Armstrong, but in order to go with the same sort of spirit about our own everyday life affairs. Readers should always know and be aware that their own readings are de/constructions, involving disassembly and construction.

References

Ashmore, M. (1989). *The reflexive thesis: Wrighting sociology of scientific knowledge.* Chicago: University of Chicago Press.

Bochner, A., & Ellis, C. (Eds.). (2002). Ethnographically speaking: Auto/ethnography, literature and aesthetics. Walnut Creek, CA: AltaMira.

Denzin, N. (1989). *The research act, 3/e.* Toronto: Prentice Hall.

Derrida, J. (1985). *The ear of the other.* Lincoln: University of Nebraska Press.

Derrida, J. (1995). *Archive fever: A Freudian impression.* Chicago: University of Chicago Press.

Derrida, J. (1998). *Monolingualism of the Other; or, The prosthesis of origin.* Stanford, CA: Stanford University Press.

Gilmore, L. (1995). *Autobiographics: A feminist theory of women's self-representation.* Ithaca, NY: Cornell University Press.

Hegel, G.W.F. (1977). *Phenomenology of spirit.* Oxford: Oxford University Press.

Marcus, G. E., & Fischer, M.M.J. (1986). *Anthropology as a cultural critique: An experimental moment in the human sciences.* Chicago: University of Chicago Press.

Neumann, A. (1998). On experience, memory, and knowing: A post-holocaust (auto)-biography. *Curriculum Inquiry, 28,* 425–442.

Reed-Danahay, D. E. (Ed.). (1999). *Auto/ethnography: Rewriting the self and the social.* Oxford: Berg.

Ricœur, P. (1991). *From text to action: Essays in hermeneutics, II.* Evanston, IL: Northwestern University Press.

Roth, W.-M. (2005). *Talking science: Language and learning in science classrooms.* Lanham, MD: Rowman and Littlefield.

Roth, W.-M., & Harama, H. (2000). (Standard) English as second language: Tribulations of self. *Journal of Curriculum Studies, 32,* 757–775.

Roth, W.-M., Hwang, S., Lee, Y. J., & Goulart, M.I.M. (2005). *Participation, learning, and identity: Dialectical perspectives.* Berlin: Lehmanns Media.

Roth, W.-M., & McRobbie, C. (1999). Lifeworlds and the 'w/ri(gh)ting' of classroom research. *Journal of Curriculum Studies, 31,* 501–522.

Varela, F. (1996). Neurophenomenology: A methodological remedy for the hard problem. *Journal of Consciousness Studies, 3,* 330–350.

Watson, L. C., & Watson-Franke, M. (1985). *Interpreting life histories: An anthropological inquiry.* New Brunswick, NJ: Rutgers University Press.

Woolgar, S. (Ed.). (1988). *Knowledge and reflexivity: New frontiers in the sociology of knowledge.* London: Sage.

II

Possibilities and
Potential Problems

Auto/biography and auto/ethnography constitute genres that come not only with possibilities but also with potential dangers. The possibilities appear clear: Because society exists in and through our membership, what we write about ourselves is also about society collectively. Both individual and collective presuppose one another. Investigating the Self, or rather, our actions, gives us access to the ways in which culture is concretely realized. At the same time, we are too close to ourselves, which gives rise to the possibility that we do not find the distance required for critically interrogating our own sense making. We may be like the proverbial fish in the water, which does not or no longer realize the medium that allows it to live. We then may become caught in illusion and delusion. Good auto/biography and auto/ethnography therefore requires critical doubt, a way of engaging ourselves that also deals with the potential dangers of illusion and delusion.

The first four contributions in this second section articulate how auto/biography and auto/ethnography provide opportunities: to gain inroads to understanding the learning of science by homeless students (Barton/Darkside), the development of teachers (Pereira et al.), as sociological method that leads to understanding the social context of students and teachers (Roth), and to understanding the very possibility of these methods that arises from the embodied nature of the researcher's experience (Breuer).

The next three contributions warn readers of the potential dangers that come with these forms of inquiry and writing research and that already have been flagged in Franz Breuer's contribution (Chapter 5): when auto/biography and auto/ethnography lead to the preoccupation with the Self over the fact that the Self is an effect of the individual|collective dialectic, these methods and genres easily obtain an air of self-indulgence, wallowing in one's feelings, and the like.

The contributions not only tell us about the opportunities and potential dangers of auto/biography and auto/ethnography, but also provide images of forms of life that are shared by some members of society. One of these experiences is poverty and homelessness, which are addressed in the chapter by Angela Calabrese Barton and Darkside (Chapter 2) and in my own (Chapter 7). All three, we have lived in homeless situations, sometimes chosen (Angie, I), sometimes not (Darkside, I). Although our writing testifies to the resilience of human beings in general, the fact that we find ourselves here ought not lead us to legitimate societies that do not sufficiently care about all their members. Most importantly, as I show in my chapter, there is also a moral imperative for not exploiting those who already have fallen on hard times by capitalizing on their frailty for our personal gains. Others grew up in situation of greater ease (e.g., Settelmaier), but these experiences, too, mediate what and how we experience later in our lives.

Two chapters provide explicit arguments in which the usefulness of auto/biography and auto/ethnography can be grounded. On the one hand, researchers have material bodies, to which the person can point by reflexively uttering "I." Franz Breuer (Chapter 5) shows how, because of the phenomena of transference and countertransference, researchers can read in the behavior of others responses to their own behavior. Each time, the body serves as the means to express associated emotions and understandings. In my own Chapter 4, I provide the complementary argument, whereby individual and collective are irremediably aspects of the same unit because they mutually presuppose each other. The two chapters, therefore, can be seen as the very foundations for auto/-methods.

The three final chapters in this second section are cautionary in nature (Rodriguez, Roth, Kincheloe). All three make salient the dangers that lie in ideology, which comes with and is reified in the process of self-inspection typical of auto/methods. Ideology is resilient, and it takes substantial efforts not only with break it but also with the instruments that are used in the breaking of ideology (Bourdieu, 1992). Only constant interrogation of one's own presuppositions, and the interrogation of the presuppositions underlying the interrogation process, has the potential of leading us out of the quagmire of ideology. Jacques Derrida, in many of his writings, has exemplified how continuous and continued efforts of writing can be used to shift and question the position from which we write.

More so than in the other sections, the contributions to this section explore different forms of writing, where the different texts and different representational means (texts, photographs) are juxtaposed. As Franz Breuer notes, multiple representations have the potential to lead to stereoscopic vision and depth information about the epistemic object. In this sense, therefore, the contributions also represent the possibilities and potential problems of auto/biography and auto/ethnography in the *medium* of representation, which, according to Marshall McLuhan's (1995) dictum, is an important aspect of the message. While many of us may be unfamiliar with techniques of reading such texts—should we read one page of opposing columns at a time? Or read first one column of text prior to the other? Or should we go back and forth between pieces of text?—the questions about how to read themselves are interesting in the sense that they bring to the foreground the normally unquestioned ways of reading in our culture. Speaking for myself, having read and constructed many texts of this kind, I do not have *a method*. I sometimes read an extended passage in one voice, column, or medium prior to moving to the one(s) juxtaposed. At other times, I move back and forth, allowing associations to emerge from the intertextuality that I practice in the process. While re-reading the penultimate copy of this manuscript, I noticed that I used the fingers of my two hands to keep track of the locations where I ended reading respective parts of the texts, which helped me to continue reading wherever I had left off. Readers may take the copresence of multiple texts and textual forms as a license to experiment with their own reading practices and even to interrogate their received, cultural forms of reading.

References

Bourdieu, P. (1992). The practice of reflexive sociology (The Paris workshop). In P. Bourdieu & L.J.D. Wacquant, *An invitation to reflexive sociology* (pp. 216–260). Chicago: University of Chicago Press.
McLuhan, M. (1995). *Understanding media: The extensions of man*. London: Routledge.

2   Greater Objectivity through Local Knowledge

Angela Calabrese Barton and Darkside

When talking about their lives, people lie sometimes, forget a lot, exaggerate, become confused, and get things wrong. Yet, they are revealing truths. These truths don't reveal the past "as it actually was," aspiring to a standard of objectivity. They give us instead the truths of our experiences.

—Personal Narratives Group, 1989, p. 261

Introduction

The focus of our paper is on using auto/biography in science education to understand coming-to-know science across difference. In this paper, we make two interrelated points. The first point is about auto/biography and why we ought to think about auto/biography as both the telling of one's story and the using of that story with others to understand and use difference productively (in science, in life). Therefore, the first half of this paper is about us telling our stories of schooling and science.[1] In these stories, we are both critical of our lives and of the social structures that help to shape our lives. And, we both are critical of the social structures that shape each other's lives, and each other's concepts of and interactions in science. This leads us to our second major point: We hope that our auto/biographies (as both telling and interacting) allow for a "greater objective" understanding of what it means to know and do science with youth in urban settings. In particular we are interested in expressing how our sharing of our stories with each other both privately (in personal conversations) and publicly (through action research and in this paper) led us to understand from multiple

23

perspectives how different people do science differently. Embedded within this point is how auto/biography dismantles the universalistic tug of science and replaces it with a push for science as local knowledge.

To accomplish these tasks, we begin with two parallel auto/biographies (telling our stories). These auto/biographies are short, and contain only a very small piece of our lives, but they are parts of our lives that we thought might help provide contexts about our own thoughts about and actions in urban science education. From there we move into a conversation about urban science education (interacting with and through our stories), especially as it plays out in two contexts in which we are both working (in different roles): school science and after school science (transforming an abandoned inner-city lot into a community garden). Following this we then move to thinking about how our different stories apart (part I) and together (part II) provide a greater objective insight into what it means to come-to-know science. Finally in the last section, we (mostly Angie) write about how this auto/biographical exercise (both telling our stories and having conversation together about our ideas) is important in science education.

Auto/Biographies and Science Education

As our stories below illustrate, we grew up (and are growing up) in two very different worlds. Our worlds now intersect through science education. We are both researchers on a project meant to explore urban science education. One of us (Angie) is "in charge" of the project, grew up in a small town, is a an assistant professor in science education, and is a white, "homed" female interested in issues of equity and social justice as it relates to science education. One of us (Darkside) works on the project as a high school student research assistant, lived his whole life so far in the city, and is a Black, homeless teenage male interested in helping to make schools a better place for inner-city youth. We met through the action research project by teens and for teens at the shelter as part of Angie's research.[2] She has been working with homeless youth and parents in science education for four years as a result of her own self-imposed experience being homeless. Darkside had been an active participant in the action research project. Midway through the school year Darkside agreed to be interviewed in-depth on several occasions so that Angie could document his ideas and beliefs about science and inner-city life. During one of these interviews, Darkside and Angie agreed that having him play a more active—and interactive—role in the project by serving as a research assistant would improve this research and connecting it to Darkside's life. This is how we came to write this paper together.

Getting to Know Darkside

Hello my name is Darkside. I am sixteen years old, and a Black Cuban American. I was born in New York City, and raised in the Bronx. I used to have two brothers Deshawn and Morrice and a sister on my father's side. And my mother's name is Mary. And my father's name is Fancisco Darkside. I have a lot of friends in my old neighborhood.

When I was three I didn't want to drink the big baby milk bottle. I would throw it out of the window because I didn't get used to them. I wanted to drink out of a cup like other adults do in a normal life. So when I was four I jumped out of the crib. I used to use it as a bungee jump. I broke it! My father spent 500 dollars because he bought it when I was a baby. When I was five I started playing with toys and action figures, like Spider Man, WWF wrestle man figures, teenage mutant ninja turtles, and X-man figures. I started playing with them when I was five to thirteen years old. Then when I was six I used to collect superhero cards like Wolverines and Spiderman, etc.

When I was seven, I used to mix the chemicals like perfume with other things to make stronger cologne. When I was eight, I used to play with flour mixing it with vinegar and baking soda and I

Getting to Know Angie

In my auto/biographical section, I would like to share four short stories with you. In order, the stories position me as a girl growing up in western Massachusetts, a science student in middle school, and a science teacher in after-school programs (two stories).

Story 1: I grew up in a large Italian Catholic family in New England. My parents had strong feelings about our educational future. They wanted to give us the chance to go to college, something that neither of their parents were able to give them (although something they worked hard to give themselves). None of my grandparents made it through eighth grade, and consequently were destined to live their professional lives as bar tenders, custodians, and shoe and refrigerator factory workers. My dad spent his initial years after high school in the army; my mom, was a secretary at Walgreens. Having been invested with the upwardly mobile attitude of working class families of the post WWII era, my parents believed intensely in the role of education to serve as an economic advancement. In this spirit, after leaving the army my father worked his way through school to earn a teaching certificate. It was not long before my father wanted and needed more schooling to support his five children (my mother's salary as a secretary would not be enough.) He moved on with his masters and a prin-

made hard dough out of it. When I was nine, I used to play with racing cars on the floor. I used to read comics like Hawkeye, Batman, Superman, and etcetera. When I was ten I used to read a lot of books and go to sleep early. I used to read the Old Testament, the literature books, etc. when I get bored. When I was eleven, I started playing Nintendo and Super Nintendo games when Super Nintendo first came out. I get addicted to Super Mario world because it was like a world that you have a hero and his brother try to save the city from being taken over by King Koompa. He was a bad villain and I beat the whole game till it gets whack. Every time I play I beat it. It got boring to me because just like playing super Mario brothers part II, III, and I. When I was twelve I go outside to play with my friends, like tag, manhunt, baseball, etc. I used to pack bags in the supermarket. I packed bags until I was fourteen.

When I was thirteen, I know it was a bad lucky number, but to me, I made it a good lucky number. But my friends and me used to play other neighborhoods in baseball to challenge them and we always win by hitting and outpitching them, and we always outscored our opponents. My father used to take me to my godfather 's building and always had to introduce me to his friends. So when he

cipalship of a high school. As my father learned how to play the education game, all the while becoming increasingly frustrated by its hypocritical nature, he made it very clear to me that in order to succeed in college I had to learn how to play the game, or as Delpit (1988) suggests, I had to learn the "culture of power." Consequently, I remember in ninth grade having my life planned out through the age of thirty with every step detailed. I wanted to make sure that those with more power would view my (intended) actions favorably.

Also, while growing up, my sisters and I spent much of our spare time learning about the natural world around us in ways we could appreciate and value. We learned to build go-carts out of old golf bag carts left in our barn by its previous owners. We made "amusement park rides" out of old "big wheels" (wooded cable spools). We fixed our own bikes, made our own forts. My older sister, Cathy, and I even had our own lawn mowing service. We spent countless hours collecting bugs, frogs, flowers, rocks, and digging up old bricks and bottles. We nurtured the lilies of the valley and ferns that grew in our "beauty center," a place of solitude, away from books, school, and adults. It was in this place that we felt safe to keep our discoveries, our secrets and our stories. It seems as though, at this early age, outside of school, my sisters and I had a voice in science. We talked

gets in trouble or my mother gets in trouble, I run to them and they help me. They will be there for me. My father makes me look like I know them all my life.

When I was fourteen, I always walk by myself, traveling to places like Manhattan, Brooklyn, Queens, and Yonkers, except Staten Island because Staten Island is out of my reach because I didn't have friends in Staten Island. I had friends in like Manhattan, Brooklyn, Queens, and Yonkers. I started my summer youth job. This was my first job I started in my life. I started getting paid for every two weeks. I still had a little job experience. I started working in American Guild of Organists. I was working as a stock boy by putting things in order, organizing, typing, and answering telephones. Every Monday I went to the summer program for teenagers from fourteen to twenty-one. It was fun and exciting because I come there every Monday to participate, do things for the community like I did a family tree and watching plays, etc. The last day I won an award as a peacemaker with a walking stick and a book about a man named Mr. Changyu.

When I was fifteen, I participated in this program called the Cultural Affairs program as an Intern from March 98 to May 98. I was happy. In June I went to the graduation ceremony and I won

about and made sense of the world in ways that we could appreciate, in ways which were intuitive. By the time I was a teenager, I knew that being a woman meant to find common ground amidst contradiction. My teachers, textbooks, and class lessons were telling me that women were not scientists. They simply did not exist in science. Yet, my love of exploring and theorizing about my world, which I was encouraged to do at home and sometimes at school, told me that I could and should be a scientist. Explorations with my sisters (all of which were explicitly encouraged by my parents) told me that I could be a scientist. My role at home in house cleaning and cooking, my parents encouragement to baby-sit for extra money, my grandmother's desire to teach me to crochet, and my own desire to learn to wear make up, shave my legs, and get married and have kids, told me I was to be a woman, a mother, a person who was not meant to pursue science. This theme of mixed messages was not new to me growing up in the 1970's in Massachusetts. Although "women's lib" and the ERA were common themes in the news, feminism was a taboo in my schools, my church, and my home. Those women were too strident, man-haters, and lesbians. Although Susan B. Anthony, Harriet Tubman, and Wilma Rudolph were three heroes I learned about in my own explorations at the library (albeit forced explorations on the part of my

awards for participating in the program from October 97 to May 98. Ms. Rhonda congratulated me for winning the awards. In the summer time, I was looking for a job but I didn't get one because it was too late. But I never give up. I started searching all over the place like the Gap, Radio Shack, etcetera. They give me applications to fill out to return them and I never get a call back. In September I was trying to get ready to go back to school for the first day, so I have to save all my money for clothes to go to school to dress for success. When I went to school on the first day, I see all new people that were coming in and getting registered for the new school. I was shocked. They give us our program cards, ID, and metro cards.

When I turned sixteen, my father buy me a ring, a pair of boots, and a coat. I was happy but I still ain't get my wish yet which was to GET OUT OF HERE. Then I signed up for the Boys Club after my birthday and I am still having the success that is being a member to the Boys Club.

I plan to graduate from high school and go to college. I want to make something out of my life. Do some good. I don't belong to gangs. My mother doesn't want to me to. It's been hard on her—my older brother died and my other older brother is incarcerated for

parents), I rarely learned about these women in schools. I never learned about women scientists, except Madame Curie (and she worked in collaboration with her husband), and I never ever learned about minority scientists. When I did learn about female scientists, (I have no memory of learning about minority scientists in school), they were not heroes like Isaac Newton, Albert Einstein, and Galileo were heroes.

Story 2: I remember in seventh grade, that I had learned in science class earlier in the year that it was not safe to smell a bottle with chemicals in it because it could kill you or at least burn your nose hairs, and that the proper technique was to waft the bottle odors by your nose with your hand. In our class, we had to make an invention, and I thought that a neat and needed invention would be to have a nose with a chemical detector in it. I thought it would be the coolest project. So, I made a nose out of plaster of Paris and glued some hair by the nostrils. This hair was the chemical detector end. Attached to the nose were a piece of chalk and a piece of the paper. This was to print out the list of chemicals that the nose smelled. All you had to do was put the nose over the bottle of chemicals in question, and it would print out the chemicals. I was so proud of my project, and I didn't even care when the class laughed because it was kind of funny. Anyway, my teacher gave me a C—because it was not real-

gang-related activity. Not being in gangs is hard because even though you stay away from violence, you also don't get their protection.

Becoming Homeless: One thing I didn't want to tell you was about becoming homeless. That is because I didn't want you to know. It makes life too hard. Especially if people at my school or my future college find out. But, I will tell you anyway. When I was in the seventh grade, my father paid the rent, but the landlord didn't take rent. He said the check was bad. But, he didn't give us any warning. Instead the sheriff came to our apartment in the middle of the night. He told us we had twenty hours to vacate the apartment. That is when they also told us the check was bad. We didn't have anywhere to go. My mother and father took us to the EAU. The EAU, they put us in a smelly, dirty, rotten place where we stayed for ten days. After that they deemed us ineligible, reason being that my parents only have a "common law marriage." What I mean by that is they were never married by the law. They lived together for fifteen years. They had three children together, but they was never married by the law. My parents applied again at the EAU for housing. This time we stayed another ten days at the same rotten place before they told us we were ineligible.

istic and did not really work. Despite the fact that the same teacher gave Vic an A+ when his project—a telephone TV where you could see the person you were talking to—was not realistic and did not really work. He only drew a picture. I made a model!

In my seventh-grade science class I learned the hard way to accept the roles and expectations for girls and science. I learned that neither my voice nor my ideas counted. When I tried to express an interest for and creativity in chemistry, my teacher punished me for not being realistic. (Even though Vic was praised for the same thing.) I found ways to combine these mixed messages was evident in my every day activities and inventions. My nose-shaped chemical detector grew out of my need to keep the body safe and to help clean the air, and was mixed with my interest in invention and analysis.

Story 3: My first "real" teaching experiences were in after-school programs. It was in one of these programs where I had been working with a group of ninth grade students from a northeastern city. I remember one day in particular because I thought, as the teacher, I had designed the "perfect" activity—one that would make the science relevant to their lives, hands-on, and just plain exciting! We were supposed to be focusing on metals and the properties of metals that particular afternoon. So, what I decided to do with my students was to have them mix To-

My parents they got some money and paid to get married. They went to the EAU and they put us in a shelter. I never went to school during that time, until we got into a shelter. I never really made such an understanding, but I can see now that my grades were bottom in the seventh grade.

I have now lived in shelters for over three years. Right now I live at the same shelter for nine months with my mother and father.

The shelter where I live is in a poor run-down part of New York City. Over two hundred families live here. Some people live here for just a couple of months. Other people, like me, live here for a year or so. This shelter has programs for youth, such as the Boys and Girls Club and the Keystone project for transforming the lot. It also has Daycare, GED classes, and WIC.

They are really strict here because you have to sign in and out every time you leave or come back to the shelter. You can't be here unless you are with your parent, and you can never have guests. The security guards mostly pick on you and make you feel bad.

School: When I was in first grade I started in the second semester in January 1987. I used to be a pain in the neck sometimes driving teachers crazy in the auditorium. The teacher told my mother

tal Cereal (a kind of cereal fortified with vitamins and minerals, including 100 percent of the daily recommended dosage of iron) with water. After the cereal was soaked through, the students were to put a magnetic stir bar into the mixture, and place their beaker containing "cereal mush" and magnetic stir bar on a stir plate, turn the stir plate on, then watch and wait!

After about fifteen minutes or so, they were to remove their beaker from the stir plate, reach into it, and pull out the magnetic stir bar. If the "experiment" worked correctly, students would have lots of little iron filings collected on the tip of their stir bar. I thought that this would be a way not only to begin to talk about iron and other metals, and such qualities as magnetism, but also to talk about nutrition, our bodies, and the manufacture of food. My students really got into this activity, mixing their cereals and pulling out stir bars. Except Rhonda. About the point in class, where we began to talk about what those little brownish things were at the tip of their stir bars, Rhonda physically separated herself from the rest of the class, opened her purse, and pulled out a pack of cigarettes. As I looked at her, she returned my glance, opened her pack of cigarettes, put one in her mouth and lit it. I stood there wondering about how I thought this activity was engaging, and was teaching the students something about chemistry and metals and nutrition. Yet, my

"Can you keep your son home because he is a pain in the neck!" Then they let me go ahead to the next grade because I had a reading level of third grade. I was smart. Then they transferred me to a different school and I passed and they transferred me again to another. I stayed there from the third grade to the sixth grade. In the third grade we used to play with toys and mixing up chemicals, like baking soda and vinegar. I was reading and I was smart and stuff, and they let me go to the fourth grade. In the fourth grade they give me a different teacher, she was smart and old but she been there for years. They called her Ms. E, but she let us do things, but she didn't let us get away with it so we behaved. Sometimes I be a class clown but I stopped.

Then in the fifth grade I had Ms. L and she was a good teacher too but some of the kids take advantage of her sometimes when we do things bad and we over doing it. Then we did the work and stuff. She gave us a lot of work, even for the vacation. In the sixth grade I had the same teacher again. She let us do things we want to do but sometime when she was absent the students be like you got other teachers that will substitute when the teacher is not here and give you work. At home, I used to mix chemicals, vinegar and

wondering was pierced by Rhonda's silence that seemed to shout, "here is what I think about your ideas about chemistry, metals and nutrition!"

Story 4: I believe I learned a very important lesson at the shelter. As part of our environmental theme, I wanted to help the children invent ways of making recycled paper. Besides, it was near the winter holidays, and I wanted the children to have their own paper to make cards to send. In their informal conversations of the past few weeks, the children had been talking about the things they wanted to get and give for the holidays. Most of these things were dream items—such as a "car for my mom"—as most of the children rarely possessed more than pocket change.

Before I arrived at the shelter, I planned to have the children collect leaves, twigs, dirt, and other natural items from around the block. I brought with me a stack of old newspapers, string, fabric, and office paper, for the recycled paper as well as popcorn, juice, and graham crackers for snack. Although I planned for the children to invent their own recycled paper, I had also planned their inventions around the ingredients I thought the children might use and how they might go about using them through the kinds of things I brought and had the children talk about. After all, I had made recycled paper successfully with several other children in the past. When the children began mixing their choice of

baking soda. I called it a Neutergin (a potion). Then I took the citywide test and I don't know what happened. I was supposed to be in the seventh grade and they told me my school was wrong.

When I graduated out of the sixth grade and I went to a junior high school that was a bad school for me because students picked up things like computers and threw it out of the window and it hit people in the head. They would throw bottles out of the window too. Things that teachers get mad at because the people who got hit with stuff like glass bottles and plants and them cube things you do math with, they complained to the principal that the students were throwing some things out of the window and hitting them with it when they walking by. Then the teacher told me I got left back again. I was supposed to be in the seventh grade, but they told me my school was wrong because they are afraid that I will get ahead of them and be smarter than they are.

Favorite Teacher: My favorite teacher was Ms. T and Ms. W because they taught me a lot of things about entrepreneur, science, global studies, etc. They taught seventh and eighth grade. Ms. T was a nice teacher in a certain way if you behave and you act bad like disrespecting her and hurting her feelings, she won't let you

ingredients for recycled paper, three boys separated themselves from the rest of the group. In their bowl instead of mixing the materials from outside with the newspapers and other materials, they instead were mixing popcorn and graham crackers that I had brought for snack along with some leftover flour from an activity a few weeks earlier. They mixed their concoction to a thick paste, spread it into a thin sheet on a large rectangular pan where they were to have put their recycled paper to dry, and then asked if they could bake it. While their concoction was baking I asked them about what they were doing. Jason informed me that they had decided to make "edible paper." When they were done, they cut their product up into tree shapes, ate some of them and made plans to give the rest of them out as edible Christmas cards.

I was fascinated with the boys' choice to make edible paper. I was also fascinated by the kinds of questions the boys were asked by their peers, and the responses they gave, when their peers learned about their covert actions. In this conversation, Jason indicated that they examined and discussed the sample pieces of recycled paper I brought for the children. The boys understood that there was a particular way to make recycled paper, and based on their analysis of the sample pieces, they described what that process was. The boys also described what it was they wanted to do

get the opportunity to do flower shop. We always make money every year to make money to go on trips and selling flower and cups and plants and clothes and stuff. Ms. W was a good science teacher because she teaches earth, environmental science and stuff and I passed it. I always passed her tests and class because sometimes we always clown around and fool around she would get mad at you and throw you out of the class. Ms. W she do things to plants, and she teaches the ocean and the three rocks: sedimentary, igneous, metamorphic rocks. I will never forget this day and so when I went to high school they teach us the same thing like they teach us in junior high.

In the ninth grade, I didn't know nobody to talk to till I met my old friend Ruben, Juan, Angel, Robert, and this friend I know from years in my neighborhood, Nat. There was a lot of people I know from my elementary school and junior high school. I did well in the ninth grade. First marking I made it on the dean's list, and the second and third I made it on the honor roll two times. Fourth and the sixth I made on the honor roll too. That was a record in my high school's history. I call it my record. I made it five times on the honor roll. In the tenth grade I had a minor set back. I could have made it on the honor

different from the prescribed activity. For example, Jason was asked why he made the edible paper. His response was that he "didn't want to make ordinary paper," that he "saw how you could do it" and had "different ideas for something [he] wanted to try." He also said that when they "took a close look at the paper" they knew it could be "done different ways," and that the purpose of recycled paper was to "make it from what you already got, using materials that already served a purpose." In making this point he picked up the sample paper I made and pointed to the pine needles in it, then compared that to the popcorn kernels in his own. Finally, Jason also told how if he gave away "edible cards" then "people could eat it," and that it would be "like a two-way present."

In some ways the very act of making recycled paper promoted the material separation of the "haves" and the "have-nots:" We were making recycled paper so that the children could have cards to give away as gifts. In addition possessing food and the times and places for eating it were strictly restricted by the shelter. In fact, as the teacher, I, like the students, was conscious of this positioning through their stories about "dream gifts." I wanted to recognize this reality, as it seemed particularly salient during the holiday season, and because I did not want to actively participate in how such material differences separate children through the have and have-not status.

roll, I could have made it on the dean's list if I didn't fail biology. In the second marking period I made it on the honor roll again. I had the magic touch. In the middle of the third marking period I was starting good until almost the end I got injured in the snow and I broke my leg.

Worst Teacher: My worst teacher in the tenth grade in my high school was Ms. F because every time I do my work other students keep on being class clowns by trying to make everyone laugh by cracking jokes on me. And I crack jokes on them back but the teacher don't say nothing to them, she says something to me that like I am the ringleader to this circus. She throws me out of class when I try to defend myself. Then she sends me to student court and I have to defend myself on trial. They didn't find me guilty or not guilty. Then I tell the principal when the students mess with me and she don't say nothing to them, she said then say something to me.

Besides recycled paper was "in," and making and giving recycled paper could be read as an environmentally friendly and even politically correct act just as it could also have been read as an act of poverty. Jason's imaginative subversion of this gift making by causing it to also be about having food in inappropriate places and times could only be admired.

Yet, Jason's actions pushed me to consider my whole analysis on another level. He addressed his desire to give a particular kind of present (rather than a prescribed one). He challenged rules about where food can be used and eaten at the shelter. Finally, he challenged the marginalization created by definitions of acceptable science through challenging the production, uses, and nature of science. Science no longer was something done by scientists far away in labs or by teachers who tell the students how to do the science through explicit directions or persuasion. Science became the active intersection between the knower and the social, political, cultural, and physical conditions and contexts embracing—but also being acted upon by—the knower.

Greater Objectivity in the Critique of Coming-to-Know-Science through Auto/Biography

Our stories contained "highlights" of our lives that we thought were important in the context of science education. What is critical to our auto/biographies is not how fully or accurately we remember our lives, and reliably report them, but rather how convincing and meaningfully we used our written lives to begin to tell a meaningful and coherent story (Polkinghorne, 1987). We use the phrase "begin to tell" rather than simply "tell" because in writing our stories and reading each others' stories we are drawn to the importance and power to use these stories in context to construct more fully —and critique more fully—our embodied understandings of science. In other words, we see two important aspects of auto/biography: telling one's story, and engaging in conversation with another about and through one's story. Therefore, in the next section of our paper we engage in a joint discussion and critique of coming-to-know science, and how auto/biography informs this process.[3] We use this conversation to suggest implicitly that multiple auto/biographical tellings by teachers, students, and researchers creates spaces for a "greater objective" understanding of what it means to come-to-know science in urban settings by bringing to voice multiple perspectives (Harding, 1991). We use a conversation format to begin this discussion so that we can open up to the reader how we both think about science and coming-to-know science differently and how such difference is both informed by our life stories, and challenged by the other's life stories. We also hope that you, as the reader, will enter into the conversation by reflecting on where your own stories and ideas fit into and are also challenged by our conversation.

* * *

Darkside: Science to me is the earth, pollution, the atmosphere. Look all around and you see science.

Angie: Hmmm. But, what makes all around science to you? I mean, what makes the earth science to you?

Darkside: I don't know.

Angie: I mean, then, why do you say "the Earth" when I say, what is science to you?

Darkside: In school, in global studies, we study the earth. So that is one reason. But also, science is all around you. It's trees. The flowers. The sidewalk. The street. The buildings. It's all science. It's how things work and how they survive.

Angie: Okay, Darkside, I agree with you, with the idea that science is all around us. But, to me, science is the process of figuring out how, as you say, things work and how they survive. I mean, I think the topic, like the earth or pollution, is important too, but more important is figuring out about the topic. So, figuring out what causes pollution, and why, what exactly pollution is made up of, and what impact pollution has on the things around it.

Darkside: Yah. Figuring everything out about pollution.

Angie: When you learn about pollution in school, do you get to figure all of those things out in school?

Darkside: We supposed to.

Angie: What do you mean, you are supposed to?

Darkside: I mean that the teacher I have, she teaches us nothing. She gives us these worksheets that don't teach us nothing. She don't care what we learn. I think she's dumbing us down, so we won't be smarter than her.

Angie: She's not teaching you enough?

Darkside: Right. She's dumbing us down.

Angie: Darkside, do you think that she is trying to dumb you down, or that she just does not know enough science to teach you?

Darkside: She's dumbing us down. She don't want us to be smarter than her. It may be she don't know enough to teach us, but she don't even give us the chance to learn extra. So, if she can't teach us, she shouldn't be there, but if she's there, she should at least let us do up to our potential. Angie, she only care about keeping us under her.

Angie: Okay. You know what I am learning from you right now Darkside? I am learning that teaching science in inner-city schools, or any schools, is as much about access and empowerment as it is about the actual content of the stuff you are supposed to learn. If teachers do not provide the right kinds of contexts for students, then how are students supposed to learn? I am also learning that science is a scary thing for teachers because if your teacher really does not want you to be smarter than she is, then something about knowing a lot of science must make her afraid.

Darkside: She might lose control.

Angie: If holding back science is about control, or I might say power, then why do you—or why did I—have teachers who did not worry about this? Like your teacher with the baking soda and vinegar?

Darkside: Well, first, Miss, is that I think an inner-city school is different about control and all. I think that kids in the suburbs just sometimes do what their told. Control in the city is different. Especially where I go to school. Gangs, and tough kids. Maybe she's afraid if kids get smarter than her, she wouldn't be able to tell them what to do. Like, I think about my teacher who taught us experiments, and she was always answering our questions, but she respected us. She helped us use our knowledge to help ourselves. It wasn't like using knowledge to control your classroom.

Angie: That is a very strong point. Teachers can hold knowledge or share knowledge for certain reasons with kids. So, I am interested in just what your science teacher was teaching you. Think about just the little bit that she is teaching you. You just said she was not teaching you enough. Is that little bit she is teaching you science?

Darkside: I guess so.

Angie: Can you explain to me what you mean?

Darkside: It is about the earth and the atmosphere, so it is science.

Angie: Okay, but remember you also said that science was about figuring out how things work. Is it that too?

Darkside: Oh, well she tells us how things work. So, yah, we learning science. Like last week, she was talking about the environment, and about how clouds form. She told us there were different kinds of clouds, and that the different kinds of clouds formed for different reasons. Thunderstorm clouds. Fair weather clouds. Rain clouds. But, then, that's it. We don't do nothing with it, except fill out of worksheets. She don't even answer our questions. I wanted to know about tornadoes, but she just telling me that I was acting out.

Angie: So, you're learning science when she talked about the clouds?

Darkside: Yah.

Angie: How about when you were doing the worksheets.

Darkside: I guess so, but it was boring. You're a teacher; don't you think that is dumbing us down?

Angie: Yes. I remember I had several of teachers that made us do worksheets, watch filmstrips, and do more worksheets. I like science because I like to figure things out. I think this is why I picked that part of science out of your definition of science. I was bored in my classes where we had to do worksheets because I didn't have to figure things out. I was only repeating what I heard. It did not really matter if I understood it. I felt like in my class where all we did was listen to the teacher and write things down, that I was only learning just a thin slice of science. One class I liked a lot when I was in high school was where we studied the insects that lived around our school. We didn't follow the textbooks. We had to use the books to find information, but what we really studied was based on what insects we found outside our building. To this day, I think I know more about insects than most other things I learned in high school science. As I think about this class, it makes me wonder about how "learning" science and "doing" science are interrelated. What do you think? Is learning science the same thing as doing science to you? or Is it the same thing as knowing science?

Darkside: Learning science and doing science are different. Like in the abandoned lot action research project, we were doing science. We were using our hands, our minds, figuring out what we need here, what we need there to make the garden. It's like, we start with the lot, and we have to decide what are we going to do with it? It is full of litter and pollution. It has got needles, trash, and all of that nasty stuff. Then, we talk about it, debate it, and decide what to do. What we did was some research on what we could do. What was cheap? What would not have too much upkeep? What would other kids not vandalize? We measured the lot, using math and measuring tapes. Then we made maps and 3-D models of what we wanted to do. In the end, we decided on a community garden. That's doing science.

Angie: Can you learn science and do science at the same time?

Darkside: Yes, that's what we was doing.

Angie: But not in school?

Darkside: No. Not in school. It is like when I was a kid; I mixed potions. I figured out what happened when we mixed vinegar and baking soda. I did that in one of my school classes too. I learned a lot in that class. That teacher was good. She respected us. It is like the lot. We are fixing it up, figuring out how to fix it. We are making it better for the community.

Angie: Okay, then is there a difference between just doing science and doing science for the community?

Darkside: Well, science for the community is for the community. Just doing science might not be for anyone. But, let me think because I would think you would always be doing science for something. Like research. You can research medicines, and that would be for people. Or, buses or whatever that would be for people.

Angie: But what about basic research? I mean, what about very basic science that is in its early stages and so people do not know what it is for.

Darkside: You mean like when people was first studying atoms?

Angie: Yes. That is a great example. What about that?

Darkside: That may not have been for people right away, but now it is.

Angie: So, is it really important in terms of doing science that it is for someone?

Darkside: Like I said before, science is something that you do in your community that you can be proud of. It is something that you do in your community to be remembered by. And, science is something that will help to beautify and change your community to make it a better place for yourself, your family and your community. You want to change the environment and make a difference. That is what we are trying to do to this lot over here. It is important to do things for your community, to make it a better place. That's what we are doing with the lot. Beautify it. Help people want to be there, to spend time there. We need to help our community.

Angie: Darkside, you know what is interesting to me about what you are saying? Well, I agree that what you are doing in the lot is science. I also agree with you that using your hands and your mind to figure out how to transform the lot is science. I also agree with you that scientists are always doing science for something, even if it is really basic research. But, one thing I never thought about before is how you talk about the science community and doing science as doing something that you can be proud of and remembered by. I never thought of those qualities as being part of science or a requirement of science.

Darkside: Maybe it is not a part of science. Maybe it is just a part of doing science. I'm doing science for my community.

Angie: So, the object of doing science is as much to figure something out for someone, like how the world works or something, as it is actually producing something useful to be remembered by? So, science has two parts?

Darkside: There is another part, and that is that it has to be good for the community. Like with the lot, we are beautifying the community.

Angie: I agree that science should have noble goals; that it should be about improving the world. I think one thing that your story helps me to see is that the local community, like the people here in the South Bronx, should be the ones to decide whether something is good. So, if some other people came in to change the lot, they should talk with the people around the community to see what they want, or they might not know if it is good for that community. I think science can be done without this quality, but it is not the kind of science that I want to support.

Darkside: I agree. You have to ask the community. You can do science without asking the community, but it might not be that good. Thinking about it, maybe you cannot even just ask the community. Maybe you have to involve the community, too in the science since it is about them. About us.

* * *

We wrote our auto/biographies and shared them with each other before rewriting this conversation shared above. We believe this order of events is important because knowing more about each other influenced how we understood each other's ideas about school and science. We believe that our conversation gets at many points about science and science education, but the most important point we want to raise is that shared stories, such as the shared stories above about science, community, school, and the lot project, provide us with a significant way to understand the world, and to challenge the understandings we bring to the world (Personal Narratives Group, 1989).

There are several stories that get spun through our conversation. We use the word "spun" to conjure up the image of spinning a web, such as a spider might do. We come to our conversation with our own histories and ideas. We give these selectively to each other; we use them to support each other and to challenge each other until we create a strong web of meaning. There are still places where individual strands (individual understandings) can be identified. There are places where the strands come together and merge. There are still other places where they intersect, but only for a moment. It is the larger web taken together as a whole image that we feel represents more completely our crafted understandings. Furthermore, we like the idea that many spiders build cobwebs, which are masses of web that are irregular or without a distinct form, and that web spinning spiders spin new webs almost daily. We would like to draw from these ideas as well—that our stories are without distinct boundaries and they change daily with our life experiences.

But, let us go back to our spun stories. First, there is the story about schooling and the differences between inner-city education and "other" education and the impact this has on the lives of youth. Then, there is the story about the purposes and goals of teaching, and how such purposes and goals are inextricably linked to larger social and political agendas. Then there is the story about silenced stories—the on-going critique present in our talk about just how much of what we know or want to know is muted by the very act of schooling. But the story we want to focus on here is the one we piece together about doing "good science" and how this idea of "good science" takes on different meanings in different contexts. In particular, sharing our stories with each other both privately (in personal conversations) and publicly (through action research and this paper) led us to understand from multiple perspectives how different people do science differently and how this is important in at least *three* contexts.

First, we talk about doing science for "ourselves" in urban settings. Doing science in urban settings for ourselves is important because doing such science enables us to act on our own needs as well as identifies us as individuals who know *how* to act on our own needs in positive and productive ways. Here, science has a utilitarian purpose.

Second, we also talk about doing science for others, and that this is important in urban settings because science is most importantly about increasing the greater good beginning with the "good for the self" then growing into "the good for the larger social community." Here, science has a social purpose.

Third, we talk about doing science for the larger community of science because such new science is where the revolution is. For example, if someone or some group were to enter Darkside's community to transform the lot, that would be science, but to be good science, that individual or group would need to engage in such a process in collaboration with those who live in the community. This would radically alter the focus and scope of the science to be done.

What is interesting about these three qualities of doing science is that they shy away from the day-to-day qualities that make science distinct from other disciplinary domains, such as particular discursive practices or ways of thinking. Our stories do not suggest that these qualities are not important, or at least not important to make subject for critique in our talk about science. However, our stories highlight the motivations for doing science in urban contexts, or what fundamental qualities we see as central to the doing of science in urban contexts because it is these qualities that are ultimately transformed into the actual science. We can return to our talk about transforming the lot to make just this point: As expressed in our conversation, one of Darkside's major reasons for helping to transform the abandoned lot into a garden is that he wants to be proud of his community. He wants people to walk by, to stop and sit down, and to enjoy what the garden has to offer. He feels he is mostly doing science because he is testing the soil, planting vegetables and flowers, cleaning up the pollution, recycling, and doing something positive for his community. He feels like he has learned some science but only science that will contribute to his local community, a place he is proud of and hopes to be remembered by. Also expressed in the conversation is Angie's desire to work with youth to help them see and use science as a tool for social action. And, also expressed in this conversation is Angie's challenge of Darkside's description of what constitutes science and Darkside's challenge to Angie to think about what qualities of youth emerge in urban contexts. These supported and challenged understandings inform our conversation about the motivations for doing science for oneself, the larger social community, and the larger scientific community, *and* they become the science in both its question and its form.

We can think of several other stories outside of our own of other people sharing their stories in scientific and engineering practice that also make this point. Seat belts in the front seats of cars only recently were redesigned to fit smaller people. The reason why this is the case is that seat belt engineers realized that the seat belts were designed for men's larger bodies. Once car companies started to include female seat belt engineers and female test drivers, they realized that driver's side seatbelts often strung across the smaller female drivers' necks (instead of their shoulder and chest). Another example involves understanding how life histories shape the science that people do. For example, Evelyn Fox Keller (1985) eloquently showed us, in her account of Barbara McClintock, how there is power in deeply understanding the reflexive relationship between personal lives and science, and how science is humanist in the sense that it reflected McClintock's empathy with the plants she studied as well as her own spirituality. Her science was a *manifestation of herself* in complex ways that included her procedures in doing science, her interpretations of her observations and her final, groundbreaking articulations of genetic theory. They were revolutionary because they were *different* and they were different because McClintock was different. Yet, the rules for practice in school science leave the practice of personal lives silenced, or at best marginalized through the presentation of limited accounts of the lives of others. Even in cases where the lives of others are brought into the account of science, these accounts brush over personal lives to elevate professional lives. We believe our stories show how the two do intermingle.

Biography and Science as Local Knowledge

Auto/biography is the highest and most instructive form in which the understanding of life confronts us. Here is the outward phenomenal course of a life which forms the basis of understanding what has produced it within a certain environment.

—Wilhelm Dilthey, 1960, p. 89

When our lived experience of theorizing is fundamentally linked to the process of self recovery, of collective liberation, no gap exists between theory and practice. Indeed, what such experience makes more evident is the bond between the two—that ultimately reciprocal process wherein one enables the other.

—bell hooks, 1994, p. 61

In science education, we hear a great deal about making science connected to everyday life. We believe our entrance into auto/biography suggests that we need to think about a different set of questions: What is everyday life? What does it mean to understand everyday life? How might thinking about "lived experience" provide a different kind of insight into science and science education?

Our reform efforts geared towards creating a science for all, like many previous student-centered reform efforts have taken seriously the call to help students understand and connect to science by explaining scientific phenomenon through "real world" experiences. Reform initiatives in science education rely on the use of personal experience because it has been shown to help students understand science better, to have more positive attitudes towards science, and to understand how science applies to their own lives (AAAS, 1989; NRC, 1996). This is significant. However, when science educators use personal experience to help students understand science, or to explain science, or to make science more real, then there is a hierarchical ranking placed on the value of students' particular experiences (Barton, 1998a). Specifically, those out-of-school experiences that are deemed acceptable in science class (i.e. the ones that fit well or neatly with the kinds of concepts taught) are more highly valued than those deemed unacceptable. Using "real life examples" in science class has favored boys (Roychoudhury, Tippins, & Nichols, 1995) and children with financial and educational resources (Apple, 1994; Giroux, 1991; Willis, 1977) through such things as machines, construction, and the world of work and men's bodies. For example, in physics classrooms, teachers (and children) talk about bicycle pumps, toasters, and electrical wiring systems to help students understand thermodynamics and electromagnetism. Yet, students' readings of their experiences often do not fit neatly or fully those prescribed experiences located within the borders of science. Valuing lived experience and their complexities, and idiosyncrasies challenges "neat science." They implode the boundaries that separate science from nonscience. As a result of these critiques, two sets of questions that have been raised include (a) "what happens when children do not have experiences with these kinds of things? How will they connect to the scientific knowledge base?" (b) How are students' lived experiences used, manipulated, forced, pulled, and tugged to *fit within the confines of science*?

These questions suggest that there is an important distinction between connecting science with "everyday experiences" and connecting science with "lived experiences." In an early essay Maxine Greene (1978/1994) asks, "What is every day life?" In response to her own question Greene writes that it only becomes meaningful to think about everyday life when we also think about how everyday life constitutes an "interpreted reality" and that such "interpretations come form many directions and perspectives," many of which uphold racist, classist and sexist practices (p. 17).

So, what does it mean to make science education connected to lived experience and how does auto/biography help us do this? Greene's ideas brings us back to the quote which opened this paper:

When talking about their lives, people lie sometimes, forget a lot, exaggerate, become confused, and get things wrong. Yet, they are revealing truths. These truths don't reveal the past "as it actually was," aspiring to a standard of objectivity. They give us instead the truths of our experiences. (Personal Narratives Group, p. 261)

What we see as important is that auto/biography becomes a piece of history, a lens by which to interpret what features of that context have significance for the author, and in what ways and through what connections (Steedman, 1986). In this sense, auto/biography brings together an understanding of personal identity and cultural context that are meant "to call to question a taken for granted rendition and logic of a time and place" (Franzosa, 1992, p. 396). In science education, we see this stance as a call to question the universal subject and disciplinary truths of science. Our stories reject a foundational epistemology in science and science education. They call for a transformed subject that challenges singular ways of knowing or being in science. This is most certainly true about the interchange that we have about what it means to "do" science and what it means to be a member of the scientific community in connection to transforming the lot. Our stories also point towards a vision of a greater objective understanding of the issues facing youth and adults as they collaboratively engage in urban science education. However, perhaps most importantly, our stories point towards how we might think about greater objectivity and science education as about local knowledge rather than universalism.

In her book of selected poems, Adrienne Rich (1972) writes about local knowledge: "Your house as a tiny flick on an ever-widening landscape, or as the center of it all from which the circles expanded into the infinite unknown." Rich's quote raises the question: When we think of local knowledge, what and who do we think of? Elspeth Probyn (1990) begins to answer Rich's question in her writings about locale and location. In writing about her own experiences growing up in England, Canada and Wales, she wrote that one of her most tremendous adolescent challenges was to accept the fact that "being from everywhere meant that on the playground you were no one (no one's cousin, or niece or neighbor since birth)" (p. 176).

For us, Probyn's and Rich's quote problematize the often implicit linkage of "local" to a particular place, a particular set of understandings, or a particular set of experiences, such as are the assumptions made in science reform efforts connecting "science with everyday life." We believe that these quotes, along with our stories about our lives and about science suggest that we need to develop a more dynamic understanding of "local" and hence "local knowledge." Doing science is always inscribed by individuals interacting dialectically with socioculture in a distinctive way to generate something (Haraway, 1997). As Darkside stated about our work transforming the lot:

Like I said before, science is something that you do in your community that you can be proud of. It is something that you do in your community to be remembered by. And, science is something that will help to beautify and change your community to make it a better place for yourself, your family and your community. You want to change the environment and make a difference. That is what we are trying to do to this lot over here. It is important to do things for your community, to make it a better place. That's what we are doing with the lot. Beautify it. Help people want to be there, to spend time there. We need to help our community.

Darkside's comments echo the feminist and cultural studies of science critique of the objectivist relationship between science, technology, and society (Ashmore, 1989; Traweek, 1988). Scientific knowledge is local and reflexive: the production of knowledge is connected with the social uses of and needs for scientific knowledge, and that knowing and the doing of science are continuously re-situated within ones own shifting context.

Thus, as students, teachers, and researchers, we have the capacity to understand critically our life experiences, and how these life experiences shape how we come to know science in local but dynamic ways (Lave & Wenger, 1991). Central to this idea is that through telling and re-telling our stories, we can connect personal "critical insight" to both the nature of our relationships with other individuals, institutional cultural values, such as those in school and in science, and political events, and the ways in which these social relationships contribute to the our own identity, values and ideological perspectives (Barton, 1998). In this way we can develop the capacity to participate in shaping and responding to the social forces that directly affect our lives in the home community, school, and science (on this point, see also Joe Kincheloe's chapter).

Challenging the Canon

We began this chapter with the thesis that auto/biography in science education is important because it provides a space to allow science to emerge from one's lived experience, a sort of auto/biography as local knowledge as science, and for the ways in which it emphasizes greater objectivity in the process of constructing a local science. This has wide ranging implications in science education. It challenges the canon that science teachers have been charged to teach. It challenges the ways in which students are expected to claim (or not to claim) that canon for their own. It challenges the kinds of research we do on how teachers teach and how students learn the subject of science. Science education, like teacher education, is an ideological education: It promotes particular images of power, knowledge and values by rewarding particular forms of individual and institutional behavior (Britzman, 1986). As we have shared, students', teachers' and researchers' experiences, like the canon of science, cannot be taken for granted and they cannot be left to lie untouched behind the tails of a universalistic subject of science. Our stories and conversations give witness to the ways in which critical examination of lived experiences leads to the breakdown of the universal subject and the knowledge-power nexus in science and science education through enabling researchers and teachers to gain the possibility of perceiving the world from the traditional viewpoint of the people who lead lives that are different from those traditionally in control of the means for imaging the world. Most importantly, embedded within the idea of "auto/biography in science education" is the belief that local people themselves are best able to define and articulate their own needs and that they ought to be the most important actors in designing efforts to address those needs.

But can auto/biography, even as telling and interaction, in science education stand alone? In some ways the researcher, or teacher, is the facilitator, the bridge builder between the author and the setting. This pushes the role of the teacher or researcher out the neutral position first because s/he has her own auto/biography from which to make sense of the world, and because s/he must be accountable to the authors and openly committed to certain kinds of social change. When working with youth and families who are homeless, or who live in urban poverty, this issue is crucial because their experiences are typically not legitimated in practice of school science or school science research. Thus, the researcher or the teacher must recognize the political nature of writing one's life, and an understanding of the intersections between discussion and action, and the ability to facilitate dialog about the social and political contexts of all of the authors' stories.

Notes

This chapter is a slightly edited version of a previously published text: Barton, A. C., & Darkside (2000). Auto/biography in science education: Greater objectivity through local knowledge. *Research in Science Education, 30*, 23–42. Darkside is the "nom de plume" of an African American student who had worked with Angie Barton.

[1] Although our stories are represented in written form, they were originally documented in written, oral, and video format (Darkside), and written format and oral format (Angie).

[2] This action research project was an after school program for teens at a New York City homeless shelter. The implicit objectives were to engage the youth in "doing science for social change." The explicit objectives were to involve the youth in studying their community, defining questions and problems to solve, and working through the process of actually solving the problems. The issue targeted by the youth described by Darkside in this paper was an abandoned city plot across the street from the shelter. The youth studied the plot and carried out the necessary activities to transform it into a community garden.

[3] This conversation is a compilation of several conversations that have been transcribed and edited appropriately for the purpose of this paper.

References

American Association for the Advancement of Science. (1989). *Science for all Americans*. Washington, DC: AAAS.

Apple, M. (1994). *Official knowledge: Democratic education in a conservative age*. New York: Routledge.

Ashmore, M. (1989). *The reflexive thesis: Writing sociology of scientific knowledge*. Chicago: University of Chicago Press.

Barton, A. C. (1998). *Feminist science education*. New York: Teachers College Press.

Britzman, D. (1986). Cultural myths and the making of a teacher: Biography and social structure. *Harvard Education Review, 56*, 442–456.

Delpit, L. (1988). The silenced dialogue: Power and pedagogy in educating other people's children. *Harvard Educational Review, 58*, 280–298.

Dilthey, W. (1960). *Pattern and meaning in history*. New York: Harper and Row.

Franzosa, S. (1992). Authoring the educated self: Educational auto/biography and resistance. *Educational Theory, 42*, 395–412.

Giroux, H. (1991). *Postmodernism, feminism and cultural politics: Redrawing educational boundaries*. Albany: State University of New York Press.

Greene, M. (1978/1994). The lived world. In L. Stone (Ed.), *The education feminism reader* (pp. 17–25). New York: Routledge.

Haraway, D. (1997). *Modest witness@second-millennium. FemaleMan-meets-oncomouse: Feminisms and technoscience*. New York: Routledge.

Harding, S. (1991). *Whose science? Whose knowledge? Thinking from women's lives*. Ithaca, NY: Cornell University Press.

hooks, b. (1994). *Teaching to transgress*. New York: Routledge.

Keller, E. F. (1985). *Reflections on gender and science*. New Haven and London: Yale University Press.

Lave, J., & Wenger, E. (1991). *Situated learning: Legitimate peripheral participation*. Cambridge: Cambridge University Press.

National Research Council (NRC). (1996). *National science education standards*. Washington, DC: National Academy Press.

Personal Narratives Group. (1989). *Interpreting women's lives: Feminist theory and personal narratives*. Bloomington: Indiana University Press.

Polkinghorne, D. (1987). *Narrative, knowing and the human sciences*. Albany: State University of New York Press.

Probyn, E. (1990). Travels in the postmodern: Making sense of the local. In L. Nicholson (Ed.), *Feminism/postmodernism* (pp. 176–189). New York: Routledge.

Rich, A. (1979). *On lies, secrets and silence*. New York: W. W. Norton & Company.

Roychoudhury, A., Tippins, D., & Nichols, S. (1995). Gender-inclusive science teaching: A feminist perspective. *Journal of Research in Science Teaching, 32*, 897–930.

Steedman, C. (1986). *Landscape for a good woman: A story of two lives*. London: Virago Press.

Traweek, S. (1988). *Beamtimes and lifetimes: The world of high energy physicists*. Cambridge, MA: MIT Press.

Willis, P. (1977). *Learning to labour: How working class kids get working class jobs*. New York: Columbia University Press.

3   **Fictive Imagining and Moral Purpose: Auto/bio-
graphical Research as/for Transformative Development**

Les Pereira, Elisabeth Settelmaier, Peter Charles Taylor

But seldom, if ever, do we ask the "who" question—who is the self that teaches?
How does the quality of my selfhood form-or deform-the way I relate to my students, my subject, my colleagues, my world? How can educational institutions sustain and deepen the selfhood from which good teaching comes? (Parker Palmer,
1998, p. 4)

Introduction

The past decade has witnessed self-study research being embraced enthusiastically by educational researchers worldwide, as evidenced by specialist research
journals such as *Reflective Practice* and *Studying Teacher Education*, an international handbook (Loughran, Hamilton, LaBoskey & Russell, 2004), and the rapidly growing *Self-Study of Teacher Education Practice* special interest group of
the American Educational Research Association.

Auto/biographical research refers to a family of related forms of self-study,
including auto/ethnography (Ellis, 1997), life history research (Casey, 1993),
testimonio (Tierney, 2000), and writing as inquiry (Richardson, 2000). Thus,
educators have a range of methodological tools for addressing Parker Palmer's
(1998) challenging "who" question, either as lone contemplatives or as interactive facilitators of change in their professional cultures. When coupled with
critical social theory, auto/biographical research heightens practitioner-
researchers' reflective awareness of their embodiment of the culture of their profession, bringing to consciousness the moral, ethical, and political values that

shape their educative relationships with students and colleagues. By understanding deeply how historical, social, and cultural forces are shaping their lives, educators may come to view their established professional practices with a fresh eye, feeling empowered to initiate transformative change such as democratizing institutional decision-making or creating learning environments in which flourish higher-level modes of thinking and feeling (Brookfield, 1995; O'Sullivan et al., 2002). Not surprisingly, critical auto/biographical research is of growing interest to culture studies researchers working with indigenous educators in transitional societies to develop postcolonial curricula that are inclusive of local cultural practices and aspirations (Luitel & Taylor, in press; Taylor, 2004).

In this chapter we focus on auto/biographical inquiry as a transformative tool for professional educators: (a) to examine critically and creatively ways in which their own moral values impact their everyday choices and decisions, and (b) to develop a practical wisdom with which to make better professional choices and decisions. We are particularly interested in the unconventional use of fictive biographical inquiry for extending educators' professional development beyond the horizon of their own lived experience to embrace the lived experience of colleagues.

Auto/biographical research adopts qualitative forms of inquiry, such as narrative and story, thereby generating knowledge that is contextual and practical in nature (Carter, 1993; Connelly & Clandinin, 1988). This knowledge is embodied in the everyday actions of practitioner-researchers striving to transform local cultures of learning and teaching through growth in their own and perhaps also their colleagues' practical knowledge. But how might this knowledge be represented (and thus communicated) other than in social actions, especially if a practitioner-researcher is serving an academic agenda that privileges a literary culture of dissertation writing? Hence we turn to the field of postmodern qualitative research, which offers an arts-based approach to research writing, including literary genres and post-epistemological research standards (Denzin & Lincoln, 2000; Geelan & Taylor, 2002; Stapleton & Taylor, 2003; Tierney & Lincoln, 1997). In this chapter we provide exemplars of postmodern auto/biographical research writing, illustrating how these genres can serve as means for constituting and representing growth in the practical knowledge of educators engaged in self-study.

* * *

Hang on! If postmodern auto/biographical writing is so powerful then why am I (Peter) privileging the conventional objective genre of science as I write this introduction? By using the passive voice of the omnipotent narrator, writing authoritatively on behalf of my invisible coauthors, doesn't the writing almost masquerade as having written itself, serving as a neutral conduit down which flows the authority of the cited research literature? Why do I not practice what my coauthors and I are "preaching" by revealing something significant about ourselves? Where are our voices and the authority of our lived experience? Am I perhaps fearful about contesting the hegemony of the conventional scientific genre? Or do I perhaps not really value the "messy texts" of postmodern qualitative research (Denzin & Lincoln, 2000)? Could it be that I am reluctant to deal with imagined editorial or peer review disapproval? On the other hand, as a transformative educator I am a strong advocate of epistemological pluralism and the deconstruction of restrictive hegemonies. And I endeavor to persuade my graduate students to commence their inquiries by excavating sedimented beliefs underpinning their professional experience. So, shouldn't I too be writing here in a way that is at least somewhat consistent with my own professional values?

It might be obvious to the reader familiar with the autoethnographic writing of Carolyn Ellis (e.g., Ellis & Bochner, 2000), the phenomenological writing of Max van Manen (1990, 2002), and the confessional and impressionistic writing of John van Maanen (1988) that I have shifted to a postmodern genre of self-conscious dialogical writing. I value this form of writing because of its educative potential, especially for my graduate students, most of whom are educators conducting auto/biographical studies of their professional practice. In my experience, carefully crafted written language creates a rich educative space for bringing the inquirer's subjectivity into the foreground, enabling it to be examined critically and reflectively, and developed further via creative and contemplative thinking. In this post-Wittgensteinean moment of history, and influenced by Don Cupitt's (2001) philosophy of bright empty radical humanism, I regard language almost as "all there is." I use language to create my social realities and relationships, my professional and private identities. And so it makes eminently good sense to me that, via artistically skilful use of language, I grow my self in all these dimensions. This is my experience now, in the moment of this act of writing. Extending this line of thinking, it follows that a unique characteristic of auto/biographical research is the self-conscious and dialogical use of language to grow the professional self.

The knowledge that emerges from this process differs significantly in epistemological terms from scientific knowledge inasmuch as it is bound to the context of the inquiry, is personal in nature, but has a moral practicality for reshaping the professional educator's social roles and relationships. The moral dimension affords the potential not only to transform the self but also to develop a praxis for transforming the social world in which the professional self is located, as has been demonstrated in several autoethnographic studies I have mentored (e.g., Afonso & Taylor, 2003; Luitel & Taylor, in press). Recently I have discovered a powerful way of organizing my thinking about the various types of knowledge that emerge from arts-based auto/biographical research. Based on John Dewey's philosophy of education for a democratic society, Henderson and Kesson (2004) have designed a professional development model of *practical wisdom*: a high level state of mind attuned to complex and morally astute decision-making and problem solving. The model advocates research as/for professional development of teachers by means of seven modes of inquiry—*techné, poesis, praxis, dialogos, phronesis, polis,* and *theoria.* Several of these modes already are well known to qualitative educational researchers, whilst others are likely to be unfamiliar. What I find exciting is that when an auto/biographical inquiry, in league with these modes of inquiry, employs language artfully to give expression to lived experience, both actual and envisaged, the outcome is a rich array of voices of the self—reflexive, dialogic, poetic, heroic, imaginative, soulful, vulnerable, etc. Their creative juxtaposition on the printed page provides a powerful educational space for the reader, as well as the writer.

As I write this introduction I have in hand two doctoral research theses I have mentored that exemplify arts-based auto/biographical research. In the first, written by Elisabeth Settelmaier (2003), the researcher used auto/biography to investigate the historicity of her own moral sensitivities/sensibilities, seeking to understand why she felt compelled to advocate the teaching of ethical dilemmas in school science. Elisabeth and teachers in an Austrian secondary school co-wrote fictive dilemma stories and evaluated their impact on student learning in the teachers' classrooms. The auto/biographical aspect of the research enabled Elisabeth to excavate her childhood memory and articulate the source of her professional values, thereby making explicit her standpoint in the interpretive aspect of the research. Without wishing to give too much away, I shall disclose that she was born in the same town as Adolf Hitler and, as with many Austrian youth, grew up in the dark shadow of their country's early twentieth-century history. Elisabeth's thesis and subsequent publications contain an extensive account of critical auto/biographical research theory and practice (Settelmaier, in press; Taylor & Settelmaier, 2004), parts of which are presented below.

Les Pereira's (2005) doctoral thesis research, a critical and fictive auto/biographical[1] study of his own school leadership practice, was completed more recently. Les commenced his inquiry within an ethnographic ethos, documenting incidents that typified the culture of the school to which he had been appointed as a culture-changing deputy principal. He adopted a writing-as-inquiry approach (Richardson, 2000) and wrote auto/biographical narratives for the purpose of reflecting critically and creatively on his evolving school leadership praxis. But he also wished to portray interpretively the thoughts and values behind the actions of school colleagues with whom he interacted as deputy principal. At a critical juncture, however, he departed from the conventional constructivist standards of interpretive inquiry that compelled him to "member-check" the credibility of his constructed representations of others (Guba & Lincoln, 1989). In order for his research role to serve authentically his leadership role (rather than vice versa) he realized that he could not subject his colleagues to this particular epistemic imperative. Given the politically and ethically sensitive nature of his transformative leadership role, Les needed to be perceived by his colleagues as engaging in authentic school-based problem solving, rather than in the seemingly inauthentic practice of a self-interested researcher. A feature of Les' subsequent research is his use and creative juxtaposition of a range of texts and voices, including auto/biographical writing, fictive biographies of colleagues, and extracts from popular literature and songs.

Elisabeth and Les, respectively, present the following sections. The chapter concludes with reflections from the three of us.

Excavating One's Own Ethical History

When I (Elisabeth) started my doctoral research, one of the first things Peter did was to encourage me to write an auto/biography, which I did only reluctantly at first. I could not really see the point in "taking time away from my study" in order to dig deep into issues that were by no means special nor very meaningful to me—How could they be meaningful to other people? At that point in time, I must admit, I was not aware that anything related to my past had any bearing on my doctoral studies. It took me several levels of auto/biographical analysis to realize that a lot of things (if not the whole of my past life) had to do with my studies—some more than others. In particular, I found that my upbringing in a particular environment had influenced me directly to develop certain values and attitudes—"sensitivities"—toward the relationship between ethics and science. I would like to introduce you to a vignette drawn from my doctoral thesis (Settelmaier, 2003), which takes you to the environment I grew up in, a small, sleepy town in Upper Austria.

How it all Began

Looking back I can see some influences during my early life that have probably made me very sensitive to ethical dilemma situations. One influential dilemma has to do with my birthplace: My father used to be a medical doctor before his retirement. He worked in medical research in Vienna, in the Netherlands, and in Britain for many years before he gave up this academic career and became the senior-anesthetist at the local hospital in a semi-rural town in Upper Austria. My parents decided to move from Vienna to Braunau am Inn, a small but beautiful, medieval town of architectural splendor, only a few years before I was born.

This decision presented me with the dubious pleasure of sharing my birthplace, with—of all people—Adolf Hitler, a fact that indeed was to be of some importance for my personal development later. It involves being confronted with a incomprehensible past at an early age, as well as being "equated" with the Nazis of sixty years ago, no matter what your personal political stance really is due to the fact that many people overseas tend to identify "Nazi" with "German" or even worse Austrian, due to a lack of historical knowledge, I believe. The dilemma with

Braunau for me was that, on the one hand, I love the place. I still have my parents and many friends there. I like the people. I love the river Inn, its quiet hidden arms, relatively intact ecosystems along the river, bird and beaver colonies, river-woods that offered us a great adventure playground in the sixties and seventies.

But times have changed: Braunau is now a border town within the European Union. In 2002 the river-woods are no longer safe for children to play in: they have become a different type of "playground"—illegal immigrants trying to cross the river into Germany play hide-and-seek with border patrols which are supposed to prevent "illegals" from "infiltrating" the German border. But this is a different story, reflecting modern-day Austria.

The peacefulness and sleepiness of the small town is deceptive: Braunau's historical background tends to relate us to a particularly unsavory aspect of the past, even though Braunau's most notorious ex-citizen spent only two years of his life there—the first two years to be precise. Regardless how old Adolf was when he left, or how much of political indoctrination he had received whilst playing in his nappies: to uncritical and unknowing overseas visitors, Braunau's reputation has been tainted for all times.

The inhabitants of this small town do not really want to be seen in relation to this particular past. There is a strong spirit of political awareness about the past as especially this webpage shows clearly http://www.hrb.at/. This political aware-ness was especially obvious when a granite boulder was to be set up in front of Hitler's birthplace as a monument against Nazism, carrying the words, "Für Frieden, Freiheit und Demokratie—nie wieder Faschismus. Millionen Tote mah-nen."[2] The population of Braunau was split because a great number of people re-jected the project, but not as might be presumed because they opposed the monument as such or because they thought that Nazism was such great a thing but much rather out of fear that Braunau could become a pilgrimage-site for Neo-Nazis or other war-tourists from all over the world. Others saw it as a clear sign: Braunau is declaring its standpoint openly. Yet others, especially the elderly, thought the past should best be left alone and not be touched, "Let's be glad it's all over!"

* * *

To me, the value of auto/biographical research writing lies in the narratives that we can produce about our lives. But why, we may ask, is this worth the ef-fort? Surely, some might say, this is nothing but self-indulgence or narcissism (Bleakley, 2000). Barone (2001) suggests that narratives are designed to do what art does so well: to lay bare questions that have been hidden by the answers. Through auto/biographical inquiry, we might start to question that which seems unquestionable to us, a given fact, something that "has always been there." We might begin to confront what the phenomenologists call our "natural attitude," that is, our everyday way of thinking and valuing whose naturalness makes this process invisible to us in much the same way that the fish is unaware of the wa-ter in which it exists.

Writing my auto/biography forced me to look closer at the reasons for choosing science or science education as a career. Throughout my twenties and early thirties I had always thought that I had chosen science purely because it sounded interesting at the time. At the age of twenty-one, I had dropped out of medical studies after six semesters because studying medicine and having two toddlers did not go together well. I wanted to study something where I could use what I had already learned in relation to medicine and something that would allow me to raise a family at the same time. I started studying genetics at first and later changed to science education because I did not want to spend my whole life isolated in a laboratory but much rather I wanted to interact with people— becoming a teacher seemed the obvious choice! Digging a bit deeper revealed to my great surprise that the foundations for this choice had been laid years ago— at the age of five to be precise:

"A small step for a man, a giant leap for mankind" (Neil Armstrong)

Cuddled into the black leather TV chair in my parents' living room, wrapped in a blanket, I am watching the black and white, fuzzy pictures delivered from the moon's surface into our home. I remember having a strange feeling about the fact that some human beings are actually "up there" and are able to look down on "us."

I was five years old when Neil Armstrong first set foot on the moon. My family had gathered around the television set, my parents, my brothers, their girlfriends. . . I remember the tension in the room during those last moments before the landing—fear something might go wrong at the very last moment. At last it was certain—humankind had achieved something unique and I remember feeling that I had just witnessed something extraordinary. Pride of what humans can do, pride of what science can help us achieve. I believe that at this very moment the foundations for my interest in science were laid. As a child, I never wanted to become a nurse, a policewoman, least of all a teacher. Marie Curie as an idol was much more like it—funny enough, events and choices made during my later life have turned me into a science teacher. What is the meaning of that?

Later I remember seeing pictures from the Houston control room. My mother pointed out a man to me, tall and blond, amongst the scientists and technicians, "This is Wernher von Braun," she said. "He originally came from Germany and is now one of the great American rocket scientists. He has contributed considerably to this event tonight." I was impressed to say the least. The fact that he came from a neighboring country with some cultural and historical commonalities left us with a feeling as if we also to some degree shared the glory of the moment.

* * *

This vignette describes a defining moment—an epiphany if you like—when I seem to have made the decision to choose a direction in my life that would somehow link me to science. Before engaging in auto/biographical analysis, I had no memory of this detail of my history. It was buried underneath memories that posed as the reasons for my choice—in fact, these "reasons" were building on a potential that was in my mind already at the time. Self-reflection unearthed something I had simply "forgotten" but that was only dormant rather than lost.

When self-reflection becomes critical it involves a searching view of un-questioningly accepted presuppositions (Mezirow, 1991). Most of what we have learned about ourselves has not been examined for unconsciously incorporated assumptions. However, as I learned during the process of writing and sharing my auto/biography with others—my mentor in particular—this process might be of benefit to others. Instead of asking, "Why would anybody be interested in my unimportant life?" we might want to ask "What experiences, issues, stories from my life can be of benefit for others? What is it, in what I say, that others might recognize in themselves? How can this affect my research and my attitude about who I am dealing with as a researcher and what I hear from the participants of my research? What can I learn from getting to know myself better?"

In these postmodern times, dealing with one's own biases before interpret-ing and representing others has become an important issue of qualitative re-search ethics (Lincoln & Denzin, 2000). The "crisis of representation" has taught us to look critically at our attempts to speak authentically about other people's experiences. Many researchers now accept that they are not disinter-ested but are deeply invested in their studies, personally and profoundly. As a form of self-study, critical auto/biographical research involves a study of the re-searcher's self in relation to "the other" (Bullough & Pinnegar, 2001). For me, understanding what had driven me to take up studies into the development of an ethics curriculum within science education became a vital issue.

One area in my doctoral research where my personal involvement in the topics of ethics and science became especially apparent, was constituted by the topics of the dilemma stories the teachers and I co-wrote. The teachers had given me their planned curriculum in advance and I tried to find topics that would fit their planned curriculum so that the stories would not be too much of an artifi-cial add-on but much rather a vital part of the curriculum. One teacher, Sandra, was planning to teach astrophysics as part of the Year 10 physics course. I im-mediately thought of a story I had heard several years before on television that had deeply impressed me—the story of an astrophysicist who had been very tal-ented and successful yet his biography was tainted with war crimes. For the re-search, I turned this story into a fictional dilemma story based on the man's bi-ography. I have summarized the story for this context.

The story is about a rocket scientist who has a life ideal: he wants to build a rocket that can fly to the moon. The political situation in his country changes, a

new regime comes into power, and he is confronted with making a choice between staying in a country where human rights violations are reportedly happening, or leaving his research behind, which means having to start anew somewhere else. The new government lures him with generous research funding into
staying and collaborating with the totalitarian regime. Whilst encountering serious obstacles in his research that can be resolved only through human experiments—the government offers him the "use" of concentration camp prisoners.
Being driven to achieve his goal to build a rocket he accepts the offer. Many
prisoners lose their lives during the experiments. Meanwhile, the government
has engaged in a war and forces him to change his research focus from rockets
that can fly to the moon to missiles that can reach the enemy's territory. Once
again he regards this "interruption" to his plans as temporary only. After the
war, the researcher is "invited" to the United States to support the US space program with the knowledge he has gained during his career in his homeland. Even
though his knowledge was derived from the sufferings of many victims in the
concentration camps, he is now a sought-after man and he does not disappoint:
The Americans are the first to reach the moon. An awe-inspiring moment, yet
who thought about (or knew about) the prize that had to be paid to reach this
goal? (Settelmaier, 2003, in press)

The fictional character in the story is based on the biography of Wernher
von Braun, the man I had come to idealize from the moment of the first landing
on the moon when I was five years old—the same man described in the vignette
above. Von Braun was one of my idols when I chose a career in science. Finding
out about who this man really was raised a question I had been struggling with
from my childhood onwards: having grown up where I have grown up—can you
ever "trust" your idols? The impact of this revelation had been strong enough for
me to choose him as an example of bad research ethics many years later by making him the main character in one of the dilemma stories I evaluated with the
students. When I was writing the dilemma stories, I was unaware of the direct
relationship between my own past and my research.

One issue I was struggling with during the writing process was to fully
grasp the legitimacy of auto/biographical research. A number of researchers
have suggested guidelines and quality standards for narrative and self-studies in
particular. I would like to draw from Barone (2001) as well as from (Bullough &
Pinnegar, 2001). Barone and Eisner list qualities that turn a narrative into an
arts-based text. They suggest that the language should be expressive, contextualized. The text should create a virtual reality and present an aesthetic form. It
should carry the author's signature and above all, it should show a degree of textual ambiguity. For me, Bullough and Pinnegar (2001) ask the most crucial

question of all: When does self-study ever become research? Answering their own question, they explain that history and biography need to be joined, "When the issue confronted by the self is shown to have relationship to and bearing on the context and ethos of a time, the self-study moves to research" (p. 15). In order to answer the famous "so what?" question about the significance of the work that "wise" readers tend to ask, they emphasize that there must be a balance in evidence not only in what data have been gathered and presented but in how they have been analyzed, in how they have been brought together in conversation. Ultimately the aim of self-study research is moral, to gain understanding necessary to make the interaction between the researcher's self and others who share a commitment to the development and nurturance of the young increasingly educative.

According to Bullough and Pinnegar self-studies should ring true and enable connection and the author's voice should appear. This brings in the notion of what Adler and Adler (1994) refer to as verisimilitude. The stories should promote insight and interpretation. History should be engaged forthrightly and the author should take an honest stand. A good self-study should be a good read, and attend to nodal moments of our biographies, thereby enabling the reader to gain insight or understanding into the self. It was my goal to make my stories accessible to others by adhering to the above quality standards.

A Moral Dilemma and the Getting of Wisdom

In this section I (Les) present one of the story lines from the research I completed for my doctoral thesis. My purpose is to illustrate how critical auto/biographical research, involving a fictive approach to writing about a moral dilemma, can stimulate the development of a teacher's practical wisdom. As Elisabeth has pointed out, auto/biographical research raises concerns for some commentators, but I think that these concerns are from a theoretical rather than experiential perspective: like a cow denouncing the taste of deer to a lion. Poststructuralist theory tells us that all writing is essentially a work of fiction; embedded in the historicity of the writer and only ever a partial description of events, a fiction. I will return to this later. For the moment, I suggest that auto/biographical research, a powerful contributor to the generation of "owned" knowledge (Grundy, 1987), provides perspectival insight that may speak to the experiences of others. For, as Roland Barthes has pointed out, the "reader" writes the meaning of the text.

The approach I outline here includes auto/biography, biography, and a special genre that I call *fictive biography*. Throughout this section, you will hear my voice along with the voices of those who inhabited my research lifeworld. Although the narrative flow of the six-part *A Story of Our Times* represents the inquiry process I followed, I have taken a step outside the process to reflect on the auto/biographical method. The structure includes two types of commentary: one, breaking the flow of the story at strategic points to elaborate on what has gone before; and two, parallel 'asides' that present reflections on the process that was undertaken. Thus *A Story for Our Times* serves as a

> ----------Aside----------
> It is significant that the journal entries were written in real time. Auto/biographical episodes are necessarily written after the event, often once the final outcome is known. Perhaps, unconsciously, there is a tying together of loose ends and structuring of the narrative to maintain a coherence of thought, action, and result.

canvas against which the accompanying commentary rests. Parts I to IV are journal entries written shortly after the events they describe have occurred. Parts V and VI, however, are significantly different. They are poetic presentations: pieces of fictive writing that contribute to a rewriting of history . . . but more of that later.

A Story for Our Times—Part I

Marie came into my office wanting to see me. It turns out Damien is getting too close to a female student. Marie tells me she has discussed it with him as his line manager; that Albert has tried to talk to him about it as a colleague; that Damien is paying no attention. The issue: leaving his class unattended to chat with the student who, while out of class to go to the toilet, detoured past Damien's class; the student not going to her own class but sitting in Damien's class while he is teaching (another year group!); meeting up with her at lunchtime for "a chat."

"I've tried to explain it to him, Les, but he's not paying any attention. I've told him that staff are talking about it—students are talking about it, but he says they should come and see him if they really care. I don't know what to do next."

During her description I find myself playing over in my head previous discussions with Marie, memories of her particular way of working. She is a very thorough "get-it-done" person, she's not a "gonna" as Steph (the Principal) would say. But she is, as Marie puts it herself, "anal-retentive." She is a "very-down-the-line" person, a "maintain-a-meter-from-the-students-during-desk-supervision" kind of teacher—(I wonder how she would respond to the sight of students rubbing the bald spot on my head, or draping over my shoulder when I'm on duty, or in classes?). But this is not the same. Marie has a point if what she is saying is true.

"It's the same as last year," she adds. "We had exactly the same issue last year . . . with another girl." I fall back into wondering if Marie and the other teachers from "the girls' table" are a little jealous over the fact that the young male teacher is not paying any attention to them—they are power brokers within the school. The dying ring of "What do I do next?" brings me back from my deliberations.

* * *

So began an episode from my life as a deputy principal. As with all pieces of auto/biographical writing, it is part of the record of my development up to this point in my life; part of my "living educational theory," as Jack Whitehead (1989) might say. For me, a key aspect of auto/biographical research is that, in examining the events of my life, I give myself the opportunity to rewrite my history, to recreate the situation from outside the oppressive immediacy of real-time experience. I have the opportunity to reflect-on-action, on my reflection-in-action, and, in developing my understandings prior to future situations, to reflect-before action (Pereira, 2005; Schön, 1983). I have the opportunity to develop my life-praxis.

This story, of how I managed the relationship between Damien and Susan, along with my subsequent attempt to understand the dissatisfaction I felt with its conclusion, provides a moral landscape as murky as the waters of Donald Schön's (1983) swampy lowlands. But it is from out of this mire that a deeper richer understanding of the moral and ethical responsibilities of a leader appears.

A Story for Our Times—Part I Continued

"I'll speak to Steph and just check that she's happy with what I'm thinking," I conclude after outlining my plan. Marie apologizes for "dumping" this on me as she makes her way off to class.

Steph agrees with me taking it over—another job! It's too late for me to catch up with Damien before the end of the day so I leave a polite note in his pigeon hole asking him to come and see me Period Four the next day when he and Marie are free.

Part II—Some Time to Reflect

Fortunately, rather than by clever planning, I had given myself some space to think about the issues as I saw them. By arranging for the meeting to occur the day after Marie raised her concerns, I had the evening to get a "center" from which to respond. My thoughts weren't clear-cut although they did widen my understanding—a little.

An Entry from My Journal

I have a lot of empathy for Damien. Marie's concerns may have some validity and, if there is any truth in her claims, Damien is playing very close to the line. He is a little bit of a maverick, displaying the self-assured self-reliance of others like him, like me, who have come from industry, who know that schools are just one part of life's experiences. He chooses to spend his lunch times, alongside two of the other young male teachers, out by the Aboriginal Centre or on the oval, where students can see him, while Marie sits at the unwelcoming *Girls' table*. And this pays off; very rarely does he have significant problems with his students. Marie's concerns seem to originate from the clarity of the line she draws in the student-teacher relationship. Marie doesn't like blurry edges.

But how does a teacher develop a relationship that opens the door to genuine learning, to discussions that have life value? Marie would probably call into question some of the relationships I have had with students—I don't think she would understand. But the quality of relationship is central for a teacher and a student. I find it difficult to believe a passion for life-learning can be achieved through the sterile solution of linear equations (my subject area) or exercises in balancing the books in accounting (Marie's subject area). Much of the interaction that develops this kind of relationship is in the incidental, off-task conversations through which a teacher gains understanding of a student's orientations, interests and standpoint in the world. And on the student's side, maybe conversations about content and assignments are seen as part of the job whereas other time is given freely, carrying with it an implication of care; it's not part of the mandated curriculum.

Marie's approach is not mine. She is very business-like: rules, policy, and guidelines. As the curriculum officer she has produced mountains of newsletters, booklets of strategies and curriculum improvement program updates that everybody commends but few have read. She is excellent at getting the paperwork done and takes her role as a teacher-in-charge very seriously. She has little time for people who don't *do their job*. It is this approach that has brought her to me, a concern for *professionalism*. She is concerned about Damien: "he's not being very professional!"

But what is professional? Marie has very clear (dogmatic?) views about what it is to be a teacher and, like everybody, makes judgments according to her beliefs. She seems to acknowledge very few wavy edges at the boundaries of her knowledge; she doesn't look for the blur, the shadow. In all of our interactions, I have difficulty thinking of a time when she wasn't looking for clarification of an issue, the admin line, policy directions, the agenda, and minutes, minutes, minutes, other than when she was passing on staff complaints—she is always a valuable staff barometer. But like all of us, there is what she says and what she does; she doesn't always live up to her own standards. I have seen her standing outside her classroom chatting with other teachers while her class is working, a concern she has raised about Damien. Students have told me she takes phone calls in class, a complaint she has made about David (another member of Marie's department). I have seen her powerful, no-nonsense persona dissolve in tears as a result of Mario's (a

----------Aside----------
I had begun writing to analyze the situation and my thoughts, and perhaps give myself some guidance as to how to proceed. But the meandering road followed by my thoughts produced a far richer understanding that, colored by moral and ethical complexities, left me with a greater sense of confusion. Rather than approaching a possible solution, at the end, I was left with the feeling of being cornered, along with Damien.

colleague's) threatening behavior and her refusal to take up my help in addressing it in a professional way.

I can't help considering the role of the *Girls' table* in bringing Marie forward. They are power brokers within the school, Steph and I have discussed this a number of times, and they don't have time for the three young male teachers on staff, of which Damien is one. Gossip can be very useful in monitoring the temperature of the school, but it can also create a reality that didn't previously exist. Their role in this is worrying for me. If there is no need for concern their involvement could create one.

But the question remains, if there is any truth in the concerns that Marie has raised, how do I guide Damien away from what could become a sticky situation? The slightest hint of this kind of misconduct is a problem. If there is no truth I will need to bring the rumoring to a halt—and there is fat chance of that. Damien and I are both trapped!

* * *

My thoughts that evening had served only to stir up the waters. In trying to work out a plan of action I had brought myself to fundamental questions on the nature of my own practice, my beliefs and the responsibilities I felt with respect to developing the school. Coupled with this, the contextual factors brought to the foreground the strategic importance of my actions. In my failure to construct a satisfactory approach, I resigned myself to a "suck-it-and-see" approach.

Part III—The Next Day

Damien grabs me as I walk through the door, still carrying my bag. "I've got your note. Can we talk about it now?" He doesn't need to ask me what it's about.

"Not really, Damien. I have scheduled it so that Marie can be there as well."

"Does she need to be? Can't we just get it over with now? I'll forego the right to have her there."

"Well Marie is your line manager, Damien, so I want her to hear what's being said." He leaves, not happy.

Part IV—Later that Day

Marie turns out to be unable to make the meeting—due to a timetable mix-up she actually has a class at that time. It's Friday, and if I don't speak to him today he's got all the weekend ahead of him. We agree to talk about it Period Three and for me to talk to Marie separately—Damien doesn't know that I am only involved because I have already spoken to Marie.

"So what's it about?" Damien asks, maintaining the pretence. I'm sitting sideways on to him on the 'customer' side of the desk. He is clearly agitated and is hoping he's wrong about the topic for discussion.

"Staff and students are talking about your relationship with a student."

"Oh, not again. This happened last year." (Ooops!) "Who's complaining?"

"Well I can't say, Damien, but concerns have been raised by several staff and a number of students." I don't say that they have approached Marie not me.

"This is bullshit. They just want something to talk about. There's nothing going on."

"Well, I'm told that," I say and outline the things that Marie has told me.

Damien lies. He says that may have happened but ages ago. He, of course, continues to get angry and maintains a complete denial. "We're just mates."

"I guess that's part of the problem, Damien. You can't be "mates" with her, she's a student and you have to maintain a teacher–student relationship."

"You're picking me up on my words," I point out that I want to make sure we are both perfectly clear about what we mean. He's not happy. I explain the danger of the situation, that a teacher can't risk even unfounded gossip. "There's nothing going on," he repeats, a little more loudly, a little more insistent.

"Does she feel the same way?"

"What?" He looks straight at me, the lines of a frown developing above his semi-closed eyes.

"Does she feel the same way? Does she have any feelings for you?" There's no answer. Silence. "She has to go to her own classes, Damien. And you have to put some space between you." He's looking down at the floor, his face still flushed from his earlier frustrations.

"So do you think I should talk to her, tell her that we should 'cool' it?" I don't ask what there is to "cool"—but as time goes on I'm getting more convinced that Marie has called it correctly.

"Damien it needs to come to an end. Perceptions do count and that is why your colleagues are concerned. They are worried you don't understand the position you are placing yourself in."

"So concerned they don't talk to me!" I don't believe it either.

"If it continues, Damien, by you or her, I will have to arrange a parent interview." He goes white. That clinched it. It'll finish.

Damien leaves. He is not happy. Neither am I.

The End . . . for now

Enter Phronesis and Fictive Biography

This incident is characteristic of many situations in the life of a school leader, situations that often prove to be highly complex, but more importantly, inherently disagreeable. Although I knew it would never be possible to resolve issues to everybody's satisfaction, if I was going to follow this career path I needed a way of making sense of the complexities of situations. I needed to be satisfied that *I* had moved towards a balanced understanding that would support a judgment that didn't leave *me* feeling morally bankrupt.

The dissatisfaction I felt over the conclusion of this issue led to my investigation of the incident through a process of writing-for-inquiry. This was carried out against a backdrop of an exploration of the concepts of techné, phronesis, and praxis, with respect to Jürgen Habermas' knowledge-constitutive interests. I had come to see praxis (practical action responsive to context) as being advised by phronesis (practical judgment/wisdom). Praxis and phronesis were tools that could assist in the transformation of my own practice. Paul Ricœur and John Wall provided versions of phronesis that supported a more creative pathway to addressing its moral imperatives while simultaneously providing a justification for the writing of fictive biographies.

Paul Ricœur's *critical phronesis* aims to mediate between different moral worlds—that of self and others. In a postmodernist fashion, Ricœur acknowledges the impossibility of reducing others to our own understandings or interpretations of them. As such, critical phronesis recognizes the "singular and capable moral 'self' or 'will' who is other from all others" (Wall, 2003, p. 324), and advocates a recreation of one's self and one's practices to account for this inevitable difference.

John Wall's formulation of phronesis builds upon the ideas of Ricœur. Whereas Ricœur saw phronesis as aiming at generating a consensus, albeit an unobtainable one, Wall sees poetic phronesis as facilitating the creation of new meaning on the basis of the differences between individual perspectives. He argues that there is a need for the creative reinterpretation of history resulting from an acknowledgement of otherness. With a phronetic approach "the self addresses its tragic incommensurability with others precisely through the innovative transformation of its own moral historicity" (Wall, 2003, p. 336). Poetic phronesis, then, engenders social inclusivity through the generation of meaning that is based upon difference.

Further, in its focus on human experience, phronesis opens the door for an exploration of alternative perspectives through the poetic use of fiction stories (Richardson, 2000) and existing works of literature (van Manen, 1990). In accepting the postmodernist warning that it is impossible to develop a

---------Aside----------

Critical and poetic phronesis proved to be powerful referents for inquiring into *A Story of Our Times*. Through their filters I was able to recognize the narrowness of my own historical perspective and to poetically reshape my own future practice. They drew a boundary around a focus ("the finite and limited practices of singular individuals" [Wall, 2003, p. 326]) and enabled me to recognize the conflict between the larger historical forces of the past and my attempts to be me. Through their lenses, the self can be seen as an ongoing poetic innovation. The over-riding features of these interpretations of phronesis have led me towards an attempt to create new meanings, to reinterpret my lived experience in such a way as to account for each of the *others*, and to develop my practice in such a way as to mediate between the moral worlds of *others* and myself. This is not an attempt at a watered-down consensus, however, but a return to my own narrative aims and practices after an exploration of, and taking account of, others.

complete understanding of any situation, and the advice of critical and poetic phronesis, I chose to write a fictional account of Damien's experience of the event, to rewrite history from Damien's perspective. My first attempt, however, was less than satisfactory. To generate another perspective I removed myself from center stage and wrote a fictive biography of Damien. However, I had unwittingly created a quasi-confession and threaded it throughout his words and actions. It served only to justify my existing belief that Damien was "guilty." The second attempt achieved a significantly different result.

Damien's Story—The First Attempt

"Shit! Shit . . . shit . . . shit!" Damien quickly folds the note and puts it in his pocket before anybody else in the staffroom spots it. He checks around to see if anybody heard him. He registers that light feeling in the stomach that is brought on by the release of adrenalin. But there's nobody to fight . . . and nowhere to run. Shit. What does he want me for? Does he know? There's been talk. Nothing's going on. No he doesn't know. He doesn't. Shit. He suddenly realizes that he has been standing at his pigeonhole, reading nothing, doing nothing, thinking everything; like the Big Bang, his mental world suddenly dilates to include an environment. Classes begin in thirty minutes. He heads out past the assembling staff, the pace of his step precluding anything other than "Hi, Damien." But, if anybody spoke, he never heard.

* * *

"Les! I just got your note."

"Oh. Hi, Damien," says Les. He hasn't made it to his office door yet and is still carrying his bag and laptop. Damien tries to read his face, unaware of the lack of color in his own. Is it about Susan? Is it?

"Can you see me now?" says Damien.

"Not really, Damien. I have scheduled it so that Marie can be there as well."

"Does she need to be? Can't we just get it over with now?"

"Well Marie is your line manager, Damien."

"I'll forego the right to have her there," he says.

Damien's Story—The Second Attempt

Damien makes a sharp exit from the deputy's office. It's five minutes to recess and he heads to the canteen to pick up his order but, uncharacteristically, turns off and makes his way back to his office. The students will discover the *Three Musketeers* are one down today; there'll be one less teacher to chat to outside the *Aboriginal Centre*. Scott and Matt will have to look after things. He knows the office will be quiet; the "Girls" will be holding court in the staff room. He flops into the chair after closing the door, and as he runs over the incident in his mind, his eyes begin to focus as his temper rises.

A parent interview! If it continues! NOTHING'S HAPPENING! What the hell's the matter with everyone? She's a kid for Christ's sake. Who the hell do these people think I am, a child molester? They're supposed to be my colleagues. What colleagues! Talking behind my back, it makes me sick. They could have told me if they were so concerned. Neither

"No, Damien. I want her to hear what's being said." Shit, shit, shit! He screams silently, heading off towards the staff room but detouring out of the door towards his office. Marie isn't there, although he hadn't decided what he was going to say, if anything. They've done it again! They're supposed to be my colleagues, my friends. That's a laugh. Running off to the deputy. Shit! They're such a bunch of morons. She's a kid! I bet it's the Girls—the bitches! Shit!

* * *

Damien is free first period. He waits outside his empty classroom catching sight of her as she's making her way to class. She sees him and redirects over to say hello. "How are you this morning? Have you got a minute? We need to talk." "Of course," she says and follows him into the classroom. She walks over to a desk and sits on top of it as Damien slides the door shut. He turns to face her after checking who had seen them. He knew this was not okay.

"I've got to go and see the deputy," he says. Not really knowing how to say it—or what he is trying to say.

"What for?" she asks smiling, her bare shoulders hunched slightly forwards from the pressure of her outstretched arms pushing against the desktop.

"I think it's about you and me." He notices the smile run across her lips.

"What about you and me?" she asks.

"Someone's complained about us being friends. They think something's going on." He chokes out a laugh feigning the nonchalance of a young cavalier.

"Who? And about what?" She asks. Was there a slight tease in there, he wonders?

"I bet it's Dryden. You know what she's like. Cold. The ice-maiden. Isn't that what students call her?" She smiles at him.

"Nothing's happened," she says. "Don't worry about it." Like last year. But this is different. Steph is firm and Les plays by the rules. He'll follow it.

"Yeh. Don't worry. I'll fill you in on it later. I just wanted to warn you what was going on," he

Albert nor Marie understand…and how could they? They have no relationship with any of their students…it's like they still teach in the twenties. But Scott, Matt, Paul? I get to know students, treat them as people, not 'things'. They understand that. Is that unprofessional? Albert and Marie would still have them lining up outside the door! Shit. Professional . . . she doesn't even know the meaning of the word. She's never been in industry. For her it's all about following rules. The rules. Whose bloody rules? She's such an idiot. I bet she's behind this: her and her mates—the "Girls." It's just like last year . . . the same thing all over again. She's been on at me since I first got here. Well, since they made me so unwelcome at "their table." She's power bloody mad. I thought we'd already cleared this up, I should have guessed. She must have some issue of her own. What's the difference between me developing a relationship with Susan and developing a relationship with Jacob? They're both Year 12's; I've been their teacher. How come they haven't mentioned Jacob? Because he's a boy? Of course I have a better relationship with Susan, I coach her soccer team twice a week after school. But I've maintained a teacher–student relationship—I don't allow her to call me by my first name at school. All the kids call me "Damien" at training. What's the big deal? How could they think I would?

says. Who am I kidding? She doesn't get it.

* * *

The first draft made me very aware of one of the dangers of fictively writing another's biography. Although I had placed Damien's character center stage, I had maintained my own position as the "hero" of the piece. It was in the second draft that I was able to step outside my predispositions, to constrain my own position to that of a minor character by writing Damien as the "hero." A completely different perspective on the whole incident came to light and made me wonder how Damien might have perceived the whole thing: my meeting with him; Marie's passing on of the problem (if he had realized this was what had happened); and the effect on his working relationships with his colleagues.

---------Aside---------
While at the same time demonstrating one of the problems of this approach, the first draft contributed to exposing another possibility. For my daughter, Christa, the smile, perceived through her own auto/biography, held a significance that I had not recognized. Had I destroyed the first draft of Damien's story, this line of inquiry may have been missed.

Phronesis' concern for gaining wider perspectives, coupled with Max van Manen's (1990) suggestions to look at the literary world, pointed me towards the auto/biographical work *To Sir, With Love* (Braithwaite, 1959). Edward Braithwaite's description of his first year of teaching in an inner-London school offered a similar scenario but generated an altogether different line of thinking that reminded me of Sting's description (1986) of his years as a teacher in England.

Part V: To Sir, With Love

♫ It's no use
He sees her
He starts to shake
He starts to cough ♫

She waited until the first few opening bars of the beautiful evergreen 'In the Still of the Night' floated over the room then turned and walked towards me, invitation large in her clear eyes and secretly smiling lips. I moved to meet her and she walked into my arms, easily, confidently, as if she belonged there. There was no hesitation, no pause to synchronise our steps; the music and the magic of the moment took us and wove us together in smooth movement. I was aware of her, of her soft breathing, her firm roundness, and the rhythmic moving of her thighs. She was a woman, there was no doubt about it, and she invaded my mind and my body. The music ended, all too soon. We were locked together for a moment, then released.

"Thank you, Pamela."

"After I leave school may I come and see you sometimes?"

"Of course, I'd be very pleased to see you any time."

♫ Temptation,
Frustration
So bad it makes him cry ♫
– Sting (1986)

"Thank you. Bye, Sir."
"Bye, Pamela." (Braithwaite, 1959, p. 187)

* * *

With this avenue of research opened, I had gained two other perspectives that served to further problematize the issue. This begged the question: how did their situations resolve themselves? Rick Braithwaite's description provided a rich educative source.

* * *

So there it was. Somewhere deep inside of me I had known it all along but had refused to acknowledge it, because in spite of her full body and grown-up attitude, she was to me a child, and one who was in my care. I could appreciate that the emotional stirrings within her might be serious and important to her—it was not uncommon for girls of fifteen to be engaged or even married—but although I liked and admired her, she was to me only one of my class, and I felt a fatherly responsibility for her as for all the others. (Braithwaite, 1959, p. 110)

* * *

Rick's awareness of his situation led him to confide in Grace, a female member of staff.

* * *

"Well Rick, are you surprised?"
"Look Grace, this is no time for jokes. I need advice because this thing is quite outside my experience."
"I'm not joking, Rick. This sort of thing happens all the time whenever there are men teachers and girl students, from the infants, right through to high school and university. Here sit down and let me bring you up to date."
We made ourselves comfortable and she continued:
"There hasn't been a really good man teacher in this school for ages—I'm not including the Old Man. We've been having a procession of all types. The fellows these girls have seen here have been, on the whole, scruffy, untidy men who can't be bothered to brush their teeth or their shoes, let alone do something about their shapeless ill-fitting clothes. Good God, those twerps tootle off to a training college and somehow acquire a certificate, a licence to teach, and then they appear in a classroom looking like last week's leftovers! . . . Then along comes Mr. Rick Braithwaite. His clothes are well cut, pressed and neat; clean shoes, shaved, teeth sparkling, tie and handkerchief matching as if he'd stepped out of a ruddy bandbox. He's big and broad and handsome. Good God, man, what the hell else did you expect? You're so different from their fathers and brothers and neighbours. And they like you; you treat them like nice people for a change. When they come up here for cookery or needlework all I hear from them is "Sir this, Sir that, Sir said, Sir said," until I'm damn near sick of the sound of it. . . . You treat them with kindness and courtesy and what's more they're learning a lot with you. Be patient with Pamela. She's only just finding out that she's a grown woman, and you're probably the first real man she's met. Be tactful and I'm sure she'll soon pull herself together." (Braithwaite, 1959, pp. 111-112)

* * *

These literary narratives supported the notion that things could be other than they first appeared and opened up another possible source of information. Peter suggested I ask one of my daughters (I have four) to write something from the perspective of a young girl, so I rang Christa and asked about her experiences. "Oh yes," she laughed into the phone. "I know exactly what you mean! Every one of my friends has had a crush on a teacher." What follows is my daughter's literary construction of Susan's story, Susan's fictive biography. Again, Sting offered a parallel insight.

Part VI—Susan's Story

Dear Diary,
You'll never guess what happened today. At lunch Penny told us that there was a HOT new English teacher. Jaz and I pumped her for info—hey can you blame us? Being the principal's daughter, she knows ALL the goss, and is the information point for the whole school. Any-

> ♫ Young teacher
> The subject
> Of schoolgirl fantasy ♫

way, the low down was: twenty-four, unmarried, just out of uni and drives a battered up Toyota.

Jaz and I couldn't WAIT for English! I walked into class trying to appear casual and stopped dead in my tracks. There was A GOD! Jaz bashed into me (also not looking where she was going) and he looked up to see what the commotion was. He gave us a smile and said "Hello." Then dimwit Justin Forbes crashed into us and we went flying! A perfect opportunity to say "Hi" and introduce myself gone down the toilet. Now I'll have to wait for him to learn my name among thirty other students! Ugh!

> ♫ Book marking
> She's so close now
> This girl is half his age. ♫
> – Sting (1986)

He did speak to me again that period, only me, not the rest of the class. He was explaining something about grammar but all I could hear was his voice drifting through my head. Then I hear "Is my English class so boring that you must day dream through it?" I snapped back to reality pretty quickly! I whispered out a quick "Sorry sir" and turned bright red! If only he knew what I was day dreaming about!

Anyways, he's got brown hair, green eyes (I got a good look when he spoke to me about day dreaming), and the most GORGEOUS smile! Not to mention a DREAMY voice.

Jaz and I saw him driving away from school and my eyes followed him down the street. So did Jaz's but she wasn't lookin' at him the way I was . . . do.

Jaz and I had planned to skip our afternoon classes tomorrow but I'll try and get her to skip the morning ones instead . . . now I'll have a reason not to wag English. Lou's having a slumber party this weekend. All girls so you know it's gonna be all truth and dare. It's not usual that I'm the one trying to keep my own secrets though.
Love and kisses,
Susie   xoxo

* * *

The fictive biographies of Damien and Susan combined with those of Rick Braithwaite and Sting, augmented the palette of colors with which this dilemma may have been painted. They served to facilitate a poetic recreation of my own auto/biography by exposing elements of that experience which I may have missed the first time. My thesis built upon this work to explore several key issues, problematized further by postmodernist perspectives: moral relativity and moral development; the privileging of perspectives; and the sense of moral selfhood in the face of internal and external pressures for a particular decision. In so doing, the space I have managed to create for the *other* has facilitated a significant growth in my owned knowledge, one of the three dimensions of practical wisdom (phronesis). But more than this, it provides an example of what some have termed a post-postmodernist approach.

Reflections

Les: If research is to maintain its value it must heed its own advice. Postmodernist and poststructuralist theorists scream a warning about the partiality of all descriptions, and constructivist perspectives advise that this is all we are able to create—the postmodern dilemma. I would argue that auto/biography as a research method provides a powerful way to explore the nexus between one's self and one's environment. While critical reflection served to lay bare the unquestioned assumptions underlying my practice as a leader, creative reflection, through the agency of fictive writing, opened a moral space that allowed me to recognize the singular experiences of the affected *other*. It is in the generation of a perspective born in the overlap of all other perspectives that a utilitarian approximation to the "truth" may be found. I move forward from this research with an understanding that every perspective, every theory, is limited in its applicability. This knowledge provides me with the ability to utilize the strengths of each perspective and the flexibility to drop each one if/when it fails to contribute to developing my understanding.

Elisabeth: Writing auto/biographically for my doctoral thesis and in particular revisiting these writings whilst preparing my contribution to this chapter has provided me with a profound insight into the fluidity of who we think we are as a person, as a teacher, as a researcher and of all the social roles I occupy in the course of a day, a month, a life. Excavating forgotten memories and rethinking taken-for-granted assumptions has brought to the fore a person whose private and professional life is closely interwoven with her life history. In my case, I could link some (if not all) of my professional decisions to the context of my upbringing, my generation, and to the wider historical context "before my time." Writing an auto/biography confronts the writer with the fuzziness of one's *self* and with the complexity of one's relationships with *others* within an historical context. It forces us to examine our values and moral sensitivities. For me, one of the most valuable experiences during the process was to use my doctoral supervisor as a sounding board: the discussions with him kept me on track, forced me to look again, dig deeper, and to sift through the material that surfaced. I believe that having a mentor, or at least a critical friend, kept me focused and helped me crystallize relevant issues from my life story.

Peter: What we have illustrated in this chapter is the exciting potential of arts-based auto/biographical research for the professional development of educators, especially those not averse to exploring Parker Palmer's (1998) question of "Who is the self that teaches?" Addressing this question entails excavating and recontextualizing the moral values underpinning one's professional identity and actions. This question, however, is not to be addressed in isolation, as a grand inward looking celebration of the disconnected self. Indeed, for socially transformative purposes, it should accompany questions of "Why do we teach what we teach?" "Why do we teach in this way?" "Whose interests are being served best?" and "How can we teach in a better way?" These are questions with a communal orientation, a sociopolitical sharpness and a moral and ethical purpose. Equally, we cannot afford to address only these latter questions. In the absence of an auto/biographical focus we shall be forever looking beyond ourselves—to colleagues, academics, bureaucrats, and politicians—for inspiration about what to value (or not value). That is the way of received knowledge, a way that is fundamentally disempowering and antithetical to the growth of our professional practical wisdom. Arts-based auto/biographical research as/for transformative professional development can and should bring the self and other into a dialectical and dialogical relationship, setting up a fruitful tension that propels us simultaneously in two directions—inward and outward—connecting within ourselves and with the community in which we are situated. To do that well we need to become fully mindful: to be sensible and sensitive, analytic and poetic, moral and aesthetic, and to be imaginative. For in the absence of envisioning a good educational journey for our students we cannot hope to reconstruct our current professional realities or participate in co-inventing new ones.

Notes

[1] *Auto/biography* here signifies a combination of auto/biographical and biographical approaches for exploring the relationship between self and other, or as Michelle Fine (1994) puts it for "working the self-other hyphen."

[2] The core of postmodernism is the doubt that any method or theory, discourse or genre, has a universal and general claim as the "right" or privileged form of authoritative knowledge. Postmodernism suspects all truth claims of serving particular interests (Richardson, 2000).

References

Afonso, E. Z. de F., & Taylor, P. C. (2003, July). *Auto-ethnographic inquiry for professional development: Re-conceptualising science education in Mozambique.* Paper presented at the annual conference of the Australasian Science Education Research Association, Melbourne, Australia.

Adler, P. A., & Adler, P. (1994). Observational techniques. In N. K. Denzin & Y. S. Lincoln (Eds.), *Handbook of qualitative research* (pp. 377–392). Thousand Oaks, CA: Sage.

Barone, T. (2001). *Touching eternity: The enduring outcomes of teaching.* New York: Teachers College Press.

Bleakley, A. (2000). Writing with invisible ink: Narrative, confessionalism and reflective practice. *Reflective Practice, 1*, 11–24.

Braithwaite, E. R. (1959). *To sir with love.* London: New English Library.

Brookfield, S. D. (1995). *Becoming a critically reflexive teacher.* San Francisco: Jossey-Bass.

Bullough, R. V., & Pinnegar, S. (2001). Guidelines for quality in auto/biographical forms of self-study research. *Educational Researcher, 30* (3), 13–21.

Carter, K. (1993). The place of story in the study of teaching and teacher education. *Educational Researcher, 22* (1), 5–12, 18.

Casey, K. (1993). *I answer with my life: Life histories of women teachers working for social change.* New York: Routledge.

Connelly, F. M., & Clandinin, D. J. (1988). *Teachers as curriculum planners: Narratives of experience.* New York: Teachers College Press.

Cupitt, D. (2001). *Emptiness and brightness.* Santa Rosa, CA: Polebridge Press.

Denzin, N. K., & Lincoln, Y. S. (2000). Introduction: The discipline and practice of qualitative research. In N. K. Denzin & Y. S. Lincoln (Eds.), *Handbook of qualitative research* 2nd ed. (pp. 1–28). Thousand Oaks, CA: Sage.

Ellis, C. (1997). Evocative auto/ethnography: Writing emotionally about our lives. In W. G. Tierney & Y. S. Lincoln (Eds.), *Representation and the text: Re-framing the narrative voice* (pp. 115–139). Albany: State University of New York Press.

Ellis, C., & Bochner, A. (2000). Auto/ethnography, personal narrative, reflexivity: Researcher as subject. In N. K. Denzin & Y. S. Lincoln (Eds.), *Handbook of qualitative research* 2nd ed. (pp. 733–768). Thousand Oaks, CA: Sage.

Fine, M. (1994). Working the hyphens: Reinventing self and other in qualitative research. In N. R. Denzin & Y. S. Lincoln (Eds.), *Handbook of qualitative research* (pp. 70–82). Thousand Oaks, CA: Sage.

Geelan, D. R., & Taylor, P. C. (2001). Writing our lived experience: Beyond the (pale) hermeneutic? *Electronic Journal of Science Education, 5* (4). Downloadable at http://unr.edu/homepage/jcannon/ejse/ejse.html

Grundy, S. (1987). *Curriculum: Product or praxis?* Lewes: Falmer.

Guba, E. G., & Lincoln, Y. S. (1989). *Fourth generation evaluation.* Newbury Park, CA: Sage.

Henderson, J. G., & Kesson, K. R. (2004). *Curriculum wisdom: Educational decisions in democratic societies.* Upper Saddle River, NJ: Pearson.

Lincoln, Y. S., & Denzin, N. K. (2000). The seventh moment: Out of the past. In N. K. Denzin & Y. S. Lincoln (Eds.), *Handbook of qualitative research* (pp. 1047–1065). Thousand Oaks, CA: Sage.

Loughran, J. J., Hamilton, M. L., LaBoskey, V. J., & Russell, T. L. (Eds.). (2004). *International handbook of teaching and teacher education practices.* Dordrecht, The Netherlands: Springer.

Luitel, B. C., & Taylor, P. C. (in press). Envisioning transition towards a critical mathematics education: A Nepali educator's autoethnographic perspective. In J. Earnest & D. Treagust (Eds.), *Educational change and reconstruction in societies in transition: International perspectives.* Perth, WA: Black Swan.

Mezirow, J. (1991). *Transformative dimensions of adult learning.* San Francisco: Jossey-Bass.

O'Sullivan, E. V., Morrell, A., & O'Connor, M. A. (Eds.). (2002). *Expanding the boundaries of transformative learning: Essays on theory and praxis.* New York: Palgrave.

Palmer, P. L. (1998). *The courage to teach: Exploring the inner landscape of a teacher's life.* San Francisco: Jossey-Bass.

Pereira, L. J. (2005). *Between the 'Real' and the 'Imagined': An inquiry into the act of transformative leadership.* Unpublished doctoral thesis, Curtin University of Technology, Perth.

Pereira, L. J., Taylor, P. C., & Pereira, C. E. (2004, December). *Rewriting history: A poetic approach to the moral transformation of leadership practice.* Paper presented at the annual conference of the Australian Association for Research in Education, Melbourne, Australia.

Richardson, L. (2000). Writing: A method of Inquiry. In N. K. Denzin & Y. S. Lincoln (Eds.), *Handbook of qualitative research* 2nd ed. (pp. 923–948). Thousand Oaks, CA: Sage.

Schön, D. A. (1983). From technical rationality to reflection-in-action. In D. A. Schön (Ed.), *The reflective practitioner: How professionals think in action.* New York: Basic Books.

Settelmaier, E. (2003). *Transforming the culture of teaching and learning in science: The promise of moral dilemma stories.* Unpublished PhD thesis, Curtin University of Technology, Perth, Australia.

Settelmaier, E. (in press). Excavating a researcher's moral sensitivities: An auto/biographical research approach. In J. Wallace & P. C. Taylor (Eds.), *Qualitative research in postmodern times: Exemplars for science, mathematics and technology educators.* Dordrecht, The Netherlands: Springer-Verlag.

Stapleton, A. J., & Taylor, P. C. (2003, July). *Representing research (&) development.* Paper presented at the annual conference of the Australasian Science Education Research Association, Melbourne, Australia.

Sting (Artist). (1986). *Don't stand so close to me* [CD].

Taylor, P. C. (2004, July). *Transformative pedagogy for intercultural research.* Paper presented at the meeting of the Culture Studies in Science Education International Research Network, Kobe, Japan.

Taylor, P. C., & Settelmaier, E. (2003). Critical auto/biographical research for science educators. *Science Education Journal Japan, 27,* 233–244

Tierney, W. (2000). Undaunted courage: Life history and the postmodern challenge. In N. K. Denzin & Y. S. Lincoln (Eds.), *Handbook of qualitative research* 2nd ed. (pp. 537–553). Thousand Oaks, CA: Sage.

Tierney, W. G. & Lincoln, Y. S. (Eds.) (1997). *Representation and the text: Re-framing the narrative voice.* Albany, NY: State University of New York Press.

van Maanen, J. (1988). *Tales of the field.* Chicago: University of Chicago Press.

van Manen, M. (1990). *Researching lived experience: Human science for an action sensitive pedagogy.* Albany: State University of New York Press.

van Manen, M. (2002). *Writing in the dark.* London, Ontario: Althouse.

Wall, J. (2003). Phronesis, poetics, and moral creativity. *Ethical Theory And Moral Practice, 6,* 317–341.

Whitehead, J. (1989). Creating a living educational theory from questions of the kind, 'How do I improve my practice?' *Cambridge Journal of Education, 19,* 41–52.

4   Auto/Method: Toward a Dialectical Sociology of Everyday Life

Wolff-Michael Roth

In this chapter, I show why and how auto/biography can be used to constitute a dialectical sociology of everyday life through my reading of a book on auto/biography as sociological method. The reflexive nature of my reading provides entries to what it meant to grow up and live in postwar Czechoslovakia, occupied by the Soviet Union, and postwar Germany, occupied by the western alliance. Sociology of everyday life ought to be of great interest to educators, particularly with respect that part of our and our students' lives that constitutes their out-of-school experiences. More so, this chapter is not only about auto/bio-graphy, as topic and praxis, but also an auto/ethnographic inquiry into reading by exposing the ways we academics read books. It is also about writing auto/biography, as I am grappling with ways of writing the genre, as exhibited in the struggle I am writing *about* and in the struggle evident in my own text.

Auto/Biography and Sociology

There are many subfields in education each characterized by its own dominant mode of inquiry, often following the dominant methods that also characterize the subfield's parent discipline. Thus, educational psychology is dominated by the quantitative experimental approaches that characterize psychology; likewise, educational sociology is generally dominated—and receives more funding than its poor sibling, qualitative sociology—by quantitative approaches. In this chapter, I explicate, through my—the reader's—auto/biographical lens, an auto/biographical approach to conducting sociological inquiry. Such auto/biographical approaches go a long way toward situating sociology in the lived experiences of people, not only women as in feminist sociology (Smith, 1987) but in the experiences of the poor (see my Chapter 7), colored, cultured, and otherwise differentiated. On another level, this chapter also pursues an anthropological project, in making explicit the ways in which academics, like I, read and explicate texts: this, therefore, is not only a text about auto/biography as method for a reflexive sociology of the past—that of others and my own—but also a contribution to an anthropology or sociology of reading that seeks, through an explication of one's own practices, details of reading in one's community more generally (e.g., Livingston, 1995; Smith, 1999). Auto/biography therefore functions as auto/-ethnography, here concerned with sociology of everyday life in its varied and multilayered forms.

Auto/biographies provide us with a means to access our everyday lives, as we lived them in some distant past. In this, they provide us with access to particular way of living in *this* culture at *that* time. Auto/biographies therefore provide us with a resource for sociological investigations of everyday life in its concrete particularities and, because of the dialectical relation between the particulars of culture and the general possibilities it makes available to individual members, an access to culture and society in general. It is an approach, which may be articulated in terms of an analogy to genetics—gaining access to understanding the parental genetic make-up through analyses of the children. Each child in a family bears the genetic imprint of its two parents, whose genes therefore constitute possibilities; their genetic make up is equivalent to a concrete general. The genes of every child are concrete realizations of the possibilities in the genetic make-up of the parents; the filial genes are concrete particulars. In a similar way, one family's way of

Memories: I don't remember much of the year 1968. I was in Yugoslavia, camping with my family. A few days after returning home, it happened. It was August 28. We were all glued to the television. Russian tanks had invaded Czechoslovakia and now were in the streets of Prague. I have a vivid image of a place with a fountain, tree-lined streets filled with people, and Russian tanks. I remember thinking, "We just came from a communist country. We could have been trapped." I also remember my outrage—How could anyone let this happen? How could the Americans let this happen? I understood only later that when there are no American interests (money, exploitation) at stake, American politicians don't care. And, after all, what is the difference between Russians "liberating" Czechoslovakia and Americans bombing the hell out of Afghanistan (or in their terms, bombing it back into the stone age) or killing 100,000 Iraqis to throw the country into turmoil?

life is a concrete particular of the cultural-historically possible ways of living at the moment.

At the beginning of my scholarly career, I was a teacher-researcher. Later, I used apprenticeship as an ethnographic method, which allowed me to access the particular understandings and cultural practices through my own unfamiliarity and subsequent trajectory of becoming a member. However, auto/biography as a method of writing research came only later. In this chapter, auto/biography provides me with a resource to generate materials that document forms of living and thinking in Germany after WWII, and what it meant to grow up during this period in a defeated country. They are first-person sociological accounts that parallel and reflexively elaborate the accounts of an auto/biographically mediated sociology of Czech culture over several decades from WWII through the quiet revolution.

I had promised to write a review essay about *Our Lives as Database* (Konopásek, 2000); but at the moment when the book review editor of *FQS: Forum Qualitative Sozialforschung/Forum Qualitative Social Research* asked me about it, I was physically tired and emotionally

Memories: Growing up in post-war Germany, I knew little about what had happened to Czechoslovakia or any other country neighboring Germany between the two world wars. The entire country, adults and kids, school system, media, and so on, seemed to be engaged in a collective forgetting. And I, as many of my friends, was not very much interested in finding out, perhaps unconsciously trying to unstuck this other *Urschuld*, this other originary guilt. Symptomatically, my parents talked very little about their own youth. From my mother, I received but sketches of her seeking cover in bomb shelters at night during air raids, trips to the countryside for a few potatoes and a good meal with distant relatives, and my grandfather's stay in a field hospital in Poland where my grandmother visited him once. My father didn't talk about his days as a member of *Hitler Jugend*, only his small-caliber rifle, built identically to the army rifle but with a different barrel; my uncle's flights over their estate, his "training flights" to Vienna to buy "Sacher Torte" for his (female) admirers. I vaguely remember that I heard about the Munich Agreement (September 29, 1938), which brought the Czechoslovak Republic to an end, the annexation of "Böhmen" (Bohemia) and "Mähren" (Moravia).

* * *

In all societies, it is the parent's fate to decide "when and how to tell *it* to the child." (Kapr, p. 232)[1]

drained. Taking on this task now seemed like a duty rather than a pleasure. I leafed through the book, began to read Preface and Prologue, and then became intrigued. I read on, jumping to the second part of the book, entitled Documents, which contained eight life narratives by participants in the SAMISEBE project. I continued to read on and on for the entire day; the next morning, I picked up

Figure 4.1. These images of going to school in post-WWII Germany also feature indirectly the country as a wasteland (left) or the poverty multi-year and multi-sibling clothing (e.g., leather shorts, very long pants [right]). But they do not feature lack of food, outdoor toilets, and other aspects of growing up that are inscribed in my body and partially available through memories.

where I had left the previous afternoon, finished the Documents, and then returned to Part I and Chapter 7 (which, in a strange way of numbering, follows Part II that follows a different numbering, "Life narratives 1" through "Life narratives 8") completed reading the book. In my busy life as academic, I hardly ever have the leisure or desire to read a book from cover to cover. This one was so intriguing that I could not but read it in one swoop.

The book drew me deeper and deeper into a sociological history of Czechoslovakia and the Czech Republic, viewed from a first-person perspective. I even went to the Internet to search for more information about the country, Prague, and the Russian invasion. And while I read, memories of my own youth in post-WWII Germany began to surface, details of everyday life that had many aspects in common with the different auto/biographical narratives, and which allowed me new perspectives of myself and German culture and social life after the war. Other themes, like the owning of houses and apartments, while not part of my own lived experience, became starting points for images, then reflections of housing in post-WWII Germany.

The auto/biographical materials and most of the essays that preceded them used a representational form that I felt worked very well, more so, which I enjoyed. Material from the auto/biographies were, most often, not mounted as data in the traditional sense, supporting what the author has to say, a piece of constructed reality for the construction of reality, but as texts that stood in relief to the main narrative, almost like the voiceover technique that I have used in the past (Roth & McRobbie, 1999) to build tension into the text by disrupting and interrupting the main narrative that threatened to take over and off to be-

Memories: Most of my classmates in Gymnasium [grammar school] lived in rented apartments. I knew people who owned houses—most of the farmers did, because they had inherited the farm or had built on the property sliced off their parents' farms. But in the city, only the "rich" owned houses—even those of us growing up in relative poverty called most of them "Neureiche," the newly rich as distinct from the properly rich, like the nobility. My parents always lived in rented houses, part of the contract my civil-servant father had with his employer, the state, and had no prospects of owning a house or even an apartment. My siblings still live in rented apartments; my mother only owns hers because of an inheritance late in her life.

come a master narrative. In this way, the reader of *Our Lives as Databases* often encounters multiple perspectives on the same situation or topic, recounted from the perspective, or rather through the auto/biography and auto/ethnography of the different participants in the collective effort. But before providing a deeper analysis of why the book works and what makes it theoretically so interesting, let me provide a brief outline of its structure and content, which are followed by the exemplary analysis of one chapter and a few points of minor criticism. In so doing, I utilize the same literary techniques employed by the authors of the book.

The Book: SAMISEBE as Praxis of Method

This book, as its editor (Konopásek) points out, is the result of a sociological project, SAMISEBE, a play on words with two reflexive Czech pronouns, literally meaning "ourselves' selves" (p. 13, note 2). Several Czech sociologists of diverse methodological and theoretical commitments, different gender and generations repeatedly met for a period of about four years to conduct a sociological study (experiment) on the changing nature of their society with the fall of communist rule by using their auto/biographies as the primary database. Despite the perceivably interesting results, the project more or less fell apart: increasingly irregular and spaced meetings, a reorganization of the members' university that turned them from researchers into teachers, and repeatedly failed attempts at garnering outside funding for their project all contributed to the demise of "the golden age of" (p. 55) a practical and reflexive experiment that had started so well. Disagreements between members and the tremendous demands on time needed to enact the collaboration contributed in non-negligible ways to the difficulties of maintaining the SAMISEBE project. Nevertheless, before the end of the project, the group was able to produce this wonderful book.

Structure

The contents page of the book provides the following somewhat unusual structure with respect to the distribution of chapters: Preface, Prologue (Chapter 1), Part I: Texts (Chapters 2–6), Part II: Documents (Life Narratives 1–8), and Epilogue (Chapter 7). The preface and prologue both introduce a lot of background on the SAMISEBE project. In Part I, five members of the group (Disman, Alan, Šmídová, Kabele, & Konopásek) provide interpretive and analytical texts that have emerged as products of their collective work. The primary auto/biographical material that these five and the remaining three members (Holý, Kapr, & Stehlíková) gathered in preparation for and as part of their meetings has been assembled, partially, in Part II of the book.

Elsewhere in my notes: I fully agree with the editor's (Konopásek) analysis that "'intertextuality', 'reflexivity', 'indeterminacy', 'multivocality' and 'relativism' are not theoretical or even programmatic principles here" (p. 53) but rather concrete praxis. Rather than saying that "SAMISEBE was born as an experiment with a rather weak intellectual basis" (p. 53), I might have said that the project began before getting lost in too much (ivory tower) reflection.

Not surprisingly, giving the intention of the project, the *Texts* draw on the auto/biographical materials, some also appearing in the Documents while others are not. However, rather than placing these texts as data and analyzing them in detail, the auto/biographical materials are placed as if in counterpoint, relief, or as voiceovers; in some instances, a text produced by the same author but in a different context is similarly set in quotation form and often prefaced "Elsewhere . . ." There is therefore an interesting interplay between the analytical texts and the auto/biographical materials placed next to them.

The technique worked for me especially in the *Documents*, where the auto/biography of one person was often augmented or relativized by auto/biographical materials from another group member, as in the following example from the life narrative of Miroslav Disman, relativized by a text by Olga Šmídová:

And this was one of the stumbling blocks of my life, because all the participants got a piece of paper certifying that they would get three pieces of cake and milk coffee and that was the let-down. The milk coffee had skin on it, and I hated skin on milk with a vengeance.

> Olga: I also remember a brief sequence. My siblings came on one Sunday for the day, I was sitting in this woman's kitchen, and I had a huge bowl of milk coffee, which I hated with a vengeance and had to drink. (p. 194)

While reading, I wondered whether a different format for the book might have worked better and might have been even more consistent with the intertextual nature of a researcher's experience, which contributes to the interpretive horizon brought to the analysis and the auto/biographical materials that constituted the (textual) objects of analysis. For example, one could have imagined that the two different texts (*Texts*, *Documents*) were arranged in double columns or facing

> My father often talked about Czecho-slovakian coffee, actually, I think he said coffee from Bohemia—he never specified whether this would have been before the war, after the Munich Conference of 1938, or during the war. My grandmother apparently somehow could get a hold of green coffee beans, which she (or, more likely, one of the young women whom she trained to run the households of rich and noble families) roasted for their consumption. . . . I never did have coffee until I was twenty.

pages, or on upper and lower part of the same page. Apart from the nightmare such arrangements might cause the publisher, would such arrangement lead to different reading experiences? How would the vicinity of the different textual materials pertaining to the same author (is he or she the same, given that there are temporal differences between the times when the texts were authored?)? How would readers proceed with the multiple texts on the same or facing pages? Would the linearity and sequential nature of ordinary reading be disrupted? What would happen to our reading if the texts of different authors—that is, authors who respond to different first and last names—were juxtaposed on the same or facing pages?

During its experiment, the SAMISEBE group conceived of the texts that they produced as constituting eight biographical layers, beginning with a first, "innocent" biography, subsequently augmented by further biographical texts, which could no longer be innocent given the discussions that had intervened. Whereas the topics at the second level remained unspecified, each author wrote auto/biographical texts pertaining to a specific theme to produce subsequent levels. These themes include "What the Czechoslovak Communist Party meant or means in my life," "How the SAMISEBE group met and worked," "My life from 7 to 9 am," "Family possessions," "The last three years," and "My friends."

Documents In the *Documents*, readers find selected excerpts from the original SAMISEBE life narratives produced by the different authors, each life narrative "augmented" by excerpts from the narratives of others. The SAMISEBE project has an iterative quality, where the narratives of one person are constantly confronted with the narratives of others, giving rise to an accelerated process of theoretical sensitivity. Across the different participants, these excerpts cover the broad range of topics that the group had addressed in their focused writing. As a collection, these *Documents* provide an intriguing perspective on Czechoslovak and Czech society—through multiple lenses constituted by the concrete lives of the different authors. These texts, though selected and assembled for the purpose a book publication, maintain all the heterogeneity that comes with different selves but also the homogeneity that comes from investigating the same collective life, society. Through this collection of auto/biographical materials on the same topic, we learn a lot of sociology that we would not get from impersonal-narrator and survey-based analyses of a society said to change following the abandonment of party rule in 1989.

When I read the "Documents," it became clear to me how little I knew about Czechoslovakia, its culture and its people. It is true, I had read every novel and short story by Franz Kafka, but little else. The country always had a good hockey team, and as far back into my childhood as I can remember, I knew the name of Emil Zatopec. I know a little more and am very familiar with composers such as Bedřich Smetana, Antonín Dvořák, Vítězslav Novák, Josef Suc, Leoš Janáček, and Bohuslav Martinů. How little this amounts to as knowledge about a society and a culture! Today, living here in Canada, I am even farther removed from the Czech Republic, which makes it rarely, if ever, into the news—just when they play hockey against our team.

Because of the widely varying age-levels represented in the group (birth-dates 1924 to 1963), the *Documents* cover different periods each associated with its own dramatic change to the political life of Czechoslovak and Czech society—the truncation of the country with the Munich Pact (1938) and subsequent control by Germany (1939), change to communist rule after WWII (1947), the Prague spring and Russian occupation (1968) and the subsequent period of "normalization," and the "Velvet Revolution" (1989) following massive, popular demonstrations. However, rather than grand narratives about what happened, which brought about so-called changes or transformations, we see events as these have been experienced by real, concrete people, how they had to move or had someone move in, who saw "columns of German prisoners, wretched, limping" (p. 197) through their villages and who "felt a lot of pity" for the prisoners. We see the "Velvet Revolution" through the experiences of someone who participated in a teachers' forum all the while wanting/having to stay out ("I wanted terribly to get involved in every activity, and on the other hand I knew that my wife was ill and that I had to stay out of it" [Kabele, p. 225]).

As a result, we read a sociology from a first-person perspective, and through a perspective where eating breakfast, illness of family members, broken heaters, water in the basement are as much part of everyday immortal society as the history of a nation through grand narratives, purged of what constitutes the very basis of these narratives. There are no mysteries in these lives—just as there are no mysteries in the lives of the exceptional people of this world—we all live concretely, moment after moment, sleep and get up, fill (eat) and empty ourselves, do one thing rather than another. And yet, in education we take these lives insufficiently into account, treating others as disembodied knowers to be filled with the stuff our institutions are about.

Reflection: Reading my curriculum vitae, many (young) colleagues seem to be mystified by my publication record. I get asked, "What do you do to be able to produce so much?" and "What kind of life do you live?" While I politely answer that there is nothing special about my life, I have an internal monologue that is about getting up, making coffee, drinking water, going to the bathroom, eating, cycling, gardening, cooking dinner, having a conversation with my wife, and going to bed. There is nothing special about my life, no special gifts (intelligence), no special office, no special anything—just plain ordinary life, day in and day out. This plain ordinariness, this lack of something special, is what is so special.

Of course, we all get up in the morning, experience mornings between nine and eleven. What is so special about this collection of auto/biographical experiences is that the authors use them as a starting point for doing sociology, a sociology that is not detached from everyday experience but rather grounded in it. *Our Lives as Database* is therefore also an attempt at sociology that describes and perhaps explains society all the while keeping in focus its members' experiences of this society. I say also, because the authors themselves have their own explanations about what they have done and what the outcomes of their work are. But, in keeping with Ricœur (1991) that actions are interpretable like texts and with Derrida (1988) that the meaning of a text is only accomplished in the act of reading, other readers will arrive at yet other significations of what the SAMISEBE group has done.

Texts In the five texts, the authors cover considerable and heterogeneous ground: Miroslav Disman, the only latecomer admitted to the original group and the émigré who brings a "stranger's" perspective, describes a very personal epistemology; Josef Alan, key figure in the group because of his institutional position as center director, analyses family relationships and membership in the communist party; Olga Šmídová builds on the stories of housing in her analysis of family strategies related to property maintenance and transfer; Jiří Kabele looks at social transition, constancy and change, of the Czech society during the "Velvet Revolution"; and Zdenek Konopásek provides a superb, theoretically well grounded reflection on the state of sociology, which he considers in terms of a "grandma" metaphor, and the contribution that an auto/biographical sociology can make to the field. (Although Konopásek confesses somewhere to be "on the right", his grandma metaphor nicely fits with a materialist dialectic, according to which parents and their off-spring co-exist at the same time, so that sociology exists both as "grandma" and as its anti-dote, the "auto/biographic" incarnation.)

In the first text, Konopásek provides an introduction to the SAMISEBE project, its history, development (including the rules that the participants created and subsequently negotiated as they went along), and a description of the emerging biographical layers. The closing chapter (Konopásek) is somewhat of a continuation of these basic texts where Konopásek provides an argument for the contribution that reflexive auto/biographies concerned with life and social transformation of a former communist country can make to understanding social life and societies in the capitalist West.

Of these texts, those written by Konopásek are different in the sense that he, more so than others, provides many links to the current state of sociology and draws less on the auto/biographical texts created in and for the group meetings. However, in my reading, these texts are necessary to provide some intertextual links between the SAMISEBE experiment and sociology as a field and its state at this historical juncture. These chapters provide the crucial link without which SAMISEBE might have remained the product of an insular effort, standing beside many other efforts without attempts to articulate similarities and differences to other concurrent efforts. Konopásek certainly is widely read in and masters the intricacies of many current discourses, whether these pertain to reflexivity, actor networks, or knowledge/power. He covers the sociological and textual terrain ground from Ricœur to Foucault, Ashmore to Woolgar, Latour to Lynch, and Beck to Giddens.

In the spirit of the entire book, these "more theoretical" chapters are part of and stand apart from the other chapters, very much in the same way that the different texts within the chapters are part of and different from the main narrative. But throughout the texts, I found much "food for thought," starting points for auto/biographical and theoretical reflections. In fact, through my the reflections on my auto/biography I realized that these texts about the constancy and change of Czech(oslovak) society, viewed through the constancy and change of eight Czech individuals, were also texts about me and about the society where I had grown up (post-WWII Germany). What we learn, sociologically, is not about one society specifically, but also about the collective human condition more generally. Let me provide by one example, pertinent in many ways to my own life because the chapter author, Disman, also immigrated to the country where I am at home now.

A Sample Chapter: The "Stranger" as Analytical Concept

One of the SAMISEBE group is Miroslav Disman, who emigrated from Czechoslovakia during the fall of 1968, and eventually became a professor of sociology at York University (Toronto, Canada). Fittingly, he uses Alfred Schutz's (1944) concept of the "stranger" to provide a particular analysis of the changing nature of self and society that is evident in his own auto/biography, thereby working towards a "very personal epistemology" (p. 59). Disman looks at the different experiences of understanding, how with the temporal distance to his native country, his past experience became progressively less an adequate tool for understanding the events in Czechoslovakia. Strangely enough, when he returned after the Velvet Revolution, he rapidly experienced a familiarity quite different from the stranger metaphor, a working of "old ready-made recipes" and "thinking as usual" (p. 60).

Reflection: I have lived nearly half of my life in Germany, but I never felt homesick to that country, the sense of longing that some people feel when away from "home" (Heimat), a stranger in a strange land. Although I feel at home here (Victoria, Canada), there are always people who attribute my ways to my German origins, while simultaneously my German colleagues attribute my ways of being to my North American context. Perhaps my three languages give me away, all of which I speak with some accent—any one with an accent is automatically a stranger, forgiven for the faux pas he or she might commit. Does being a stranger provide a particular analytical vantage point, as Disman and Alsop (this volume) indicate?

But when he subsequently returned for a second time eighteen months later, he realized that he did not understand; he was a stranger in his own country. He could not take for granted understanding and being understood. "Even the language, seemingly my own language becomes a problem. The 'chance of understanding and being understood' could not be taken for granted anymore" (Disman, p. 61). He writes about being able to understand the political and ideological attitudes of his friends, but not able to comprehend where these had come from. And he realizes that even after an extended time, "There are still many areas where I feel that virtually all of them have a different understanding than I have, and that their understanding is different in the same way" (p. 64).

Memories: After a long absence, I had returned to Germany for a three-month fellowship. I remember one Saturday afternoon I took a stroll through the city of Kiel. Something felt strange, inexplicable. I could read the signs, hear and even deciphering what passers-by were saying—and yet I felt as if I had dropped into a foreign land, where I did not understand. Until I realized that all shops and businesses were closed. Although there were people in the street, the city was unexpectedly dead in a way—where I call home, people would go in and out of stores, be walking with their purchases.

As I read Disman's chapter, I was thinking not only about my own experiences of immigrating to the country where my parents had met, married, and conceived me, but particularly about the concept of understanding and its relation to familiarity. I had noticed (attributing much of it to my job, teaching, which allowed me to interact extensively with people) that in many social situation I was increasingly able to participate in conversations about culturally and societally significant events, television shows, books, and so forth. I could increasingly predict, or more, know without reflection, what was sensible to say and hear being said. At the same time, my experience during the stay in Germany showed that I was losing or had lost this sense for what would sensibly come next. On the surface and upon quick reading, Disman articulates experiences over other émigrés, who, upon returning to the country they left, find that it is no longer the same.

I found the chapter interesting, as well as the others, because on closer inspection, I realized that the author used the concept of understanding somewhat loosely—thereby raising questions that an epistemology of *understanding* would have to address. This concept wreaks havoc, both in everyday and many professional discourses, because it is used to cover both pre-reflective intuitions about how the world works and explanations of the world in terms of theoretical constructs. Disman makes a correlative distinction between *understanding* of social situations, which has to be experienced (p. 60), and factual knowledge, which is easy to transmit and easy to comprehend (p. 59). And, in a most curious phrasing and reversal of the terms understanding and comprehending, Disman claims, "I could understand the present political and ideological attitudes of my friends, but I was still not able to comprehend where these attitudes had come from" (p. 62).

It is helpful to conceptualize understanding and explanation (comprehending) as two aspects of a dialectic unit. Understanding arises from lived experience, including its pre-articulate and inarticulate aspects. This understanding requires explanation to be further elaborated and articulated; but the effort of explanation has understanding as a prerequisite. This is the case not only for the social situations that Disman refers to but also for the supposedly most rational of human beings, natural scientists. As I repeatedly saw in my research, when scientist were unfamiliar with the biological systems represented in a graph, details of the pertinent data

Memories: Two years prior to my fellowship stay in Germany, a cousin had visited me in Vancouver. We had long conversations about politics, philosophy, and life. As I was listening to her, I heard and understood the words and remembered that nearly twenty years earlier, I had thought and talked like this. Although this talk sounded familiar, voices from a long forgotten past, it felt strange now, a little removed from reality. It was not that she was removed from reality, she was there with me in a very concrete way, but that the language and the culture it embodies seemed to be so much more philosophical compared to the pragmatism that is—now—my own. That is, there are moments when I hear and recognize the words but do not understand.

collection procedures, instrumentations, and other "anecdotal" aspects of the research, they found it difficult and even impossible to interpret (explain) the graph (Roth, Bowen, & Masciotra, 2002). On the other hand, when scientists successfully interpret a graph, I could show that they drew heavily on "anecdotal" experiences, which provided the very ground that the explanation (interpretation) seemed to require.

The epistemology of the stranger, therefore, has to include the concept of understanding, which goes beyond merely recognizing or making cursory connections between signs. What Disman and I experienced, which we articulated as not understanding, is the bodily experience of living practical life with those whose language we seemed, on the surface, to comprehend. What we lacked were these crucial aspects of everyday practical life, which is co-extensive with our understanding.

Linked to the problem of understanding and explaining, are those of Self as constant and changing and the Self-Other dialectic. The SAMISEBE project is about the articulation of experience and about reflecting on similarities and differences between different auto/biographies. That is, the group members are engaged in the dialectic of understanding and explanation, the latter articulating the former, the former being the requisite of the latter. How we read and understand some text changes over time, as we never look back at the same original text but always through an ever-expanding interpretive horizon, including our own and other's readings. Given that the members of the group worked with their experiences and with an ever expanding set of texts articulating this experience, it is not surprising that Disman felt both the SAMISEBE group and his Self as changing ("The entire SAMISEBE Group is constantly changing" [p. 65], "Disman writing this postscript is different from the Disman who joined the project" [p. 65–66]). But I return to this issue below.

Why Auto/Methods Work as Sociological Method

A central questions to be asked is why and how the praxis of collective writing and analysis of auto/biography works and legitimately contributes to sociology. In the following, I first sketch the argument that the editor Konopásek makes, which constitutes, by and large, a very nice argument. Nevertheless, I had the sense that two main aspects that seem central to me to sociology and auto/biography or auto/ethnography have not been sufficiently articulated and theorized: the relationship between individual and society, on the one hand, and the relationship between Self and Other, on the other hand. Because I have made this observation in several disciplines recently, I articulate some of the basic features that I think need to be more in the foreground in (qualitative) social research. I begin by providing a review of the editor's own argument and proceed to articulate further positions that one might include in an argument for auto/biographical sociology.

The Insider Argument

Konopásek's argument for SAMISEBE—collective auto/biography as sociological method—fundamentally revolves around the reflexive nature of sociology as stated in the following syllogism. Sociologists take society as the central object of study. Sociologists are members of society. Therefore, (a) sociologists also study themselves and (b) use their knowledge qua members of society to interpret their data, even if these are not auto/biographical. The syllogism constitutes the fundamental assumption underlying the ethnomethodological approach (Garfinkel, 1967). Classical ("Grandma") sociology, however, attempts to separate the sociologist-subject from his or her object (society), even masked the relationship by interposing objective "scientific method," a praxis that distinguished what people do in everyday life (including sociologists qua citizens) from what sociologists qua scientists do. Konopásek points out yet another connection between sociology and its object: society in general but the ruling powers in particular always also pick up elements from sociology thereby inscribing ideologies into everyday life (Smith, 1999).[2] Governments ask for statistics, which sociologists provide in the guise of particular discourses, which become reinscribed into society to be found again by sociologists. Necessarily, any interview would reveal such concepts (discourse, language) in everyday description of reality, thereby reifying the very concepts that a scientific sociology has created in the first place.

Konopásek (pp. 160–163) characterizes the SAMISEBE method along three fundamental dimensions. First, SAMISEBE explicitly mobilizes the personal experience of sociologists, which allows a blending of professional and bio-graphical discourses and interpretations. This blending does away with the traditional separation between what and who represents and what and who is represented, between subject and its object. Second, the SAMISEBE method is based on an interactive and reciprocal logic. This means that "different" "others," different along the dimension of age, sex, professional histories, political inclinations, thematic preferences, and positions in university hierarchy provide texts and interpret their own and those of others. This grounding in differences among participants provides, thus Konopásek, the SAMI-SEBE group *"with mutual control over our own biographical and socio-logical practices"* (p. 161, emphases in the original). Third, SAMISEBE is open ended, thereby reflecting the open-ended nature of all auto/biographical work.

Memories: I remember that in the early days of my own research in the classroom of other teachers, I frequently felt outraged about the actions of one teacher or an-other—"How could he do this?" and "How could she say that?" But as I became a more seasoned researcher, I turned this outrage against myself asking "How do I come to question, 'How could he do this?' and 'How could she say that?'" Turning the outrage against myself became an excellent methodological tool to deal with my presuppositions. What makes me see one lesson in a favorable light but upset with another? What are the experiences and horizons that constitute the other part in the dialectic relation with "reality" from which emerge what and how I perceive social events?

This reflects the open-ended nature of all interpretive work, especially when human actions are viewed in terms of the metaphor of the text and, most generally, human existence itself.[3] Konopásek argues that these three characteristics do not only complement but also "guarantee" one another in the sense that mobilization of individual experience (Point 1) and interactivity (Point 2) require time, thereby supporting the open-endedness (Point 3). Similarly, interactivity requires attention to research and social practices, thereby supporting the blending of professional and biographical discourses.

There are, of course, not only advantages that come from being a member of society and also an analyst of this society, because the preconstructed can be found everywhere. That is, because sociologists appropriate concepts (dis-courses) as members of (immortal) society, they run the danger of simply reify-ing these concepts. "Embedded in, or taken by, the object that it takes as its ob-ject, [an un-reflective scientific practice] reveals something of the object, but something which is not really objectivized since it consists of the very principles of apprehension of the object" (Bourdieu, 1992, p. 236). The sociologist, taking as his or her task to know an object (social world) of which he is the product, is likely to raise problems and employ concepts that are products of the same ob-ject. Konopásek concludes, "Hence, of course, the somewhat banal flavor of most conclusions brought about by standard sociological study" (p. 146). Simply watching out does not improve the situation. What is required has variously been described as "radical doubt" or "suspicion of ideology" and involves a struggle:

> To avoid becoming the object of the problems that you takes as your object, you must re-trace the history of the *emergence* of these problems, of their progressive constitution, i.e., of the collective work, oftentimes accomplished though [sic] competition and strug-gle, that proved necessary to make such and such issues to be known and recognized (*faire connaître et reconnaître*) as *legitimate problems*, problems that are avowable, pub-lishable, public, official. (Bourdieu, 1992, p. 238)

Dialectics

The SAMISEBE project makes complete sense to me; I even envied the indi-viduals as a collective to have been in the right place at the right time to partici-pate in the praxis of reflexive auto/biographical sociology. But some of the cen-tral issues—perhaps just in my thinking—that ought to have been addressed seemed to have eschewed the authors—the dialectics of individual and society and Self and Other. A discussion of these dialectics could have contributed enormously to a project that embodies this problematic in its very banner, auto/biographical sociology. Not only is auto/biography also oto-biography, (NLat. < Gr. *ous*, ear), for the ear of the other and necessarily in the other's lan-guage (see my introduction), but the "/" of the auto/biography confronts those biographies that the authors wrote about themselves with those written by their respective others. The "auto-" (Gr. *autos*, self, same), what relates to the self, also confronts the "socio-" (Fr. < Lat. *socius*, companion, fellow), the other, and therefore society. And even before making an auto/biography available to oth-ers, the Other has intruded via language, which always comes from the other and is for the other, both binding the Self to and alienating it from the Other (Der-rida, 1998). Auto/biography is always and already hetero- (or allo-?) biography

In the following paragraphs, I unfold some of the issues that in my view are part of the very reasons why auto/biography as sociological praxis works and why it has a lot to contribute.

Self and Other Psychology generally (there are some exceptions) theorizes the human being independently of the social and material world in which it is embedded. Most poignantly, (radical) constructivist psychology argues that the individual is informationally closed, produces ("constructs") its own information, as it is involved in the construction of conceptions of the world, which it can test only for their viability. Such approaches take the individual, the *cogito ergo sum*, as the starting point and the central mystery and problem is how human society comes about, or more precisely, how we come to understand others. Social constructivist approaches somehow make the reverse argument claiming—often using cultural-historical approaches as their rhetorical referents—that knowledge is socially constructed before the individual appropriates it. Both approaches suffer from the problem of essentializing individual or collective and subsequently thinking the respective other term in terms of the first.

An alternative to such approaches has been elaborated in *Soi-même comme un autre* (Ricœur, 1990), which elaborates the problem of the individual in the form of two dialectics: the dialectic of identity based on its two major meanings of identity, sameness (Lat. *idem*) and selfhood (Lat. *ipse*), and the dialectic of self and other than self. Rather than immediately positing the subject, expressed in the first person singular of the "I think" and "I am," Ricœur emphasizes the primacy of reflective meditation, which "*is the price to pay for a hermeneutics characterized by the indirect way of positing the self*" (my translation, p. 28). The very conception of sameness–selfhood and Self–Other as dialectical units implies that neither term takes ontological priority. At the same time, from an ontogenetic perspective, Self and Other emerge together as individuals understand themselves as Selves in the very moment that they understand respective Others as Selves who experience the reciprocal Self-Other relation. Self and Other have the same origin, emerging from the same originary moment of

Reflections elsewhere in my notes: While reading *Our Lives as Databases*, I had the strong sense of the presence of the dialectic of continuity and change, self and other, self as constant and changing. I am thinking about our use of the "I" to refer to myself throughout different times of the day and during different stages in "my" life. Although we experience ourselves differently, we use the same "I." Although "I" am saying that "I" am different, know that I understand differently through my experiences with Germans, there are moments when I think of "myself" as a boy as if it was the same me.

prise de conscience. That is, subjectivity and intersubjectivity emerge simultaneously. My reasons for acting are always reasons that are, in principle, intelligible to you, my other; your reasons for acting are, in principle, always intelligible to me, your other. My understanding of the world is, in principle, always also intelligible to you, my other, as your understanding is, in principle, intelligible to me, your other. Even in the most intimate case of relating to oneself, the hand-to-hand touching, the other, the foreign, is already present:

This experience is already haunted, at least, but constitutively haunted, by a hetero-affection related to the spacing, then to the visible spatiality: From where the intruder, host, a desired or undesired host, a helping other or a parasite to be rejected. (Derrida, 2000, p. 205, my translation)

This Self|Other dialectic makes auto/biography—autos, oneself, implies the other, the hétéro or allo—immediately a plausible way of sociological investigation, as we find in ourselves always also an aspect of the Other. Self and other are so different, but they are also so much the same; they are part of the same, they have an identical origin. Our experience in and of the world is one concrete case of a generalized possibility to experience in and of the world. At the same time, investigating the biography of others (allo-biographies?) provides us insights about ourselves. Collective analysis of the biographies of others provides new insights, of the analysis of our auto/biographies: cross-fertilization, allogamy. These dialectical relations do not facilitate the work but rather seem to proliferate the contradictions inherent in the Self|Other dialectic:

It was, above all, the presence of *our own* auto/biographies (the biographical narratives of each one of us) in the collection of analyzed texts that complicated the whole thing so much and that compounded and amplified the usual interpretive difficulties of sociologists-biographers. Precisely because of the reflexively-auto/biographical nature of our research, we continuously felt very close and intimate connections between sociological analysis on one hand and the sum total of our experiences, or "biographical knowledge," on the other hand. (Konopásek, p. 42)

The second important aspect coming from Ricœur's reflections is the dialectic of identity, identity meaning same (idem-identity) and self (ipse-identity). The tension between these two aspects exist in simple everyday experiences and expressions, such as when we point to an old photograph and say, "This is me at the age of twelve." "This" is the indexical term used to designate something in the vicinity of the speaker, here an image. Although the image is present, it is an (iconic) index to someone living at another time, speaker's-age-minus-twelve years back. "Me" refers to the speaker at the moment of the utterance. The tension arises from the fact that the sentence establishes an identity "is" of the person living today and the one living speaker's-age-minus-twelve years back. These two persons are both the same and different ("Disman writing this postscript is different from the Disman who joined the project" [Disman, p. 65–66])—a description that makes little sense in classical logic but is a fundamental constitution of dialectical logic.

Auto/biography is inherently about change, growing up, moving about; and yet, despite these changes, we human beings feel that there is something, deep down within ourselves that remains the same and that allows us to say "This is me at the age of twelve." Further, despite the fact that we are different selves when we are in the presence of our colleagues during a faculty meeting, of our parents during a Sunday visit, or of our teammates on a sports team. That is, idem identity can remain the same all the while its ipse part, the Self, changes both in time and with situation. That people are different, even in unexpected ways, does not come as a surprise.

Individual and Society   The relationship between individual and society does, for the most part, not play a central role in much of the scholarly literature that I face in the domains of research where I work (education, science and mathematics education, social studies of science, pragmatic linguistics). Yet there exist, from my perspective, reasonable approaches for theorizing these two entities: both Bourdieu (1997) and Holzkamp (1983) base their theories in dialectical conceptions of individual human beings and the (social and material) world that surrounds them. Thus, both scholars clearly articulate in their own characteristic ways (a) the co-emergence of individuals and their lifeworlds and (b) the emergence of the dialectic between individual and society as part of human development. In both instances, individuals and their social worlds are folded into one another (there is no nice equivalent to the German *Verschränkung*).

Let me begin with the historical process that folds together individual and society into a dialectic relation, a process that also involves the very emergence of human (social) psychology as experienced phenomenon (Holzkamp, 1983).[4] In the process of human evolution, there was a moment when the ability to use tools (chimpanzees use them, too) and divide labor (wolves and other animals practice it) together provided pre-humans with some advantages that became factors in natural selection processes. With increasing tool production and division of labor, there followed a qualitative shift in dominance from environmental determination to the active adaptation of the environment to human needs and into a process of generalized societal provision. Now, individuals no

longer needed to be concerned with their direct survival in a (hostile) environment but could guarantee their survival by contributing to the collective effort of
maintaining society. Individuals are now "able to individually realize and to
share in the societal developmental processes" (Holzkamp, 1991, p. 56). But
participation in collective processes always also presupposes mutual intelligibility, intersubjectivity, a mutual understanding that the contribution to the survival
of the other also and inherently has my own survival as a consequence. Furthermore, my individual contribution does not require to be specific, so that each of
my contribution to society is but a concrete realization of the generalized contributions required for the continuation of society—even to the point that some
contributions do not need to contribute to society at all (writing a diary) and
even harm collective life (murdering someone else).[5] It comes as no surprise that
communist party rule could continue even though many, as analyzed by Alan,
did not become party members, refused invitations to become party members,
participated only in a passive way, or were ejected from the party altogether.

Nowadays, an individual is born into a society that has not only emerged
from pre-human forms of organization but also has continued to evolve culturally and historically. Bourdieu (1997) makes a strong argument for the continued relevance of the material basis of human nature (thought and culture), which
arises from the openness of each human body to the regularities of the (social
and material) world. These influences are formative but only in the sense of being one aspect of a dialectic: the other aspect is the human being who has to perceive the world. This perception itself is a function of the individual's experience, so that individual and his or her world develop together. The world
perceived by the individual becomes the ground for his or her actions, but these
perceptual abilities have been influenced by the world. The way I perceive and
understand the world is always and already shaped by this world, the patterns of
its social and material events. At the heart of individual development is the same
fundamental organism-environment dialectic that already characterized the
thoughts of biologists, philosophers, and social psychologists alike.

This dialectical relation between individual and collective has its consequences. That is, the reasons for action (German, *Handlungsbegründungen*) are
always mine, in a concrete way, but each reason is simultaneously a concrete realization of the generalized reasons that are available and intelligible at the collective level. More so, these reasons do not just exist in an abstract sense but
each individual makes available these groundings to others together with his or
her actions. Our own views, their contents and the limited nature, are also symp-
tomatic for more general phenomena that transcend the individual me, not only
within a particular society or culture, but also across cultures. From a dialectical

perspective to concrete everyday life, neither the sameness of individually and concretely experienced action possibilities are then surprising. Auto/biographical sociology therefore always involves access to the concrete action possibilities and reasons for actions that exist not only for the individuals and the collective, but also, and in the same concrete ways, at the societal level more generally. Because our participation in society allows us to understand not only ourselves but also others although they are different, auto/biographical sociology in a group such as SAMISEBE provides a considerable sampling of concrete everyday understanding of society.

Concluding Thoughts

Our Lives as Database is the result of a sociological experiment, SAMISEBE, which existed not because of some planning and theorizing, but as concrete practice of auto/biographical method in one sociology department. The book opens up a fascinating world not only onto Czech(oslovak) society but also onto sociology as a discipline. More so, it provides much material for beginning one's own auto/biographical reflections and to further develop some of the themes that the different authors individually and the project collectively unfolds before our eyes. We can engage in our own reflections to test the viability of Konopásek's claim that these reflexive auto/biographies from the East provide some means for understanding ourselves in the West.

This chapter, in a very explicit way, also contributes to a sociological anthropology of reading. It is one (concrete) example how a member of society— though not naïve with respect to the disciplinary foundations of *Our Lives as Database*—interacted with the material text that the book provided. My auto/biographical notes, the thoughts they articulate, and the intertextuality they bring about all are the outcome of one concrete reading that reflects an aspect of sociology, much of it of German society in the 1950s and 1960s, when I grew up in a culture that actively practiced forgetting—among others, the atrocity of the camps such as Auschwitz, which currently celebrates its sixtieth anniversary of liberation. But the auto/ethnographic part also accounts for my experiences of estrangement and being a stranger, and therefore is reflexively related to the chapter of another émigré in this volume, Christiane K. Alsop.

Notes

This chapter began its life as a review essay (Roth, 2002), but since then has undergone substantial changes and revisions.

[1] All references to chapters in *Our Lives as Database* only use author name and page number.
[2] The inscription of ideologies from the sciences has also been described as the reflexive scientization of society (Beck. 1992).
[3] I do not endorse Konopásek 's statement *"Text is real, reality is textual"* (p. 165), for as I have argued elsewhere, there are considerable parts of our experience (including expertise) that do not lend themselves (easily) to description and therefore resist the textual metaphor (Roth, 2001).
[4] I only sketch the form that the analysis takes, for there is insufficient space here to articulate the entire argument. For an English introduction by Holzkamp himself see *Societal and Individual Life Processes* (Holzkamp, 1991). For a more elaborate explanation and exegesis of Holzkamp's work see the book on German critical psychology by his friend Charles Tolman (1994).
[5] What the American society has not realized is that even murdering someone is a generalized action possibility that exists at a societal level. Thus, killing killers will change little, because it does not deal with the contradictions in the society that makes killing a generalized possibility. This is just what we can see: despite being companion to other (totalitarian) societies that maintain the death penalty, murder rates remain among the highest in the world.

References

Beck, U. (1992). *Risk society: Towards a new modernity*. London: Sage.
Bourdieu, P. (1992). The practice of reflexive sociology (The Paris workshop). In P. Bourdieu & L.J.D. Wacquant, *An invitation to reflexive sociology* (pp. 216–260). Chicago: University of Chicago Press.
Derrida, J. (1988). *Limited inc*. Evanston, IL: Northwestern University Press.
Derrida, J. (1998). *Monolingualism of the Other; or, The prosthesis of origin*. Stanford, CA: Stanford University Press.
Derrida, J. (2000). *Le toucher, Jean-Luc Nancy*. Paris: Galilee.
Garfinkel, H. (1967). *Studies in ethnomethodology*. Englewood Cliffs, NJ: Prentice-Hall.
Holzkamp, K. (1983). *Grundlegung der Psychologie*. Frankfurt: Campus.
Holzkamp, K. (1991). Societal and individual life processes. In C. W. Tolman & W. Maiers (Eds.), *Critical psychology: Contributions to an historical science of the subject* (pp. 50–64). Cambridge: Cambridge University Press.
Konopásek, Z. (Ed.). (2000). *Our lives as database—Doing a sociology of ourselves: Czech social transitions in auto/biographical research dialogues*. Prague: Karolinum Press.
Livingston, E. (1995). *An anthropology of reading*. Bloomington: Indiana University Press.
Ricœur, P. (1990). *Soi-même comme un autre*. Paris: Seuil.

Ricœur, P. (1991). *From text to action: Essays in hermeneutics II*. Chicago: University of Chicago Press.

Roth, W.-M. (2001). Phenomenology and mathematical experience. *Linguistics & Education, 12*, 239–252.

Roth, W.M. (2002). Auto/biography as method: Dialectical sociology of everyday life. *FQS: Forum Qualitative Sozialforschung / Forum: Qualitative Social Research, 3*(4). http://www.qualitative-research.net/fqs/fqs-eng.htm

Roth, W.-M., & McRobbie, C. (1999). Lifeworlds and the 'w/ri(gh)ting' of classroom research. *Journal of Curriculum Studies, 31*, 501–522.

Roth, W.-M., Bowen, G. M., & Masciotra, D. (2002). From thing to sign and 'natural object': Toward a genetic phenomenology of graph interpretation. *Science, Technology, & Human Values, 27*, 327–356.

Schutz, A. (1944). The stranger: An essay in social psychology. *American Journal of Sociology, 49*, 499–507.

Smith, D. E. (1987). *The everyday world as problematic: A feminist sociology*. Toronto: University of Toronto Press.

Smith, D. E. (1999). *Conceptual practices of power: A feminist sociology of knowledge*. Toronto: University of Toronto Press.

Tolman, C. W. (1994). *Psychology, society, and subjectivity*. London: Routledge.

5 Scientific Experience and the Researcher's Body

Franz Breuer

This contribution deals with the epistemological relationship between research-ers and their research objects. I presuppose the existence of simultaneous proc-esses on two levels: (a) a discussion of methodologies and methods mainly con-cerned with the concept of empiricism in science that occurs in different variations in different disciplines—natural sciences versus social and behavioral sciences; and (b) how scientists evolve relationships between their own bodies and their research objects and what consequences for researchers' personalities, habitus, and behavior derive from this relationship. My considerations devel-oped within the disciplinary context of psychology in Germany. The mainstream enacts research methods based on those that are typical in the natural sciences. I critically reflect on some implications of the structure of research linked to this model type. In contrast, I regard research in the social and behavioral sciences as oriented toward some fundamental ideas, in which auto/ethnography and auto/-biography play an important role. In the following, I outline two epistemological traditions and their ideas about empirical evidence, how empirical evidence has to be constructed, and how scientific data are collected. I contrast the natural science tradition against the tradition in the social and behavioral sciences. In the natural sciences, researchers collect data with complex and implication-laden (technical) instruments and try to avoid and extinguish any human influence and trace. In the social and behavioral sciences, the role of the epistemic subject and its object of understanding are viewed as anthropologically and interactively related and exchangeable, and researchers' personhood and material bodies are involved in the gathering of empirical data.

Auto/biography and auto/ethnography are interesting prototypes of the latter tradition. Understanding subjects put themselves in the place of their objects, focus on personal self-experience, and take themselves (one could say their bodies) as the locus of scientific data collection. Epistemologically, one takes a perspective of self-detachment and self-reflection to interpret these personal data as cases of transindividual experience and tries to understand subtle empirical phenomena by accessing the Self in a particular, profound (introspective) way. The artfulness of the approach lies, for example, in the personal ability to deal with these Self-related phenomena in a reflective and reflexive manner.

My own credo regarding scientific production of understanding is this: Acquiring scientific knowledge is a specifically human (historically, socially, and culturally mediated) activity in which epistemic subjects (researchers) engage their sensual and cognitive potentialities in learning processes. The materiality of the body as condition of consciousness implies a holistic participation of researchers engaged in the endeavor of understanding their research objects. In this, researchers are human beings with sensual, intellectual, and personal abilities and characteristics, biological and cultural attributes, socialization, habitus, social charisma, and sensibility. In the context of the social and behavioral sciences, I presuppose the general possibility that the positions in the subject–object constellation are exchangeable; in other words, I presuppose the isomorphism of subject and object. I also presuppose that research settings are interactive and embedded in the materiality of their everyday contexts (in the aforementioned sense). I finally presuppose that understanding is produced rather than constituting an image of the world (Bergold & Breuer, 1992; Breuer, 1991). Reflecting on one's personal role as the researcher (role, influences, perceptions, and reactions) offers a promising epistemological perspective for understanding Self and research object in the context of the questions pursued and the research fields and processes.

Scientific Experience

The term *scientific experience* is not clearly defined philosophically or methodologically. It is reasonable to refer not to one scientific experience but to different concepts of experience (Wohlgenannt, 1969). These concepts are strongly influenced by the research domain and by the orientations to particular methodologies and methods that are subject to historical changes. In the philosophy of science, these problems are discussed explicitly in methodological terms. Implications concerning sensual and bodily characteristics of the researcher, however, have been made salient only in exceptional cases. The issue can be reconstructed only indirectly from the history of concepts and historical developments of scientific practices and their ruling criteria. The body is seen as irrelevant and, programmatically, is a non-problem in scientific self-reflection, which is simultaneously an articulation and aspect of the problem.

In the following, I first describe some aspects of the development of the (early) modern natural sciences. I focus on (a) how the concept of the object of research changed, (b) the change of the concept of experience and empiricism, and (c) the methodologies linked to this concept. The natural science understanding of science has implications for the role of the researcher in the research process, which can be linked also to the forms in which the habitus of individual scientists is expressed.

Prevalent notions in the empirical social and behavioral sciences (I mainly refer to psychology) regard the adoption of the (successful) epistemological model of natural sciences as the ideal. However it is questionable whether the attendant arguments crucial for this preference are indeed valid for the social and behavioral sciences. The unresolved dispute about whether psychological research belongs to the natural or social and behavioral sciences (or even social and cultural studies [e.g., Bruner 1990; Groeben, 1986]) is indicative of the fact that very different positions and perspectives are brought to bear on the epistemic issue. This issue can be articulated by contrasting different concepts of experience and empirical research. I discuss some problematic aspects concerning the adoption of the natural science concept of research by the social and behavioral sciences by focusing on the material nature of researchers' bodies and the implications that derive from it.

Historical Changes of the Notion of Experience in the Natural Sciences

In the natural sciences, epistemology is characterized by the historical relations of rationalism and empiricism, which include confrontational, interactional, modifying, and integration-oriented aspects. Do (objective, subjective) ideas, categories, thinking, or theories and hypotheses have primacy with regard to scientific understanding? Or are there empirical phenomena and their representations as sensations or perceptions at the outset of knowledge? Plato and Aristotle are quoted as representing oppositional ideas. The former advocated pure thought as the route to truth and saw body-centered perception as obstruction. The latter took an opposing standpoint. Accordingly, there is no other route to knowledge than via sensory perception of the empirical world. The world of concepts and ideas is recognized as a secondary creation, an abstraction, and it is accepted that sensory perceptions are not immune to failures (e.g., Feyerabend, 1975).

Historiographies of modern natural sciences often describe Bacon, Kepler, and Galileo as significant protagonists whose work led to new epistemological ideas and processes. On the one hand, they represent an empirical point of view, as they emphasize the importance of phenomena and sensory perception to the development of understanding and theory. On the other hand, they discussed the role and nature of sensory perception and the concept of empirical research from a rationalist point of view. Unbiased perception and its connection with common sense are no longer significant from an epistemological perspective. A (non-articulated) concept of critical empiricism emerges: There is a suspicion against everyday perception, which is seen as an obstacle for perceiving the world as it really is. In contrast, a theoretically informed observer becomes more and more important. Galileo, for example, is somebody who was able to *see* the free fall of an object dropped from a tower as a phenomenon inside a moving system where everything including the observer moves.

The suspicion against sensory perception manifests itself, among others, in the increased use of instruments and procedures that improve human perception and even displace it. This also leads to a loss of simplicity (or an increase of theory), for researchers have to know the inner workings of the instruments and apparati to dissociate their effects from the signals to reveal the real, object-related and theoretically relevant data:

Let us consider observations by telescopes in astronomy or microscopes in biology as an example! There is no experience that can be made from observation without the observer knowing the functioning of his observation instruments. For example somebody who cannot distinguish an aberration or a contamination of his microscope from the observed object also cannot distinguish between true and wrong conclusions concerning the subject. (Janich, 1981, p. 75)

Human cognition constitutes, in the words of Francis Bacon, an "uneven mirror." In the natural sciences, understanding-related ambitions go in the opposite direction: Efforts are made to achieve an "even mirror," an "objective" perception, ideally without the effects of a biasing sensual human subject. Or, at least, a self-reflective theory is sought that accounts for the knowing subject's presuppositions and biases so that these can be, somehow, subtracted from the obtained sensual perception. The new science emerging at the time was "not only empirically oriented but also critical against empiricism" (Kutschmann, 1986, p. 157). The notion of empirical research itself became conceptual and shifted away from an Aristotelian notion of human experience. The viewpoint of understanding in early modern natural sciences can be denoted as empiricist with a refined, rationalist background: "Only theory allocates empirical experiences to positions where they can verify or falsify" (p. 163).

A strict separation of theoretical and empirical notions turned out to be impossible (e.g., Popper, 1980). Based on ethnographic descriptions of the construction of scientific knowledge and scientific practice, historical and sociological investigations of science show that instrumental approaches in the (natural) sciences cannot guarantee the purification of knowledge and objectivity. Natural scientists normally ignore presuppositions, practical routines, and communicative constitutions and conditions of scientific facts. Yet the mundane character of scientific research, its embedding in cognitive traditions, technical procedures, cultures, and speech communities, cannot be abstracted from fact even in the purest of natural sciences (e.g., Fleck, 1979; Knorr-Cetina, 1985; Kuhn, 1962).

Changes in the Human–Nature Relationship

The aforementioned historical changes in the epistemology of the natural sciences are concomitant with changes in the conception of the relation between human beings and the non-human world. Any relationship, similarity, correspondence is questioned and a separation is realized. Three aspects are crucial. First, the researcher gives up an anthropocentric perspective on life—e.g., regarding the qualification of the observer's place (Copernicus) and the abstraction of time from ordinary temporal experience (Newton). Second, there is an associated dis-anthropomorphization of nature. This means giving up notions of similarity between domains of being (e.g., with respect to animistic interpretations of nature, mythological ideas, conceptions of an entelechic, purposeful character of nature). Third, this leads to a questioning of the physical-sensual abilities of perception, which can be prototypically demonstrated with Locke's tenets of "primary and secondary qualities." Human senses (smell, taste, sound, color, or gestalt) are *secondary* characteristics (*re*presentations) that have only limited validity concerning the *real* character of objects. Accordingly, the human mind has to transcend them to get to their nonsensual, primary qualities (e.g., quantitative measures of extension, movement, strength).

Bod(il)y Consequences

As a result of these developments, knowledge deriving from a knowing body is increasingly questioned as deficient and arbitrary. Therefore methodical purification of natural scientific production of understanding aimed at extending, completing, specifies, in extreme cases even substitutes, human sensual perception through the use of instruments, implements, and apparati. As a consequence, scientific research becomes artificial. The involvement and impact of the scientist's bodily sensual characteristics decreases: because of their imperfection, faultiness, unreliability, human bodies are increasingly and programmatically excluded. The ideal aim was to gain *disembodied* insights to nature and to reach a self-exegesis of nature. Researchers' sensual bodies became appendices to apparati and their role was narrowed to anticipation, planning, and arranging the instruments to focus on natural phenomena without actually interfering with their measurement. The bodily characteristics emerged in the following way:

Bodily feeling and sensing, active sensuousness of perception is frozen and shut down for the benefit of an increased activity of mind; inversely compassion of the soul and apathy or synharmony of mind are shut down or at least discriminated. The claim of finding out about undisguised nature "as it is" demands the in-active body and the a-pathic mind: Either determines the bodily existence of modern scientists. (Kutschmann, 1986, p. 134)

As a result, the scientist's body steps into the background, takes on a "shadowy existence" (p. 329). After analyzing the biographies of three distinguished scientists (Girolamo Cardano, Johannes Kepler, Isaac Newton) in an exemplary fashion, Kutschmann sums up the personal and habitus-related characteristics of the modern scientist:

- the typical habitus of modern scientists . . . [is] noncommunicative, rather unimposing, prospering in clandestineness. (p. 390)
- relatively little tied to one place: His place . . . could be anywhere. (p. 390)
- the body . . . disappears in favor of a diffuse, always seesawing mental state. (p. 392).
- a most sensitive and sensible, and simultaneously labile character whose basic structure is dominated by perpetual agitation, skepticism, and concern. (p. 396)
- the natural scientist is—as far as possible—meant to strive toward not believing in his senses, for putting the perception of nature on an objective, technically repeatable footing. (p. 399)
- the clinical picture of . . . the modern natural scientists is dominated by mental and neurotic diagnoses. . . . hypochondria, . . . bewilderment, . . . delusional ideas. (p. 400)
- the scientist loses the feeling of his bodily authenticity. (p. 404)

Methodological Developments in the Social and Behavioral Sciences

The dissociation of human beings and nature—or subject and object—in the natural sciences has its analogy in the social sciences and humanities, sometimes with a several-century delay and with different emphases according to the discipline. The "act of separation" is concretely realized (a) in the dis-anthropomorphization of the person as an object of scientific insight and (b) in the adoption of the natural science ideal of the disembodied researcher. Both tendencies are prevalent in the respective disciplines. The former manifests itself in the rethinking of the notion of the research object—the idea of the person. It is an object, belonging to nature external to it—it is an exorcism of the idea that humans are in the image of god or the abandonment of the assumption of the subject–object isomorphism. The human body now is described as "mechanical" or "rational machine," as a "chemical laboratory," "electronic computer," "energetic closed loop," "cybernetic system," "profane flesh," or "object." The latter tendency shows itself in the establishment of an idea of science and a methodological ideal that rival those in the natural sciences with respect to skepticism toward the body, a substitution of senses by apparati, and a purification of method. Such an understanding of research methods now also is the predominant orientation in the social and behavioral sciences.

"Empathic Potencies" of Understanding

An alternative to the outlined natural-scientific empiricist epistemology is the possibility to understand nature in principle. It is the concept of "empathic" potencies of understanding: "Concerning this matter I have in mind the sensual, libidinous and imaginative acquirements as imagination and the ability to desire, as well as . . . the mimetic metamorphosis and imaginary assimilation" (Kutschmann, 1986, p. 211), which are "characterized by the fusion of the epistemic subject and its object at the site of the body" (p. 212). However this possibility of experiencing has been denied in the history of natural sciences and did not influence its development. This empirical approach plays a different role in social and behavioral sciences because of different epistemic relations. An analogous denial of the role of empathic understanding therefore is problematic.

There are good reasons—in terms of a rationally enlightened position—to question the belief in the world's anthropomorphic texture with respect to the relation between human beings and the non-human world. Concerning the construction of knowledge about the human nature, this demythologization requires a qualification. The basic idea of anthropomorphism of the object of research—or rather, the inherent identity of structure between epistemic subject and epistemic object—is not inappropriate in the social and behavioral sciences. Quite to the contrary: there would have to be very good reasons to deviate from presupposing the anthropological isomorphism between the epistemic subject and epistemic (human) object.

Scientific epistemology is therefore subject to a different horizon of consideration and adequacy than in the natural sciences. Body-centered epistemic methods—as implied by the empathic principles that accompany an anthropological isomorphism—are quite common in everyday face-to-face interaction. They are therefore interesting as research objects in their own right. They are also constitutive for interpersonal contacts—we always think of the other in terms of our Selves. There is no contact without such affinities and fusions—regardless of whether the particular subject|object intents it, whether he/she concentrates his/her attention on it, or whether he/she realizes it. This latter aspect is crucial for the social and behavioral sciences. Here we can find a difficulty that researchers face only scarcely and reluctantly. Purification of method according to the standard paradigm in the natural sciences creates a contextual abstraction and artificiality—thus runs the general argument. On the one hand, this abstraction and artificiality belies the interactive and everyday character of the investigation's setting that cannot be eliminated. On the other hand, abstraction and artificiality render a generalization of results impossible in principle.

This criticism is not new. The German psychologist Klaus Holzkamp (1972b) elaborated the most incisive critique along these lines. He articulated the complicity required by research participants as a precondition for conducting experiments with human beings. He also made salient the structural characteristics of the researcher processes designed to define initial conditions, reduce the system of life conditions, and attenuate the stimulus situation (Holzkamp, 1972a). All of these processes make generalization beyond the narrow context of the experiment doubtful. Furthermore, however strong the disembodiment claims may be, experimental procedures make interaction inevitable, which inherently activates bodily resonances in the epistemic subject (researcher) and the epistemic object (participant). These resonances within the researcher find no explicit representations or position in currently accepted research procedures; they are suppressed and remain unaccounted for. They become, however, effective as factors that influence cognition—they literally come from behind.

An alternative approach focuses on the positive aspects of the body as locus of knowledge and knowledge construction, for example, in the psychological concept of *countertransference* (Devereux, 1967). From this perspective, the research methods constitute, among other things, ways for investigators to deal with (emotional) uneasiness, irritations, and disturbances that are triggered by the confrontation with research objects. *Anxiety*—which stands for all positive and negative human emotions—constitutes an important modality of the resonances that the researcher experiences; and these resonances are exploited as a *positive* aspect of method. Reduction of anxiety is a necessary moment of research for dealing with an object scientifically through one's own personhood. This approach leads to a reflection of Self and thereby offers an epistemologically productive role to the resonances experienced in and through the body of the researcher.

Two Social-Scientific Concepts of Experience

A historical contextualization and confrontation of the two approaches for synthesizing a viable concept of experience in the social sciences and humanities can be found in *Die Einübung des Tatsachenblicks* ("Exercising the factual gaze") (Bonß, 1982). Based on authors such as Alfred Schütz, Berger and Luckmann, and Foucault, the author attempts to construct a more precise concept of empirical research in the social sciences by following a historical and philosophical approach. He analyzes the idea of empirical research with respect to its social, temporal, and factual relativity. Bonß conceptualizes it as an "experience of an external world as 'reality' developed from a construction of meaning in societies" (p. 21), which both enables and constrains communication. "What is 'real' to a Tibetan monk may not be 'real' to an American businessman" (Berger & Luckmann, 1966, p. 15).

Proceeding in the manner of history and philosophy of knowledge, Bonß (1982) opposes two empirical types that are relevant for social sciences; these "are produced according to different rules and cannot be reduced to each other" (p. 10). First, there is the "empiricism of facts" or "empiricism of nature." The outside world is modeled as a subject-independent, nonsocial structure. It is founded on a strict separation between pre-scientific and scientific experience, highly determined by apparati; in the social sciences, it is mainly represented by "statistical, matter-of-fact approaches" that can be characterized by "desubjectivation, decontextualization, and quantification" (p. 59). Experiences of reality in the lifeworld are reduced to their "instrumentally manageable aspects" (p. 85). Second, there is an "experience of totality" or "social empiricism." Here, the outside world is modeled as a subjective, symbolic reality under the maxim to scientifically reconstruct "perceived experiences," "without leaving out the character of experience concerning the social reality" (p. 45), characterized by conditions regulating the communication of perception. In the social sciences, this is prototypically represented by "monographic approaches," "where the explanation and definition of empirical entities is not given by the categories of number and measure but by so called 'qualitative approaches' that create empirical facts related to subject and situation by inductive generalization" (p. 98). This procedure is also characterized as a concept of a "hermeneutical-inductive 'securing of evidence'", as "paradigm of evidences," which "recalls in its cognitive core . . . a kind of knowledge that is almost as old as mankind itself, namely of the symbolization processes of hunters and trackers, who can ascertain species, size, and appearance of animals from tiny traces" (p. 112).

Fact-oriented approaches to empirical research are—in agreement with their natural science model—intentionally articulated in terms of the removal of the researcher from the process of empirical production (though Bonß does not describe the dimension of bodily materiality as an independent perspective in his argumentation). At the same time, empirical production in the context of a holistic experience is characterized to a higher degree by intentional personal participation of researchers in the reality they analyze. This comprehensive concept realizes different kinds of researcher participation, interest, or exposition of being affected, all of which imply bodily involvement.

Fieldwork as a Prototype of Knowledge Construction in the Social Sciences

One approach to empirical research in social sciences typifies Bonß's *holistic experience*: the ethnographically oriented stay in the field by means of which investigators inquire foreign—i.e., socioculturally strange—communities. Historically, the researcher's bodily presence in the field became the standard approach only with the work of Bronislaw Malinowski conducted among the cultures of New Guinea and the Trobriand Islands. Before that time, ethnological investigations were based on the basis of data collected by someone else—e.g. notes of missionaries, soldiers, administration officials, adventurers, globetrotters, or instructed employees. Today this latter practice is often depreciatingly denoted as *armchair ethnology* (Fuchs & Berg, 1993; Geertz, 1988).

The researcher may realize the stay as participating observer or as observing participant. This is a situation where the epistemic subject transforms something foreign and alien into its own category system, figuratively denoted by the term *othering*. This figure represents the prototypical case of understanding in the social sciences—a hermeneutic procedure. In ethnology, some questions regarding knowledge are carried to extremes that are likewise fundamentally relevant in other social science research contexts—e.g., the problem of representation or the role of differences in the face of structural identity. However, this frequently does not become evident. There has been controversy concerning the role of fieldwork as method and participant observation: the role of researchers in the field, their abilities of perception and categorization, the matter of linguistic representation of a foreign culture and the like (e.g., Breuer, 1989; Clifford & Marcus, 1986). In the following I articulate an alternative analysis of this method, which emphasizes the role of the body to knowledge construction.

Fieldwork often takes the researcher far from home, away from the familiar culture and social environment, convenience, and accustomed ways of life and into isolation and solitude, combined with strains and deprivation. This situation is a profound, and in fact existential, characteristic of ethnographic research: it involves "a painful kind of self-awareness" (Kohl, 1993, p. 114), a "secondary socialization," and a "remake of his infantile situation" (Stagl, 1993, pp. 16–17). The researcher's experience became part of the official discourse with the jolt to the research community provided by the posthumous publication of Malinowski's New Guinea and Trobriand Island diaries (Malinowski, 1967). This discussion made salient that ethnologists produce their data, descriptions, or theories as a result of their experiences of a foreign culture and society in a very direct sense *with* and *through* their bodies (cf. Geertz, 1988). They, with their entire bodies, are virtual instruments in the construction of knowledge. The specific characteristics stemming from this approach are due to two conditions that simultaneously provide anthropologists with a temporary affiliation in the foreign cultures and lead to a decentering, a critical, analytical view of them. Their ontological isomorphism with research participants and their anthropological competence as socialized insiders in communities—though foreign—are basic requirements for participation. Their primary socialization in a specific context of an occidental culture and their scientific education provide a background that shapes their experience and perception of and agency in the foreign cultures.

Their status as guests with limited durations of stay, as wanderers between two sociocultural worlds, leads to a certain distance taking and inherent foreignness between participants and researcher. This space is also responsible for a particular epistemological stance. The situation is inherently fragile, as the researchers may abandon their guest status, loose distance, and *go native* permanently. This situation constitutes a subjective entanglement in the sociocultural context where researchers stay with body and mind. Accounting for this subjective entanglement in the data analysis and considering its epistemological consequences constitutes, from a nonsectarian position on research method, an important condition for gaining viable knowledge about foreign cultures.

Auto/Ethnography

In auto/ethnography, researchers constitute their own object of research so that the knowing subject and the research object become one. Auto/ethnography concerns knowledge of the Self, which is not easily constructed, but which is, according to a German saying, "the first step to improvement." In addition to the idiosyncratic and mere private knowledge of Self, auto/ethnography concerns the position, behavior, and experience of Self as an interesting, significant example of universality, the concrete realization of culture in a concrete, situated, and embodied person. If it is true that talking about others implies talking about oneself, then, conversely, talking about oneself also implies something about others. Subtle descriptions from a first-person perspective can be particularly interesting in cases that focus on topics not normally talked about in conventional research narratives because they concern something unpleasant or tabooed.

Auto/ethnographic descriptions concern for example the (linguistic) explication of practices, patterns of behavior, self-perception, emotion, and assessment that normally (in the practice and consciousness in a everyday context) remain in the background and are unconsciously or only implicit consciously known; or they concern phenomena that one knows privately but that usually are not brought up in public. For this purpose the described subject|object phenomena can come from different fields of the author's experience and activity—for instance from personal private contexts of the researcher (e.g., Ellis [Chapter 17]; Kraft Alsop [Chapter 20]) or from professional contexts, especially from situations of social science research (field-stay, production of scientific texts, etc. [e.g., Lee/Roth [Chapter 19]; Noy [Chapter 18]). This way of focusing demands from the researcher an effort to explicate, requiring self-awareness and viewing the Self virtually from the outside by a process of *decentration*, that is, a process of rendering foreign that which up to now was taken for granted (Breuer, 1999; Raeithel, 1983).

"Disturbances" in Object and Subject

A specific variant of the social science effort concerning self-reflection is a depth-psychologically founded conception of the subject–object relation (Devereux, 1967). This approach does not represent mainstream ethnology, but rather a separate version of the discipline: ethno-psychoanalysis (e.g., Heinrichs, 1985, 1993). This approach takes an explicitly body-centered perspective concerning the research process. A principal starting point is the identification of different types of data:

1. The behavior of the subject.
2. The "disturbances" produced by the existence and observational activities of the observer.

3. The behavior of the observer: His anxieties, his defensive maneuvers, his research strategies, his "decisions" (= his attribution of a meaning to his observations). (Devereux, 1967, p. xix)

In the mainstreams of the social and behavioral sciences, these dimensions receive researchers' attention in decreasing order. First, there is a focusing on the object's behavior, which can be regarded as setting the observational standard of the researcher. Second, researchers attend to the "interferences" deriving from the relationship between the researcher and the researched, that is, researchers attempt to account for their effect on the observed persons (generally denoted as "reactive effects"). Fact-oriented empirical approaches deceive themselves by adhering to the fiction of noninterference: There is in fact a lot of orientation to the research situation, both by the researcher and the research participant (Roth & Lee, 2004). There are also indications that researchers attempt to efface their bodily presence. Researchers frequently are serious, businesslike, role-specific, neutral, controlled, and self-effacing by producing relevant facial expressions. They attempt to act as non-persons, to stage a presence as if covered with a cloak that renders them invisible, pretending to overcome the patterns and rules of behavior that mediate everyday social interactions. But research participants take into account such behaviors of the researcher in their own actions and behaviors. The tendency of the research object to react to the researcher's presence makes the model of disembodied knowledge production problematic in principle. The general attempt to deal with this problem is to control and minimize the "disturbing" or "tampering" effects—or quite simply just to ignore them.

A productive alternative to knowledge production takes these phenomena as in principle inevitable elements of social science research, which therefore is understood as an interactive process (e.g., Bergold & Breuer, 1992). What research participants do is then understood as reactions to "guests," "curious strangers," "acceptably incompetent people," "potential helper," or "unmarried, good looking women." These reactions to the researcher are to be understood as informative and meaningful, providing information about the object, for example, concerning their categorizations or patterns of behavior and preferences. To do this, researcher need to be conscious and sensible with regard to their presence as stimulus, an increased attention to this aspect and a certain autonomous possibility of regulation (Breuer & Roth, 2003; Heeg, 1996).

Researchers least attend to the final point listed above: "Unfortunately, it is about the third type of behavior that we have the least information, because we have systematically refused to study reality on its own terms" (Devereux, 1967,

p. xix). Devereux proposes to focus exactly on this aspect and to cultivate it: reactions are triggered by the bodily presence of the researcher in contact with the research object—including, for example, disturbances, emotions of different quality, various associations. In psychoanalysis, these phenomena are part of *countertransference*, that is, effects on the analyst's body emerging from the contact with the object of analysis that derive from the unconscious. Affective emotional reactions of the researcher (anxieties, uncertainties, embarrassments, desire, or attractions) are related to preferences, inclinations, dislikes, defense- and avoidance-strategies, and dis/attention in the research process. They are thus part of the method-related decisions researchers make or ought to make.

Devereux proposes not to engage yet another objective turn, discounting or eliminating the researcher's body in this new perspective. Such attempts would fail, because of the inherently unavoidable effects of countertransference. To the contrary, if researchers do not consider the effects, there is a high probability that they influence decisions about method without being aware of it. Devereux argues that researchers have to attend to these effects and deal with their own reactions to the research object; this then enables them to treat their own bodies as texts. In this way, the researcher's body can be used productively, as epistemic windows, as data in the process of gaining scientific knowledge. "When ignored, or warded off by means of countertransference resistances masquerading as methodology, these 'disturbances' become sources of uncontrolled and uncontrollable error, although . . . when treated as basic and characteristic data of behavioral science they are more valid and more productive of insight than any other type of datum" (Devereux, 1967, p. xvii).

Epistemological Subject–Object Boundaries

Historically, the idea of empirical research in the natural sciences developed from a notion of perception as sensual and embodied to one that was disembodied and instrumental, with considerable consequences concerning role and bodily habitus of the researcher. This process is highly questionable in the context of the social and behavioral sciences; it is even inappropriate and unproductive. More adequate appear to be empathic approaches and "body-activity," especially when used self-reflectively. At this point in my argument, I turn from a descriptive to a methodologically prescriptive level. Devereux's methodological recommendations for the behavioral sciences address this problem in terms of the partition between the epistemic object and the epistemic subject.

Phenomena of the outside world are registered, perceived, recorded, and understood by an observer in a certain, system-dependent way. Devereux analyses the locus where the epistemic subject and its object meet in terms of the statement "and this I perceive" (p. 281), which formulates a protocol statement concerning a perceptive event. He characterizes this as the point, where the "observer . . . begins" (p. 281), "at which one's real or claimed knowledge and explanations cease" (p. 285), and where, for example, physical or electrochemical concepts come to their limits of application and the epistemic subject passes into a "mental phenomenon." At this point a partition is made between the observer and the thing observed. "The partition is, by definition, 'mobile' and its 'shifting' is not continuous" (p. 279); it depends on theoretical background concepts in their broadest sense—on disciplinary perspectives, methodologies, methodical procedures etc.

In scientific observations, instruments play an important role (with regard to technical apparati as well as to the "apparatus" of human perception). Devereux asks "whether it is more meaningful to speak of a partition between the object and the apparatus or of one between the apparatus and the observer" (p. 281). In answering the question, he refers to a thought experiment of the physicist Niels Bohr concerning the exploration of an object with a stick:

If the stick is grasped firmly, it becomes an extension of the hand; the locus of the partition is therefore at the 'other' (distal) end of the stick. . . . In Bohr's example, a stick held rigidly is less part of the object than of the observer. Held loosely, it is more part of the object than of the observer. These two ways of holding the stick are paradigmatic of all behavioral science experimentation and observation. (pp. 281–282)

Devereux provides several examples to illustrate this and to show the variety of possible readings. For instance the physicist who measures the environmental temperature with a mercury barometer: The locus of the partition in this case lies at the end of the mercury column (or between the light reflected there and the observer's retina). In contrast to that the psychoanalyst is seen as a prototype of "proximal" perception:

[D]eliberately channels stimuli emanating from the patient *directly* to his own unconscious. . . . He allows his patient to reach—and to reach into—him. He allows a disturbance to be created within himself and then studies this disturbance even more carefully than he studies the patient's utterances. . . . He says: "And this I perceive" only in respect to these reverberations "at himself." . . . The disturbance occurs "within" the observer and it is this disturbance which is then experienced as the real stimulus and treated as the relevant datum. (p. 301)

On Epistemological Methods in the Social Sciences and Humanities

The object–subject partition can vary on a scale of bodily "distal" to "proximal reading." The variation is conditioned by disciplinary, theoretical, methodological, method-related, and personal concepts. The predominant tendency concerning the empirical concept of modern behavioral sciences apparently moves toward the distal end of the scale. Among other things this is linked to the historical developed, critical self-reflection of the position of the epistemic subject and his/her sensual or perceptive abilities. A simple transposition of this idea to the behavioral sciences is suspect: reasons would have to be stated to deal with human and social objects in the same epistemological manner as with inanimate nature. The situation of gaining knowledge here is fundamentally different. Regarding method and methodology, the following issues have to be considered: (a) structural isomorphism between subject and object of research, owning basically the same anthropological characteristics, dimensions of possibilities, and the like; (b) unalterable interactivity between subject and object in the situation; and (c) inevitable amalgamation of the research situation with everyday contexts of both types of participants.

A self-reflective consideration of the epistemological position and role of the epistemic subject proposes not a maximization of "distal" methods but rather a "proximal" approach—the focusing and cultivation of a body-centered and self-reflective orientation for gaining knowledge. Such a reorientation will not find it easy to assert itself in the mainstream communities of the social and behavioral sciences—and life will not be easy for the researchers. The personal demands on self-clarification and self-reflective use of the knowing body have to be set high in this context; and these demands will be met with considerable difficulties and resistance in the scientific community. As is known, self-reflection is a hard task for everyone—the observation of distal others is much easier. There are also few examples and models of social scientific usable method-related concepts that help making such an approach attractive and realistic. Psychoanalysis is a prominent example for focusing on the self-experience of the epistemic subject as a means of gaining knowledge. But psychoanalytic forms of analysis are not useful to every social scientist. There are other scientific traditions and methods that offer ideas concerning the researcher as a relevant social and personal actor in the context of investigation as well as the associated self-attention and self-focusing. Auto/ethnography is an important and creative alternative.

Conclusions

Here I present some suggestions for where our journey might be heading, though there is insufficient space to articulate these ideas in detail. Fundamentally, I suggest considering the basic characteristics of the situation in which the social and behavioral scientists find themselves when collecting data. There are subject–object isomorphism, interactivity, and experience of everyday aspects. Furthermore it is important to reflect the epistemic subject as an embodied person with specific biological, personal, social, cultural, biographical, sensual, and cognitive traits, concepts, points of view, and perspectives and to focus on these not in a negative sense of biases and errors but rather in a positive, productive sense. Which insights are possible when we actively regard, use, and reflect these conditions that otherwise would be hidden without such a source and perspective? All data is principally readable with respect to the knowing subject and to the research object: It offers information concerning the object of knowledge and concerning the system that investigates the object.

Regarding the reading of data at the scientist's body, we are confronted with attention, sensibility, perception, ways of describing and representing, documentation, and reflection of resonances and transactions that are triggered by the contact with the object. Among other things, there are effects that result from the researcher's presence in the field and among participants. I offer three illustrative examples of alternative methods.

First, there is reflection of the course and history of the embodied researcher's cognitive and emotional engagement with the research object, the topic. Which presuppositions, biographical experiences, and the like (also and especially those beyond scientific conceptualization) can be found at the beginning of the research and what can be said about their development over time? Which decisions have been made concerning focusing on certain topics, demarcating, or ways of working? In my research group I have had good results with keeping a personal research diary as a possibility to cultivate the reflection of these aspects. The diary documents the entire research process in a broadest sense including its personal and conceptual parts. I also offer my students and coworkers supervisory assistance as part of the research process, where personal resonances are articulated and reflected together.

Second, there is reflection of the contact and contact history with the field; this contact requires interaction and intervention. Which relationship, position, and role does the researcher take with respect to participants and field, and how do these develop in the course of the research history? Among other things, the field is characterized by a repertoire of admission criteria, potential roles for curious strangers, guests, guest members, or counselors. The duration of the field stay also deserves consideration, as it involves increasing familiarity or loss of confidence, and increasing expectations. Participants may confront the researcher with wishes, desires, needs, reservations, or rejections. Whether or not the researcher accedes to these, they can be read as information concerning the researcher as a person and as information about the field.

Third, researchers may reveal characteristics of their own perspective as constructed and bound to their being in the world. They achieve this by enacting systematic confrontation, comparisons among alternative or competing positions, viewpoints, or perspectives. Divergent information is thereby created that leads to stereoscopic vision, which enables researchers to relativize and decenter their own understanding. The system-dependent aspects of the researchers' perspectives become more concrete, allowing them to perceive their own behavioral patterns and to gain depth with respect to their understanding of the research object.

Notes

This is a considerably modified version of a previously published German text (Breuer, 2000), with kind permission of the Steiner-Verlag, Stuttgart. My thanks go to Barbara Dieris and Wolff-Michael Roth who translated and adapted the text into English. We translated all quotes from German sources, but relied on the original in the cases of *From Anxiety to Method* (Devereux, 1967) and *The Social Construction of Reality* (Berger & Luckmann, 1966).

References

Berger, P. L., & Luckmann, T. (1966). *The social construction of reality: A treatise in the sociology of knowledge.* Garden City, NY: Doubleday.

Bergold, J., & Breuer, F. (1992). Zum Verhältnis von Gegenstand und Forschungsmethoden in der Psychologie. *Journal für Psychologie, 1*, 24–35.

Bonß, W. (1982). *Die Einübung des Tatsachenblicks. Zur Struktur und Veränderung empirischer Sozialforschung.* Frankfurt: Suhrkamp.

Breuer, F. (1989). Die Relativität der Realität. Zur erkenntnis- und praxisbezogenen Produktivität differentieller Sehweisen der „Wirklichkeit." In I. Beerlage & E.-M. Fehre (Eds.), *Praxisforschung zwischen Intuition und Institution* (pp. 57–69). Tübingen: DGVT.

Breuer, F. (1991). *Wissenschaftstheorie für Psychologen. Eine Einführung.* Münster: Aschendorff.

Breuer, F. (2000). Wissenschaftliche Erfahrung und der Körper/Leib des Wissenschaftlers. In C. Wischermann & S. Haas (Eds.), *Körper mit Geschichte. Der menschliche Körper als Ort der Selbst- und Weltdeutung* (pp. 33–50). Stuttgart: Steiner.

Breuer, F., & Roth, W.-M. (2003). Subjectivity and reflexivity in the social sciences: Epistemic windows and methodical consequences. *Forum Qualitative Sozialforschung / Forum: Qualitative Social Research, 4*(2). Available at: http://www.qualitative-research.net/fqs-texte/2-03/2-03intro-3-e.htm

Bruner, J. (1990). *Acts of meaning.* Cambridge, MA: Harvard University Press.

Clifford, J., & Marcus, G. E. (Eds.). (1986). *Writing culture: The poetics and politics of ethnography.* Berkeley: University of California Press.

Devereux, G. (1967). *From anxiety to method in the behavioral sciences.* The Hague: Mouton.

Feyerabend, P. (1975). *Against method: Outline of an anarchistic theory of knowledge.* London: NLB.

Fleck, L. (1979). *Genesis and development of a scientific fact* (T. J. Trenn & R. K. Merton, Eds.). Chicago: University of Chicago Press.

Fuchs, M., & Berg, E. (1993). Phänomenologie der Differenz. Reflexionsstufen ethnographischer Repräsentationen. In E. Berg & M. Fuchs (Eds.), *Kultur, soziale Praxis, Text. Die Krise der ethnographischen Repräsentation* (pp. 11–108). Frankfurt: Suhrkamp.

Geertz, C. (1988). *Works and lives: The anthropologist as author.* Cambridge: Polity.

Groeben, N. (1986). *Handeln, Tun, Verhalten als Einheiten einer verstehend-erklärenden Psychologie. Wissenschaftstheoretischer Überblick und Programmentwurf zur Integration von Hermeneutik und Empirismus.* Tübingen: Francke.

Heeg, P. (1996). Informative Forschungsinteraktionen. In F. Breuer (Ed.), *Qualitative Psychologie. Grundlagen, Methoden und Anwendungen eines Forschungsstils* (pp. 41–60). Opladen: Westdeutscher Verlag.

Heinrichs, H.-J. (1985). Gespräch mit Georges Devereux: „Es gibt eine kulturell neutrale Psychotherapie." In H.-J. Heinrichs (Ed.), *Das Fremde Verstehen. Gespräche über Alltag, Normalität und Anormalität.* Frankfurt: Fischer.

Heinrichs, H.-J. (1993). Über Ethnopsychoanalyse, Ethnopsychiatrie und Ethno-Hermeneutik. In W. Schmied-Kowarzik & J. Stagl (Eds.), *Grundfragen der Ethnologie. Beiträge zur gegenwärtigen Theorie-Diskussion* 2nd ed. (pp. 359–380). Berlin: Reimer.

Holzkamp, K. (1972a). Zum Problem der Relevanz psychologischer Forschung für die Praxis. In K. Holzkamp, *Kritische Psychologie. Vorbereitende Arbeiten* (pp. 9–34). Frankfurt: Fischer.

Holzkamp, K. (1972b). Verborgene anthropologische Voraussetzungen der allgemeinen Psychologie. In K. Holzkamp, *Kritische Psychologie. Vorbereitenden Arbeiten* (pp. 35–73). Frankfurt: Fischer.

Janich, P. (1981). Natur und Handlung. Über die methodischen Grundlagen naturwissenschaftlicher Erfahrung. In O. Schwemmer (Ed.), *Vernunft, Handlung und Erfahrung. Über Grundlagen und Ziele der Wissenschaften* (pp. 69–84). München: Beck.

Knorr-Cetina, K. (1985). *The manufacture of knowledge. An essay on the constructivist and contextual nature of science.* Oxford: Pergamon.

Kohl, K.-H. (1993). *Ethnologie—die Wissenschaft vom kulturell Fremden. Eine Einführung.* München: Beck.

Kuhn, T. S. (1962). *The structure of scientific revolutions.* Chicago: University of Chicago Press.

Kutschmann, W. (1986). *Der Naturwissenschaftler und sein Körper. Die Rolle der inneren Natur in der experimentellen Naturwissenschaft der frühen Neuzeit.* Frankfurt: Suhrkamp.

Malinowski, B. (1967). *A diary in the strict sense of the term.* London: Routledge & Kegan Paul.

Popper, K. R. (1980). *The logic of scientific discovery.* London: Hutchinson.

Raeithel, A. (1983). *Tätigkeit, Arbeit und Praxis. Grundbegriffe für eine praktische Psychologie.* Frankfurt: Campus.

Roth, W.-M., & Lee, Y. J. (2004). Interpreting unfamiliar graphs: A generative, activity-theoretic model. *Educational Studies in Mathematics, 57,* 265–290.

Stagl, J. (1993). Szientistische, hermeneutische und phänomenologische Grundlagen der Ethnologie. In W. Schmied-Kowarzik & J. Stagl (Eds.), *Grundfragen der Ethnologie. Beiträge zur gegenwärtigen Theorie-Diskussion* 2nd ed. (pp. 15–49). Berlin: Reimer.

Wohlgenannt, R. (1969). *Was ist Wissenschaft?.* Braunschweig: Vieweg.

6   Unraveling the Allure of Auto/Biographies

Alberto J. Rodriguez

In this chapter, I propose linking feminist poststructuralism with Bakhtin's concepts of *voice* and *ventriloquation* for critically engaging with auto/biographical texts. I argue that by becoming better aware of the teller's intentionality and her/his insights gained from telling a (re)constructed version of self, the listener and the teller can engage in personal and socially transformative dialog. This dialog can assist the teller/listener to move from superficial affirmation of (re)-interpreted lived experiences to more socially responsive action.

Sharing a Chosen Story of Self

Giving a keynote address at a teachers-as-researcher conference: [1] Most people at one time or another have experienced how uncomfortable feeling hungry can be, but have you ever felt hungry for days? Being hungry for days grabs a person's soul and wraps it with a shroud of fear to the point that you do not feel hungry anymore—you only feel the fear of being hungry and desperate all over again the next day.

There were times I felt that way during my last year of high school in the South American country where I was born. Being one child among five and the only one to make it so far in high school at that time, I was running the risk of becoming another statistic in the unflattering reports that document what happens to the children of divorce, the children of single mothers, and the children of the poor. I was lucky and resilient enough, however, to bounce back—fear can also be such a great motivator.

I held on until the next little bit money came in, borrowed my friends' textbooks, and my last year of high school turned out to be my best! My grades had been good all along—even before my parents' divorce—and I ended up getting a scholarship to study abroad. Just when I thought I could get out the cycle of misery I inherited, while pursuing my undergraduate biology degree in Canada, I discovered for the first time that the color of my skin was brown.[2] I discovered that this shade of skin color made me an object of hate, and that being a second language learner, poor, and an object of hate would work against my desire to obtain a post-secondary education. Like it or not, I began to see that I entered a competitive system where by virtue of who I was (and who I represented historically), I was to run an uphill race with invisible but just as heavy balls and chains attached to my ankles. Balls and chains that—although they had been forged long ago in the times of slavery—I was to wear anyway because the shade of my skin color and my "foreigner" status gave me unwelcome title to them. It became obvious that working hard was not enough, being financially supported by a scholarship was not enough, being willing to leave everyone I ever knew behind at the age of eighteen was not enough, I was now required to run in a ridiculous race where the winners had long been chosen. They have been chosen by virtue of their light skin color. A skin color that gave them title and privilege just like mine gave me racist slurs, threats, educational disadvantages, and just simply more searches at the airport.

Meritocracy—the notion that all one needs to succeed is to work hard enough in our society is such a well-crafted and color-blind myth. And busting open this myth in terms of equity, student achievement, and education reform in science is one the goals of this keynote address.[3]

* * *

After reading this auto/biographical account, what do you make of it? What was the purpose of sharing this story? What was my intentionality? What new insights did I gain from the telling of this (re) constituted version of self now that I am a middle class, Latino, science teacher educator and researcher?

In this chapter, I propose that these are the types of questions that the teller (the author of the auto/biography) and listener (the reader) must ask to engage critically with auto/biographical text. At first glance, my intentionality may appear obvious to some. In particular, the last paragraph speaks of "busting open the meritocracy myth." I appear to be saying that the meritocracy myth perpetuates the notion that working hard enough is all one needs to succeed while turning a (color-) blind eye to the myriad of social inequities and oppressive social norms that prevent many from participating in a democratic society. If this is obvious—good, but how often is the teller's intentionality clear in the auto/biographies we read? Why is this important to know, and why should we take steps to seek this type of conceptual and ideological clarity?

In this chapter, I offer an alternate way of reading/doing auto/biographical work by drawing from feminist poststructuralism and Mikhail Bakhtin's theory of the novel. First, arguments will be presented to illustrate how these two theoretical frameworks can be used to unravel the (re)constructed Self behind the stories we *choose* to tell. This approach is particularly important in science education research because it may provide insights for enhancing the educational opportunities of traditionally disadvantaged students (i.e., females, the poor, and students from diverse ethnic backgrounds). The essay closes with an analysis of the auto/biographical excerpt described above in order to illustrate how the proposed approach can be used to deconstruct auto/biographical work in education.

Making Links with Feminist Poststructuralism

> No theoretical version of self can be separate from questions of the vested interests attached to such versions. (Kelly, 1997, p. 50)

The use of auto/biography in educational research has increased considerably in recent years. From provocative essays *in Representation and the Text: Reframing the Narrative Voice* (Tierney & Lincoln, 1997) to useful "how to" books such *as Writing Educational Biography: Explorations in Qualitative Research* (Kridel, 1998) it is evident that auto/biography—as a research tool—continues to gain favor in the qualitative researcher's toolkit.

There is something alluring about auto/biographies. Something in the ways the stories are told often engages us to the point that we relive vicariously the teller's experiences through the listening. This may be due in part to the degree to which our own lived experiences resonate with those of the teller. It may also have to do with our capacity to empathize with the teller's struggles to make sense of complex and demanding contexts that can be easily found in everyday teaching. There is a danger, however, in allowing us to be swept by the teller's captivating narratives without asking what the teller's motives or intentionalities are. *Intentionality* is defined here in terms of the consciously driven ideological, political, pedagogical, and theoretical motives behind the desire to tell a chosen story of self.

This notion is at the crux of this chapter, and this is one place where feminist poststructuralist scholarship can help us problematize the allure of auto/biographical research. Perhaps Ursula Kelly (1997) puts it most succinctly when she asks, "Whose interests and what ideologies are promoted and secured by a particular version of self?" (p. 50). Those who tell/listen to auto/biographies must ask this question in order to move from superficial affirmation of (re)constructed stories to personal growth—a new critical awareness of who we are and of our role in sustaining or transforming current social inequities. This is also an area where feminist poststructuralist research warns us about the romantic allure of telling/listening to auto/biographies and about the over/covert hegemonic power relations they may serve. Kelly makes this point clearly:

Unproblematic or romantic notions of the power of story and/or the educationally redemptive powers of auto/biography—even when applauded by those whose agenda may appear more radical—must be approached cautiously, for notions are never innocent; they always participate in larger ideological constructs. (p. 49)

Therefore, I am simply proposing that the author's intentionality for sharing a chosen story of self should be as important as the telling itself. Educators/researchers always have reasons for conducting a study or telling a story that go beyond the obviously apparent. This *intentionality* should be made visible to readers in order to reveal often taken-for-granted political and ideological agendas. The following excerpt from Bill Pinar's (1994) provocative collection of essays raises related questions in regard to the notion of intentionality,

Auto/biography is interesting when its telling enlarges and complicates the telling subject, and the listening subject. We are not the stories we tell as much as we are the modes of relation to others our stories imply, modes of relation implied by what we delete as much as by what we include. (p. 218)

If this is the case, why do we seldom see authors explicitly explain why they have chosen to share a particular story about themselves? What are the political, ideological, or pedagogical motives that the author wishes to convey by sharing a slice of their lived experiences? If our stories in auto/biographical research constitute us not only by what we say but also by what we imply, as Pinar mentioned above, why not just explicitly let the readers know what *we* hoped to imply? This, of course, will not prevent listeners from forming their own interpretations, but it will surely add to the wealth of information needed to critically construct meaning.

Pinar's description of what makes auto/biographical accounts interesting or useful raises another central issue. Namely, in what ways has the author's (re)constructed self changed after the telling? If the telling subject is constituted by the listening subject, as Pinar explained, then the telling subject must have also undergone a process of transformation—a new sense of awareness of one's sociocultural location in the present by understanding one's historical past.

These newly gained insights by the telling subject should also be shared with the listening subject as part of the narrative (data) listeners need to construct meaning of the stories they hear. I am by no means implying that authors come to a completely self-aware state by virtue of telling auto/biographies. We are indeed constituted by the discourses we have at hand, and how and what sense we make of our lives at any time in the present may very well be constructed differently later, as we come to new understandings of discursive practices in new contexts. As Davies (1993) states "the process of retrieving one's own stories . . . is partly a process of retrieving the detail of one's specific personal history . . . using currently available discourses to (re)tell them in terms that those current discourses make possible" (p. 177). Therefore, educators who use auto/biography as a research/pedagogical tool have a responsibility to their readers to share what new insights (if any) they have gained from the process of (re)constructing a slice of their selves. This too can be part of the telling in hope to further engage the listener in critical and transformative discourse.

So far in this paper, it has been suggested that by allowing the readers of auto/biographies to become more aware of the author's intentionality more spaces for critical engagement with the author's lived text are possible. I have also suggested that those who conduct auto/biographical research have a responsibility to readers to make new insights (if any were gained from the re-telling of their lived experiences) part of the narrative. In this way, richer contextual data can be made available for readers to move beyond empathy or superficial affirmation of their own lived experiences as these resonate with the author's. Hence, critical engagement in the telling and listening of auto/biographies could enable us to take a more active role in the improvement—e.g., of equity in science education. Science education in the US is a field where equity issues continue to draw the attention of government officials and educators. More and more people are becoming aware that pervasive gaps in achievement and participation exist between the haves and haves not and students from traditionally marginalized cultural backgrounds including Latinos/as, African American, and Native Americans (Rodriguez, 2004).

Further support for a feminist poststructuralist critique of auto/biographical studies can be found in the work of Mikhail Bakhtin's theory of the novel. In the next section, links between these two theoretical frameworks and the telling/-listening of auto/biographical studies are presented.

Making Links with Bakhtin's Theory of the Novel

> We impoverish the past and do not enrich ourselves. We are suffocating in the captivity of narrow and homogeneous interpretations (Bakhtin, 1981, p. 140, From Notes Made in 1970–1971)

This powerful statement by Russian literary theorist and philosopher, Mikhail Bakhtin (1895–1975), provides a springboard for exploring how two of his major constructs, *voice* and *ventriloquation*, intersect with feminist poststructuralism to unravel the telling/listening of auto/biographies in educational research. Bakhtin defines voice as "the speaking personality, the speaking consciousness" (Bakhtin, 1981, p. 434). Thus, according to Bakhtin, a speaker's voice always has a particular "intonation" that echoes the values of the speaker. "Intonation is the sound that value makes" (Clark & Holquist, quoted in Wertsch, 1991, p. 51). For Bakhtin, "words belong to nobody, and in themselves they evaluate nothing. But they can serve any speaker and be used for the most varied and directly contradictory evaluations on the part of the speakers" (1986, p. 85). Bakhtin further explains that

The word in language is half someone else's. It becomes "one's own" only when the speaker populates it with his own intention, his own accent, when he appropriates the word, adapting it to his own semantic and expressive intention. Prior to this moment of appropriation, the word does not exist in a neutral and impersonal language (it is not, after all, out of a dictionary that the speaker gets his word!), but rather it exists in other people's mouths, in other people's contexts, serving other people's intentions: It is from there that one must take the word, and make it one's own. (1981, p. 293)

This way of thinking intersects directly with feminist poststructuralism. It was already mentioned above that "notions are never innocent; they always participate in larger ideological constructs" (Kelly, 1997, p. 49). Hence, our voice, or our speaking consciousness, or our subjectivity, is constituted in language and dependent on the sociocultural contexts in which it currently operates. As Chris Weedon explains, "poststructuralism proposes a subjectivity which is precarious, contradictory and in process, constantly being reconstituted in discourse each time we think or speak" (1997, p. 32).

It is important to note at this juncture that even though Bakhtin provides a useful framework for the analysis of an author's "intention," "values," on "intonation" in a story, he does not use these notions with same kind of ideological and socially transformative focus being proposed in this essay. As a matter of fact, the use of the word ideology has a less political meaning in Russian than it does in English, and perhaps because of the political atmosphere in Russia at the time, Bakhtin used this term in a broader sense (Morris, 1994). For Bakhtin, ideology represents the author's system of beliefs or worldview. In this essay, however, the word ideology is used with its fullest political meaning. It is also here that feminist poststructuralism is most useful for helping us explore how our ideologies reflect our discursive practices; that is, the ways our everyday lives, through interactions with others, serve to sustain or disrupt oppressive patriarchal, ethnocentric, or cultural social norms. Therefore, the term intentionality is being suggested to draw more attention to the need to question the auto/biography author/teller's consciously driven ideological, political, pedagogical, and theoretical motives behind her/his desire to tell a chosen story self.

Bakhtin provides another useful construct for the analysis of an author/teller's intentionality. This construct is *ventriloquation*. According to Bakhtin, an author is in a privileged position to express her/his point of view, values and belief systems by "speaking through" a character in the story. He claims that

the author manifests himself and his point of view not only in his effect on the narrator, on his speech and his language (which are to one or another extent objectivized, objects of display) but also in his effect on the story—as a point of view that differs from the point of view of the narrator. Behind the narrator's story we read a second story, the author's story; he is the one who tells us how the narrator tells stories, and also tells us about the narrator himself. (1981, p. 313)

Thus, through ventriloquation, the teller of auto/biographies directly or indirectly positions her/his voice in the sociocultural context of the listener, but to what purpose? By asking the Bakhtinian question, "Who is doing the talking?" and "Whose voices (values, world views, beliefs, etc.) are represented in the narratives we hear?" we can come to better understand and critique the teller's intentionality. In addition, by following a feminist poststructuralist approach, we can press Bakhtin's question further by not only asking "Who is doing the talking" but by asking "Whose interests are being represented and served by the voices embodied in auto/biographical stories?" If the teller makes more directly apparent her/his intentionality in their chosen story of self, and the listener is more vigilant and expectant of this, a richer and more meaningful engagement with auto/biographical work becomes possible. This approach to the telling and listening of auto/biographies in educational research will not only be useful to the listener, but to the teller as well. This approach increases the potential for the teller himself/herself to generate new insights. In other words, instead of providing an auto/biographical account that may ultimately serve to reaffirm a (re)constituted version of self, the teller could share his/her intentionality as well as new insights gained from the telling. This, in turn, will create a semiotic space for the teller and listener where multiple meaning is possible, and where the potential to question taken for granted power positions and oppressive social norms is brought to the for.

Unraveling a Chosen Story of Self

The reader is encouraged to read again the auto/biographical account presented earlier. In this section, that story will be deconstructed using the poststructural and Bakhtinian approaches discussed thus far.

One of the main characters in the auto/biographical text presented here is the eighteen-year-old Latino who saw finishing high school and going on to college as the key to break the cycle of poverty in which he was trapped. Through the narrating voice of this character, I ventriloquate my present voice as a middle-class Latino science teacher educator. By purposely selecting this particular story about my past—and not other—and by condensing it in such a way, I present the listener with arguments that in fact support my present ideological framework and commitment to working for social justice. My intent should be obvious—to provide evidence through my own lived experiences that the meritocracy myth is a social construct that needs to be rethought and that we all need to become more active in social transformation. In short, pursuing a college degree is hard enough for everyone without having to contend with racism and other oppressive social norms.

Ventriloquation therefore is a powerful tool in the written word because it enables the teller, as mentioned earlier, to express his views, values, and belief systems. By becoming more critically aware of this inescapable fact, the listener can avoid being swept by the allure of auto/biographical work and allow his/her own voice to enter in transformative dialog with that of the teller. As Bakhtin explains, "there is no such a thing a voice that exists in total isolation from other voices" (in Wertsch, 1991, p. 51). A speaker's voice is always engaged—in dialog—with another. One of the main questions being explore here, however, is what needs to be done to ensure that the dialog of voices take a transformative turn and not just a comforting and affirming stance.[4]

Another way to illustrate the importance of critically engaging with auto/-biographical work is to consider the same text without sharing my experiences with racism and my views on the meritocracy myth. In this way, I could have written a story that reflected a more politically safe and palatable narrative for members of the culture of power. If this story is read with these omissions, it could easily be used to reify the roughed individualism and meritocracy myths that permeates the culture of power. In other words, the poor boy from South America made in the land of milk of honey just because he worked hard enough—not like those other "lazy" people who don't want to work—who don't want to learn.[5] This type of appropriation of someone's text is dangerous, and it serves to preserve the status quo because it ignores the countless *Others* who did not make it. For example, in the United States, Latinos/as constitute the largest growing ethnic group, yet gaps in academic achievement and unequal access to educational opportunities still persist between members of the predominant culture and students from diverse cultural backgrounds (Rodriguez, 2004; Secada, et al., 1998). Blaming the victim must be a comforting practice. It places the focus on the *Other* and away from us—away from paying attention to how our positions of privilege unequivocally implicate us.

Auto/biographical work that are based on uncomplicated hero/heroine narratives can be used, then, as powerful tools for superficial self and/or collective confirmation that everything will be "fine" because everyone can "make it" in spite of unbelievable odds. This pacification of the mind can be avoided by the teller making his/her intentionality more readily apparent, and by the listener demanding this to be so. It is through the potential space for critical dialog between the teller's and the listener's voices that meaning and personal/social transformation is possible.

What new insights did I gain from the sharing of this (re)constructed version of self that can advance my own and the listener's understanding of our current discursive practices? The telling of the above auto/biographical story in a public forum again was as difficult as the first. This makes me wonder to what extremes one must go to draw attention to the social inequities people of color, the poor, and women continue to face on a daily basis. While there has been some improvement in bridging the achievement gap, and while women now represent the largest group enrolled and attaining bachelor and master degrees, we need to still be concerned about the small percentage of women pursuing and attaining science, engineering, mathematics and computer technology degrees (Rodriguez, 2004). Sadly, little has changed since I once was the poor boy trying to make it through high school and college. I sometimes even see the rage of the poor boy I was reflected in the eyes of my own son and daughter. Good students who thankfully have not experienced the debilitating force of poverty, but who have already seen the ugly face of institutionalized racism in the form of tracking and have heard the hateful sound of racial slurs.

What new insights have you gained from listening to this (re)constituted version of myself, and how does it resonate with your own voice, your own experiences, and your commitment to social justice?

Conclusion

The use of auto/biographical work in educational research continues to gain popularity. This research tool has much potential for self and collective professional growth. However, the allure of telling/listening to auto/biographical work could also serve to (re)inscribe current oppressive and hegemonic practices. In this essay, it was proposed that one way to establish a critical dialog between the teller and listener of auto/biographical work is by linking elements of Bakhtin's theory of the novel (voice and ventriloquation) with elements from feminist poststructuralist thinking. This critical engagement enables the listener to discern the teller's intentionality for sharing a (re)constituted version of self. It was also argued that the teller has the responsibility of sharing new insights (if any gained) from the (re)telling a chosen version of self. As feminist poststructuralists point out, we are constituted by the present discourses we have at hand, and the sharing of what we learned from telling our stories about a past event may be as important as the telling itself.

The critical analysis of auto/biographical work is particularly important in the field of education, because it may contribute enhancing the educational opportunities of traditionally marginalized students (female, poor, and/or minority students).

Ironically, the last word goes to Bakhtin. In the following quote, Bakhtin once more makes clear the importance of paying attention to the teller's intentionality. It is this type of critical engagement that can enable us to move away from superficial affirmation of alluring auto/biographical text to generating insights for self and collective growth:

To study the word as such, ignoring the impulse that reaches beyond it, it is just a senseless as to study psychological experience outside the context of that real life toward which it was directed and by which it is determined. (Bakhtin, 1981, p. 292)

Notes

A previous, somewhat different and shorter version of this chapter was previously published as Rodriguez, A. J. (2000). Linking Bakhtin with feminist poststructuralism to unravel the allure of auto/biographies. *Research in Science Education, 30*, 13–21.

[1] This chapter was developed from a keynote address was given at the Teachers as Researchers Conference in Miami, Florida. The conference was sponsored by the Dade County Public Schools District and the National Science Foundation's Urban Systemic Initiative in August 1997.

[2] In Latin American countries, racism is not so much an issue of struggle as it is in North America. Socioeconomic status plays a larger role in the struggle for social justice between the haves and have-nots of Latin America countries.

[3] A version of this keynote address was published in Rodriguez (1998).

[4] A brief summary of the "Busting Open the Meritocracy Myth" article (Rodriguez, 1998) was published in the National Education Association magazine *NEA Today* (January, 1999). I received dozens of letters from teachers and administrators mostly in support of the article, but a few letters were written by people mainly interested in defending their on-going racist practices. These individuals used a myriad of derogatory terms to refer to minority students "lack of abilities" and/or "lack of motivation" to do well in school.

[5] Due to space constraints other important Bakhtinian concepts such as speech genres and dialogicality are not discussed here. For more examples in the use of these concepts see Wertsch (1991) and Wortham (1999)

Acknowledgement

The author would like to thank Dr. Cathy Zozakiewicz for reading versions of this manuscript and for sharing her vast understanding of feminist post-structuralism.

References

Bakhtin, M. M. (1981). *The dialogic imagination: Four essays by M. M. Bakhtin* (M. Holquist, Ed.). Austin: University of Texas Press.

Bakhtin, M. M. (1986). *Speech genres and other late essays* (C. Emerson & M. Holquist, Eds.). Austin: University of Texas Press.

Davies, B. (1993). *Shards of glass: Children reading and writing beyond gendered identities*. Cresskill, NJ: Hampton.

Kelly, U. (1997). *Schooling desire: Literacy, cultural politics, and pedagogy*. London: Routledge.

Kridel, C. (1998). *Writing educational biography: Explorations in qualitative research*. Levittown, PA: Falmer.

Morris, P. (1994). *The Bakhtin reader: selected writings of Bakhtin, Medvedev, and Voloshinov*. London: Edward Arnold.

Pinar, W. F. (1994). *Auto/biography, politics and sexuality: Essays in curriculum theory 1972–1992*. New York: Peter Lang.

Rodriguez, A. J. (1998). Busting open the meritocracy myth: Rethinking equity and student achievement in science. *Journal of Women and Minorities in Science and Engineering, 4*, 195–216.

Rodriguez, A. J. (2004). *Turning despondency into hope: Charting new paths to improve students' achievement and participation in science education.* Southeast Eisenhower Regional Consortium for Mathematics and Science Education @ SERVE. Tallahassee, Florida.

Secada, W., Chavez-Chavez, R., Garcia, E., Munoz, C., Oakes, J., Santiago-Santiago, I., & Slavin, R. (1998). *No more excuses: The final report of the Hispanic dropout project.* Washington: U.S. Department of Education.

Tierney, W. G., & Lincoln, Y. S. (1997). *Representation and the text: Re-framing the narrative voice.* Albany: State University of New York Press.

Wertsch, J. V. (1991). *Voices of the mind.* A sociocultural approach to mediated action. Cambridge, MA: Harvard University Press.

Wheedon, C. (1997). *Feminist practice and poststructuralist theory.* Cambridge, MA: Blackwell Publishing.

Wortham, S. (1999). The heterogeneously distributed self. *Journal of Constructivist Psychology, 12*, 153–172.

7   Auto/Biography and Ideological Blindness

Wolff-Michael Roth

Auto/biography is an emergent literary form for writing scientific texts. Much of the literature on the topic focuses on the writer and the writing of auto/biography and auto/ethnography, and their possibilities as praxis of method. However, readers, too, have lived their lives, which are now inscribed in their bodies as experiences. These experiences are central to the way in which we relate to the world; they in fact mediate how the world looks to us. Thus, in reading an auto/biographical report, my own auto/biography mediates how I interact with the text. In this chapter, I use auto/biography as an entry point to reading auto/biography. More so, I use auto/biography reflexively to deal with some potential dangers in the auto/biographical method.

In the summer of 2003, I read *The Sneaky Kid and Its Aftermath* (Wolcott, 2002), a first-person account of the (sexual) intimacy between a researcher (Harry Wolcott) and his research participant (Brad, the sneaky kid). Two years after the events, the sneaky kid returned with a vengeance, beating up the researcher and burning down his house. After a few pages, I noted that I became angry. I read on because I had promised to review this book for *FQS: Forum Qualitative Sozialforschung/Forum Qualitative Social Research*. But the further I got into the book, the more I wondered about the ethical issues—the sexual relationship between researcher and researched and the exploitation of a down-and-out person by someone from the ruling class. In the attempt to analyze the source of my ethical unease, I came to understand that there were some parallels between the sneaky kid, who was living with hardly any comfort in a shabby cabin on Wolcott's property, and myself at various stages in my life. I felt that

Wolcott not only made the sneaky kid pay his rent in terms of sexual favors, but the author also multiplied various forms of capital that he invested. I had grown up in extreme poverty, and repeatedly lived in poverty during my adult life. I resented not only the exploitation of another's situation but also the fact that Wolcott claimed to have done nothing wrong, shedding all responsibility for his actions.

Writing a review filled with resentment is not a good way to do scholarship. But I wanted to voice my critique nevertheless. However, because author and literary figure bear the same name, the auto/biographical nature of Wolcott's account raises problems for the critique and deconstruction of this literary form. Any critique of the protagonist potentially can be read as a critique of the author and therefore as an ad hominem attack. To mark the difference I propose to differentiate the two for the purpose of deconstruction (here, Harry Wolcott and Wally Haircut, respectively). In my reading, the relationship between Wally Haircut and Brad is highly unsymmetrical in terms of Foucault's knowledge/-power concept and Bourdieu's analyses of the relations between economic, social, cultural, and symbolic capital. Wally Haircut, I suggest, had everything to gain in these dimensions and his research participant, the "sneaky kid," had everything to lose. This is just how it turned out. I develop these problematic issues using the following auto/biographical episodes that pertain to poverty and freedom as concrete, lived experiences. Ultimately, this chapter is about (a) the confusion of authors and protagonists, (b) the confusion between authorial intentions and reader receptions, (c) the relationship between biography and understanding text, and (d) the relationship between researchers and their participants.

* * *

A day in the summer of 1963 It is evening, I am sitting at the kitchen table with the farmer and his family, chopping big slabs of homemade sausage putting them on the homemade, wood-fire backed rye bread, wolfing them down. Equally important, I was taking great gulps of the homemade apple cider, which I had been allowed to draught myself from the giant barrels in the cellar. I had been looking forward to this meal all day. In fact, I worked on the farm only for this reasons. A small ten-year old boy then, I had been loading hay with a pitchfork onto a cart with wood and iron-rimmed wheels all day. The cart was subsequently drawn by a couple of the milk cows back to the barn in the village—this farmer, as others in this village, was too poor to own horses or a tractor. I had been looking forward, because I had to work to have a piece of meet or sausage, which my family was too poor to buy, like butter and many other things that we only knew as luxury items,

Figure 7.1. In post-WWII Germany, I began working on farms at the age of nine just for a meal with meat. There was little machinery, cereals were mowed and subsequently threshed by hand. Oxen pulled the hay-filled carts, loading and unloading of which provided me with some employment.

which we could never afford. Now, tired and getting sleepy from the strongly alcoholic cider, I was happy. It was heaven, and I knew I could and would come back another day, to work without pay, just to have a meal with meat and the apple cider.

A day in the summer of 1979 I have just finished my M.Sc. thesis on the "Stopping Power in Protons from 20 to 120 keV," waiting for my last oral examination, wondering what I will do with my life. Beginning a job as an industrial physicist, leading a smug middle-class life including the annual vacations somewhere in France or Italy, and spending the next thirty-five years at it does not seem to be a an interesting alternative. I spent much of the last several years reading physics and philosophy somewhere along a river or in a cabin, photographing interesting scenes and events and developing my own photos, painting old farm and fishing houses. Continuing at the university by doing a Ph.D. is therefore not an option, because I have come to reject schools or universities as places of learning (my conviction, "If you want to stop learning something, go take some classes in it!"). The two most viable cultural "career alternatives" (Wolcott, 2002, p. 50) at this moment are, (a) working for a year and then buying a few square meters of land and a trailer, then stop working and live a sparse life growing vegetables or (b) hitchhiking to and living somewhere in Central America on less than five dollars a day. Two months later, I will have begun to enact the second option.

A day in the summer of 1986 I am sitting at a table in one of those restaurants that offered an all-you-can-eat salad bar for three dollars. I had been eating for an hour, chosen (cottage and other) cheeses to get protein, and fresh vegetables for the vitamins. I am so full, I can hardly move. But I know I will not have anything to eat for the next twenty-three hours. In the evening, it will be water. In the morning it will be water again, I do not have the money for coffee, tea, or whatever else people normally drink and eat in the morning. Should I feel hungry during the day, I will drink water again. Three dollars a day is all I have during the summer, sleeping on wilderness campgrounds where I can stay for free, or sleeping in a car that I cannot drive because I do not have the money for the gas.

Sometimes I get lucky and find a person who wants someone they can trust to sit their apartment for a week. Sometimes I sleep in an office at the university, but sleeping outside is much more pleasant. I often bathe in a lake; sometimes I take a shower in the physical education facility. I wash my clothing in the lake, or in a shower, and dry them outside in the campground. But I do not borrow money to "be better off"; I am too proud to ask friends (any relatives live continents away) and live on the little I have. I do not have much money, but I am free. "Freedom's just another word," Janice Joplin used to sing, "for nothing left to loose." I do not know that other summers will be coming, finding me in the same sort of situation, a little more or a little less money per day. Nothing left to lose and therefore free.

A day in 1991 The assistant headmaster at the private school where I work asks me to report to some function that he had volunteered me for, as he had done with all the other teachers. I have no intention to follow his "invitation," which, immediately after I declare it, results in an angry outburst on his part. After a little while of back and forth, I tell him that I will be reporting to my office, that I will be doing a normal workday, but that I will not be going to do what he had asked us to do. I said, "If you don't like it, give me the pink slip," and walked away. I do not know if he will fire me; he has been easy at firing people and paying them up to two years of salary as separation pay. I do not worry, for I know I have come to the school with nothing but what fit into my little car, and I will be able to leave with as

Figure 7.2. For many years, we did not have the means to own a television set. My siblings and I sometimes were allowed to go to the neighbors to watch a late-afternoon or early-evening show.

much, too. I know that I needed little, and that I can sleep again in the car and on campgrounds until I will have found something else. Again, Janice Joplin's words come to me, "Freedom's just another word for nothing left to loose."

A day in the summer of 2003 I am sitting on the beach not far from my home, reading *The Sneaky Kid and Its Aftermath*, I book that I have promised to review. The book makes me think about the relationship between Brad, a young man who apparently dropped out of society, living a life that shares some similarities with moments of my own life, and professor Wolcott, well situated in his bourgeois lifestyle, through whose actions research, ethics, career, sexual relationships and so forth got tangled up. I am thinking about myself, someone who has lived like Brad, both outside and inside society, but who now is a professor. I wonder, "How do my experiences—more cross-cultural and cross-class than those that Wolcott ever appeared to have had—mediate the reading of *The Sneaky Kid* that I enact?" Why am I not convinced by professor Wolcott's argument that there is nothing unethical about him having a sexual relationship with an informant, with *this* informant? Even though I now live comfortably in a home with a garden, where I grow all the vegetables that my small family needs for the year, I know that I am not afraid to be back where I was, without the home and garden. It is not the home and garden that makes me happy, fulfilled, enjoy life, but knowing that whatever the circumstances, I can live with the circumstances. The idea to live without the traps and contraptions of a middle-class life, which I have only accessed over recent years anyway, does not worry me. It is true that I do not want my wife or my son to be in this situation. But for myself, I do not worry about it.

* * *

In the hermeneutic sciences, there is general acceptance of the presupposition that lived experiences shape who we are and who we become; how we read and understand a text is an outcome of a transaction between the text and ourselves. If I, the author of this text, claim to have sympathies for Brad, who, in *The Sneaky Kid and its Aftermath* beat up another protagonist, Harry, then readers may feel that this makes sense because of apparent similarities between the "I" in the previous paragraphs and Brad. It is also self-evident that auto/biography is a reduction that cannot ever capture the fullness of present or past experiences and that time changes how we understand past events. Thus, whether I, the author of this essay, would use auto/biographical episodes at another point in my academic career is far less clear, in particular because "in every writing, and consequently, in every experience . . . there is this experience of incineration" (Derrida, 1995, p. 209) that makes us forget how things were at a previous moment in time. Although perceptive readers may discover similarities between the events represented in the previous paragraphs and Brad, one of the two main protagonists in *The Sneaky Kid and its Aftermath*—opting out of "normal" career trajectories and freedom that comes from owning little and having nothing left to loose—the relationship between Brad's lived experiences and mine remains open. This is so, because the relationship between my lived experience and the above accounts remain open, as does the relationship between Brad's experiences and the account provided in *The Sneaky Kid*. It remains open not only to me, the author of these paragraphs, but also to you, the reader. In reading these lines, you are countersigning this text in the way I countersigned *The Sneaky Kid*. Neither Wolcott's nor my text can ever be a means for the "transference of meaning, the exchange of intentions and meanings" (Derrida, 1988, p. 20), for both texts, as texts in general, "free meaning from its tutelage of the mental intention" (Ricœur, 1991, p. 149).

Writing comes with a responsibility, especially auto/biographical writing, "because a [auto/biographical] *récit* . . . is not simply a memory reconstituting the past; a *récit* is also a promise, it is also something that makes a commitment to the future" (Derrida, 1995, p. 206). This responsibility relates to the author. But there is also a responsibility on the part of the reader. If my auto/biographical paragraphs were part of a novel, you (the reader) could talk about the protagonist as making stupid mistakes or decisions, about feeling sorry for himself, or about his narcissism. You could do so even if the novel was written in the first person. If, however, the author claims that the text is auto/biographical, then the issues become more complicated. Any comment about stupid mistakes, feelings, or narcissism all of a sudden can be construed as ad hominem attacks on the author. For the critique and deconstruction of auto/biographical texts, I therefore propose separating the living author and his or her protagonists (even in the case of a [purported] auto/biography) and any claim of overlap (i.e., truth) as impossible because of the ontological gap between any entity and its representation. To clearly differentiate between the author and the first-person protagonist of *The Sneaky Kid and its Aftermath*, I change the latter's name to Wally Haircut.[1]

Dialectic Perspective on Experience

There is no universal set of things to be desired or events to fill one's days and dreams, just as there is no absolute set of things to be learned. What people learn or want or do or dream about is embedded in particular macro- and microcultural systems. (Wolcott, 2002, p. 7)

Wolcott wrote these lines first in a report to the U.S. National Institute of Education, continues, which, because nobody seemed to react to the report, he published in the *Anthropology and Education Quarterly* immediately after having become the editor of that journal. The story was subsequently republished in different venues, as a chapter in a book on complementary methods of research, as a chapter in one of his own books, now again in this book. It constitutes a central aspect of the author's professional career since the early 1980s. The report contains the story of Brad, a "sneaky kid," who squatted in a little cabin on Wally Haircut's twenty-acre homestead. Brad mostly lived on the seventy dollars worth of food stamps, and income from occasional jobs in the community or for the author. I am certain that my experiences as a child, working for a good meal, living in a tent as a graduate student with one meal a day, and similar experiences mediated my reading of the *Sneaky Kid*.

Wolcott continued his account in the *Sneaky Kid* chapter that opens this book, "What he [Brad] had learned to want was a function of his culture, and he drew narrowly and rather predictably from the cultural repertoire of the very society from which he believed he as extricating himself" (Wolcott, 2002, p. 7). Brad was a free spirit, but in living outside society, he squarely lived inside it.

Because Brad did not need more than the food stamps, he was free to do as he wanted, much as I was free and without committing myself to banks or other lenders. Brad did not have many needs—he supplied himself with things by stealing, something that I had never done, and therefore was free. But, as Wolcott recognizes, these choices, living in the woods or on a wilderness campground, are not just personal choices but are some function of the existing culture. There is something true about this statement, though I disagree about the "function," because I recognize the dialectical relationship between the generalized action possibilities at a collective level and the concretely realized actions at the individual level. More importantly to me, Wolcott attributes these ideas to his alter ego, Wally Haircut, having arisen from the interviews that he conducted with Brad. But such ideas have existed before. The integral relationship between the possibilities open to individuals and the possibilities existing collectively at the level of society is a core issue of dialectical materialist thought originated by Karl Marx, and which was subsequently developed by Russian social and cultural-historical psychologists (e.g., Leont'ev, 1978) and philosophers (e.g., Il'enkov, 1977).

From a dialectical materialist position, societal life and individual life are dialectically related. For society to survive it has to be concretely realized by individuals; but individuals need to embody society in their actions to survive. In their actions, individuals therefore always concretely realize action possibilities that exist at the collective level. Theories that isolate the inner nature of humans from societal relations and that reduce human inner life to mere "inwardness," in which human beings are understood as maintaining their lives in given social and material environments, are therefore simply false.

Human thinking, in its specific and determining characteristics, must be understood not merely as the analysis/synthesis of individually posed problems, but rather as appropriation of societal modes of thinking with which the individual realizes socially developed forms of analysis/synthesis in his or her individual thinking and only in this way becomes able to contribute to the development of these thought forms" (Holzkamp, 1991, p. 59)

Therefore, the social nature of human beings consists not of anthropological and psychological constants, but rather of a historically contingent developmental potential that makes it possible for individuals at each cultural-historical moment of societal development, with its expanded social appropriation of nature, also to change their own nature.

Whereas we act freely, we do realize existing possibilities at the collective level. In every act, I realize cultural possibilities that I have come to enact because of my interactions with others and with all the objects that already had a

Figure 7.3. A tent—doghouse (Ger. Hundehütte) we used to call it—usually served as my home when I had no home.

place in culture. When I lived in cars and on wilderness campgrounds (Figure 7.3), or went hitchhiking toward Central America, I did not do something that existed outside of society. I concretely realized a possibility at the collective level—there were places where you could eat as much as you could for three dollars a day, there were tents and cars that provided shelter against adversities and bad weather, there were farms that could afford paying a lad's day of work with a meal, and there were lads such as I who did want to work for a meal. Later, when I was hitchhiking toward Central America, I concretely realized possibilities that existed at the collective level—there were people with cars, there were people inviting me, I had a sleeping bag that allowed me to sleep in the ditch beside the road when I did not have an invitation to stay with someone. In a similar way, Brad, the sneaky kid, enacted possibilities that existed at the collective level, drawing on whatever resources that he had at hand. He could go and get his monthly ration of food stamps, he could do odd jobs (getting thumped in your butt is really something odd for many people) for a little money, or he could provision himself by taking food and other cultural items without paying for them. Even the recognition of something as a resource cannot be abstracted from the culture that stands in a dialectical relation to its concrete enactment through Brad.

Although we make individual choices, these choices are already under-standable by others. When we chose to act one way rather than another, it is be-cause we are already using elements from our cultural repertoire to account for making the choice for ourselves and inherently for others. There is therefore no subjectivity without intersubjectivity. Individual subjectivity always involves the transgression of pure individuality in the direction of participation in collective subjectivity and therefore has interpersonal character. At the very moment when I articulate something very subjective, for example, "I feel sad," I have to use a language that I inherited from the other, which is already culturally existent, which is already understood by others. At the very moment I index myself as a person through the use of the reflexive "I," I use a sign, which in its very nature is non-identical with what it refers to, it is "not-I." "I" is both personal and so-cial, there is no "I" without a "you," there is no Self without the Other, there is no subject without an object (other), no individual without the collective.

Similarly, by interviewing Brad, publishing a report and article from it, Wally enacts general cultural possibilities. Even the author's apparent refusal to do much reading but rather to focus on writing (Wolcott, 2001) is a general cul-tural possibility, though failure to appropriately situate your writing in the intel-lectual history of culture may be penalized in the review process. Even the nasty part of the *Sneaky Kid* story, which I unfold in this review, the (homo) sexual re-lationship between a researcher and his participant, is part of the general possi-bilities, which have been concretely enacted by Wally and Brad. Whether these actions were or are ethical or unethical, moral or immoral, or normal or per-verted will not be the point of my review. Others have engaged Wolcott. On the other hand, *The Sneaky Kid and Its Aftermath* can be read as the protagonist Wally Haircut's long justification of an event in the quest for redemption. The point of my essay lies in articulating a critique of asymmetrical relationships that lead to further asymmetries, accountability and responsibility for actions, and the need to contextualize studies in the existing literature. But before getting there, I will articulate the dialectic of reading and review the structure and con-tent of the book.

Dialectic of Reading

Every qualitative researcher knows that texts are inherently overdetermined—there is no *one* sense (some people say meaning), *one* message, or *one* reading possible. Rather, any particular sense, message, or reading emerges from the dialectic of *reading*, which can be analyzed using reader and text as two aspects of the same unit. In fact, there is nothing that moves from the text to the reader, like a message or idea, there is no transfer of an author's intended meaning to the reader. Rather, by engaging with a text, readers articulate their existing practical understandings of how the world works *in front of the text*. There is no message *in* or *behind* the text not even *between the lines*, but only an unfolding of understanding in the transactions between reader and text. But each reader has developed in a culture (and therefore developed culture), has concretely realized cultural possibilities and become an individual through his or her experience in an already patterned, cultural-historical world. Thus, my reading of *The Sneaky Kid and Its Aftermath* is *a* reading of the book rather than *the* reading of the book; it is a concrete realization of the possibilities of reading this book—and therefore tells us something about the culture of which Wolcott, I, and my readers are co-constitutive members.

The possibilities for my reading emerged from my life experiences, themselves concrete expressions of the possibilities to enact a life in our culture. Thus, my experiences of freedom while living on a bare minimum are important and perhaps defining moments for the kind of reading that I will present here. The exact relation between my reading and these experiences can never be established however appealing the connection may appear, because every trace of past experience has the nature of "cinder [which is] something that remains without remaining, which is neither present nor absent, which destroys itself, which is totally consumed, which is a remainder without remainder" (Derrida, 1995, p. 208). Other moments that bring forth my reading are the vast amount of literature that I have come to know through reading. Elsewhere, Wolcott (2001) acknowledges that he does not read extensively, because, he argues, as an academic, one is either a reader or a writer. The use of sociological and social psychological theory could have led to a more reflexive text, and, because of the dialectic of understanding and explaining, would have assisted in the analysis of the incident involving the sneaky kid and the subsequent fall out that it caused in the scholarly community.

Perhaps my reading is more sympathetic to Brad despite his crime, burning down Wally Haircut's house, because I have lived in down and out situations, because I lived inside society all the while living outside of it. Perhaps my reading is more sympathetic to Brad because I understand the insider/outsider relation not only through my lived experience but also through my theoretical, cultural-historical, dialectically informed lens. Perhaps my reading is not more sympathetic to Brad at all; I may have simply disliked the way in which Wally Haircut talks about himself, a way that can be read as self-glorifying and redemption seeking arising from his relationship with the *Sneaky Kid.* But whatever an empirical study (anthropology of reading) would reveal, my reading is a concrete realization of the possible readings and therefore tells us something about our (scholarly) culture more generally.

Structure and Content of *The Sneaky Kid and Its Aftermath*

This book is essentially about one (ethnographic?) study, the events it engendered, and the resources for actions it provided in subsequent situations. In Part One of the book entitled "The Sneaky Kid," Wolcott writes an ethnographic study and describes some of the events that followed it. The basic story is that of an influential article that had been printed in the widely used *Complementary Methods for Research in Education* (Jaeger, 1988), and read by many graduate students. Drawing on his interviews with a young squatter on his extended property. Brad, the "sneaky kid," Wolcott developed a story about the difference between schooling and education. The story itself, reprinted once more as Chapter 1 ("Adequate Schools and Inadequate Education: The Life History of a Sneaky Kid") in this book, is an interesting case study but a little bit of existing social theory would have pushed the analyses to be more revealing.

In a subsequent auto/biographical study, Wolcott revealed, among other things, that his protagonist, the ethnographer Wally Haircut, had initiated and had a homosexual relationship with Brad, his research participant. The piece mainly focused on cultural alternatives to career options. In Chapter 2, ("The Brad Saga Continues"), Wolcott relates much of the material from this article. The chapter also includes more of the juicy details of the relationship between Brad and Wally Haircut, including explicit and graphic descriptions of the sexual relation (Brad's having an erection, him being excited) and that Brad not only consented to sex but also enjoyed it.

The relationship with Brad had repercussions not only in the educational field, but also in Wally's personal life. After having gone for two years, Brad returned and burned down the author's home, which the latter shared with his lifelong partner Norman. The events surrounding Brad's return constitute the core of Chapter 3 ("The Return"). Brad, who had been diagnosed with paranoid schizophrenia, admitted to arson (for which he was tried and sentenced) and to assault (he had beaten Wally with a piece of wood). The trial and surrounding events are told in Chapter 4 ("Out"), in which Wolcott presents Wally Haircut as the victim further victimized in the process of the court proceedings. As I am reading these lines, and generally empathetic with the plight of others, I notice that I am not feeling sorry for Wally, and will articulate a theoretically informed analysis of answerability and responsibility in the fifth section of this essay.

Following these revelations and in response to disapproval in the educational community, Wolcott took the opportunity of writing an invited chapter on validity in qualitative research to reflect on the ethics of being intimate with one's research participants. The contested nature of Wolcott's position and his writings constitute Chapter 5 ("More Truths, More Consequences"). This chapter, together with the material appearing in the first and second chapters, constitutes the "Brad Trilogy." Wolcott presents Wally as a victim, this time in the professional community, where some members found sexual intimacy between researcher and researched objectionable.

The second part of the book, "Where Do Our Studies Go?," is devoted to more of the aftereffects of the original events. Chapter 6, ("The Rebound"), is entirely focused on the contested reprinting of the original Sneaky Kid piece in *Complementary Methods for Research in Education.* In Chapter 7 ("A Play on Words: The Brad Trilogy as Ethnodrama") the author relates how the trilogy came to be turned into a play. This play is reprinted in the appendix. The interesting point in my reading is that the character of the play and the character of the earlier story are both characters always different from the living person Harry Wolcott who wrote the latter and added the former to make a book.

In Chapter 8, ("Drawing Lessons") the author reflects on possible lessons that can be drawn from his articles and the events that surround it. In it, Wolcott continues to tell the story of the ethnographer Wally Haircut as double and triple victim.

I had really looked forward to this book (Roth, 2003) and began reading it with the expectation of reading an important contribution to the literature. As my reading proceeded, Wolcott convinced me more and more strongly that his protagonist Wally Haircut delivers an apologetic, self-indulgent, egocentric, uncritical, and ideological account of the events surrounding and following the original research. I felt less and less sorry for Wally Haircut and his adventures and thought that he really needed to stand up and articulate the responsibility that came with each of his actions. In the following sections, I discuss but a few points of my reading.

Some Thoughts

After some of my resentment had receded, I began to draw on my scholarly experience to write about what I felt was exploitation and a lack of responsibility and answerability. I had a sense that many of the authors I was familiar with—Bourdieu, Foucault, Holzkamp, Bakhtin, and Ricœur—would provide me with sufficient theoretical material to show how Wolcott had been exploiting the kid for immediate personal benefit—the sexual relation—and subsequently built a professional career on it.

On the Dialectic of Actions

Actions have the interesting property that in their execution, not only does the subject engage with the object and thereby change the sociomaterial world, but also the subject produces and reproduces him or herself—a form of "consumption" of the subject by the community. Furthermore, each action also creates sociomaterial resources that are subsequently available to the interacting subjects themselves. Two subjectivities, like Wally and Brad, are therefore not independent from one another but, in collective action—e.g., participating in interviews, having a sexual relationship, or being employer and employee—the two not only produce outcomes (changes in the world), which become resources for further action, but also produce and reproduce themselves and their relation.

In the process of establishing new levels of intersubjectivity, two or more interacting subjects become a little more like the other; in the very notion of intersubjectivity, two or more persons come to understand a situation in the same way, or assume that they understand in the same way, developing a common element. When we now look at Wally and the sneaky kid together in the cabin, they produce many hours of interview material. (While I am reading about the shabby cabin, images of living in a tent on a lake [Figure 7.2] constantly invade my attentional space.) They also produce and reproduce themselves as individuals all the while uniting to form a unique whole in their sexual embrace. Finally, they also produce exchange relations as Wally decides when the sneaky kid Brad would be paid and for which actions he would be paid, his "doing odd jobs," doing the interview, and, who knows, for the sexual favors as well, implicitly or explicitly.

These actions come with, as I show below, a responsibility or answerability, which Wolcott has not accounted for. These actions and their outcomes become resources for further actions on the part of both Wally and Brad. Wally publishes and republishes the original piece, as elaborations or sequels. Brad, the sneaky kid that he has always been, cannot get over the relationship, and returns with a vengeance. Although they both used the outcomes of the relationship as resources for further actions, the way they deployed these resources was quite different, because of their vast differences in the capital that they each had brought to the situation. The relationship between Wally and Brad was always asymmetrical, from the initial advances throughout the relationship, when the author paid for interviews, reading through the articles, and the other jobs that Brad was asked or offered to do. Wolcott acknowledges the asymmetry between

Brad and Wally in descriptions such as, "I tried to be as fair and consistent with him as I could in our every interaction" (SK, p. 44), and he presented Wally as "lay[ing] down the law" (SK, p. 45).

On the Movement and Translation of Forms of Capital

Actions bring about changes in the world; they have outcomes, which provide resources for further actions. These outcomes can also be accumulated, constituting forms of capital. Social agents are

bearers of capital and, depending on their trajectory and on the position they occupy in the field by virtue of their endowment (volume and structure) in capital, they have the propensity to orient themselves actively either toward the preservation of the distribution of capital or toward the subversion of this distribution. (Bourdieu & Wacquant, 1992, pp. 108–109)

There are three fundamental species of capital: economic capital, social capital, and cultural capital. Social capital is the sum of resources (actual or virtual) that accrues to individual and groups due to the network of formal and informal relationships of mutual acquaintance and recognition. Cultural capital, which could also be called an informational capital, represents the non-economic forces such as family background, varying investments in and commitments to education, social class, and other cultural resources (language, theories, beliefs). Economic capital constitutes, among others, the financial resources available to and accessible by social actors. To these forms we can add another one, symbolic capital, which is the "form that any one of these three species takes when it is grasped through categories of perception that *recognize* its specific logic" (Bourdieu & Wacquant, 1992, p. 119). The forms of capital cannot only be transformed into one another but can also determine the relative forces, position, and strategic orientation of two or more interacting individuals.

In the present situation, actions provided quite different resources for Wally Haircut and the sneaky kid. The former uses his existing cultural capital to transform the interview material into a report. Because the report was apparently not sufficiently read, Wally subsequently used his social capital, his relations to others in his discipline and his institutional placement as editor of the journal *Anthropology and Education Quarterly* to get the piece published in this journal. He used his social capital subsequently to get the piece repeatedly republished. How much this social and cultural capital has transformed itself into monetary capital is not easy to establish. Wally repeatedly makes the point that he did not gain financially—for example, when Brad's mother hypothesized during the court proceedings against Brad for his arson. But he described repeatedly how spending some money on Brad really would be covered by the money received for the original report, how he held back money until Brad had completed a job, and so forth. Wolcott also tells us proudly of the 5,000 copies that he sold of his book containing the trilogy, which certainly resulted in a nice royalty check from his publisher. In *Ethnography: A Way of Seeing* (Wolcott, 1999), the author repeatedly admitted to the pressure in academe to publish or perish—in contrast to many other places in this world, North American universities make careers and salary progress dependent on "productivity," which is measured in part by counting publications (and sometimes even page numbers). At the time Wally interviewed Brad, he was about fifty years of age. He had another fifteen years to go in academe, and therefore, the articles, books, and notoriety that he got out of all of this are an important aspect of the professional career to be accounted for. Here, although I am of the same age as Wolcott at the time, and also being an academic, I do not identify with him. Although I am better off than when I was down and out, I still empathize with the feelings and experiences of those who, too, are down and out rather than with my "peers."

Wally Haircut had all the cultural capital to transform not only the interviews into a written piece that was repeatedly republished, but he also had the cultural capital, the intellectual resources, to transform the experience in other ways. For example, by talking to his long-term partner Norman about his sexual encounter, Wally transformed this experience into a virtue. Wally justifies having this dual relationship, saying that Norman was not interested in sex that Wally, despite his fifty years, still wanted. So Wally uses his existing cultural resources to transform what could have been seen as an infidelity into a virtue—in fact, this entire book is about translating and legitimating something many people will find objectionable into a virtue. That is, Wally had sufficient resources to put the sexual relationships behind him and continue with his life after Brad's departure.

Brad, on the other hand, did not have the same kind of resources. In terms of cultural capital, Brad could barely write, and Wolcott makes the point by transcribing a letter in all its orthographic shortcomings (SK, p. 25). We know little about the kind of relationships Brad had before he got to "meet the author," we know particularly little about any sexual relationships he may have had. We know that Brad had been shipped back and forth between his parents, and going from school to school, there were few opportunities to appropriate cultural capital of the type that Wally had. I agree with Wolcott who suggests that (a) there is a difference between schooling and education, (b) "School is a lousy place to learn anything in" (Becker, 1972), and (c) we learn more in school but at the interstices of formal schooling and outside school. But despite all of this other education Brad has had, when the two encountered one another, Wally was not only a bourgeois professor with more than a decent income (living on a twenty-acre property) and sufficient financial capital to pay Brad for his various jobs but also was a cultural and social capitalist in comparison to Brad. The defense attorney suggested, "[Wally] seeks help for Brad, but it's help with a hook . . . to get him well to continue the sex. Get well here, where I am, where the sex is" (SK, p. 93). Wally did use his social and financial capital to help Brad, but it was help with a hook. There was always a hook, Brad had to finish the job—but we only have Wally's word (in a double sense) for what it meant to "finish the job."

With little capital to mediate the products of their relations, Brad ends up hating the professor, who, in Brad's words, "screwed with my head, my ass and my life too much" (SK, p. 98). Brad used his cultural capital as a resource to interpret their joint actions as screwing with his head, ass and life. That is, Brad used his cultural capital to translate the events as having been screwed, in more than one way. It is exactly when there are substantial differences in the cultural capital that come with formal and informal education among the culturally rich that ordinary people feel "screwed in their heads." It is exactly because those culturally rich have "their way with words," that inequality is produced and reproduced in such relations. Having a homosexual relationship, in Brad's words, "was a low-down, dirty, disgusting perverted thing to do and that is what I have to live with for the rest of my entire life" (SK, p. 98). Brad did not have the cultural resources to interpret the relationship at the moment of the encounter, and especially not afterward, during the moments that the desire to pay back Wally Haircut some of the pain that he had received. Was it the first sexual relationship Brad had? Was it the first homosexual relationship that he had? During the trial for arson, Brad asked the judge to be sent to the hospital rather than the prison where he could be sexually victimized. Has he had such experiences during his stay at reform school? Brad certainly did not have the cultural capital to mediate this encounter and the aftermath that it had for him. He returned with a vengeance, and not only was "burning down the house" but also was "burning down the bridges." Rather than increasing the possibilities for acting, his actions decreased his possibilities, his room to maneuver. There was no way back, no way out of the cul de sac into which he was headed. Wally had "screwed with his head," and the cultural resources available to Brad for interpreting it became a referent for his subsequent actions.

On Knowing what the Other Feels

From a dialectical perspective, all of our feelings and experiences are concrete realizations of culturally possible feelings and experiences. There are limits, however, to auto/biography as a means to find out about feelings in general and the feelings of others, in particular. What did Brad feel during the sexual relationships? "I have no way of telling whether he was as stimulated as I [Wally] was," writes Wolcott (SK, p. 43), "but there is no faking an erection, and he was always there with his." But in part, as medical and anecdotal evidence shows, such erection is mediated by pressure on the prostate, which a penis in a man's rear end does in fact exert (Perry, 1982). Even an innocent medical examination of the prostate can result in erection and ejaculation. There is no way of telling that Brad's erection did not come, involuntarily, from the stimulation provided by Wally's actions. This did not seem to be Wally's main concern, which appeared to be that the "sex with Brad was an absolute delight" and that he "was highly stimulated by his youthful body" (SK, p. 43). Wally is singularly concerned with his own satisfaction, stimulation, and gratification. He admits that Brad did not indicate overt sexuality. We also read that Brad did not want to go to prison, because he would be sexually victimized. This does not sound like a Brad who particularly likes having a homosexual relation, or, if he did at the moment, used his cultural capital to translate the experience into something that prospectively he viewed as horrible.

But Wally has his way with words, "It is curious how Brad repressed any indication of overt sexuality, guarding the idea that he felt he was constantly preoccupied with sex, for he was so daring in other ways" (SK, p .43). So Brad did not indicate sexuality, he "repressed any indication" of it, but "there is no faking an erection" (SK, p. 43). Wally is very close to saying that Brad said no, or said nothing, but really meant saying yes? For those who do not yet know, this is a typical male argument to explain why they pursued sexual aggressiveness although the other person, usually female, does not want to grant them any favors. So Brad repressed his desire, but could not fake an erection—all the more reason for Wally to experience "absolute delight" (SK, p. 43).

Wally insists that Brad "consented to the sex," but Wolcott does not provide us with a cultural analysis of the situation, the differences in capital that the two had coming to the situation, and the differences in capital with which the two would come out of it. Wally insists that Brad had consented to the sex all the while insisting that Brad had delusions, fantasies, and "mental problems" (SK, p. 81).

On the Role of Theory

There is a dialectic of (practical) understanding and explaining (Ricœur, 1991). To explain a situation, we already have to have a practical understanding of it and a practical understanding of explaining. Practical understanding therefore begins, envelops, and terminates structural analysis, and therefore our efforts at explaining. But practical understanding, to develop and unfold, requires explaining, structural analysis. Without structural analysis, practical understanding remains undeveloped, constituting a form of ideology that is in an unquestioning and unreflective way brought to the lifeworld situations we face. Practical understanding alone leaves us stuck in the life problems as we face them, without the possibility to make the structural changes required for lasting change to come about (Holzkamp, 1983). Auto/biographies run the risk of getting stuck in this problem and remaining accounts of particulars rather than telling us something about our culture more generally. In my reading of *The Sneaky Kid and Its Aftermath*, there is too much ideology and too little cultural-historical, critical analysis. Let me make a case.

"Truer words were never spoken" (SK, p. 86). Wally Haircut has a particular relation to truth and to interpreting events, including the court proceedings dealing with Brad's arson and other documents. Throughout my reading of the case, I felt that existing theory would have enhanced the analysis. The analysis of the court proceedings could have been done in the light of the analyses of similar material presented in *Discursive Psychology* (Edwards & Potter, 1992) or *The Spectacle of History: Speech, Text, and Memory at the Iran-Contra Hearings* (Lynch & Bogen, 1996). Both books provide excellent case studies of how contentious issues are worked out in interaction (the basis of all culture), how truth is constituted rather than being an ontological category that is apparent in statements such as "Truer words were never spoken."

In the absence to such references, the analysis remains at the level of common sense. It comes as no surprise that Wally "came away with no respect for the courts" (SK, p. 86). There it is, the courts, the highest accomplishment of his democratic country, where the judicial system has evolved to deal in an impartial way with issues, even those that involve the most powerful, deserve no respect from Wally Haircut. Poor Wally! He has had to account for his acts, and thereby had to take responsibility for them in a public forum, where he could no longer adhere to the delusion of being the innocent victim, and then walks away "with no respect for the courts." He had "always assumed the system to be much better" (SK, p. 86)—better for Wally, allowing him to walk away from being accountable?

Again, there was an issue of money. A copy of the proceedings would have cost Wally $4,000 if he had to pay for a transcription. Luckily, the appeal required an official transcript, and Wally could get a copy of the official transcript for a total of $397. Again, the situation had worked in his favor, Wally saved money (financial capital), got away cheap, and then used it to promote his own cause, the publication of this ranting justification entitled *Sneaky Kid and Its Aftermath*. His social capital, knowing the publisher who invites him to write the book, allowed him to further increase his various forms of capital. "No doubt things could be worse," but everything had a pretty good positive twist for Wally.

While reading, I highlighted the comment "about the implicit messages the jury was receiving as to what was ahead and how, as good citizens, they ought to be thinking about it" (SK, p. 87). However, communication can never be the transference of meaning. Message has its etymological origins in the Latin *mittere*, to send. From a classical information theoretical perspective, a message is a piece of information sent by a sender via some medium, a telephone cable, a courier, to some receiver. To make any sense at all, sender and receiver have to be tuned in the same way, have commensurable coding and decoding procedures. Human communication is not that simple, if we think of language as being the medium. There is no unique coding and decoding in place—the very notion of sign (a vehicle) implies uncertainty, difference, "difference" (Derrida, 1981), variability, ambiguity, trace, cinder, and so on (Malpas, 1992). Now the very opposition of implicit and explicit messages no longer makes sense—the issues would have deserved much more complex (existing) cultural tools for interpretation. There is more than one sense to any word, any sentence.

On Answerability and Responsibility

I read the entire book as the protagonist Wally Haircut's attempt to extricate himself from this answerability: Brad was of legal age, "he had consented to the sex. Only later did Brad express misgivings about it" (SK, p. 81). (As indicated, Brad did not have the same sophisticated cultural capital that Wally had to deal with "being screwed.") This part of the argument repeatedly shows up in the text. Brad was of legal age, though Wally claims that the court got it wrong when it accepted it to have been nineteen rather than the twenty Wally claimed. No doubt, Brad *was* of legal age, but he was also not fit to be accepted in the army. Despite his nice body, fit for an actor, or so Wally whispered into Brad's ear, he was unfit for the Marines, having been classified as a ninth grader at the reform school. But Wally abrogates his responsibility and answerability, Brad was of legal age and he consented. (Let us leave aside for the moment whether Brad really liked "being screwed.")

Even if we know someone else, and know ourselves, we still have to grasp the "truth of our interrelationship, the truth of the unitary and unique event which links us and in which we are participants" (Bakhtin, 1993, p. 17). Accordingly, to understand an object means that we have to understand our "ought" in this relationship, the attitude or position that we ought to take with respect to it and other individuals. For our participation in interaction, we are responsible; each act "presupposes my answerable participation, and not an abstracting from myself. It is only from within my participation that Being can be understood as an event, but this moment of once-occurrent participant does not exist inside the content seen in abstraction from the act *qua* answerable deed" (p. 18). We are answerable for each act, every moment of our lives, every act is an answerable act: life itself "can be consciously comprehended only in concrete answerability" (p. 56).

Wally was and is answerable in more than one way. He was initially in the situation with Brad. The two were doing whatever they were doing (interviewing, engaging in exchange relations, having sex), or, drawing on Brad's language (cultural resource), "screwing with [Brad's] head." Wally is answerable now for his actions then, in the cabin Brad had built. He is also answerable now for the ways in which he (unrepentantly) promotes his own case, proclaims his innocence, his victim status, rallying whatever resources he had been culling from the situation in the first place. He is responsible for his physical and verbal actions, the categories he used to describe and transform the original experiences that had so much of an aftermath. From an ethnomethodological perspective, the use of even simple, mundane descriptive categories makes available (possible) a variety of inferential trajectories *in situ*; these are grounded in the various salient features bound up with or constitutive of these descriptive categories for the practical organization of what relative mundane knowledge is at the moment. These categories and this knowledge have their responsibilities, for the various salient features "provide grounds for moral properties, for finding that certain kinds of events or actions may or may not have taken place, for determining culpability, even for defeating the applicability of the category or description in the first place" (Jayyusi, 1991, p. 241). The categories are bound to and used in knowledge contexts in which description and appraisal and all conceptual, moral, and practical issues are irremediably interwoven.

Auto/Biography and Auto/Ethnography—Pitfalls

In this book, Wally Haircut conforms with the cross-cultural stereotype of the U.S. American—boisterous, loud, vain, conceited, playing the "poor-me-I-am-hurt" card when he realizes that others don't buy into his argument, holding others hostage with his money, being the sole owner of truth. A dialectical approach to culture would have better helped Wolcott in constructing an explanation of the sequence of events, especially for garnering some of the support for Wally's case. Wally not only has a unitary conception of truth—a cultural ideal that has had important implications for Western ethos—but also that he is its beholder. The dialectical approach would have allowed Wolcott to work toward a cultural dialectic of knowledge and desire or toward a cultural-historical analysis of the dialectic of capital and its exchange and transformation. He could have relativized both Wally Haircut's desires and knowledge, and arrived at a more sophisticated analysis of *The Sneaky Kid* and its aftermath. After reading Wolcott's previously published *Ethnography: A Way of Seeing* (Roth, 2003), I was looking forward to reading this latest installment from the author. However, the book was a disappointment, my reading produced disappointment.

Using one auto/biographical and auto/ethnographical account as a scientific text interacting with my own auto/biography, I articulate some of the potential dangers in this praxis of method. One of key dangers of this praxis is the potential for becoming entrapped by ideology and thereby by produce|reproduce inequality and injustice. The dangers that come with looking inward to the exclusion to looking around, not only oneself but especially across the borders, are especially salient to me on the day of this writing in the early months of 2005, as the fighting in Iraq continues despite the American gifts of "freedom" and "democracy" the country has received. And yet, one half of the American people have re-elected George W. Bush on his record of his service and despite his unpopularity in almost every other country in the world. Looking inward comes with dangers, and both auto/biography and auto/ethnography tread a fine line in unearthing the particulars of our lives and getting caught in the everydayness of its ideology.

Notes

Parts of this chapter have been published as a review essay: Roth, W.-M. (2004). Auto/biography as scientific text: A dialectical approach to the role of experience. *FQS: Forum Qualitative Sozialforschung/ Forum Qualitative Social Research, 5*(1). http://www.qualitative-research.net/fqs-texte/1-04/1-04review-roth-e.htm

[1] In the novel *Pale Fire*, Vladimir V. Nabokov (1962) made the relationship between author and his work the central theme. The novel consists of a 999-line poem, apparently by an academic named John Shade, followed by a 200-page commentary by his colleague Charles Kinbote. Who the narrator within the novel is has become a topic of scholarly debate. Did John Shade invent Charles Kinbote or Charles Kinbote invented John Shade? Perhaps another colleague, V. Botkin, invented both of them? Perhaps John Shade's dead daughter Hazel' ghost prompted both John Shade's poem and Kinbote's commentary to it? (e.g., Boyd, 2001). In, *Ulysses*, James Joyce (1986) devoted the entire Chapter 9 (pp. 151–179) to a theory of the special relationship between Shakespeare and the ghost in *Hamlet*. Accordingly, Shakespeare was said to have played the Ghost in Hamlet, crying out on stage to his two son's, as actor to Prince Hamlet and as father to Hamnet Shakespeare who had died around the time that Hamlet was first played. It has been suggested that Shakespeare has been something like the ghostly father of Joyce and, similarly, Nabokov the ghostly father of *Pale Fire* (Rosenbaum, 1999).

References

Bakhtin, M. M. (1993). *Toward a philosophy of the act*. Austin: University of Texas Press.

Becker, H. S. (1972). A school is a lousy place to learn anything in. *American Behavioral Scientist, 16*, 85–105.

Bourdieu, P. (1986). The forms of capital. In J. G. Richardson (Ed.), *Handbook of theory and research for the sociology of education* (pp. 241–258). New York: Greenwood.

Bourdieu, P., & Wacquant, L.J.D. (1992). *An invitation to reflexive sociology*. Chicago: University of Chicago Press.

Boyd, B. (2001). *Nabokov's Pale Fire: The magic of artistic discovery*. Princeton, NJ: Princeton University Press.

Derrida, J. (1981). *Dissemination*. Chicago: University of Chicago Press.

Derrida, J. (1988). *Limited inc*. Chicago: University of Chicago Press.

Derrida, J. (1995). There is no one narcissism (autobiophotographies). In E. Weber (Ed.), *Points. Interviews, 1974–1994* (pp. 196–215). Stanford, CA: Stanford University Press.

Eco, U. (1976). *A theory of semiotics*. Bloomington: Indiana University Press.

Edwards, D., & Potter, J. (1992). *Discursive psychology*. London: Sage.

Holzkamp, K. (1983). *Grundlegung der Psychologie*. Frankfurt: Campus.

Il'enkov, E. (1977). *Dialectical logic: Essays in its history and theory*. Moscow: Progress.

Jaeger, R. M. (Ed.). (1988). *Complementary methods for educational research*. Washington, DC: American Educational Research Association.

Jayyusi, L. (1991). Values and moral judgement: Communicative practice as a moral order. In G. Button (Ed.), *Ethnomethodology and the human sciences* (pp. 227–251). Cambridge: Cambridge University Press.

Joyce, J. (1986). *Ulysses*. New York: Random House.

Leont'ev, A. N. (1978). *Activity, consciousness and personality*. Englewood Cliffs, NJ: Prentice Hall.

Lynch, M., & Bogen, D. (1996). *The spectacle of history: Speech, text, and memory at the Iran-contra hearings*. Durham, NC: Duke University Press.

Malpas, J. E. (1992). *Donald Davidson and the mirror of meaning: Holism, truth, and interpretation*. Cambridge: Cambridge University Press.

Merleau-Ponty, M. (1945). *Phénoménologie de la perception*. Paris: Gallimard.

Mikhailov, F. (1980). *The riddle of self*. Moscow: Progress.

Müller, A.M.K. (1972). *Die präparierte Zeit: Der Mensch in der Krise seiner eigenen Zielsetzungen*. Stuttgart: Radius.

Nuckolls, C. W. (1995). The misplaced legacy of Gregory Bateson: Toward a cultural dialectic of knowledge and desire. *Cultural Anthropology, 10*, 367–394.

Perry, J. D. (1982, November). *The functions of erection reconsidered*. Paper presented at the Annual Meeting of the Society for the Scientific Study of Sex, San Francisco, CA. http://www.incontinet.com/articles/art_sex/foferect.htm.

Ricœur, P. (1990). *Soi-même comme un autre*. Paris: Seuil.

Ricœur, P. (1991). *From text to action: Essays in hermeneutics II*. Chicago: University of Chicago Press.

Rosenbaum, R. (1999, December 6). The novel of the century: Nabokov's Pale Fire. *The New York Observer*, p. 31.

Roth, W.-M. (2003). "If somebody's with something every day they've gotta learn something—Or they're just out to lunch": The dialectics of ethnography as a way of being. *Forum Qualitative Sozialforschung / Forum: Qualitative Social Research, 4* (3). http://www.qualitative-research.net/fqs-texte/3-03/3-03review-roth-e.htm.

Wolcott, H. F. (1999). *Ethnography: A way of seeing*. Walnut Creek, CA: Altamira Press.

Wolcott, H. F. (2002). *The sneaky kid and its aftermath*. Walnut Creek, CA: Altamira Press.

8   Auto/biography and Critical Ontology: Being a Teacher, Developing a Reflective Persona

Joe L. Kincheloe

There is nothing new in asserting that the ways one teaches and the pedagogical purposes one pursues are directly connected to the way teachers see themselves. At the same time the ways teachers come to see themselves as learners, in particular the ways they conceptualize what they need to learn, where they need to learn it, and how the process should take place shape their teacher persona. Too infrequently are teachers in university, student teaching, or in-service professional education encouraged to confront why they think as they do about themselves as teachers—especially in relation to the social, cultural, political, economic, and historical world around them.

Teacher education provides little insight into the forces that shape identity and consciousness. Becoming educated, becoming a critical practitioner necessitates insight into the construction of selfhood and personal transformation. Auto/biography in this context becomes an intensely practical dimension of teacher education, as pre-service and practicing teachers begin to discern the construction of their selfhood in relation to larger social structures and epistemological dynamics. Auto/biographical research as conceptualized here empowers one to act in a more informed manner, to engage in critical action that transforms not only one's own life but also the lives of others.

Thus, this chapter explores the nature of a critical form of auto/biographical research, a postformal auto/biography, and its pragmatic uses in teacher education and pedagogy. Scholarly teachers who are researchers are well served to explore this construction of selfhood and pedagogical orientation. At one level this is a form of ontological knowledge—an awareness of what it means to be a teacher, to be human. Thus, this chapter explores how auto/biographical research in a critical ontological context provides insight into the construction of teacher selfhood in relation to social, cultural, political, economic, and historical domains. Such a project, I believe, negates any tendency for auto/biographical research to lapse into a narcissistic enterprise. Too often auto/biographical research has focused on an abstracted self in a manner that can be described as self-absorbed. Postformal auto/biography is focused on understanding one's social construction for the purpose of gaining humble new insights that facilitate one's ability to become a responsible and transformative member of larger communities where socially just activities are coordinated—activities that address oppression and alleviate human suffering.

The Scholar-Teacher as Auto/biographical Researcher: Postformal Inquiry

In more constructivist and critical forms of inquiry researchers who do not understand themselves tend to misconstrue the pronouncements and feelings of others. The complexity and multiple readings characteristic of such multilogical research are remote to more positivistic scholars, as they seek comfort in the prescribed methods, objectivity, and depersonalization of traditional social scientific research (Lemke, 1995; Van Hesteran, 1986). In a sense, the objectivist tradition provides a shelter in which the self can hide from the deeply personal issues that permeate all socio-educational phenomena. Such personal issues would, if it were not for the depersonalization of traditional inquiry, force an uncomfortable element of researcher self-revelation (Rasberry, 2001; Schneider & Laihua, 2000). Critical teacher researchers seek insight into how their own assumptions (and those of the individuals they research) came to be constructed. They transcend formalism's concern with problem solving by seeking to determine the etymology of the problem—in other words, they want to learn how to think about their own thinking (Romano, 2000).

The effort to explore the construction of subjectivity and its relation to research, an essential characteristic of *postformalism*, involves individuals' attempts to disengage themselves from socio-interpersonal norms and ideological expectations (Kincheloe & Steinberg, 1993). This postformal concern with questions of meaning, emancipation via ideological disembedding, and attention to the process of self-production rises above the formal operational level of thought and inquiry and its devotion to proper procedure. A brief description of postformalism is in order. Objectivist, formal thinking and research imply an acceptance of a positivist mechanistic worldview that is caught in a cause–effect, hypothetical-deductive system of reasoning. Unconcerned with questions of power relations and the way they structure our consciousness, formal objectivism accepts a decontextualized, depoliticized way of knowing that breaks a social and educational system down into its basic parts to understand how it works. Emphasizing certainty and prediction, formal objectivist knowledge work organizes verified facts into theory. The facts that do not fit into the theory are eliminated, and the theory developed is the one best suited to limit contradictions in knowledge.

In this context, postformalism works to produce insights that move beyond these limitations. Postformalist researchers strive to construct knowledge that

- is consistent with a critical ethics of difference—a theoretical orientation that accounts for cultural difference, the complexity of everyday life, and the demands of a rigorous democratic education. Grounded in a detailed awareness of a bricolage of indigenous knowledges, African-American epistemologies, subjugated knowledges, and the moral insights of liberation theology, the postformal ethic of difference seeks more complex approaches to understanding the relationship between self and world. How do students and teachers come to construct their views of reality, postformalists ask in this ethical context? Guided by the critical ethics of difference, teacher-researchers come to understand the social construction of world and self. In this context they focus on the forces that shape individual perspectives. Why are some constructions of reality and moral action embraced and officially legitimated by the dominant culture while others are repressed?

- resonates with emancipatory goals—those who seek emancipation attempt to gain the power to control their own lives in solidarity with a justice-oriented community. Here postformalists attempt to expose the forces that prevent individuals and groups from shaping the decisions that crucially affect their lives (Apple, 1999). In this way greater degrees of autonomy and human agency can be achieved. In this first decade of the twenty-first century we are cautious in our use of the term emancipation because, as many critics have pointed out, no one is ever completely emancipated from the sociopolitical context that has produced him or her. Concurrently, many have used *emancipation* to signal the freedom an abstract individual gains by gaining access to Western reason—i.e., becoming reasonable. The postformalist use of *emancipation* in an evolving criticality rejects any use of the term in this context. In addition, many have rightly questioned the arrogance that may accompany efforts to emancipate "others." These are important caveats and must be carefully taken into account. Thus, as postformal auto/biographers search for those forces that insidiously shape who we are and respect those who reach different conclusions in their personal journeys. Nonetheless, postformalism considers the effort to understand dominant power and its effects on individuals to be vitally important information needed in the effort to understand selfhood and construct vibrant democratic communities.

- is intellectually rigorous and internally consistent—does the knowledge in question provide a richer insight into a phenomenon than did other constructions? Is the postformal construction thorough in answering all the inquiries it raises about the phenomenon? Is it sensitive to the complexity in which all phenomena all embedded? Does it expand our consciousness in relation to the phenomenon? If the individual constructing a body of knowledge can answer these questions in the affirmative, she is on her way to a rigorous and consistent construction.

- avoids reductionism—the rationalistic and reductionist quest for order refuses in its arrogance to listen to cacophony of lived experience, the coexistence of diverse meanings and interpretations. The concept of understanding in the complex world viewed by postformalists is unpredictable. Much to the consternation of mechanistic researchers there exists no final, transhistorical, non-ideological meaning that we strive to achieve. As such postformalists create rather than find meaning in enacted reality, they explore alternate meanings offered by others in similar circumstances. If this was not enough, they work to account for historical and social contingencies that always operate to undermine the universal pronouncement of the meaning of a particular phenomenon or experience. When researchers fail to discern the unique ways that historical and social context make for special circumstances, they often provide a reductionist form of knowledge that impoverishes our understanding of everything connected to it. The monological quest for order is grounded in the positivistic belief that all phenomena should be broken down into their constitutive parts to facilitate inquiry. The goal of integrating knowledges from diverse domains and understanding the interconnections shaping, for example, the biological and the cognitive, is irrelevant in the paradigm of order and fragmentation. The meaning that comes from interrelationship is lost and questions concerning the purpose of research and its insight into the human condition in general and individual subjectivity in particular are put aside in an orgy of correlation and triangulated description. Information is sterilized and insight into what may be worth exploring is abandoned. Ways of making use of particular knowledge are viewed as irrelevant and creative engagement with conceptual insights is characterized as frivolous. Empirical knowledge in the quest for order is an end in itself. Once it has been validated it needs no further investigation or interpretation. While empirical research is obviously necessary, its process of production constitutes only one step of a larger and more rigorous process of inquiry. Postformalism subverts the finality of the empirical act of knowledge production in its quest for transgressive auto/biographical insight.

Thus, postformalism grapples with purpose, devoting attention to issues of human dignity, freedom, authority, and social responsibility. Many conceptions of postformalism contend that an appreciation of multiple perspectives necessitates an ethical relativism that paralyzes social action. Our conception of postformal perceiving and inquiring is tied to the construction of a system of meaning that is used to guide the research/cognitive act. Never content with what they have constructed, never certain of the system's appropriateness, always concerned with the expansion of self-awareness and consciousness, postformal auto/biographers engage in a running meta-dialogue, a constant conversation with self, a perpetual reconceptualization of their system of meaning.

Theorizing Postformal Auto/biographical Research:
Paying Homage to William Pinar's *Currere*

Any notion of postformal auto/biography is indebted to William Pinar's notion of *currere* (Pinar, 1994; Pinar, Reynolds, Slattery, & Taubman, 1995). In his thirty-year effort to analyze the way individuals experience education, Pinar connected his understanding of phenomenology to psychoanalysis and aesthetics to produce a unique analytical form. *Currere*, the Latin root of *curriculum*, concerns the investigation of the individual experience of the public. Utilizing this analytical synthesis, Pinar argued that we are better prepared to approach the contents of consciousness in the way they appear to us in educational contexts. Such exploration allows us, Pinar argued in a manner that would help shape postformalism, to loosen our identification with the contents of consciousness so that we can gain some distance from them. From our new vantage point we may be able to see those psychic realms that are formed by conditioning and unconscious adherence to social convention.

With Pinar's insights in mind a postformal auto/biography takes a direct cue from *currere*. When *currere* is combined with a critical reconceptualization of Howard Gardner's notion of intrapersonal intelligence (I prefer *insight* over *intelligence*), interesting insights for auto/biography begin to emerge. Postformalism asserts that a critical form of intrapersonal insight involves not only the ability to discriminate among feelings, isolate and define emotions, and use such insight in the attempt to shape one's behavior, but also the ability to analyze the social and political dimensions of those emotions and feelings. In postformal auto/biography I offer an etymological dimension of cognition that asks what are the psychological and social origins of my perceptions of the world, my understandings of my own identity.

In this context, postformal auto/biography's thinking about our own thinking induces teachers and students to reexamine their personal constructions of the purpose of schooling; it induces men to expose the ways the privileged position of masculinity has shaped their self-images; it induces heterosexuals to refigure their identities vis-à-vis confrontation with the dynamics of heterosexism and sexual preference; it induces workers to reconsider the workplace and its social dimensions as a profound influence on identity formation. Hyperreality's crisis of meaning and identity is also a crisis of thinking. As a society, we still have little idea how electronic culture's information saturation and the power relations embedded within such a process shape our consciousness. Postformalist thinking about thinking appropriates the ideology critique of *currere*, pushing what we call sophisticated cognitive activity into an analysis of the production of the self.

Postformalism thus views *currere* as a method that explores the influence of ideology vis-à-vis subjective educational experience and its relationship to auto/biographical research. In this context teachers and students are encouraged to reflect on their past lives in schools and their interactions with teachers, books, the symbol structures of schooling, and other education-related artifacts. Pinar urges students and teachers to remember, observe, and record; focus specifically, he advises, on present responses to what is remembered. In this context he induces individuals to ask: "What do I do with what I have been made?" "What happens when students and teachers find in this process that they are racist, misogynist, class-biased, or homophobic?" Upon such discoveries the individual must begin to deal with such socially constructed legacies, utilizing logic, emotional empathy, prayer, or whatever means that work to reform such tendencies.

Currere and Auto/biographical Research

Through *currere*, Pinar wants us to become action researchers of ourselves—I refer to this as a form of postformal auto/biography that helps teachers develop a reflective persona. Teacher and their students in this context begin to systematically analyze how sociopolitical distortions have tacitly worked to shape their worldviews, perspectives on education, and self-images. With a deeper appreciation of such processes, practitioners recognize the insidious ways power operates to create oppressive conditions for some groups and privilege for others. Thus, a critical form of postformal auto/biography opens up new ways of knowing that transcend formalist modes of analysis. Such teacher-researchers of selfhood cannot help but turn to auto/biographical analysis in their inquiry. Aware of past descriptions of higher order thinking, such teachers are alert to connections between biography and cognition. That is, teachers in this situation become researchers of the formation of their own socio-cognitive structures.

Such inquiry produces a meta-awareness of an omnipresent feature of postformal teachers. They are always in the process of being changed and changing, of being analyzed and analyzing, of being constructed and constructing, of learning and teaching, of disembedding and connecting. Indeed, the purpose of a

currere-informed teacher research is not to produce reductionist forms of certi-
fied data and validated educational theory—it is to produce a meta-theoretical
form of insight about the interaction of Self and context supported by reflection
and grounded in sociohistorical insight (Carr & Kemmis, 1986; Carspecken,
1999; Kincheloe, 2005; Schratz & Walker, 1995).

Thus, critical inquiry is connected to *currere* and its concern with conceptual sophistication, with a more contextually embedded form of knowledge produced by teachers and subsequently by their students, and with an academic discipline's relation to one's ever-evolving auto/biography. Such concerns inform a
postformal conception of a deeper level of understanding or a higher order of
cognitive activity. In such a context teacher-researchers must confront not only
what they see but also *why they see what they see*. When postformal
auto/biographers learn why they see what they see, they are thinking about
thinking, analyzing the forces that shape their consciousness, and they are placing what they perceive in a meaningful context. They come to learn that all seeing is selective, filtered not only by the ways that power has constructed our
subjectivity but also by how we respond to such power plays.

Postformal teachers learn that they see from particular vantage points in the
web of reality, coming in the process to realize that there is no value-neutral way
of perceiving. The postformal observer employs this meta-awareness in combination with Pinar's instrumental concept of the self-application of disciplinary
knowledge to tease out what is significant in a classroom situation. This recognition of significance emerges from a larger postformal appreciation of context—
an understanding of the historical, philosophical, and sociological dimensions of
what is going on in schools. For example, an observation might be significant in
that it illustrates the contemporary embodiment of the postindustrialization purpose of schooling as a method of social classification, the influence of positivism in shaping the way student evaluation is conducted, or the power of an-
drocentrism to shape the profile of a "successful" school administrator.

With these ideas in mind postformal auto/biographical teacher-researchers
develop approaches to pedagogy and teacher education that encourage practitioners to construct their own self-knowledge while developing strategies to help
students do the same. Such pedagogy understands that the development of self-
knowledge, an understanding of the social construction of self is a key purpose
of a rigorous and critical education. Postformalists imagine teacher education to
provide teachers the skills for assisting students in the analysis of their interpretations of cultural meanings. In this context a central dimension of postformal
auto/biography emerges: with these analytical skills teachers and their students
gain the ability to intervene into their own consciousness construction. Such in-

tervention enables teachers and students to engage their experiences in ways that both affirm and question it. In such a process postformal auto/biographers are always attentive to the objective of encouraging self and social transformation in a way that promotes humility, community building, and social justice.

Postformal Auto/biography and Critical Ontology

In the effort to better understand the social construction of selfhood postformalists have developed the notion of a critical ontology. In a critical ontology postformalists drawing on *currere* employ auto/biographical research for the purpose of attaining new levels of consciousness and more informed "ways of being." Teachers and students who gain such a critical ontological awareness understand how dominant cultural perspectives have helped construct their political opinions, religious beliefs, gender role, racial positions, and sexual orientation. A critical ontological vision helps us gain new understandings and insights as to who we can become. Such a vision helps us move beyond our present state of being—our ontological selves—as we discern the forces that have made us that way. The line between knowledge production and being is blurred, as the epistemological and the ontological converge around questions of identity. As we employ the ontological vision we ask questions about ethics, morality, politics, emotion, and gut feelings, seeking not precise steps to reshape our subjectivity but a framework of principles with which we can negotiate. We hermeneutically engage this framework of principles with our specific historical circumstances, our socio-cultural situatedness. Thus, we join the quest for new, expanded, more just and interconnected ways of being human.

Critical ontology strives to free ourselves from the alienation of the machine metaphors of Cartesianism. Such an ontological stance recognizes the reductionism of viewing the universe as a well-oiled machine and the human mind as a computer. Such positivistic ways of being subvert an appreciation of the amazing life force that inhabits both the universe and human beings. This machine cosmology has positioned human beings as living in a dead world, a lifeless universe. Ontologically, this Western Cartesianism has separated individuals from their inanimate surroundings, undermining any organic interconnection of the person to the cosmos. The life-giving complexity of the inseparability of human and world has been lost and social/cultural/pedagogical/psychological studies of people abstracted—removed from context. Such a removal has brought about disastrous ontological effects. Human beings, in a sense, lost their belongingness to both the world and to others around them. Postformal auto/biographers understand that they must engage in their labors with a compelling knowledge of this alienated backdrop.

Education and social psychological scholar Philip Wexler (2000) picks up on these ontological issues, arguing that an intuitive disenchantment with this Cartesian fragmentation and its severing of the self-environment relationship is fueling a diffuse social revaluation. He employs revitalization for describing the decentered mass movement taking place throughout Western societies. It constitutes an attempt, he contends, to resacralize our culture and ourselves. Such an effort exposes the impact of Eurocentrism and positivism on what human beings have become, as, at the same time, it produces an ontological "change from within." Understanding the problems with the culture of positivism's lack of self-awareness or concern with consciousness and interconnectedness, Wexler's resacralization picks up on both premodern and postmodern wisdom traditions to lay the foundation for profound ontological change. In the emerging ontology, the Cartesian bifurcation of the mind and body is repaired, and new relationships with the body, mind, and spirit are pursued. In the transcendence of modernist notions of bodily ego-greed, a new understanding of the body's role in meaning making and human being is attained.

Picking up on these insights a postformal critical ontology positions the body in relation to cognition and the process of life itself. The body is a corporeal reflection of the evolutionary concept of *autopoiesis*, self-organizing or self-making of life. Autopoiesis involves the production of a pattern of life organization. Cognition in this ontological context involves the process of self-production. Thus, life itself, the nature of being, is a cognitive activity that involves establishing patterns of living, patterns that become the life force through self-organization. If life is self-organized, then there are profound ontological, cognitive, and pedagogical implications. By recognizing new patterns and developing new processes, humans exercise much more input into their own evolution than previously imagined. In such a context human agency and possibility is enhanced. Of course, in this context the importance of postformal auto/biography reveals itself. To tap into this autopoietic dynamic individuals must gain a meta-understanding of who they are in relation to their environment(s) and patterns of life. To move to a new level of human *being*, teachers and students must develop rigorous understandings of these processes and the possibilities they herald.

In light of these autopoietic insights postformalists come to understand that evolution is not as random as previously thought. Life is self-produced in forms of escalating diversity and complexity. The interaction of different living forms can catalyze the self-production feature of living systems. In both its corporeal and cognitive expressions the autopoietic life process reaches out for difference and novelty to embrace its next ontological level (Capra, 1996; Kincheloe & Steinberg, 1997; Steinberg, 2001). Teachers who understand this critical onto-logical process can use these notions to rethink their lives and their teacher per-sona. With these understandings, we can self-organize and reorganize the aca-demic cosmos in ways that account for new levels of complexity where new patterns and processes allow us to rethink the nature of our being and the possi-bility of our becoming. Curriculum in this context takes on an unprecedented importance, as it pursues ways of knowing and being that shape the evolution of the human species. In this way postformal auto/biography becomes self-ex-ploration on a mission to push ourselves into new domains of being.

The Power of Historicity in Critical Ontology and Postformal Auto/biography

As postformal auto/biographers gain insight into the social construction of knowledge, understanding, and human subjectivity, they gain a consciousness of their own and other's historicity. What many researchers have referred to as the crisis of historicity is really nothing more than the development of this con-sciousness, this understanding of historical, social, cultural, ideological, and dis-cursive construction of knowledge and selfhood. The effort to distinguish be-tween different social realities and different interpretations of the world around us is more difficult than originally assumed. With such an understanding in mind postformalists always have to deal with levels of complexity ignored by less informed researchers. As postformalists negotiate their way between the constructed and discovered dimensions of knowledge work, they come to appre-ciate the blurred line between the historical and historiographical.

Naiveté results when historicity is dismissed in auto/biography. Postformal-ists argue that any research must understand the historical situatedness of both the researcher and that being researched. The historicization of research allows postformal auto/biographers to ask questions of knowledge production that have previously gone unasked and, thus, to gain insight into previously invisible proc-esses shaping the ways we use to describe and act in the world. In this way the auto/biography becomes thicker, more insightful, savvier, more rigorous, and less self-absorbed (Bridges, 1997; McCarthy, 1997).

The understanding of the social construction of self and historicity in rela-tion to auto/biographical research cannot be separated from hermeneutics. In this context the auto/biographer employs *critical hermeneutics* to understand the his-torical and social ways that power operates to shape meaning and its lived consequences. Critical hermeneutics alerts us to the ways power helps construct the social, cultural, and economic conditions under which meaning is made, research processes are constructed, and selfhood is produced. In this context critical hermeneutics facilitates the auto/biographer's attempt to identify socially oppressive forms of meaning making and research processes. Postformal auto/biographers understand that constructivism and historicity are unhelpful concepts when power and its effects remain unrecognized.

Peter McLaren (2001) points out that merely focusing on the production of meanings may not lead to "resisting and transforming the existing conditions of exploitation" (p. 702). Postformalists take his admonition seriously and assert that in the critical hermeneutical dimension of auto/biography the act of understanding power and its effects is merely one part—albeit an inseparable part—of counter-hegemonic praxis. Critical hermeneutics understands that meaning doesn't "just happen." Instead, meaning is imposed on the world and if researchers are not aware of such dynamics they will unconsciously join in this imposition. Joining in the imposition is disguised by the assertion that meaning exists in the world independently and unconnected to the subjectivities of researchers and other "knowers." All objectivist researchers do, they innocently and reductionistically maintain, is discover this independent meaning and report it to their audience. In this hermeneutic context auto/biography takes on an expanded importance, as it becomes a necessary precursor for a researcher engaging in any method of research. In this context auto/biography informs the researcher of her own location in the social web of reality and how this location helps shape how she makes meaning of the world.

This insight into the importance of auto/biographical research is irrelevant to positivist researchers. Power in the positivist construction of knowledge, it is argued, plays no role in the process. Postformalists employing critical notions of historicity and constructivism know better. The objective knowledge and the validated research processes used by reductionists are always socially negotiated in a power-saturated context. Assertions that knowledge is permanent and universal are undermined; the stability of meaning is subverted. Forces of domination will often reject such historically conscious and power-literate insights, as such awareness undermines the unchallenged knowledge assertions of power wielders. Postformalist auto/biographers know that critical hermeneutics is dangerous when deployed in the sacred temples of knowledge production. It is no surprise that this form of philosophical inquiry is typically excluded from the canon of official research (Lutz, Jones, & Kendall, 1997). The critical dimension of research is dedicated to engaging political action in a variety of social, political, economic and academic venues.

Postformal Auto/biography and Critical Ontology:
From Reductionist Alienation to Human Possibility

In a critical ontological context, research—auto/biography in particular—
becomes a profoundly exciting enterprise because it is always conceptualized in
terms of what we can become in both an individual and a collective context.
Here the notion of auto/biography with a purpose arises. When criticality meets
auto/biography we research ourselves not simply for self-knowledge but for a
transformative outcome. We engage in auto/biography to become something we
are not yet—we apply the critical concept of immanence to ourselves. In our
auto/biographical socio-ontological imagination we can transcend the Enlightenment category of abstract individualism and move toward a more textured
concept of the relational individual. While abstract individualism and a self-
sufficient ontology seem almost *natural* in the modernist Western world, such is
not the case in many non-Western cultures and has not been the case even in
Western societies in previous historical eras. In ancient Greece, for example, it
is hard to find language that identified *the self* or *I*—such descriptions were not
commonly used because the individual was viewed as a part of a collective who
could not function independently of the larger social group. In the commonsense
of contemporary Western society and its unexamined ontological assumptions
this way of seeing self is hard to fathom.

Western Enlightenment ontology discerns the natural state of the individual
as solitary. The social order in this modernist Eurocentric context is grounded on
a set of contractual transactions between isolated individual atoms. In other
works I (Kincheloe, 1993) have referred to Clint Eastwood's "man with no
name," a cinematic character who did not need a "damn thing from nobody" as
the ideal Western male way of being—the ontological norm. Operating in this
context, we clearly discern, for example, cognitive psychology's tradition of focusing on the autonomous development of the individual monad. In postformalism's critical ontology a human being simply cannot exist outside the inscription
of community with its processes of relationship, differentiation, interaction, and
subjectivity. Indeed, in this critical complex ontology the relational embedded-
ness of self is so context dependent that psychologists, sociologists, and educators can never isolate a finalized completed *true self*. Since the self is always in
context and in process, no final delineation of a notion such as ability can be determined. Thus, we are released from the rugged cross of IQ and such hurtful
and primitive entities as *intelligence*.

One can quickly discern the political consequences of such a Cartesian ontology. Human beings in Western liberal political thought become abstract bear-

ers of particular civic rights. If individuals are relational, context-embedded beings, however, these abstract rights may be of little consequence. A critical ontology insists that individuals live in specific places with particular types of relationships. They operate or are placed in the web of reality at various points of race, class, gender, sexual, religious, physical ability, geographical place, and other continua. Where individuals find themselves in this complex web holds dramatic power consequences. Their location shapes their relationship to dominant culture and the social psychological assumptions that accompanies it. A prime manifestation of ontological alienation involves a lack of recognition of the dramatic effect of these dynamics on everything that takes place in the psycho-educational cosmos. These ontological understandings help postformal auto/biographers frame their research.

In the context of postformalism's critical ontology the abstract, autonomous self with a fixed intellectual ability becomes an anachronism. As an effort to appreciate the power of human beings to affect their own destinies, to exercise human agency, and to change social conditions, postformal auto/biographers study selfhood in light of the sociological, cultural studies, cultural psychological, and critical analytical work of the last few decades. Much of what dominant psychology and education consider *free will* and expressions of *innate intelligence* are simply the effects of particular social, cultural, political, and economic forces. While we can make decisions on how we operate as human beings, they are never completely independent of these structuring forces. This is true no matter who we are or from where we come—no person can operate outside of society or free from cultural, linguistic, ideological influences.

From Auto/biographical Research to a New Vision of Selfhood

Postformal auto/biography becomes the first step in a larger critical effort to construct the conceptual foundations for a new mode of selfhood when it employs an understanding of complexity theory, Humberto Maturana and Francisco Varela's *Santiago Enactivism* as the process of life, critical theoretical foundations, the critique of Cartesianism, and poststructuralist feminist analysis. Such a configuration cannot be comprehensively delineated here, but postformal auto/biographers can begin to build theoretical pathways to get around the Cartesian limitations on the ontological imagination. Given that living things constantly remake themselves in interaction with their environments (Maturana & Varela, 1987), auto/biographical research is grounded in an appreciation of the human ability to use new social contexts and experiences to reformulate subjectivity. Here the concept of personal ability becomes a de-essentialized cognition of possibility. No essentialized bounded self can access the socio-cognitive potential offered by epiphanies of difference or triggered by an "insignificant" insight.

As postformal auto/biographers begin to identify previously unperceived patterns in which the self is implicated, the possibility of cognitive change and personal growth is enhanced. As the barriers between mind and multiple contexts are erased, there is an increased chance that more expanded forms of *cognitive autopoiesis*—self-constructed modes of higher-order thinking—will emerge. A more textured, thicker sense of self-production and the nature of self and other is constructed in this process. As we examine the self and its relations to others in cosmological, epistemological, linguistic, social, cultural, and political contexts, we gain a clearer sense of our purpose in the world especially in relation to justice, interconnectedness, and even love. In these activities we move closer to the macro-processes of life and their micro-expressions in everyday life.

A key aspect of life processes is the understanding of difference that comes from recognizing patterns of interconnectedness. Knowing that an individual from an upper-middle class European background living in a Virginia suburb will be considered culturally bizarre by a group of tribespeople from the Amazon rainforest is a potentially profound learning experience in the domain of the personal. How is the suburbanite viewed as bizarre? What cultural practices are seen as so unusual? What mannerisms are humorous to the tribespeople? What worldviews are baffling to them? The answers to such questions may shock the suburbanite into reorienting her view of her own "normality." The interaction may induce her to ask questions of the way she is perceived by and the way she perceives others. Such bracketing of the personal may be quite liberating. This auto/biographical interaction with difference is an example of *structural coupling* that creates a new relationship with other and with self. A new inner world is created as a result of such coupling (Sumara & Davis, 1997; Varela, 1999).

Such explorations on the ontological frontier hold profound pedagogical implications. As teachers and students relate their auto/biographical research to the rigorous study of diverse global knowledges, they come to understand that the identities of their peer groups and families constitute only a few of countless historical and cultural ways to be human. As they study their self-production in wider biological, sociological, cultural studies, historical, theological, psychological, and counter-canonical contexts, they gain compelling insights into their ways of being. As they engage the conflicts that induce diverse knowledge producers to operate in conflicting ways, students become more attuned to the ideological, discursive, and regulatory forces operating in all knowledges. This is not nihilism, as many defenders of the Eurocanon argue; this is the exciting process of exploring the world and the self and their relationship in all of the complexity such study requires. In light of such teacher and student auto/biographical work, the curriculum can never be the same.

The processual and relational notions of self structurally couple with the socio-cultural context and can only be understood by studying them with these dynamics in mind. If our notion of the self emerges in its relation with multiple dimensions of the world, it inherently is a participatory entity—it is more open to change than reductionist scholars have traditionally maintained. Such an interactive dynamic is always in process and thus demands a reconceptualization of *individualism* and *self-interest* (Pickering, 1999). The needs of self and others in this context begin to merge, as the concept of self-reliance takes on new meanings. Notions of educational purpose, evaluation, and curriculum development, for example, are transformed when these new conceptions of the personal domain come into focus. In this first decade of the twenty-first century we stand merely on the threshold of the possibilities this notion of selfhood harbors. A postformal notion of auto/biography moves us into this exciting domain.

Auto/biography, Critical Ontology, and the Power of Enactivism

A critical ontology understands that any effort will not work if it seeks to explain complex cognitive, biological, social, or pedagogical events by the reductionist study of their components outside of the larger processes of which they are a part. It will not move us to new levels of understanding or set the stage for new, unexplored modes of being human. The social, biological, cognitive, or educational domain is not an assortment of discrete objects that can be understood in isolation from one another. The fragmented pieces put forth in such studies do not constitute reality—contrary to Western commonsense. The deeper structures, the tacit forces, the processes that shape the physical world and the social world will be lost to such observers. As I argue in the introduction to *The Stigma of Genius: Einstein, Consciousness, and Education* (Kincheloe, Steinberg, & Tippins, 1999), Albert Einstein could not have produced his general theory of relativity without this understanding of connectedness, process, and the limitations of studying *things-in-themselves*.

For 250 years physicists had been searching for the basic building blocks of gravity—some contended it was a particle (a graviton), others argued it was a gravity wave. Einstein pointed out that it was neither, that it was not a *thing* at all. Gravity, he maintained, was a part of the structure of the universe that existed as a relationship connecting mass, space, and time. This insight, of course, changed the very nature of how we conceptualize the universe. It should have changed how we conceptualize epistemology, cognition, pedagogy, and ontology. Of course, it did not—and that is what postformal auto/biographers are still working on. The emphasis on studying and teaching about the world as a compilation of fragmented things-in-themselves has returned with a vengeance in recent educational reforms. The idea of education and learning as a form of self-transformation is a dangerous proposition in the era of *No Child Left Behind* and right-wing educational reform in the US.

In this context the work of Maturana and Varela is instructive to those concerned with auto/biographical research. Their *Santiago Enactivism* employs the same relational concept Einstein's used in general relativity theory to explain life as a process, a system of interconnections. Indeed, they argue, that the process of cognition is the process of life. In enactivism mind is not a thing-in-itself but a process—an activity where the interactions of a living organism with its environment constitute cognition. In this relationship life itself and cognition are indelibly connected and reveal this interrelationship at diverse levels of living and non-living domains. Where mind ends and matter begins is difficult to discern, a situation that operates to overturn the long-standing and problematic Cartesian separation of the two entities. In the enactivist conception, mind and matter are merely parts of the same process—one cannot exist without the other. Such an understanding changes the nature of the auto/biographer's task forever. A critical ontology seeks to repair this rupture between mind and matter, self and world. In this re-connection we enter into a new phase of human history, new modes of cognition, and dramatic changes in pedagogy.

According to the enactivist, perception and cognition also operate in contradiction to Cartesianism, as they construct a reality as opposed to reflecting an external one already in existence. The interactive or circular organization of the nervous system described by Maturana is similar to the hermeneutic circle, as it employs a conversation between diverse parts of a system to construct meaning. Autopoiesis as the process of self-production is the way living things operate. Self-construction emerges out of a set of relationships between simple parts. In the hermeneutic circle the relationships between parts *self-construct* previously unimagined meanings. Thus, in an ontological context meaning emerges not from the thing-in-itself but from its relationships to an infinite number of other things. Such relationships, therefore, become central concerns of the postformalist auto/biographer. In this complexity we understand from another angle that there is no final meaning of anything; meanings are always evolving in light of new relationships, new horizons. Thus, in a critical ontology our power as meaning makers is enhanced. Cognition is that process in which living systems organize the world around them into meaning. These understandings mark the death knell of traditional forms of auto/biography.

Specifically, Maturana and Varela argue that human identities do not come with us into the world in some neatly packaged unitary self. Since they "rise and subside" in a series of shifting relationships and patterns, the self can be described using the Buddhist notion that the "self is empty of self-nature." Understanding this, Varela (1999) maintains, self-understanding and self-change become more possible than ever before. The self, therefore, is not a material entity but takes on more a virtual quality. Human beings have the experience of self, but no self—no central controlling mechanism—is to be found. Much is to be gained by an understanding of the virtual nature of the self.

According to the enactivists this knowledge helps us develop intelligent awareness—a profound understanding of the construction and the functioning of selfhood. Intelligent awareness is filled with wisdom but devoid of the egocentrism that undermines various notions of critical knowing. In such a context intelligent awareness cannot be separated from ethical insight. Without this ontological understanding many of pedagogies designed to empower will fan the flames of the egocentrism they attempt to overcome. If nothing else a critical ontology cultivates humility without which wisdom is not possible. Postformal auto/biographers are on a quest for a humble form of wisdom about who they are and what they may become in relation to others.

Enactivism, the Relational Self, and the Reflective Teacher

From an enactivist perspective, learning takes place when a self-maintaining system develops a more effective relationship with the external features of the system. In this context enactivism is highlighting the profound importance of *relationship* writ large as well as the centrality of the nature and quality of the relationships an organism makes with its environment. In the development of a critical ontology we learn from these ideas that political empowerment vis-à-vis the cultivation of the intellect demands an understanding of the system of relationships that construct our selfhood. We can talk ad nauseam about auto/biographical reflection, but it means little if undertaken outside of this notion of relationship. In the case of a critical pedagogy these relationships always involve students' connections to cultural systems, language, economic concerns, religious belief, social status, and the power dynamics that constitute them. With the benefit of auto/biographically understanding the self-in-relationship, teachers gain a new insight into what is happening in any learning situation—their own or their students. Living on the borderline between self and external system and self and other, learning never takes place outside of these relationships. Such knowledge changes our orientation to curriculum development and pedagogy. The reflective teacher has much more to reflect upon.

A critical ontology is intimately connected to a relational self (Noddings, 1990; Thayer-Bacon, 2000). Humans are ultimately the constructs of relationships, not fragmented monads or abstract individuals. From the enactivist perspective, this notion of humans as constructs of relationships corresponds precisely to the *virtual self*. A larger pattern—in the case of humans, consciousness—arises from the interaction of local elements. This larger pattern seems to be driven by a central controlling mechanism that can never be located. Thus, we discern the origin of traditional psychology's dismissal of consciousness as irrelevant. This not only constituted throwing out the baby with the bath water but discarding the tub, bathroom fixtures, and plumbing as well. In this positivistic articulation the process of life and being and the basis of the cognitive act are deemed unimportant. Auto/biography informed by critical ontology is always interested in these processes because they open up previously occluded insights into the nature of selfhood, of human being. An understanding of *autopoiesis* in this context allows postformal auto/biographers to perpetually reshape themselves in their relationships and resulting patterns of perception and behavior.

There is no way to predict the relationships individuals will make and the nature of the self-(re)construction that will ensue. Such uncertainty adds yet another element of complexity to the study of sociology, psychology, and pedagogy, as it simultaneously catalyzes the possibilities of human agency. It causes those enamored with critical ontology yet another reason to study the inadequacies of positivist science to account for the intricacies of the human domain. Physical objects do not necessarily change their structures via their interaction with other objects. A critical ontology understands that human beings do change structurally as a result of their interactions. The human mind thereby moves light years beyond the lifeless cognitivist computer model of mind; human being takes on far more complexity than originally suspected.

Thus, the human self-organization process—while profoundly more complex than the *World Wide Web*—is analogous to the way the *Web* arranges itself by random and not-so-random connections. The *Web* is an autopoietic organism that constructs itself in a hypertextual mode of operation. Unanticipated links create new concepts, ways of perceiving, and even ways of being among those that enter into this domain of epistemological emergence. Such experience reminds one that a new cultural logic has developed that transcends the mechanical dimensions of the machine epistemologies and ontologies of the modernist industrial era. Consider the stunning implications that when numerous simple entities possessing simple characteristics are thrown together—whether it be websites on the Internet or individuals' relationships with aspects of their environments—amazing things occur. From such interactions emerge larger wholes that are not guided by central controlling mechanisms. Self-awareness of this process of creation may lead to unanticipated modes of learning and new concepts of human being. Reflection moves to a new level of complexity. Auto/biographical research enters a new domain.

References

Apple, M. (1999). *Power, meaning and identity: Essays in critical educational studies.* New York: Peter Lang.

Bridges, D. (1997). Philosophy and educational research: A reconsideration of epistemological boundaries. *Cambridge Journal of Education, 27,* 177–189.

Capra, F. (1996). *The web of life: A new scientific understanding of living systems.* New York: Anchor Books.

Carr, W., & Kemmis, S. (1986). *Becoming critical.* Basingstoke: Falmer.

Carspecken, P. (1999). *Four scenes for posing the question of meaning and other essays in critical philosophy and critical methodology.* New York: Peter Lang.

Kincheloe, J. (1993). *Toward a critical politics of teacher thinking: Mapping the postmodern.* Westport, CT: Bergin and Garvey.

Kincheloe, J. (2005). *Critical constructivism.* New York: Peter Lang.

Kincheloe, J., & Steinberg, S. (1993). A tentative description of post-formal thinking: The critical confrontation with cognitive theory. *Harvard Educational Review, 63,* 296–320.

Kincheloe, J., & Steinberg, S. (1997). *Changing multiculturalism.* London: Open University Press.

Kincheloe, J., Steinberg, S., & Tippins, D. (1999). *The stigma of genius: Einstein, consciousness, and education.* New York: Peter Lang.

Lemke, J. (1995). *Textual politics: Discourse and social dynamics.* London: Taylor and Francis.

Lutz, K., Jones, K., & Kendall, J. (1997). Expanding the praxis debate: Contributions to clinical inquiry. *Advances in Nursing Science, 20,* 23–31.

McCarthy, M. (1997). Pluralism, invariance, and conflict. *The Review of Metaphysics, 51,* 3–23.

McLaren, P. (2001). Bricklayers and bricoleurs: A Marxist addendum. *Qualitative Inquiry, 7,* 700–705.

Maturana, H., & Varela, F. (1987). *The tree of knowledge.* Boston: Shambhala.

Noddings, N. (1990). Review symposium: A response. *Hypatia, 5,* 120–126.

Pickering, J. (1999). The self is a semiotic process. *Journal of Consciousness Studies, 6,* 31–47.

Pinar, W. (1994). *Auto/biography, politics, and sexuality: Essays in curriculum theory, 1972–1992.* New York: Peter Lang.

Pinar, W., Reynolds, W. Slattery, P., & Taubman, P. (1995). *Understanding curriculum.* New York: Peter Lang.

Rasberry, G. (2001). *Writing research/researching writing: Through a poet's I.* New York: Peter Lang.

Romano, R. (2000). *Forging an educative community: The wisdom of love, the power of understanding, and the terror of it all.* New York: Peter Lang.

Schneider, J., & Laihua, W. (2000). *Giving care, writing self: A "new" ethnography.* New York: Peter Lang.

Schratz, M., & Walker, R. (1995). *Research as social change: New opportunities for qualitative research.* New York: Routledge.

Steinberg, S. (2001). *Multi/intercultural conversations: A reader.* New York: Peter Lang.

Sumara, D., & Davis, B. (1997). Cognition, complexity, and teacher education. *Harvard Educational Review, 67,* 75–104.

Thayer-Bacon, B. (2000). *Transforming critical thinking: Thinking constructively.* New York: Teachers College Press.

Van Hesteran, F. (1986). Counselling research in a different key: The promise of a human science perspective. *Canadian Journal of Counselling, 20,* 200–234.

Varela, F. (1999). *Ethical know-how: Action, wisdom, and cognition.* Stanford, CA: Stanford University Press.

Wexler, P. (2000). *The mystical society: Revitalization in culture, theory, and education.* Boulder, CO: Westview.

III

Understanding Teaching
and Learning to Teach

Auto/biography and Auto/ethnography constitute important means for teachers to collect materials that server them for reflection on their practice. Auto/-biography and auto/ethnography do not substitute for reflection but establish a representation of the previously lived experience, which subsequently interrogate critically. It is through the process of critical interrogation that the practical and primary understanding is developed. However, the primary understanding precedes, accompanies, and concludes and therefore envelops the critical interrogation. Here is how it works.

Without lived experience, there is no primary understanding that the person can reflect upon. Only after having exposed themselves to the irremediably unfolding events in the classroom, from which there is no time out to reflect, do teachers have a ground on and through which reflection on teaching can be developed. However, this experience, to become object of reflection, has to be objectified—raw experience in the making cannot serve as object because it has not yet been completed. Auto/biography and auto/ethnography both constituted forms of inquiry and writing that produce these primary objectifications, which then, in a second step, become the object of critical interpretation (reflection).

Such interpretation, however, does not float in thin air. It is always already grounded in the practical understanding of the situation one is reflecting upon. This led Martin Heidegger (1996) to stipulate—amply supported in later research (e.g., Garfinkel, 1967)—that such reflection is *existentially* based in primary understanding rather than the other way around. Reflection, however, is not *acknowledgment* of primary understanding but constitutes a development of

177

possibilities that already exist in primary understanding and its rendering in the language of auto/biography and auto/ethnography. That is, through reflection teachers appropriate what they already understood in practice but in an expli-cated way.

It is easy to confuse different levels of experience—teaching and reflection of teaching in the present case. Whether or not the two are related is a matter of empirical inquiry and cannot be taken to exist a priori. Here is why. During teaching, teachers use language to get their job done. This language is their pri-mary tool for practical pedagogy. It is their tool in and through which pedagogy is enacted. When teachers reflect, however, their objective is a different one. Now they want to explicate what they have been doing. The language they use now is *for the purpose of explication* it is *about* teaching. For the sake of this discussion, we can think of this language as a secondary artifact (Wartofsky, 1979), a tool for reflecting the use of the primary tools, here again language. What makes the situation difficult for practitioners and researchers alike is the partial overlap of the (primary) language used in the practice of teaching and the (secondary) language used in reflecting *about* teaching.

Kenneth Tobin writes about his experience as a teacher in the process of development—despite a thirty-five-year history as a teacher. Tobin shows that auto/biography does not have to be heroic. Quite the contrary is the case. Throughout his compelling piece, we see a teacher who, despite his long experi-ence and success in different educational settings, experiences frustrations, set backs, and failure. Tobin also shows us a different side of what it means to teach "methods" to students in the academy and engaging in teaching in the very situations that you want your preservice teachers to learn in. Margery Osborne uses her experience of teaching children about optics to reflect on our (the teachers') perceptions of children. As the children observe the world (light) through lenses and mirrors, what they see are bent and reflected images, chang-ing the way we perceive what appeared to be a familiar world. Osborne suggests that the same happens when we observe children; our images of what children want may have little to do with what children want and need. Reflecting in this way on their daily work allows teachers to grow and, using their auto/biogra-phies as a method of representation, reflect on the changes they have undergone.

David Geelan writes about how reforms and innovations in education fre-quently meet with unanticipated resistance from students and teachers. Drawing on an experience, where he was involved in team-teaching science with a num-ber of teachers at the school who were not science specialists, he uses auto/biography to answer questions about the ways in which students, teachers, administrators and parents negotiate new sets of roles and expectations for schooling in such an innovative climate. In his use, auto/biography constitutes a way of understanding the interplay of the large number of institutional, social and personal factors acting in this very complex situation. He explores the ways in which auto/biography contributed to his understandings as these developed in the course of reflecting on his professional practice and that of his colleagues.

Judith McGonigal shows us not only how she used scientists' auto/biographies with the children in her care but also how auto/biography can help in constituting a new identity for herself and therefore for teachers. It is through accounting for what had happened to her, and reflecting on this account, that McGonigal personalizes and relativizes what change can mean in science teaching and science teacher education.

Auto/biography has an important place in allowing the Other to understand the respective Self. Sherry Nichols and Deborah Tippins have taken yet another turn in their approach to teacher education. Here, educators use auto/biography in a novel form, biomythography through photo essays, to help future teachers develop images of Self as science teacher.

References

Garfinkel, H. (1967). Studies in ethnomethodology. Englewood Cliffs, NJ: Prentice-Hall.
Heidegger, M. (1996). *Being and time* (J. Stambaugh, Trans.). Albany: State University of New York Press.
Wartofsky, M. (1979). *Models: Representations and scientific understanding*. Dordrecht, The Netherlands: Reidel.

9   Becoming an Urban Science Educator

Kenneth Tobin

I relocated to an inner city university because of my commitment to make a difference as an urban science educator. I believe the greatest need for educational change is in urban schools where science education invariably falls short of its potential for social transformation. It was time for me to address directly some of the more challenging and enduring problems in science education. I was fed up with studies that claimed to have resolved the equity issues in our major urban centers when it was patently clear to anyone who visited schools in those cities that problems were manifest and unresolved.

Initial Urban Experiences

Being in the city was radically different than anything I had experienced. For six months I lived in the suburbs and had a short commute to the university. I remember clearly my initial train rides. As we approached my destination the train became crowded with high school students headed for the nearby City High School (CHS). The students were unlike any I had taught or observed. All were African American and many were from conditions of relative poverty. As I listened to them interact in the crowded conditions of the train I could scarcely understand their dialects. I wondered then whether I'd ever be able to teach students like these. At my station I disembarked, walked along the platform, up a smelly and heavily littered stairwell, and into a dilapidated street just six blocks from my office. The strangeness of the environment was greater than I expected and was analogous to being in a new country with a distinctive culture. So much was novel. But I was no tourist. I lived and worked here.

My sense making was saturated with deficiencies as I compared this with other places in which I had lived. Even though I chose to come to this urban community to practice science education I perceived the environment and its inhabitants through jaundiced eyes and seemed to notice the squalor, disrepair, dirt, trash, neglect, and signs of poverty. To be here was different to such an extent that my life experiences and professional praxis were out of alignment with my expectations and capacity to cope successfully.

Learning to Cope

"You've gotta develop an attitude." Once more I was on a train, this time in New York City, and a young woman was advising me about riding the trains and walking the streets. I was accomplished in neither of these activities and I was explaining to her that my presence in the streets of Philadelphia was too interactive. I needed to build a way of being that acknowledged others and did not engage them overtly. I knew what she meant about having an attitude but decided that a useful goal was for me to better understand city neighborhoods. I was now living in the city and decided to walk to my office, a four-mile hike that allowed me to traverse a variety of neighborhoods en route to the university. In addition, I began an urban ethnography in which I explored local neighborhoods every Saturday and Sunday morning.

I felt heroic in those days and was very conscious of the unusual nature of what I was doing and the associated risks. Being in the streets revealed just how much I had to learn. I could see no alternative than to gain first hand experience and knowledge of neighborhoods like those of the students I was to teach. Usually I did not feel comfortable and I was alert for possible dangers that might await me. My tendency to feel heroic was potentially problematic, because romanticizing events with me as hero and urban inhabitants as victims could distance me from those I sought to educate. However, over time I learned to feel at ease in being in the streets, interacting with others, navigating my neighborhood, and walking to different parts of the city. I began to fit with the environment and no longer felt separate, like a stranger giving meaning to all that happens. The strange was becoming familiar and I could make sense of the smells, sounds, and sights of my urban environment. I regard my learning to become streetwise as a necessary component of becoming an urban educator and I am certain I could not effectively teach in this community without first knowing what it means to live here.

Although I was learning a great deal about living in an urban community I was doing very little to learn about the teaching and learning of science in inner city schools. A growing concern was what to do in my science methods courses. Although I had lots of advice to offer my prospective teachers I was not all that confident that my knowledge was grounded either in good theory, research, or praxis. Most of my prospective teachers were struggling to enact much of anything I suggested and I began to wonder if it was their relative inexperience, the problems of finding suitable cooperating teachers, unteachable students, or the fallibility of my knowledge of what to suggest.

By just a few weeks into the fall semester of 1998 I realized that most of what I knew about science education was mainly applicable to middle class values and settings. Even though I had undertaken research in numerous countries my experience in all of them was essentially middle class. Furthermore, my teaching of science methods courses had focused on the teaching of middle class students in suburban-like schools. What I had to do was very clear. I had to learn to teach science in urban schools where most students were African American, living in conditions of relative poverty. Otherwise my teaching about science teaching would amount to little more than empty exhortations. I resolved to begin a program of science teaching at CHS, beginning with the most challenging group of students in the school. I declared that I would teach at the school for at least four years so that I would not be regarded as a researcher undertaking a short-term study; leaving an unchanged system after attaining my goals.

City High School

My first visit to CHS, where I am presently teaching, also involved deficit seeing. CHS is nothing like the high schools I have experienced in Perth, Tallahassee, or even in a big city like Miami. It is an urban high school with an enrolment of more than 2,000 students, 98 percent of whom are African American and from conditions of poverty. Just like the city, my initial impressions of the school were negative. My tendency was to notice the undesirable features of what was there and those missing features that would in my opinion have enhanced the school. As I walked on the pavement alongside CHS I was reminded of a prison by the expansive brick and concrete wall, just a few barred windows, and a heavy metal door at the front of the school. The building was not an architectural masterpiece and from my perspective it was welcoming neither to students nor to faculty.

I am not sure when the switch in my perceptions of the school occurred or what catalyzed the change. However, now I look forward to going to the school and as I enter the building I admire the ceramic murals and other decorative contributions of graduating seniors. Learning to regard a school as more than bricks, cement and metal bars requires a perspective of a school as a social organization, a perspective that evolved as I became part of the school community.

The school district adheres to a policy of creating *small learning communities* (SLCs) within each school. The idea is to allow students to experience a small school and to thereby create a feeling of family, belonging, school loyalty and shared values. At CHS the ten SLCs each contain approximately 200 students. Students can select an SLC according to their career or academic goals. However, not all students choose the SLC in which they will spend their high school lives. Some fail to meet the entry requirements and others are unable to maintain satisfactory performance levels. In these circumstances they are assigned to an SLC.

My teaching took place in an SLC known as *Opportunity*. The school bulletin lists *Opportunity* as "an academic and resource program to assist students who need to acquire additional academic credits because of extended absences or other extenuating circumstances. These credits will enable the students to achieve appropriate grade level or graduation requirements." However, the description in the bulletin is at odds with the perspectives of most students in *Opportunity*. Tyrone, a ninth grade student, told me that "*Opportunity* is the bottom of the trash can." Tyrone also thought that the change to a block schedule, with its longer periods, resulted in a great deal more time being wasted in each of the class periods. He emphasized that "I don't like it because what they are teaching me is too easy. I'm finished in about twenty minutes and sitting there for about fifty-five minutes doing nothing." Tyrone also was riled because he wanted to listen to music on his Walkman when he finished his work. He insisted that others could not hear the music and would not be disrupted.

This Kid is Trouble

The first time I set my eyes on Tyrone I had an instinct to back off. He did not look like the type of person I would want to mix with. His dreadlocks were arranged asymmetrically, his clothes looked like battle fatigues, and his broken front tooth gave him an appearance of a fighter. I was with Spiegel[1] in the main office. "That kid gets in trouble because people are afraid of him. He looks bad so they just get him out as soon as they can." Spiegel's words echoed my thoughts. Tyrone was headed toward the main office. Following some distance behind him was an angry male teacher who began to raise his voice as soon as he reached the office door. "What's the problem Tyrone?" Spiegel spoke quietly as Tyrone passed by. "He's suspending me because I went to get my coat." Tyrone replied softly. His response had credibility but events moved too quickly to learn more. The raised voice of the teacher became a shout and an assistant principal also began to berate Tyrone for his defiance. Within minutes a stream of colorful language flowed from Tyrone's mouth as he was ushered into the assistant principal's office. "They just don't know how to handle kids like Tyrone," said Spiegel with a resigned shrug of his shoulders.

Enforced Absence

Tyrone felt that teachers and NTAs[2] stereotyped most males as thugs and used that as a basis for suspending them from school. He explained to me that his long running battle with the NTAs resulted in him being absent so often that he was now repeating grade nine for the third time. I regard Tyrone as an enigma. He is very intelligent, wants to work hard, and succeed. But at the same time he has a spirit that will not be suppressed. He will not allow others in authority to dominate him and he does not condone duplicity when he sees it. Although some might describe him as being smart mouthed, Tyrone regards himself as principled. If an NTA calls him a bastard he will reciprocate with similar or even more profane language. His inability to "let it go" has cost him dearly with those in authority and he is continually getting suspended. Because of his appearance he is accosted frequently by NTAs and teachers and, because of his enduring spirit, his reactions are such that he earns suspensions of five days routinely. These absences soon sum to another failed semester.

On the Way to the Forum

I invited Tyrone to participate in a pre-session at Penn's Ethnography Forum. He agreed to participate and I came to the school to walk with him to the session. I located Tyrone in the lunchroom where he was speaking with a friend. He indicated that he would join me downstairs in the science lab in five minutes. At the designated time Tyrone arrived, but as we were about to leave Cowan (an NTA) burst into the room. "You and I have business," he shouted motioning Tyrone into the hallway. Although I felt outraged by the event, I waited for Tyrone to return, but to no avail. He was suspended for five days for "dwelling too long on the second floor" and was ushered from the school building. Tyrone later told me what happened. As he walked down the stairs to meet with me, as we had arranged, Cowan called on him to stop. Without explanation Cowan demanded his identity card, effectively suspending him until the card was returned. In this instance Tyrone was stopped because Cowan expected that he was breaking a school rule. Tyrone would have none of it and walked away to keep his appointment with me. When Tyrone was taken into the hallway to discuss the dwelling charge and subsequent walk off his reaction to Cowan's aggression involved his use of profane language and an automatic five-day suspension. Needless to say Tyrone did not make it to the Forum and it took an intervention from me to have his suspension lifted after three days.

Because I have developed a close relationship with Tyrone it is easy to see how Cowan in this and other instances has catalyzed problems based on his preconception that Tyrone is a troublemaker who needs to be controlled proactively. However, I can appreciate another side of this issue because I have been a beneficiary of proactive intervention from an NTA.

Proactive Intervention

My least successful activities are those in which I address the entire class. Invariably someone begins a conversation that is sufficiently loud to be a source of distraction to other students and me. This is a basic classroom management issue. But what is the best way to enforce silence when I am speaking? On this occasion I was speaking to Dante about his annoying habit of speaking loudly to a peer whenever I spoke to the class. I believe that Dante was testing me and I was aggravated by his increasing tendency to be disruptive. However, my making his behavior an issue gave him a public forum to impress his peers.
Dante looked at me with disdain and commenced a rebuttal, "You speaking so loud I have to . . ."

"Choose you next words carefully." The softly spoken voice of an NTA stopped Dante dead in his tracks.

"My bad," Dante said immediately.

The tall young African American NTA smiled reassuringly at me and left the class without another word. Unnecessary conflict was resolved before it began. If the NTA had not arrived at the most opportune of times I would have had a serious problem on my hands. I would have had to deal with Dante's verbal onslaught. I am certain that he would not have complied with any request I made of him following his anticipated outburst. I had made a serious error of judgment by raising the issue at that time and I was moments away from possible humiliation.

Refusal to Comply

One thing I learned from Tyrone is never to ask these students to do something if you cannot deal with the consequences of them refusing to do what is requested. What could I have done with Dante? Students like him are not afraid of the law and do not respect authority. Hence, threatening detention is no deterrent as most refuse to attend. In fact, if a student fails to attend a detention, s/he is suspended for five days. These students are not only unafraid of being suspended; many relish the thought of having a reason not to come to school and to stay at home or in the streets. If an optimal learning environment is to be established it is important to build a community that is self-regulating. In such a community the participants want to learn, and trust and have respect for one another. The students can develop the rules and the custom of adhering to them, not breaking them.

Why Make this the Line in the Sand?

"Dr. Tobin this is marvelous. What are we doing here?" The principal entered the room and was focused on three roof to floor length pendulums, two the same length, and one slightly shorter. The three were connected close to the roof by looping them over a long dowel rod. Three students were exploring resonance. "It's not going as well as it might look," I remarked as she entered the room. Fifteen students were present and only five of them were engaged in productive activity. Furthermore, the noise level was unacceptable to me and I was trying to get it down as she entered the classroom.

The principal looked around the class and noticed Clarence wearing his cap reversed. Although Clarence was working, the principal managed to catch his eye and pointed to her head with her forefinger. Clarence continued to work, shaking his head ever so perceptibly, but with resolve. "Young man. Give me the cap. I'll give it back." The principal moved toward Clarence who once again shook his head ever so slightly. At this stage I felt decidedly aggravated. There was going to be trouble here. So far the principal had broken two of the cardinal rules Tyrone has taught me. She chose to make an issue of something trivial and in so doing interrupted one of the few students who was working. Also, she made a request without thinking through whether she could deal with the consequences of Clarence not doing as she asked. I groaned inwardly. "Outside young man!" The principal raised her voice and the stakes. Clarence once again shook his head and continued to work. The principal strode into the hallway and Clarence continued to work.

"You need to go see the principal man. Don't make this into a bigger problem than it has to be." Clarence looked at me in stunned silence. Betrayal! He slammed his chair back and walked defiantly from the room, his cap still on his head. The principal began to scold him as soon as he reached the door, but Clarence would have none of it. He continued to walk past the principal and had to be apprehended by an NTA.

Teaching Science at CHS

When I spoke to Spiegel about coteaching we agreed to focus the curriculum on a form of science that would be relevant to the students and had the potential to transform aspects of their lives. I had in mind investigations focused on the students' neighborhoods, somewhat akin to the science that my colleague Angela Calabrese Barton (see Chapter 2) undertook with students from a homeless shelter. I thought of this as street science and envisioned the students mainly learning science outside of the classroom. When I discussed the focus of the curriculum with the principal of CHS she was not enthusiastic and viewed my suggestions as examples of low expectations and stereotyping. "Will it prepare these young people for higher studies in chemistry? If your students wanted to study more science they would be disadvantaged." The principal was resolved and I did not want this to be the issue that prevented me from teaching in *Opportunity*. Accordingly, I agreed to teach a half-unit on chemistry followed by a half-unit on physics.

Getting Started

My initial chemistry activities involved as much hands-on activity as possible. I wanted the students to associate science with doing. However, many students did not enjoy doing science and preferred to sleep, not participate, or talk socially with their peers. Most would not wear safety glasses and if I insisted they would not participate. Also, with few exceptions, the students would not persist with an activity beyond the first day.

The first activity on chromatography involved the students in separating the colors from marker pens. For the remainder of the week I wanted them to use a range of solvents to separate out colors in M&Ms, lipstick, and other types of pen. The students complained that the activities were boring and that we had done this yesterday! Similarly students refused to continue into a second and third day their investigations of chemical reactions between soluble salts (involving temperature changes, color changes and precipitates). The students wanted fresh activities that were interesting to them and did not develop a curiosity about the chemistry associated with their experiences. It did not appear as if they were able to generate open-ended questions and certainly they did not regard questions as springboards for scientific inquiry and hands-on investigations. In fact, when I asked questions designed to stimulate inquiry the students answered them using as few words as possible.

Relevance of the Enacted Curriculum

Every day I questioned the relevance of the science I was teaching the students in *Opportunity*. Sometimes they questioned it too. During an initial discussion of Newton's second law of motion an announcement from the principal interrupted the lesson to provide details about the Stanford-9 testing that was to occur later in the week. One of the students seized the opportunity to declare that he had taken the SAT-9 three times and there never had been a question on Newton's laws. Several peers, who joined him to challenge the relevance of studying Newton, force, and motion, received his assertion enthusiastically.

A second example arose the next day when we looked at the physics of delivering a fastball in baseball. One of the less involved students suddenly showed interest and asked how it was possible to hit a fast pitch for a home run. I decided that the next day students would read a short piece on everyday applications of Newton's second law and respond to questions in writing. The idea was intended to address several goals. First, the students did not appear to learn from oral description of applications or from demonstrations. Second, when students were given questions to respond to in writing they tended to answer in as few words as possible. Third, students had little persistence in answering extended response questions and were easily distracted.

As the students entered the room I handed them a single page to read. The gist of the science was that Newton's second law could be re-organized to show that force times time is equal to mass times velocity. The implications of losing momentum in a short time interval were described in terms of punches in boxing, hits in football, collisions involving automobiles, motorcyclists and cyclists, use of seatbelts and safety, uses of helmets in various sports, and the design of running shoes. Although this list does not reflect my concerns about sex equity, I did endeavor to include examples that would appeal to males and females. The reading concluded with five questions that required the equation $F \cdot t = m \cdot v$ to be applied qualitatively to a variety of everyday experiences.

As is customary in the class there were numerous students who refused to engage from the beginning of the lesson. I planned to begin with $f = m \cdot a$, replace "a" with "v/t" and then use algebra to arrive at the appropriate form of the equation. Then, in a discussion, we would apply the equation to selected examples from the everyday lives of students. I began with baseball since we explored this the day before when we also debated how auto design could minimize the impact force on passengers during a collision. A very small number of students (two of twenty, both females) showed intense interest, responded to my questions, and nodded their heads at my explanations. However, from the outset, most students were disinterested and only too willing to be distracted at the slightest opportunity. Having fully applied the concepts in several contexts and placed the key points on the chalkboard I asked the students to read the brief description and respond to the questions.

The initial problem for those who appeared willing to participate was that they did not know what to do. Because the questions were embedded in the text they could not identify them easily or discern how many were to be answered. I responded proactively by calling to the attention of all students the location of each question. Unfortunately, few students were attentive and I had to interact with each individual. As I did this I took care to explain that each question was an opportunity to show how science can be applied. I wanted students to understand that each question could be answered by applying several interconnected ideas and that short answers may not provide a complete response to a question.

With twenty minutes remaining in the lesson I decided to have a discussion of answers to the questions. The first question asked whether laws should require boxers to wear gloves having a greater mass than eight ounces. I then wrote an extensive answer to the question on the board so that the students had a model of how ten points could be distributed for the response. Less than five students copied my response despite the fact that I had informed them that questions like this would be on their tests. As I worked through each question I searched for ways to involve students. However, even though almost an hour was allocated to consider and respond to the questions there were few students who attempted to answer them and were motivated or prepared to contribute.

When I dismissed the students, I had an empty feeling in my stomach. Who had benefited from the last seventy-five minutes? As I looked across to Spiegel he shrugged his shoulders. "I am fed up with this group," he said. My sentiments, exactly. But I did not share my reservations with him. "We have got to get to these students," I said with fierce determination. "We cannot give up!"

I Took them Outside

I was very apprehensive about taking the students outside. For the most part they were unruly even when I took them down to the computer lab. Taking them into the streets seemed to be an invitation for trouble. Yet, I was a firm believer in doing science out of doors if that were possible. Accordingly, I decided to enact a series of outdoor activities.

We had been doing sound for some time and the students were not as engaged as I had hoped. The unit on music was not the success I expected it to be and the students were seemingly bored. We had used a slinky to show longitudinal and transverse waves and also had discussed the difference between standing and traveling waves. The students had seen resonance in open and closed pipes and it seemed appropriate to discuss the velocity of sound waves and also to discuss other properties of sound waves such as reflection. We then discussed reverberation, echoes, and ways to measure the velocity of sound.

The students contributed very little to the plan to measure the velocity of sound, although they certainly had the ability to work out a suitable design. Instead, in an interactive way, I led a discussion by explaining what we would do and asking students questions to solicit as much involvement from them as possible. Soon we had the design worked out. I found two large pieces of pine to strike together at one-second intervals to create a loud "clap."

The few students in attendance were quite docile. I demonstrated echoes by hitting the wood together some fifty to sixty feet from a school wall. The echoes were discernible but not discrete because there were so many walls in the vicinity. Then we went to a quiet side street that was flat. I asked for volunteers to move away from Spiegel who had agreed to clap the pieces of wood. Only Tyrone volunteered to walk with me down the street until we were far enough away for the sound to take a half-second to reach us. The rest of the students preferred to watch from a distance and crowded under a tree.

When we returned to the classroom I was reminded of the low level of mathematical competence of most of these students. The distance traveled by sound in a half second was 171 meters and none of the students was able to calculate the velocity, or at least have an intuitive idea of what it was. Accordingly, I showed them how to use the data to calculate the velocity. Then, so that they could show what they learned about the velocity of sound, echoes, and reverberation, I asked them to write a narrative, draw an illustration, or prepare a poster to hang from the ceiling. Although several students commenced the activity, when the folders were submitted at the end of the semester, only a few included their efforts and none had completed the task.

An interesting irony about the outside fieldtrip is that my fears of losing students could not have been further from what happened. We left the building with eleven students and returned with thirteen having picked up two who were late and otherwise unable to enter the building.

Persistent Problems

Sporadic Attendance

I did not satisfactorily contend with the students' sporadic attendance at school. Only a small proportion of the students in my class at any given time was there the day before or the day after. Hence it is difficult to identify issues that are relevant to those in attendance. Since I cannot easily predict who will be present on any given day the enacted curriculum tended to be planned to keep moving forward. The average level of absenteeism in my class was approximately 40 percent with a range from close to zero to almost one hundred percent absent. Out of a class of thirty-five students only fifteen might be present on a given day. Of those fewer than three would be in the class at the official start time of 8:15 A.M. and even twenty minutes into the class students would be straggling in. Of those who did come, none would have their materials out ready to begin work and many brought neither paper nor writing tools to class.

I regard it as a high priority to plan for sporadic attendance and late arrival. It is all very well to declare this as a symptom of a dysfunctional school, but it is quite another matter to cope with the consequences day after day. One way to address this problem is to have an individualized program that students can access automatically when they arrive in class. If the system includes all assignments and handouts the students who have missed class can be held responsible for their own progress. The use of computer and Internet technology might provide convenient access to assignments from remote locations such as home, public libraries and computer laboratories.

Sleeping Students

As many as six or seven students would come into class and put their heads down to go to sleep. What should I do about sleeping students? I can put them outside but then someone else has to deal with the problem. I can give them a detention, or I can suspend them. None of these possible solutions has more than momentary appeal. Perhaps I could set up my own detentions; however, this has not been an option because I am only at the school for three hours a day. There are many reasons for students sleeping in class. Punishing them for sleeping or having their heads down does not take into account the reasons for their actions. We need to better understand why students have their heads down and address the problems rather than continually deal with the symptoms. Not only that, I prefer to establish a system whereby students accept responsibility for their own actions, including their need for sleep and their use of class time. I would like to see them as autonomous, including their acceptance of responsibility for participating in class, completing assignments, and learning at acceptable levels.

Failure to do Homework

Getting students to do their homework was a problem for me because I was the only teacher in *Opportunity* who set homework and expected it to be done. A minority of the students did their homework, but peer pressure reduced the numbers and also made those who had done it reluctant to go public. Should I go over homework when students have not attempted it? Should I ask students who were here yesterday to complete the homework while I re-teach yesterday's lesson for those who were absent? What about students who are absent for several consecutive days? Should each student have an individualized program? I decided for the future that an individualized approach might be planned and enacted in such a way as to address many of the problems I encountered.

Not having a suitable textbook to take home until midway through the semester limited the types of activity I could set for homework. When we finally got a textbook it was more than twenty years old and unsuitable for many reasons that included the content having little relevance to current times and a failure to include minorities and females in substantive ways in texts and pictures. Also, for many students the conceptual difficulty and reading level were too high. The fact that there were few books in their homes and my students being unwilling to access books from public and school libraries exacerbated this problem.

Signs of Progress

Reggie looked stern as he walked directly toward me. I noticed his bandaged left hand and thought about the stories of him slugging the officer who had pulled him over during a car chase earlier this week. I didn't flinch as his right fist brushed against my jaw. He broke into a broad smile as he grabbed at my gut. "You outta shape man!" He gave me a hi-five and continued down the hallway. Reggie was back in school and five months ago this incident could never have happened. Students were beginning to acknowledge my existence.

Options to Consider

Teach Those Who Want to Learn

Some of the conventional wisdom of teaching does not appear to work well with these students, at this time. For example, monitoring of the students while they work is sometimes constructed as "being in their faces." I had developed the habit of moving around the class, getting to see what each person is doing, looking at his/her work, and as necessary providing scaffolding to facilitate the learning of individuals and groups. Also, if students appear to be unsettled I often will stand close to them to encourage their participation by my proximity. Students often show their displeasure with me roaming from group to group and will exclaim: "Back off man! Get out of my face." When Tyrone observed my teaching on videotapes he also advised me to "Back off. Only teach them when they want to be taught." I have taken this advice seriously and now approach most students only when I am invited.

Tyrone's advice to teach only those who want to be taught is also a potential way out of the relative failure of whole class lecturing. When a whole class presentation is seen as desirable it might be that those who are interested in learning can be invited to a part of the classroom where a focused presentation can be given to these students. Students who elect not to participate can be offered an alternative activity such as copying notes or reading and responding to questions. Providing students with alternative ways of participating is an approach that has potential. I will ensure that at any time students have the option of doing what they are good at doing and can pursue their interests. For example, all students seem to know how to read[3] and answer questions from the book. As sad as it may seem, allowing them to read and write science is one way to increase the rate at which students participate and presumably learn. Let them start from what they can do and over time, when they learn how to participate consistently, then they can learn new ways to participate.

I have now changed the focus of my attention from the whole class to individuals. I endeavor to recruit one student at a time to join a community of learners in which science activities are constructed around the interests and values of the students and what they can do. For example, in a lesson on motion the students were building and racing balloon-powered cars. Thirteen students were present, seven were seemingly asleep and, of the six awake, four were participating. When I began five months ago my efforts would have been directed toward getting the seven sleeping students awake and involved. Now I realize that my efforts are better spent teaching the four participants. Facilitating those who want to learn has become my goal as I endeavor to build a community of learners. As for those who are not participating? That is their decision. The door is always open if they take the initial step to get started. Of course, I do not abandon them and still make invitational overtures to them to get involved. However, I do not let that be my principal goal, as it was when I first started. It is better to focus my energy on those who will participate and want to learn than to antagonize those who are determined to resist and disrupt the learning of others.

Enact Multiple Activities in Each Lesson

For each lesson I now think in terms of multiple ten- to fifteen-minute activities in which students participate. Creating variety through the use of short activities separated by well-managed transitions appeals as a possible way to increase student participation and achievement. In my classes I soon realized that students needed to learn to concentrate and sustain their participation. I was unsuccessful in implementing anything close to six activities in a ninety-minute lesson, but I regarded the inclusion of short, varied and interesting activities as a way to address the goal of having students learn to learn.

Encourage Alternative Ways of Participating

Creating a management system to allow me to focus my efforts on students who want to learn makes a lot of sense. In *Opportunity* my biggest challenge is to effectively deal with those who are unwilling or unmotivated to learn on a particular day. Rather than placing the onus on me to get students to participate, I would prefer to allow them to choose to participate in alternative ways. If alternative activities are available and the students have the responsibility for all assignments there is merit in providing them with autonomy and the associated responsibility. In addition, I recommend an opt-out alternative that students can select occasionally, perhaps to a limit of five times per semester (still with the proviso that all assignments are their responsibility). The opt-out activity could involve participation in non-science activities of the students' choosing as long as the activities do not disrupt others in the class.

Setting up a Portfolio System

The students rarely bring notebooks or pens to class. If they have them, they don't get them out. Dealing with this problem every day suggests that something proactive needs to be done. I envision each class having color-coded folders in which students place their notebooks (paper) and pens for science. Their folder would be stacked on a shelf with the students' names prominently displayed on the spine.

Having such a system will solve numerous problems. All assignments can be placed in the folders and students can have the responsibility to complete them even when they are absent (in which case they complete them when they return to school). Completed class work and homework also can be left in the classroom portfolio. This system will provide me with access to student work and allow me to provide them with regular feedback.

Involve Others to Support Learning

To the extent possible parents, siblings, guardians and persons from the community can be involved in supporting learning. Many of the students in my class have jobs and need to earn money to support themselves and their families. Some need to support their own children. However, as Tyrone pointed out to me, "a lot of people from around my way dropped out of school. Now they see the value of education and make sure I go to school." He also pointed out how influential his brother is in keeping him at school. His brother is incarcerated but has been educated while in jail and is insistent that Tyrone go to school, attend class regularly, and make an effort to learn. It was my experience that every time I contacted a parent/guardian I made progress in getting a student better focused on learning. It is easy to assume that the parents or guardians are not interested in the education of the students for whom they have responsibility. Such an assumption is another example of the seriousness of negative stereotypes that eventually inhibit the learning of students such as those in *Opportunity*.

Searching Backward while Looking Forward

Since I began teaching the students from *Opportunity* I have done whatever I can to increase the quality of participation and learning. When I took over the class I endeavored to teach chemistry in ways that were engaging. It did not take me long to notice that the students resisted any efforts on my part to enact a curriculum that was inquiry-oriented and focused on the attainment of goals like those included in the School District's standards. For more than five months almost every effort of mine was unsuccessful in promoting the meaningful learning of science for most of my students. I now realize that there is little difference between what I was able to accomplish as I enacted the curriculum and what Spiegel achieved during my observations of his class prior to beginning my teaching. Just as I had a jaundiced view of Spiegel's teaching, I am certain that any observer of my teaching would conclude that my expectations for participation and achievement are too low and that these are the primary causes of the problems I experienced. However, such judgments would be harsh and do not take account of my goals and the difficulties of attaining them with these students.

Had I not had the experience of teaching these urban high school students my advice to prospective teachers encountering problems such as those I have experienced would have been to enact problem centered learning, emphasize inquiry and hands-on activities and, to the extent feasible, participate in field trips.

Certainly I would have advocated small group work and minimized activities associated with reading and answering questions from a text. I would have encouraged the students to connect their science activities to technology and the lifeworlds of their students and I would have expected all of my suggestions to work. Failure would have been interpreted as an inability of prospective teachers to teach appropriately. However, for more than five months I floundered. Every day I enacted activities that I expected to be successful, but they fell short of my expectations and eluded the students' interests. It is imperative that I communicate these findings to student teachers because they should not feel that the research and theory they read necessarily applies in all contexts. It is critical that prospective teachers understand the significance of elements of social class (especially poverty) and ethnic diversity as factors that will shape enacted curricula, the participation of students, and what teachers can accomplish.

My decision to begin with more orthodox forms of science was a setback to the enacted curriculum because I never could actually connect with the students' interests and performance capabilities. The initial activity on chromatography captured the students' interests because of its novelty. But students had no interest in follow-up activities, possibly because the topic was imposed on them. It would have been preferable if I had found out about their interests and built a science curriculum around them. Not only that, getting the students involved in selecting what to study would have been good pedagogy and a demonstration of my trust in them.

Science as I knew it and had experienced it in schools, did not seem to have a place at this time for these students. No matter how I restructured my ideas about what should work or interest them, the few successes were at best short term and were limited to just a few students. It was not as if I didn't ask students about their interests, how to improve the class, and what they wanted to get from the course. Questions associated with these issues were asked of students frequently and I tried to learn from their responses. However, I was not able to discern any promising starting points from the students' suggestions and interests. Instead I enacted a litany of activities that fell short of my expectations and their interests. It is possible that my lack of experience with these students prevented me from hearing their interests and translating them into science activities.

I wondered about the extent to which the institution of public schools was a problem when I read a draft of a chapter written by Deborah Stern in which she described a curriculum oriented toward social justice at a small alternative school for high school dropouts. Her description of inner city public high schools as over crowded and over regulated institutions where students are largely invisible is consistent with my experiences at CHS. Despite the schools-within-a-school policy that led to the development of heavily tracked small learning communities like *Opportunity*, the students at CHS do not participate in curricula that are emancipatory and socially transformative. Stern's students examined issues of social justice using resources such as newspaper articles about people like them, issues that arose in gangs, crime, court decisions, jail, and life and death in urban communities. Her students could relate to such issues.

What are comparable topics in science? I have searched for doorways into the lives of these students; doorways to connect what they do at school and how students live their lives. What Barton and Darkside have done in New York City is most impressive, and I have endeavored to learn from their valiant efforts to break from the mould (see Chapter 2). Their redefinition of science has enormous potential for us to connect social justice, science and the students' lives. But they have accomplished very impressive results outside of a traditional framework of public schools. Whereas Barton can work with volunteers I teach students who have been assigned to the low track and are required to be at school. It remains to be seen whether or not I can redefine science and elicit comparable levels of cooperation from students like those in *Opportunity*.

Whatever we try in *Opportunity* fits within a framework of other activities that are undertaken in the school. These students have to learn to learn. Yet there is irony in me making that statement. They are streetwise and have survived in very difficult circumstances. Of course students from *Opportunity* know how to learn. What they are not good at doing is joining in small group conversations and learning from the conversations of others. This too is nonsense! The most formidable challenges I had in *Opportunity* involved some of these students when they embarked on tirades to justify a perspective or course of action. The students are extremely articulate and they interact in their dialect at a speed that is overwhelming when the conversation involves a topic that interests them. In terms of science the most vocal they ever got was when they refused to participate in street science activities on the several occasions I tried to get them involved and when they protested the relevance of studying Newton's laws. In fact during their protests about learning Newton's laws I stepped back in astonished admiration of how a group of previously sullen non-contributors could spring to life to display an awesome array of discursive resources on which the learning of science could build. No matter how hard I tried, I could not re-create occasions like those they produced with relative ease. I could not find doorways through which they could enter to participate in science. It could be the institution or, more than likely; it is just that I am not yet streetwise within the domain of *Opportunity*. I am still on a journey of learning to teach science to students like those I have described in this paper. Until I become streetwise there is a great deal of potential in those students that will remain invisible to me, even as I continue to see deficits. It is not that I am unwilling to see their potential to learn; it is that I am yet unable to see what is there for others to see and exploit to benefit the students.

For as long as I have been in teacher education I have emphasized the importance of building relationships with students and negotiating the right to teach them. I was adamant that students do not just bestow the right for people to teach them. All teachers must earn that right and that involves students constructing themselves as learners with respect to would-be teachers. What I did not understand was just how difficult it was to earn the trust and respect of these students. For several months I found many students ignored me when I spoke to them. Most did not respond to my questions or oral remarks and few initiated any approaches that could be construed as positive. Only now can I say with confidence that I am building rapport with a significant number of students. I regard rapport as a precursor to trust and respect—so there is a considerable distance yet to traverse.

Yesterday as I crossed the street to go to my office a student from *Opportunity* called from the car window: "Heh old head! How's it goin' man? There's my science teacher." I was delighted to see Reggie in the passenger's seat with his Dad. Both wanted to shake my hand. "You will be back this year won't you Tobin?" I nodded my head, my affirmation signifying more than just an answer to his question. For me this was a big occasion and I was proud. Reggie acknowledged his teacher in the street. For me there is no higher status than to be acknowledged as Reggie's science teacher. In terms of my becoming an urban science teacher, this is one of many milestones that are still to be passed.

Coda

Communicating what I learned from research on my teaching of science in an urban setting has involved me in writing and presenting numerous papers, some as sole author and others with co-authors (colleagues, coteachers, and students). Each of the papers emphasizes different themes and voices and is written in a different style. As I look back on the different ways of writing about research it is a propitious moment to consider the relative merits of each.

Auto/Biographical Writing

Writing this autobiographical paper was an emotional experience compared to writing in other genres in which affective state is relatively unimportant. I began to delve deeply into the troubled lives of some of the students I am teaching and explored their involvement in activities that included drug use and dealing, prostitution, crime, and violence. The prevalence of such issues caste a shadow over the transformative potential of science education. I wondered where social justice could fit in the curriculum and how it could intersect with science. Inevitably the focus returned to my own role and shortcomings as an urban science teacher. Influenced by my recent reading of an auto/biography of a runaway street kid (Lau, 1995), I began to see for the first time that I had failed to be a stable source of support for the learning of the students who needed me most. I realized that my middle class life and value system saturated what I considered to be rational decisions. As my auto/biography unfolded the emerging story line focused on my learning to teach in urban settings. Ironically, when I began the paper I was not conscious of this as a goal, let alone a focus for my writing. My purpose in doing the study in the first place was not to learn to teach science in urban settings but to find out how to teach science successfully in urban environments. There is a critical difference in these goals statements. I assumed I already knew how to teach science and it was just a question of adapting or applying what I knew to urban contexts. Doing the study and then writing it as auto/biography has deepened my sensitivity to the ontological differences between knowledge that can be spoken and written and knowledge that must be enacted. There is no doubt that my experiences at CHS were all about learning to teach urban students and had little to do with adapting existing knowledge.

Having created the desired focus for the paper I turned to issues of voice. Initially I was constrained by the conventions of interpretive research and a commitment to the use of verbatim transcripts as thick description, particularly when I was examining issues about teaching and learning. However, with encouragement from Michael Roth and Judith McGonigal, I focused on the genre of auto/biography and used my own words to tell a story that was consistent with the data. Once I had adjusted the voice to be consistent throughout the paper I gained a deeper appreciation of the significance of auto in auto/biography.

The writing of the paper made a significant difference to the way I think about my roles as teacher, teacher educator and writer. I believe the best way to learn to teach in given circumstances is, with the assistance of others from whom to learn, to teach in those circumstances. The fallibility of knowledge of teaching as it is written and spoken was never more evident to me than when I tried to apply what I knew in urban settings. Now I cannot imagine teaching a science methods course without having an active classroom in which to show what can be accomplished and associated field experiences in which prospective teachers can create their knowledge of teaching science by teaching science.

As a writer I have seen that auto/biography is a powerful way to connect to others having an interest in science teaching and learning. Possibly because of the emotional involvement of the reader with unfolding events there is more of a connection with the issues expressed in auto/biography than in other forms of my writing. The genre allows me to portray my perspectives on those issues from my praxis that I regard as having most salience to the larger domain of science education.

Metalogue and the Voice of Participants

An earlier paper (Tobin, Seiler, & Smith, 1999) was written with an experienced urban science teacher (Seiler) and a prospective teacher from my methods class (Smith). We used metalogue to allow each of us to participate in a conversation that retained our discrete voices on issues we regarded as critical to learning to teach in inner city schools. Bringing these differing perspectives into the foreground is vital in research in science education where, for too long, researchers have reported central tendencies and assertions built around the preponderance of evidence. Our style of writing allowed us to include assertions about which we agreed and personal perspectives that reflected our different roles and experiences as educators. The presence of multiple authors and voices allowed us to learn from one another in the writing and to communicate with readers in ways that would not be possible using auto/biography. In addition, my learning from writing the metalogues and subsequent writing set a stage for writing this auto/biography.

Another application of metalogue allowed me to highlight the student voice in a paper that focused on student resistance in urban science classes (Tobin, Seiler, & Walls, 1999). One of the authors, Edward Walls, was a student in two of my science classes. His candid perspectives and our associated discussions allowed us to learn much more about teaching science to low track students in an inner city high school than otherwise would have been possible. The inclusion of Walls as a researcher in the study allowed us to access and write about issues and perspectives that otherwise would have been beyond our reach.

Wolff-Michael Roth and I used metalogue to develop and explicate a perspective that knowledge of teaching is re-presented only while teaching (Roth & Tobin, 2002). The context was studies that we had undertaken separately, in which we were teacher-researchers. The interactions between the two of us were a significant resource for our own learning. From our respective studies we each prepared vignettes that were appropriate for writing a paper about coteaching as a vehicle for learning to teach. Then we identified several issues that were salient in the vignettes and took turns writing in a collaborative manner about each of them. In so doing we were able to explicate and elaborate our emerging theory through the contexts portrayed in our selected vignettes. We both learned from the process and communicated to readers our understanding of teaching as praxis in a variety of practice settings. Those insights were a foundation for the rationale for this auto/biography. Initially I was privately resistant to the idea that my difficulties in teaching science to inner city students had anything to do with knowledge limitations. However, in working through the theoretical issues pertaining to the nature of knowledge of teaching and how to construct it I began to see that my ultimate success in teaching in *Opportunity* would depend on my learning to teach there. Hence, writing for publication, giving seminars to colleagues and teachers, and making presentations at national meetings all set a stage for writing and learning from an auto/biography.

. . . and Finally

Writing to learn is something we often hear in the context of literacy people advocating participation in writing activities for elementary and high school students. However, the phrase applies very aptly to me. Writing in research is not just for others. The process of writing a paper necessitates levels of analysis, interpretation and synthesis that do not occur for me unless I write. What is apparent as I enter a phase of my career when it is safe to deviate from traditional ways of writing, is that alternative writing genres not only allow researchers to present different aspects of what has been learned from research, but also facilitate additional learning for the researcher. In this context, and with an added reminder of the need for the use of multiple writing genres in research, I strongly recommend auto/biography as a way to learn from research and report what has been learned to readers.

Notes

This work was made possible in part by a grant from the Spencer Foundation. The authors are grateful for the assistance provided by Wolff-Michael Roth and Judith McGonigal for their incisive comments on successive versions of this paper. A previous, slightly different version was published as Tobin, K. (2000). Becoming an urban science educator. *Research in Science Education, 30*, 89–106.
[1] Spiegel is the regular teacher of the classes I taught for a five-month period on which this auto/biography is based.
[2] Non teaching assistants (NTAs) are male and female personnel who are hired to maintain order in a school. They keep unauthorized personnel from the school building and enforce rules and orderly conduct.

[3] Many students read well below grade level and it is important to have available in class a variety of appropriate texts that incorporate a range of reading levels.

References

Lau, E. (1995). *Runaway: Diary of a street kid.* Toronto: Coach House Press.

Roth, W-M., & Tobin, K. (2002). *At the elbow of another: Learning to teach by coteaching.* New York: Peter Lang.

Tobin, K., Seiler, G., & Smith, M. W. (1999). Educating Science Teachers for the Sociocultural Diversity of Urban Schools *Research in Science Education, 29,* 68–88.

Tobin, K., Seiler, G., & Walls, E. (1999). Reproduction of social class in the teaching and learning of science in urban high schools. *Research in Science Education, 29,* 171–187.

10   A Rose in a Mirror

Margery Osborne

The ancient Hindu philosophers expressed a definition of human nature by using the metaphor of the mirror. In the *Baghavad Gita*, there is a marvelous image of the soul which is said to be "the reflection of the rose in a glass." Like most religious philosophy, this one is concerned with the problems of death and consolation. The theory of immortality in this philosophy is expressed by saying that when death occurs, you take away the mirror—but the rose is still there. This image seems to me a very powerful one. It's not the same as the Christian idea of the soul, of course, but it emphasizes the thing I want to talk about, which is that you can't dissociate the person from the world he lives and functions in and that you can somehow measure the person by the degree of his involvement in that world. The soul is not contained *within* the body but outside, in the theatre of its commitments. (Hawkins, 1974, p. 51)

I wish to reflect on this idea of a person constructed in the "theatre of its commitments," that it is how we act, and act in the world outside of ourselves, that matters. I write, drawing on my own history in science, for I once was a crystallographer, and the imaging technologies in which I am presently involved, about how these are shaping the work I do with children and teachers in schools. The metaphor of the rose in a mirror is a particularly provocative one for me as it both connects with the science I used to do and presently do since both are intimately about optics. I wish to explore the metaphor and the meanings it invokes to talk of science and science education and their relationship to biography.

To do this I write first about some qualities of mirrors and lenses drawing on my own history as a scientist who thought and taught a lot about optics. I do this to make some points about the subject|object relationship in the doing of science and of research and finally as it concerns the enterprise of education. To this end, I describe two incidents from my participant research with preschool and first grade children. In this work I purposely tried to make the science we did reflect the science I did as a crystallographer. It is in this context that the children act and both stories are illustrative of what this environment was like. In the first story the children are looking at lenses and discussing the qualities of them and the things they are able to see as they gaze through them. This conversation echoes the qualities of lenses I describe in the abstract as an introduction to the story. In the second story I argue that the way I shape the classroom is in effect a lens through which we can view children. Again what we see through such a lens has the same qualities as the things the children and I talk about in the first story. Finally I return to the work of scientists and write about how there is a tension between the inward oriented and the outward directed facets of "doing science" that I experienced and that I try to shape my classrooms to reflect. I argue that thinking about a resolution between these may illuminate our understandings of science and scientists (including child scientists). But it does so in a way that is fundamentally problematic for understanding as a process suggests reflection on something in existence while science and both children and the people doing science do not just exist, they are in the process of doing things that are new, constructing the new in terms of their own identities and also in terms of the worlds they create.

Mirrors and Lenses

When looking at something we use tools to visualize it (even if we are just talking about our eyes). These lenses allow one to see certain things, sometimes at the expense of other things and the things that are seen are always distorted or displaced even if only by a little bit. Lenses also allow us to see things that we were not expecting, new stuff. They are tools constructed by the viewer to gaze at an object usually designed for a purpose but sometimes acting in unpredicted ways. They reflect qualities of the designer and qualities of the perceived task as much as of the thing observed. When I say "reflect," this is purposeful for under certain conditions lenses do reflect, if the angle is right or they are made of certain things or depending on lighting conditions, they reflect rather than transmit light. In which case what is seen is the viewer not the object to be looked at. Sometimes this is desired, easily recognizable but sometimes it can take us by surprise. We have all experienced the shock of thinking we are looking out a window at someone and realizing we are seeing ourselves reflected back instead.

There is a moment in this of disorientation and sometimes almost nausea and then we quickly avert our gaze and return to our lunch or whatever task we were involved in beforehand.

On the other hand there is a paradox here for although I can assert that the construction of the tools we use to see things reflect our perceptions of those things and our goals in looking and therefore reflect ourselves, to do this they have to mimic, complement, overlap the qualities of the object itself. This is what Luce Irigaray (1985) refers to in her metaphor of the speculum—the device used to look internally at a woman must be shaped like the vagina. In essence this is a projection of an image of the object that includes our beliefs about the nature of the object in the creation of the tool. The tool used to gaze at an object must complement, or mirror both the object and the subject in some fundamental ways. Such tools constructed for looking at another can be turned back to help us look at ourselves because they contain qualities of both subject and object. In *The Order of Things*, Michel Foucault (1973) muses on such ideas. In his discussion of Velasquez' painting "Las Meninas," he evokes the reciprocity of looking: we can look at the painting, and it in effect looks back at us. I argue a similar point; the act of looking at another should enable a heightened awareness of self, a self-reflexivity.

Understanding these aspects of visualization technologies suggests the relativity of the subject/object relationship and also tells us that what we see is dependent upon how we look. This is very different from the post-enlightenment science mythology that is often depicted as a search for truth using visualization techniques which reify a particular subject|object perspective. Recognizing the role of technology and the relative positionality of objectification is at the core of my current attempts to reconceptualize science and the roles of scientists and teachers (Barton & Osborne 2002; Osborne & Barton, 1999; Osborne & Brady, 2002). The science derivative from the use of visualization technologies does not appear to challenge such central tenets of science as an immutable subject object relationship. Many would argue that the core of post-enlightenment science is about seeing and about the objectification of the other. Looking *at* images is centrally about this. But it is not—in recognizing that those images are, at least in part, images of ourselves. To make an image that represents something that the creator feels is important involves developing an empathetic oneness with the object. Collapsing subject into object. It is that process, which is really a dialectic, which I wish to examine as well as its problematic aspects and to do this I will tell two stories.

The first story I tell is about teaching first and second graders about some qualities of the physics of optics and visualization. In their talk of the lenses I give them, the children play with the ideas of perspective, context and meaning and are also acting in the complex ways I describe scientists acting at the start of this chapter. There is much to be thought about in the things they notice about distortion, genesis and the content of the images they see.

Looking through Lenses with Children

This story is constructed from transcripts and videotapes of lessons I taught in a public school classroom in Michigan. In many ways the science I describe doing with children in my work is pragmatist in nature—it is driven by the children's purposes and personal orientations. This particular class is of first graders with about 80 percent from various countries around the world other than the United States. Four are English-as-Second-Language students. We have been studying plants for the past month or so, first by comparing a number of potted plants and then by growing our own bean seeds and grape hyacinth bulbs. We have been drawing our plants and learning the names of the various parts and discussing the things plants need to live and grow. Today I intend to have the children begin to track the growth of their bean seeds that have just sprouted. To this end I have given each a six-inch clear plastic ruler with beveled edges. I purposely chose these rulers for their optical qualities as well as for their use in measuring. The children immediately, as I hand them out, hold the rulers to their eyes and discover this.

Margery:	What are these things? What are these things that you are holding in the air?
Kids:	Rulers!
Margery:	What do you mean rulers?
Claire:	Measure things. . . .

The other children are yelling, "Rulers! Rulers!"

Margery:	What?
Claire:	Measure things. . . .
Cory:	What the. . .?
Claire:	It's the thing we measure with.
Yu:	Look at the rainbow.
Margery:	You measure with it. What do other people think? Is that what a ruler is, you measure with it?
Kojo:	Yeah!! If its bigger, if it grows bigger, or you can measure the carpeting, if you're gonna buy a new one.

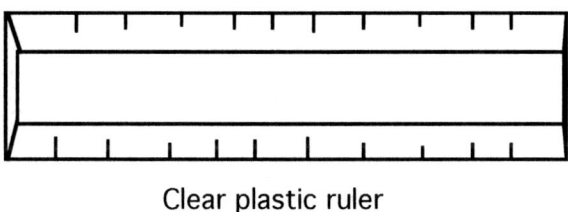

Clear plastic ruler

Figure 10.1

All the children are exclaiming about the things they see now so I ask, "Well if these rulers are for measuring how come people are looking through them? What did you see when you looked through them? What did you see Kyong Min?"

Kojo:	I see two Kyong Min's!
Claire:	I see her forehead.
Kyong Min:	I see Kojo and he had two heads [uses hands to indicate they were positioned one on top of the other]
Margery:	You were looking at Kojo and he had two heads one on top of the other? What do you see Claire?
Claire:	I see red and orange there.
Margery:	Why do you think they are orange? [Many kids are yelling, I see . . . I see . . .]
Claire:	I saw things that were orange and they were smeared.

Many children are talking. I hear things like: "I see two heads!" "Look at the lights;" "Its bigger;" "Its a rainbow;" "You're going up and down;" "Oh my god!" "Wow!" "You look weird!" "You're skinny;" "You're red." And they are also debating what they mean by words like skinny and smeared. I get their attention back again and get them all seated so we can talk. Chun So, a little Korean girl who rarely speaks is first.

Chun So:	I saw Farzoneh's face look so big. [Giggles.]
Margery:	You saw Farzoneh's face look so big? It made her face look big. Did other people see that?
Kids:	Yeah! Yeah!
Titon:	If you look here the floor will be like that [Points to lower facet of the ruler and points up when describing the placement of the floor].

Margery:	You look here, in the bottom?
Titon:	Yup.
Margery:	And the floor is ?
Titon:	Like this [Indicates on an incline].

In this discussion the children and I name the tools we are using as rulers but we are using them as lenses. This is something of an unexpected use or at least I had not expected them to find this use so immediately. As lenses the rulers have rather complex qualities. They act to image something in a different place from what is expected much like something seen in water appears in a different spot than predicted. They double things because there are actually three lenses at angles to each other and when held correctly some act as lenses and some as mirrors. They change the color of things because they act as prisms. They distort (smear) an image and they magnify. All this can have the effect of making us aware of the object, think harder about the object and think comparatively about what it really looks like. It is also possible to forget the reality of the object gazed at and to just look at the illusion and think it is real.

The next day we return to our discussion of the little rulers. I ask Mike to tell us what he was able to see.

Mike:	Double everything but when I looked at the carpet it looked like two sets of stairs.
Margery:	Yu what did you see?
Yu:	I see'd weird something [He gestures with his hands].
Margery:	Um hum, three of Tatiana?
Yu:	Um hum, and when I looked at the lights and the mirror I saw rainbows.
Bulli:	When I was looking through it on the floor, the man? [A visitor to the classroom that day.] He looked *so* big.
Chen:	Yeah!
Margery:	He is pretty big anyway though. Did he look like he reached up to the ceiling? [Many exclaim "Yeah!!!"]
V.J.:	I looked at Kojo and he went like this. [Makes wiggly hand motion.]
Margery:	Oh yeah so he's kind of distorted?
Tatiana:	I saw the desk tiny and the chairs tiny.
Claire:	Everything looked orange and smeared.

The conversation moves to a close with Cory telling us a silly joke and I move on to measuring the plants "I want you to look *at* the ruler not *through* the ruler. And think about what it looks like. In your group, I'm going to give you five minutes to do that."

I think in this last segment of the story two important things happen. The children discover the rainbow fringes that form around the objects they are looking at through the rulers and I tell them to look at the rulers (lenses) rather than through them. The rainbows become very important in a subsequent conversation a year after this incident as does remembering to look at the tools as well as just looking at the content of the image.

The next part of this story is constructed from transcripts of a class I taught in March the following year. This class was a first and second grade combination with six children returning from the previous year. The class I describe is the final class of a yearlong unit on soap bubbles and experimental design that I talk about at length elsewhere (Osborne, 1999). In this class we are discussing holograms as well as soap bubbles for we are going on a field trip to a local science museum that had just mounted a hologram exhibit. We start by examining examples on my credit cards.

I ask what they see when they look at the holograms on the cards. Abeni says that it is shiny and has rainbow colors. Tity says that it's silvery all over. Sueh-yen saw that it reflected light. He also saw that the bird changed shape as he moved it and the background reflected his face. I ask the kids if they had seen Star Wars and if they had an idea what a hologram was. Shumshad says that it looks real and it moves. Emily says that it's not real though.

We start to talk about where the different colors come from. The children say the light and I respond that the light doesn't appear to be different colors to me. Dan counters that yes the lights are different colors. He points to different lights in the room that are different levels of white. Emily says that the light sort of reflects itself to make colors. Thomas says that we could do an experiment with a prism, the light may not be different colors but the prism can show us. I ask him if he is saying that the white light can be many colors and he says that it can be the colors of the sun. I ask what are the colors of the sun and he starts to list: blue, purple . . . while different children agree and disagree, listing their versions of the colors of the spectrum. I ask Thomas if he is talking about a rainbow to which he says yes. He says that the white light can make the rainbow light and with a prism you might be able to see it.

The children are remaining very aware that they are talking about the lens itself rather than the image. They are reminding themselves of this by remembering that the images they see may look real but are not by thinking hard about the differences between the image and the object itself. This gets increasingly interesting as we proceed in this conversation because the children start to suggest theories for why they see the things they do. Sometimes these theories involve suggesting special properties of the object but equally as often the children seem to be musing on the properties of lenses.

I ask what other people think—how did the hologram get its colors. Paula says that on the hologram the colors come from the light reflecting on the silver pattern. Emily says that there is:

An invisible rainbow and it can go through our school roof and it can go through anything and when it touches that, that silvery piece it would shine 'cause you know how a rainbow is like this [makes are arc with her hands in the air] and a sun is right up here [points in the distance] and it moves around in a circle. It could reflect 'cause if they were on opposite sides, it could just go like that and it [the rainbow] would still go down.

I ask if the invisible rainbow comes from the sun or if it is always in the sky and we can't see it because the light goes through. "It's in the sky 'cause the light goes through," they respond. Danping disagrees. "I don't think there's such a thing as an invisible rainbow. I think on the credit card there's sort of like a plastic piece that's cut out like an eagle and they put some kinds of things on it and then when the light shines on it, it just comes out like a rainbow." But the light is white, I say. She responds, "I know but when the light shines on the plastic, I think they put something on the plastic to make it shine, so it makes it shine like a rainbow." The children's suggestions for the genesis of phenomena occur by pointing out associations. The causality is assumed. The mechanism or theory is overlaid on the top.

Now Shumshad agrees with Danping: "A little bit." He says if they cut out a piece that's silver and put some kind of "medicine or something that's kind of shiny and then they put a plastic piece on the card and then if you move it, it will go. " The children start debating the names of the colors again and whether or not the light from the sun is really white or yellow. Suni in particular seems to have been tutored by his father on this: "all the colors mixed, make the sunlight, make white light." I ask how the colors get out of the white light. He says that they separate but he doesn't know how they do that. Then he says that the sunlight isn't really white light but is yellow.

Cory says he agrees with Suni and reminds us of what we did last year with the rulers. How he looked up through the rulers and saw rainbows around everything. I let them try out the rulers. I ask what they see. Alyosha says that he saw a blue line under the thing that he was looking at. Danping says that now she disagrees with her idea from before "now I know how they make the rainbow, I think on the plastic, they just fold a little bit so if they fold over here and over here then these two will be different colors, if they didn't fold any, this whole piece of the bird (pictured in the hologram) would be a different color."

Sakti says that she saw different colors when she looked at the light. Meiying did also. Kwanhyo says that she saw a rainbow all across the room. Thomas says that he was disappointed because he didn't see as many colors as he usually does. He only saw red and blue. I say that they aren't very good prisms.

Suni declares that he has just figured something out. "If you put light through glass you can see the colors because glass makes the color of the light separate into other colors that are mixed to make that color, that's what I think glass does." Danping says glass needs to have corners to do that. Abeni claims that the thickness of the glass or plastic has something to do with it. I point out that the rulers aren't very fat. She says that different parts are fatter or thinner. Emily says that you see the colors only when you look through the places where the thickness changes. Tity says that you can see colors by looking through the edges too.

Sueh-yen points out that the rulers and the prism have three sides and he thinks this is important to make rainbows. Shumshad thinks that the reason he couldn't see a lot of colors with the rulers is because of "the little lines that measure." Emily says that if she crosses her eyes everything is outlined blue or sometimes yellow. This also makes it hard to see. Alyosha tell us about a rainbow he saw in Yugoslavia that happened after a rainstorm. He thinks that it is light shining through the water from the rain that makes the rainbow.

Cory saw a prism at his Grandmother's and she told him that if you don't keep it in the light, the rainbows might go away. He says that she said this because once she kept one out of the light too long and then when she did put it in the light there were no rainbows. You have to keep them in the light to get rainbows. I ask him about the rulers, why they work then and he says he doesn't know. I ask him why we don't see rainbows all the time and he says he doesn't know.

The children in this story clearly recognize that the lenses they are gazing through cause distortions, which in turn tell them things about light and about the nature of the lenses themselves and their creators. Especially in this last conversation, the children are musing upon the relation of parts to the whole. They discuss how the prisms they are gazing through distort the light, break the light into component parts. This breaking up of the whole gives us insights into the whole and into the workings of the lens but it remains important to remember the parts are not the whole. In many ways Cory, in his recounting of his grandmother's magical tale about the origins of rainbows reminds us of this—no matter how close we look and how much we think we have found explanations for what we see, there is still a mystery buried within that invokes tales of magic to satisfy our need for understanding.

The second story is about the nature of the lenses we use to gaze at children both as teachers and as researchers. Like Hawkins, I would say that the context we place children into, the "theatre of their commitments," is all-important. The people they are and the people they portray are fundamentally shaped by these commitments. That context, which as a teacher I hold the power to shape, is my "lens." As I gaze through that lens at a child my question is what can I see about him or her. But also I should remember to look at the lens itself and think about what it portrays about me and my goals and values and also to remember the distortions I introduce.

Gazing at Children

The following story occurred at the beginning of my work in an "at-risk" public pre-school classroom. I have been going there and acting as an aide, working the "water table" three times a week for most of the school year. In addition to myself there are thirteen children, ages three and four, a classroom teacher and an aide. Occasionally there are other special people such as twice a week a speech therapist.

I set up the water table when I come in the classroom—school has already been in session for a half hour before I get there but Mary Jo (the classroom teacher) has left getting the water table ready to me today. I take the cover off and arrange newspapers on the floor and get a stash of paper towels for emergency use. I put the last on my seat—I sit at the head of the table and the children stand around the sides. I put in a few things (a number of funnels, some rigid plastic tubes of varying diameters and some measuring cups of different capacities), leaving others (measuring spoons, curved tubes and bulb turkey basters) in plastic tubs that I keep at my feet so I can hand them out at strategic moments (to divert children from various conflicts or to stimulate someone who is loosing interest back into the activity or when I see a child is needing some thing in particular for an activity they have constructed). The rules are: "Only four children at a time" and "no splashing, water stays in the tub!"

I sit down to play and begin by trying to pour water from a container into a plastic tube so that it fills another container. Angela and Tiffany are the first to join me. I send them back to get smocks on and when they return, they settle in to pouring water from small containers into large—filling up the large and then pouring those into the basin of the table with much satisfaction. Tiffany grabs a tube and begins stirring the water as she adds it to a jar. She is talking about

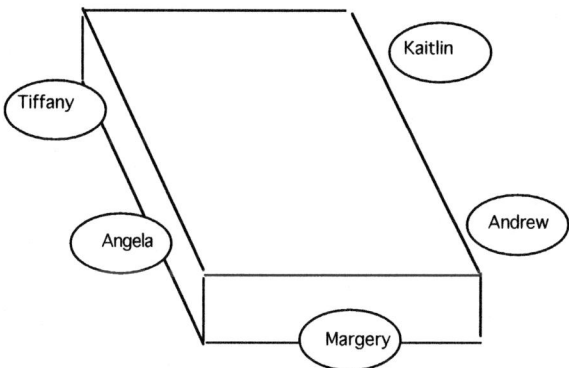

Figure 10.2. The water table.

making oatmeal and Angela chimes in. I ask them, "Do you like oatmeal?" and this begins a lengthy conversation about the likes and dislikes of everyone and anyone. Conversations with three year olds are patchwork quilts of things they do and know, things they have seen and basic fantasy. I wonder about Tiffany—does she make oatmeal for her baby sister (which is what she is telling me)? I know she does take care of the baby. Mary Jo calls her the "primary caregiver" of her family. Her mother spends the day in bed and is out all night and she has no father. Angela on the other hand is a mystery to me. She comes to school with her hair freshly put into twisty ponytails, carefully finished with *Goody™* barrettes. Her clothes are clean and she is too. The criteria for qualification for "at-risk" services are manifold.

I get out a couple of the bulb basters and start squeezing water from across the table into Tiffany's pot. Bulb basters are very difficult for small children to use! They require a certain inversion in logic as well as physical skills and strength. Tiffany though knows what to do—she expertly puts hers underwater and pushes down the bulb with all her weight. I'm very impressed. Then she does it again and the water in the tube gushes out and all over the floor. While I'm cleaning this up with my stash of paper towels, Andrew and Kaitlin arrive.

Kaitlin joins in with Tiffany making fantasy cooking projects with the water. Each has a large pot that they add water to using various smaller containers, stirring after each addition, discussing and critiquing each other from across the table. Probably an interesting discussion I think, too bad I can't pay attention to it for now Andrew is here.

Andrew has no smock, his sleeves aren't pulled up and he actually hasn't stopped running but he is *in the water*! He seizes a funnel (not from anyone but he still seizes it, he would never just pick it up) and starts pouring water into it. He intently watches the water come out the other end. He puts the end in the water, pours water in the top and watches the water go down in the top part, he does it again and watches the water around the bottom, he moves it to a jar and does it again, he turns it upside down and tries it that way. He notices nothing else including my grabbing his arms and shoving them in the smock, my picking him up and moving him to another place at the table, or the other children's activities. Suddenly he grabs a tube out of Angela's hands. She opens her mouth to protest but before that can happen I hand her another tube from beneath the table. I was ready for that one. Andrew fits the tube to the funnel and starts pouring. The other children are beginning to look a little worried. I see them watching him out of the corners of their eyes but so far they don't say anything. Every once in a while they look at me though, checking my reactions. Personally I'm still trying to use a bulb baster to fill Angela's large container (I've decided not to try to reach over to Tiffany any more and anyway she's busy with Kaitlin).

Suddenly Andrew jams the end of the tube into the drain hole in the table so that the tube-funnel combination stands upright. He pours water in the funnel and the quarter teaspoon or so of sand caught in the drain hole explodes out in a cloud. Andrew doesn't notice. He grabs another funnel and fits it into the first and pours again. Then he grabs a tube, fits it in with another funnel and pours again. He grabs another funnel and sticks it in, grabs my bulb baster and sticks it in. Now when he pours the water into the top he creates a fountain effect. The construction is well over his head. To pour into the top funnel he has to reach up and over with a full plastic container. Water runs down his arm. He misses and pours water over the girls who watch him with both awe and outrage. He drops the container. All peripheral, he pays attention to nothing but what he is doing. What *is* he doing?

I ask him. "I'm making something," he replies.

Kaitlin, who has been huddled around her funnel protecting it, gives up and starts to wash her "dishes" at the sink, which is just behind her. Angela leaves also, walking off to another center. Tiffany starts mopping up the floor with paper towels. Andrew is still pouring. Suddenly his eyebrows go up. He runs, *runs* across the room and grabs a piece of the plastic marble slide.

This is not really allowed although never articulated as a rule—no one has thought of doing this before. It wouldn't really matter though if it had been, he is so fast it is impossible to stop him before not only has he done what he set out to do, but also he's gone a couple more steps further along in his construction plan.

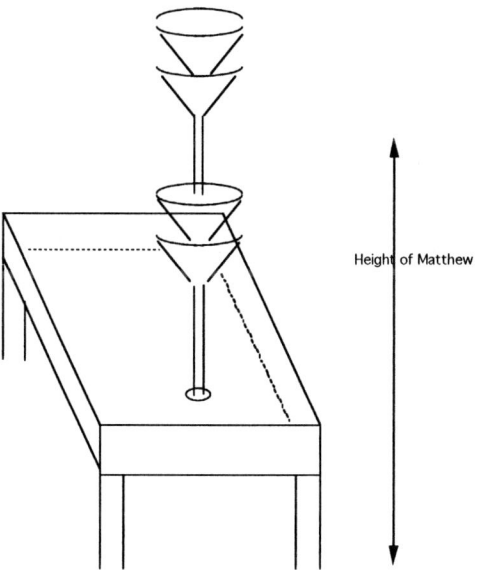

Height of Matthew

Figure 10.3. Andrew's construction.

A couple of the little girls have wanted to bring plastic figurines to the table but it was easy to prevent this—I could see them thinking about it before they even started to try to act on their thoughts. Andrew is way ahead of me. The last thing I want to do is to try to correct him when he has already moved beyond the act.

He starts trying to catch the water as it pours off the sides of his fountain with these pieces. Then he starts just pouring water into the pieces. Then he runs to get more pieces. I can see another construction is about to take shape but just at this point Mary Jo turns out the light—clean up time for snack begins and its the end off our explorations. Andrew has been totally immersed in this for thirty minutes.

Andrew is three years old in this story and four by the end of the school year. He lives with his father who is in his forties and works two jobs. He also lives with an older sister who is seven. When his father is working the night shift he sleeps at his grandmother's home. His mother never sees him although she is in the area. He and his sister where taken from her care by the Department of Family Services. The pre-school program here is configured as a "family" program, including four home visits a year by Mary Jo, the classroom teacher. At

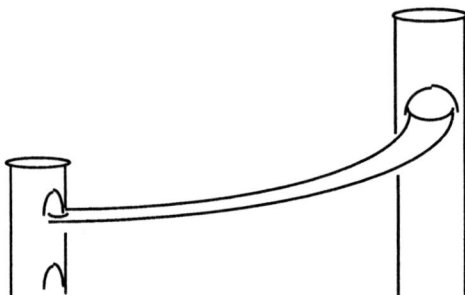

Figure 10.4. The marble slide.

home his environment is rather restricted, Mary Jo describes it as "Spartan," clean and very neat. His activities center around the computer; he is playing games of any type for all hours. At school he would choose to do this also. There are two computers in the classroom and Andrew would gladly monopolize both simultaneously, running back and forth between them primarily clicking buttons without waiting to see what happens.

Mary Jo has tried many strategies to get him to try other things than the computers but all seem to end in some sort of disaster or other with other children upset and Andrew in time out, sucking his thumb and withdrawn. In fact when ever Andrew is off the computer the other children quickly leave whatever activity he is engaged in. His ferocious intensity and inability to stick to one activity alienate everyone. Andrew is emotionally and socially immature and Mary Jo would like to have him "worked up" and assessed for hyperactivity. He is also extremely bright and verbally advanced. When he chooses to he reads quite well and he conducts classroom conversations during group time like an adult.

Andrew: [Standing at center of sitting children and leading group time.]   Angela, can you sit still?

Angela: [Squirming on the floor in distress.] No! I want Mary Jo to tie my shoe!

Andrew: Well gooood luck! She's in a bitch of a mood you know.

His ability to think creatively and remember esoteric facts and ideas is remarkable:

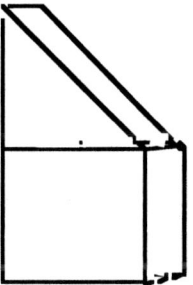

Figure 10.5. Andrew's second construction.

Andrew:	Look Margery, this is my shape shifter. [He holds up two plastic counters, a square and a triangle attached. He pushes it at my face, holding it kind of like a gun.]
Margery:	Oh yeah, how's that work? [I wince and jerk my head away, thinking he's going to make ray gun noises and talk magical superhero powers.]
Andrew:	Like this. [He holds it up again and rotates it four times around an imaginary, stationary center.])
Margery:	Oh! What's that called?
Andrew:	An octagon.

Note the same creative use of materials for purposes they were not intended for as in the water table story. This creative use of materials can also be termed inappropriate—it depends on context and who is looking (and passing judgment).

Margery:	Andrew what are you doing?
Andrew:	Making a castle. [Andrew has taken a stack of cardboard cards, carefully cut to size and with holes punched in so that they can be used as book covers, and is pouring puddles of glue on each and then pressing them together making a mountainous pile.]
Mary Jo:	Andrew that's too much glue!
Andrew:	[Squeezes the pile so that glue runs all over the floor.]
Mary Jo:	Andrew, get a towel and clean that up.
Andrew:	[Throws his pile of cards on the table and runs to get more glue.]

Mary Jo and Mary, the classroom aide, are deeply troubled by Andrew. The father, John, resists the label hyperactive and Mary Jo can do nothing without his assistance in that line. She has sent the program social worker to talk with him but he insists the child is fine at home. Mary Jo contemplates suggesting that he be removed from the program and put in a smaller scale more highly disciplined environment. She asks me what I feel about this. I argue against it for I believe that such an environment would squelch the creativity he exhibits, would further inhibit any social development. Mary points out that the continuous negative reactions, which he elicits in teachers and children, have a worse effect. I have to agree. Mary Jo talks about how she believes he is emotionally damaged as well as hyperactive, "The worst thing is I feel my every response to him just makes that worse, I damage him more."

I feel inadequate. As a university person I know they would like me to be a source of fresh ideas, some sort of solution. Over the weekend I wrack my brains, I know that in the first grade classrooms I am used to working in I dealt with behavioral problems all the time. The kind of science I advocate and practice with children is extremely open-ended and encourages the children to shape activities in their own ways. This often seems to encourage them to act out in a manner more restrictive, procedure oriented science activities do not. In those classes, I would try to work with the "difficult" children by giving them more responsibilities, giving them leadership roles and special tasks and hoping this would help them invest more deeply in the science. What if I tried this with Andrew? How would I do this in this classroom?

I carry this worry about with me for days. What would I do? What could I do here? Then I have an inspiration. I'm in the local pet store thinking about the undergraduate courses I teach and they had a cage of baby hedgehogs put out by the small mammals. I am looking at these and thinking about whether I would like to have one—they are quite attractive and they cause me to muse on the image of Beatrix Potter putting out bowls of milk for hers. At any rate they are rather expensive and those little spines worry me. My eyes drift over to the guinea pigs. There are two quite nice baby ones but they have no price. At that moment the owner wanders by and asks me what I'm thinking about. That's when it happened. I bought one. I come up with a plan. Mary Jo and I suggest to Andrew that he can have the guinea pig. I will bring it in and he will care for it as well as taking charge of who can play with it and when. When we ask him if he likes this idea he eagerly agrees.

I bring in the animal after a couple more days of talking things over with Andrew, helping him to think through his role and responsibilities. In the hall with no other children around we look at her in her cage. Andrew: "Give her to me!!" I sit him down and show him how to hold her. He is upset about the wood shavings that fall on his clothes. I brush them off. He is worried about her little claws. He gets agitated at her motions. I take her back. He never touches her again.

Discussion

During my years as a research scientist in geology and crystal chemistry, the feelings and sensations I had when I was doing my work were complex. They included feelings of joy, sensuality, beauty as well as those we associate with rational problem solving and intellectual success. These, as a package, shaped and sustained my absorption in my activities. They were projections of a depth and intensity of my person and my engagement but also involved a loss of a sense of self in a task. This combination of qualities in truth captures aspects of science rarely portrayed in our teaching in schoolrooms and suggests something of the paradox at the core to "doing" science. That science is done for itself by people immersed in it and it is also accomplished by people guided by goals, trying to accomplish important tasks—people both unaware of themselves in the world and people with a heightened awareness of context. These qualities are not separate: they are closely intertwined. My absorption in the science occurred because of its immersive qualities but these enriched and were juxtaposed to the intellectual problem solving inherent in laboratory research. I loved that too. I experienced this dualism as an enriching tension between work and play, rational and irrational, thought and feelings. I wish to suggest that the children in my stories portray both facets, that which reflects the self-in-the-world and that which reflects a loss of self. The tension which enriched the science I did/do is a large part the force behind the classrooms which I try to construct, re-enchanting the enterprise of science and science education through art and literature, re-infusing it with feelings and beauty.

This tension in the doing of science is a progressive one—it fuels the drive towards self re-creation as well as scientific discovery. It is progressive in both the substance of the science and also for those "doing" the science—for the science that is done reflects those who create it. I would argue, from reflecting on my own experiences, that unless we recognize that the doing of science involves more than mastery aimed at problem solving, that it involves, in a reciprocal and creative way, a being-in-the-world and in-the-making, we do not understand the science, the child or the process of education. David Hawkins, in the quote about the rose in the mirror above was making a plea to enrich science education, to make it more reflective of the science that scientists do. I would echo this plea for it is in the "theatre of our commitments" that we come to be, as well as it being within that terrain that we become capable of understanding others. This statement is more than important; it is essential. In these days of phrases such as "science for all," access and equity are of course central; but so is understanding others who come from different backgrounds or hold different values from ourselves. I think for us, as teachers, the only real place we can do this is in the terrain of our classrooms, in an environment where we encourage real, "authentic," engagement with each other and our curriculum.

I think my point in telling these stories of children in my classrooms and of Andrew in particular is to emphasize that I in shaping my classrooms as I do, I construct a "lens," so to speak, for gazing at a child. The materials I give Andrew and the behaviors I think should follow from them are of my choosing and even when I am trying to be sensitive and open, I am not. Andrew, for all my trying so hard to "see" him remains invisible to me. It is this failure that is so extreme in this instance that causes me to reflect upon the lenses I have constructed and upon myself in creating them. Just as the children in my first story recognize that the lenses they are gazing through cause distortions, which in turn tell them things about the object they are gazing at and about the nature of the lenses themselves and their creators, I can recognize that here and apply it. The context we put children in, the things we let them do are a lens or a mirror. Through such lenses we can see the children, in varying degrees of distortion, and see ourselves.

One would think that the point of creating these "lenses" to gaze at objects, children, science, or ourselves is to garner some sort of "truth," some insight into the inner being and potential of another. We can think that such a pursuit is harmless but it is truly only benign when we perpetuate a fiction, that the observer is not going to do anything with the observations they make and the subject of observation is unaffected by the observation. Being passive is certainly neither part of the role of the teacher nor of the scientist; and is not the point of what happens in classrooms or in research. Both are caught up in the creative function of constructing something new and creating lenses to view subject matter and children is instrumental in that. In creating the contexts for doing science in my classrooms, I state that I am purposely trying to recreate the places I worked within as a scientist—places where experience is complex and both directed towards inner motivations and outer ones. The two stories I tell exemplify this in many ways. The question is what do these lenses tell us about the children, the science and ourselves, what is such information being used for and how does being in these settings effect what is being looked at?

Now this creation and utilization of lenses used to view another is at the core of the subject object relationship I talk about at the start of this piece. If I am to argue that the subject–object relationship is based upon both self-presentation and perception which are purposeful—both the object and the subject want to do something—I am asserting the relationship is motivated by a *need*. Sartre differentiates between *desire* and *need*. In *Being and Nothingness* (1965) he claims that acts of free will are motivated by desire. In *Search for a Method* (1963) he modifies this to need. The difference between desire and need, it seems to me, is one of an intellectual desire versus more emotional, felt need. To desire is in your head, to need is in your stomach. Most importantly need addresses a vanishing point—needs can never be satiated. Desires can and then one can move beyond them. I think of Sartre's need as similar to bell hook's (1990) *yearning*—a longing which emanates from the heart as well as the mind, which shapes thought, actions, emotions and which is not satiated even when directly addressed. Similarly James Garrison (1997) describes this as *eros*—a passionate desire, a love that "begins in need and lack." The subject/object identity shifts in response to how this need is acted on and perceived.

Martin Heidegger (1962) argues that to separate subject and object, as is implied in metaphors about the subject "seeing" the object, is artificial. The subject and object occupy the same world-space, life-space: "By drawing a distinction that I (the subject) am perceiving something else (the object), I have stepped back from the primacy of experience and understanding that operates without reflection." Heidegger does not deny that we exist purposefully in this world, that we are trying to do certain things. He claims that this purposefulness involves decisions—what to do and what not to do, how to go about doing these things. These decisions are founded upon uncertainty, they reflect needs for things that we do not already have and therefore do not know. We make decisions on a basis of things felt, not articulated. This process of becoming both cognizant of our needs and questioning those needs is the essence of arguments of critical theorists such as Jürgen Habermas (1991) as well as Hannah Arendt (1964/77; 1978). In essence when lenses become mirrors we are doing this.

To conclude, I would like to describe a conversation I had recently with a friend of mine who is an electrical engineer. My friend, David, has been very kindly supplying my graduate students and myself with small digital video cameras which we give to children in schools and which they devise uses for in their science explorations. We had been talking about this metaphor of the rose in the mirror that David Hawkins recounts from the *Baghavad Gita*. We were looking at a digital photograph of a rose and I asked David if he thought there was anything transcendent about the image of the flower. We had just been talking about my garden but in relating this it is possible to substitute the word classroom for that of garden and to think about children when flowers are mentioned. I had stated that there is a difference between the things people do for a purpose, that are driven by a purpose, and those that they do as recreation—that these are a conceit. In thinking of my garden I start to reconsider this statement. I say, "Well I think about this every time I go out in my garden—is it a total conceit to put so much effort into creating a place of beauty (and really private beauty too)? You know though Kant (and Aristotle) equate beauty with truth. Marxists would say beauty is a conceit, postmodernists that truth is (or the search for it). Look at this image . . . is there something transcendent about the flower? About the image? So is it a symbol or a representation and of what?" And David, being a scientist, responds that there is no transcendence of ideas and, echoing Gertrude Stein claims that a "flower is a flower." He goes on:

The observer brings his or her own meaning to the flower (meaning that depends on his or her experience). The observer cannot simultaneously view the flower in all possible ways. In this sense truth cannot be beauty because the beauty of the flower encompasses all perspectives, which cannot be represented by anything less than the flower itself. Is truth so embedded in reality? Then where is falsehood? I like being an engineer since I've decided that engineers have no need of truth. Engineers are big on information, however, which is a clear mathematical concept (the amount of information in the flower is the number of bits it takes to represent it. This would be about ten power ten bits for the full three-dimensional flower, although I could compress this a lot by knowing it is a flower. It happens to be 25.5 kilobytes (8 bits/byte) for the flower image you sent. Thus one might say that there are 25.5 kilobytes nuggets of truth. Actually it could be compressed. One could define truth to be the same thing as information and say that the truth in the flower is it's minimal representation on a optimized computer. A hot area of debate is whether or not this concept of the flower is well defined. The flower is decaying in time and it takes time to characterize it. Characterization may also destroy the flower. Thus the flower is in some sense immeasurable. In this sense, may be it is transcendental.

Well being something of a Deweyian, I would argue that the whole point of experience is to give our lives, our social lives meaning but unlike David, I would say the point of searching for meaning is to assert "truths" (even if relative ones) which guide our actions. Our transcendence is in the realm of our actions–we transcend ourselves by what we are able to do. But in another sense David's idea, that the flower is immeasurable and therefore transcendent, when applied to our ideas of children and our trying to understand them is a very beautiful thought. It suggests to me that our images of particular objects as well as our understandings transcend the particular as they act as metaphors, as they become evocative of things greater than themselves. This is where wisdom lies, and what, I think, both teaching and research should be about and is the point in concerning oneself with the role of biography in either.

References

Arendt, H. (1964/77). *Eichmann in Jerusalem: A report on the banality of evil*. New York: Penguin Books.

Arendt, H. (1978). *The life of the mind*. New York: Harcourt Brace Jovanovich.

Barton, A. C., & Osborne, M. D. (2002). Transforming the "harsh world." In W.-M. Roth & J. Désautels (Eds.), *Science education as/for sociopolitical action* (pp. 167–184). New York: Peter Lang.

Foucault, M. (1973). *The order of things: An archaeology of the human sciences*. New York: Vintage Books.

Garrison, J. (1997). *Dewey and eros: Wisdom and desire in the art of teaching*. New York: Teachers College Press.

Habermas, J. (1991). *Moral consciousness and communicative action*. Cambridge, MA: MIT Press.

Hawkins, D. (1974). *I, thou and it. The informed vision: Essays on learning and human nature*. New York: Agathon Press.

Heidegger, M. (1962). *Being and time*. New York: Harper.

hooks, b. (1990). *Yearning: Race, gender, and cultural politics*. Boston: South End Press.

Irigaray, L. (1985). *The speculum of the other woman*. Ithaca, NY: Cornell University Press.

Osborne, M. D. (1999) *Constructing knowledge in the elementary school science classroom: Teachers and students*. New York: Falmer.

Osborne, M. D., & Barton, A. C. (1999, April). *Constructing a womanist science*. Paper presented at the annual meeting of the American Educational Research Association, Montreal, Quebec.

Osborne, M. D., & Brady, D. J. (2002). Imagining the new: Constructing a space for creativity in science. In E. Mirochnik & D. Sherman (Eds.), *Passion & pedagogy: Relation, creation, and transformation in teaching* (pp. 317–332). New York: Peter Lang.

Sartre, J.-P. (1963). *In search of a method*. New York: Vintage Books.

Sartre, J.-P. (1956/1965). *Being and nothingness*. New York: Citadel Press.

11 Using Webs of Narrative to Explore Negotiation of Meaning and Practice

David R. Geelan

Reforms and innovations in education frequently meet with unanticipated resistance from students and teachers. A new school in an Australian city has implemented a coordinated package of innovative approaches to middle (age thirteen and fourteen) schooling including integrated curriculum, portfolio assessment, a team approach to teacher collaboration in curriculum development and an ethos of caring and responsibility. During 1996 I was involved in team-teaching science with a number of teachers at the school who were not science specialists. In this chapter, I use auto/biography to answer questions about the ways in which students, teachers, administrators, and parents negotiate new sets of roles and expectations for schooling in such an innovative climate. Auto/biography is one way of richly understanding the interplay of the large number of institutional, social and personal factors acting in this very complex situation. I explore the ways in which auto/biography contributed to the understandings I developed in the course of reflecting on my own professional practice and that of my colleagues, and to communicating these understandings to other teachers involved in similar innovations.

Introduction: Reflexivity and Teaching/Learning/Research

From a perspective that recognizes the reflexivity of living in human relationships (Steier, 1995), I regard teaching as part of the emergent activity of teaching/learning/research. In the community of the classroom, learning is co-

constructed by all participants. Teachers learn from their colleagues and students
and conduct research (both formal and informal) as they aspire to improve their
practice. Students teach their teachers and fellow students and conduct experiments in learning and social interaction. Separating this rich blend of activities
into teaching, learning, and research may be useful to help us talk about them,
but I experience being with students as teaching/learning/research.

Enactivist epistemological perspectives (Davis, 1995) suggest that our actions arise out of the totality of our being, in engagement with our environments.
I experience teaching in this way—I bring all of myself to the classroom (as well
as to my research and writing), and act and react out of who I am. The process is
only partially rational and intentional, and draws on experience, subconscious
processing and relationship reflexes. I bring to the classroom the love of my
family and the conversations that I have had over many years with my wife Sue.
I bring the thousands of novels and other books I've read, and all the lives I've
vicariously lived through fiction. I bring my experience of playing computer
games and conversing with people all over the world in online forums. I bring
my religious faith, as well as the questions and conflicts engendered by my
struggles to believe and accept. I bring my political views and commitments,
and my connections with pop culture through movies and music.

But teaching is also thoughtful, intentional, and reflective. Reflection is a
more active process of weaving my teaching experiences and commitments into
the fabric of who I am. Reflection on past classroom actions and their consequences informs my understanding, and future actions grow out of that understanding. Max Van Manen says it better than I can:

[P]edagogy requires a reflective orientation to life. . . . By thoughtfully reflecting on what
I should have done, I decide in effect how I want to be. In other words, I infuse my being
and my readiness to act with a certain thoughtfulness. And yet, how I am now as a
teacher will not be clear until I have had further opportunities to act in more appropriate
ways. How I am as a teacher depends on what I do, on my possibilities for acting
thoughtfully. But my possible actions do not magically arise, they depend on the thoughtfulness that I have been able to acquire in recollective reflection. (Van Manen, 1991, p.
116)

If knowledge is defined in enactivist terms, as a disposition toward certain
(emergent) ways of acting in certain contexts, then how will my actions (including mental representations) be informed by my professional and personal
auto/biography? In what ways do my teaching/learning/research, inside and outside classrooms, inform and enrich my Being, in order that I can enrich others?

Experience and Resistance

This research into my *lived experience* (van Manen, 1990) as a team teacher in Arcadia High School[1] grew out of my earlier critical action research study (Geelan, 1994, 1996) on my attempts to support my students in becoming active learners. On that occasion I found that my teaching innovation was largely unsuccessful, and that students and teachers became frustrated by the challenges to their existing school roles and expectations. The pressures placed on students by expectations—their parents' and their own—placed a low value on greater quality of understanding and the development of transferable learning skills, and a high value on good grades. The students felt that by attempting to change their learning roles from passive to active (and my teaching role from *dispenser of information* to *facilitator of learning*) I was abdicating from my key responsibility—helping them to memorize the information they would need for success in their examinations.

I continue to value active learning and students' development of skills and attitudes to learning that will better fit them for a world in which they will need to continue to learn at a rapid rate in order to survive. I suspect that if such changes to the expectations of students are to occur, however, it will not be because teachers have unilaterally chosen to change their own roles; rather, it will be through a process of negotiation and role redefinition that includes all stakeholders, including parents. The results of my earlier research supported this view, and the commitments, approaches and perspectives of those who planned Arcadia High School suggested that such an approach to educational innovation would be attempted at the school.

Context and Complexity

Arcadia High School opened in 1995 with 600 students in Years Seven and Eight (approximately ages thirteen and fourteen). The school is in the rapidly growing western corridor of an Australian state capital, and was needed because an expanding population meant that the two local secondary schools and five primary (elementary) schools were overflowing.

A visionary team of educators led by the foundation principal Terry Jenner chose to make this school something fairly new for this state—a middle school. In the state where Arcadia was developed, Year Seven is the final year of primary school, and Year Eight is the first year of secondary school. The change in culture and approach between the two levels of schooling is quite dramatic: In primary school, students spend their day largely with a single teacher, in one classroom, whereas in secondary school they may have up to six different teachers and move to a new room for each subject. Primary schools are generally smaller, around 300 students, while suburban secondary schools can have up to 2,000 students.

The team involved in the development of the Arcadia program decided that Arcadia would be a middle school, relieving stresses on both the local primary and secondary schools and, more importantly, easing the transition for students. The program developed was similar to that in primary schools—students had a homeroom and a homeroom teacher who taught them all learning areas (subjects) except fine arts, technology (industrial arts), sports, and languages other than English (LOTE).

It was felt that such a structure had significant potential to support students in developing transferable learning skills and a high level of literacy. Other innovations introduced to support this approach included portfolio assessment, which was intended to de-emphasize grades as a motivator and to value work the students did outside exam conditions, and teacher collaborative planning, which was intended to support teachers in providing a genuine integrated curriculum.

My role within the school during its inaugural year (1995) was as a teacher educator involved in professional development courses with some teachers in the school. Because there were several teachers who were interested, a university course was run on the school site rather than at a university campus. This gave me a strong feeling for both the exhilarating successes and the frustrating challenges of attempting to bring together a mixed community of primary and secondary teachers (because there were no middle schools in the area, there were no trained and experienced middle school teachers), and to blend and balance the two cultures in ways that would best support students' learning and personal growth.

Naturally, there were clashes of style and approach between the two groups of teachers—at one point in May these became so severe that it appeared the school community might just fly apart from the centrifugal force of conflicting expectations. By the end of 1995, however, the school reached a synthesis that had many teachers raving over the new freedom they felt to teach in innovative and creative ways.

In 1996, the school added Year Nine (that is, the previous year's Year Eight students moved into the new grade), which meant that the student population increased by a third, to more than 900 students. This meant that the teaching staff also increased by a third, from thirty-five to almost fifty.

In consultation with my doctoral supervisor, Peter Taylor, I chose to conduct my doctoral research in the school because I felt that what was happening there was exciting, and that it related strongly to my own educational commitments and values. The teaching/research activities I undertook at Arcadia offered an opportunity to put into practice the new understandings gained from the earlier research. I also wanted to take advantage of a Ph.D. scholarship to conduct some long-term, close-up, intensive study of teaching and learning in classrooms—I knew that in the full life of an academic I may never again have such an opportunity.

For this reason, I volunteered to team teach at Arcadia for two and a half days each week throughout the 1996 school year. The teachers had been either primary or secondary teachers, and most of the secondary teachers had specialized in areas such as English (language arts) and social studies. Many of the teachers expressed their unease about teaching science. As an experienced science educator, I offered to help out in this area. While teaching, I would observe my own teaching practices and those of my colleagues, and the reactions and interactions of the students. I would attempt to record the happenings, emotions and implications of the classrooms by writing *impressionistic tales* (Van Maanen, 1988). I taught in five different classrooms, with five very different teachers. Only one had been at the school in 1995, so in their various ways, each had to experience for herself the process of a dramatic change of educational culture and expectations.

Impressionistic Tales of the Field

During the teaching year at Arcadia, I wrote a large number of *impressionistic tales* (van Maanen, 1988), usually immediately after some critical incident in my teaching or in the school. The tales consist of short narrative pieces in a variety of literary genres—journalistic reportage, reflective analyses, fictionalized incidents, or pieces of fiction. They were intended to capture not only the incidents that occurred, but also—by analogy with impressionist paintings (Taylor, 1997)—the feelings and ideas which these incidents aroused in me, and the ways in which they affected my construction and understanding of my teaching and my students' learning.

The tales formed one important set of data for the research study. They were complemented by other data—interviews and surveys—as a form of data triangulation (Lincoln & Guba, 1985). Only the tales, and some discussion of the standards applied to them, will be represented in this chapter—the full study is described and analysed in some detail in *Weaving Narrative Nets to Capture Classrooms* (Geelan, 2004).

Content Lumps

"I didn't think there'd be much dissonance between what I'm trying to do—you know, integrated curriculum, student centered learning and negotiation—and what the rest of the teachers at Arcadia are doing."

In Peter's office, Thursday morning, we're reflecting—or at least, I'm reflecting, and he's listening—on my expectations of the school, and some of the frustrations I'm already starting to feel with the progress of my research.

"I expected a fair bit of freedom in developing curricula for my classes. Listening to the discussion within the school last year, I expected the curriculum to be much more fully integrated than it is: The various learning areas inform one another more than they would in a traditional high school, but there are still separate sections of the day dedicated to particular disciplines. You know, it's like 'Put away your maths books now, it's time for science.'"

"Why is that, do you think?" asks Peter. "Is it because of constraints on the timetable, or demands from the Education Department?"

"I think one reason there's not much integration of science with other subjects is that Fred Simmons, the Head of Department for science, has a really strong content-based view about what's important in junior secondary science. He's had years of experience in traditional science teaching, and he talks about 'non-negotiables.' These are supposed to be the things students need for upper secondary science, and he defines them in terms of particular facts and pieces of 'content.' rather than skills and attitudes. Because these content lumps are usually pretty scientistic and abstract, it's almost impossible to integrate them with the particular integrated module the students are studying."

Peter listens and nods. "What will that mean for your teaching, and your work with the team and the other teachers?"

"My role in the school gets tricky: I want to improve students' learning opportunities, and I think one important facet of that has to be discarding most of this 'non-negotiable' stuff. I mean, one, students don't retain it anyway, and we re-teach it in upper school, two, it wrecks their positive attitudes toward science, and three, it gives them a very positivistic view of science . . . do I have to go on? I'd far prefer to concentrate on the integrated modules, and draw in scientific ideas and ways of working and experiences when they're relevant and when they'll fit."

"Can you go ahead and do that? Surely you've got a fair bit of autonomy within the five classrooms, and even in the whole team?"

"Yeah, I guess I can do some of it, although not as much as I'd like to. I guess I feel like I'm a guest in the school, and it wouldn't be appropriate or fair for me to attack Fred's approach or subvert it. I need to talk to him and try to broaden his approach, but my own teaching will still be constrained by his influence."

"That is a bit frustrating," agrees Peter. "How will that impact your research? Does it make it impossible to do what you wanted to do?"

"No, not really—well, maybe. But I think it can also be seen as a positive thing. If one important use of this study is to explore what it means and how it feels for a teacher to innovate in the classroom, to improve students' learning opportunities, then it's realistic that there be some constraints and opposition. The interest comes in trying to develop ethical, effective, creative solutions."

* * *

In hindsight, although I continue to be personally committed to an approach to science education that is more strongly integrated with students' out-of-school experiences and with their other school subjects, I am disturbed by the arrogance toward Fred that is evident in the comments recorded here. I have a particular understanding of the nature of science and school science, which I think is defensible (otherwise why would I hold it?), but my readiness to dismiss Fred's knowledge and experience in his professional area now strikes me as deeply lacking in the very qualities of tactfulness and thoughtfulness (Van Manen, 1991) that I was trying to incorporate in my teaching practice. That is to say, perhaps my educational concerns about my students and the image of science that the school represented to them were appropriate (that's another argument), but it remains incumbent on me to extend the same concern toward colleagues with whom I disagree. While I (self-)righteously conceded that I would not undermine Fred's work in the school, I was also very convinced that he was one of the obstacles to reform, and I was the cure!

This is ironic, given that I entered the school with a theoretical perspective described as "critical constructivism" (Taylor & Campbell-Williams, 1993), which combines personal constructivism's emphasis on the constructed nature of knowledge (Glasersfeld, 1989) with social constructivism's understandings of the collaborative nature of learning (Tobin, 1990). It adds elements of Jürgen Habermas' critical theory, yielding a perspective on the nature of education as a socio-political process.

Habermas (1978) identifies three forms of human interests. The *technical* interest has been the dominant paradigm in Western culture. It is concerned with understanding for control, with predictability and uniformity. It is the rationality of the physical sciences. The *practical* interest embodies a concern for understanding and relationship, and for communication. The *emancipatory* interest is concerned with power—with challenging reified structures of power and institutional control. My *practical* interest in developing rich communicative relationships seems, in retrospect, to have been confined to the students and to the teachers who agreed with my way of thinking.

My critical constructivist perspective underpinned both the teaching innovations I attempted and my research methodology. This meant realizing that, like those of my students, *my own* knowledge and understandings were constructed. Steier (1995) refers to this understanding as reflexivity. From a reflexive perspective, it is no longer possible (if it ever was) for the researcher to stand off from the life in classrooms and observe "objectively." As I've said elsewhere:

> If constructivism is to mean anything, it must mean that the theorist is irrevocably involved in life, in social interaction, in learning—in the very things the theory purports to explain. This being so, there is no meta-theoretical perspective, no 'outside' from which to understand the activities of teaching, learning and research. They must be understood from "inside" through social relationships which define both the mode and the content of our discourse. (Geelan, 1997, p. 25)

Steier suggests that if a concern for reflexivity is taken seriously, then teaching, learning and research merge to become collaborative social learning. This has been my experience during this study and since—I am teacher and researcher, teacher and learner, learner and researcher. I, like my students and colleagues, am seeking to understand and to shape my behavior and practices on the basis of my new understandings in an iterative process that never ceases while we breathe.

St. Therese and the Nature of Science

Therese looks from Carolyn to me, and back again. Most of the other students in the room have missed the inconsistency—frankly, most of them stopped listening ten minutes ago. But Therese is bright, and even though she considers science "a waste of time," she's almost always listening and thinking, even when I think she's just adding another layer of intricate doodling to the inside of her folder.

"That's not what Mr. Geelan says science is about," she murmurs, without bothering to raise her hand. Carolyn—the class teacher—has just come out with the statement that "science is true facts about the world," and Therese remembers that a few weeks ago, in one of my fairly frequent digressions into the nature of science, I claimed that science is a way of understanding the world that doesn't necessarily yield truth.

Now Carolyn's looking at me too, and I try to explain again what I understand the nature of science to be. My perspective owes something to Paul Feyerabend's *anything-goes* approach, something to postmodernism and constructivism and something to the sociology of science. It's eclectic and rather complex, and I'm trying to describe it as clearly and simply as I can, without using any of those terms.

But even as I'm explaining, I'm thinking "Do the students really need this? Is it appropriate for their age and stage of development to try to grapple with epistemological and ontological questions that I came to much later? Or would it be more comfortable and productive for them to believe in the sacredness of scientific knowledge for a little longer?" I can't decide what is most appropriate, and the situation has arisen in the classroom right now, so I try to make the best of it.

"Well, I think about it this way," I begin.

How do I do this without openly disagreeing with Carolyn?

"Science is a word that's used to talk about two things, and they're both important. Science is a body of knowledge—ideas and theories. These are really ways that people have found to think about what they see in the world. But science is also an activity—it's something people *do*, as well as something they know. In our school science lessons, we try to introduce you to some of those scientific ways of thinking about the world, and we also try to let you do what scientists do—explore the world in thoughtful, careful ways."

"I don't want you to think that science is just about memorizing a heap of facts—that, number one, isn't very useful, and number two, doesn't make you a scientist, or even scientifically literate. Science is about learning a special set of ways of working and thinking. They're related to ways we work and think in other learning areas, but also a bit different. For example, in English, we look at a novel or a poem or a story and try to understand what it's about, and how it makes us feel."

Carolyn breaks in, "But in English there's really no one right answer, where in science there is . . . isn't there?" I don't want to deal with that right now, so I turn from the class to her and say "I'm getting to that, but I want to do this a particular way," then continue.

"What Ms Young was talking about was the first of those two things about science—scientific knowledge."

I continue with my explanation, in a lecturing mode that's unusual for me, and I'm very aware that, fascinating and important as this stuff is to me, and although I think I'm explaining it pretty clearly, most of the students' eyes have glazed over. Some are staring out the window at the gentle grey drizzle, one or two have their heads down on their desks, and Tony is flicking bent staples at Jules when neither teacher is looking. I've been seeing the staples appear, but I want to catch Tony in the act—perhaps then the inevitable visit from his mother will be at least marginally less unpleasant. Unless I have some pretty direct evidence, it'll just be "You're picking on him" again. I'm not, but Carolyn is, and that makes my position morally difficult when I'm talking to Tony's mum.

Carolyn says, "So, you're saying scientific facts aren't really true?" While I'm trying to get my thoughts together, Therese blessedly breaks in. "No, Miss Young, it's more like they're true at one place and time, but not always. They're sort of like fashion." Carolyn completely ignores her and keeps looking toward me, and I try to explain the ideas Therese has just put together so cogently. I also try to acknowledge Therese and her contribution, by alluding back to them in my comments, and earn a grudging smile before she drops her head forward and hides behind her long dark fringe—a frequent refuge.

Carolyn says, "Oh, okay, I think I understand," but her expression makes it clear that she doesn't, and doesn't really believe me anyway. Therese has a better understanding of this stuff than Carolyn ever will—but she still thinks science is a waste of time.

Anyone Can Teach Science?

I presented a paper at a local science education conference this month—it was called "Anyone Can Teach Science." I was trying to organize for myself, and hopefully for the teachers and researchers at the conference, how I felt about the teachers with whom I was working at Arcadia, as science teachers. None of them have any formal training in either science or science teaching, and in talking to them I found that several expressed misgivings about the Arcadia middle schooling model that required them to teach science. That's one of the reasons the study took the shape it did—I was responding to these teachers' perceived inadequacy in teaching science.

Most research that has looked at this issue—what a teacher needs in order to be a science teacher—has concentrated on knowledge of science: science content, "facts" and information and skills. I certainly observed any number of howling factual errors from the teachers I worked with, and if I hadn't been in the room these would have been "transmitted" to the students.

They frequently were anyway—there are only so many times you can cor-
rect a person publicly without undermining them totally.

But there are at least two other ways to look at what science teachers need.
One is provided by Lee Shulman's handy scheme, dividing what teachers know
into *content knowledge*—the scientific information to be taught, *pedagogical
knowledge*—generic knowledge and skill about teaching in general, and *pedagogical content knowledge*—specific skills, strategies, ideas and information required to teach particular content, in this case science. I would argue that all the
teachers I worked with possessed adequate, and in some cases excellent, pedagogical knowledge. Teachers often rely on books and CD-ROMs and on discussion with colleagues to expand their understandings of science content. But several of the teachers expressed their own lack of pedagogical content knowledge
in the area of science.

The second way of looking at what teachers need is really what got me into
trouble in the school. Recent theories in science education, particularly those
that take constructivism as a referent, have tended to devalue the memorization
of science facts and to value students' individual and social construction of
knowledge and sense-making schemes, based on their laboratory and out of
school experiences. At Arcadia, too, teachers were encouraged to integrate science with the other learning areas. Because having a large body of content
knowledge is devalued, this perspective has tended to encourage the idea that
anyone can teach science—you don't need to be a science specialist. But I'd argue that this kind of teaching requires, not less knowledge of science, but more:
Social constructivist learning approaches and curricular integration go well beyond the knowledge of facts, to a really quite sophisticated understanding of the
nature of science and science education. I know that I really only developed
such an understanding (if indeed I have it!) during my M.Ed. studies, after completing a science degree and then spending several years teaching science. I tried
to support and encourage the teachers I was working with to teach and understand science in these ways, but their own perception of their need—and therefore of my role—was in content knowledge. They saw me as a provider of facts
and resources, whereas I saw myself as a model for more constructivist modes
of science education. The conflict was fundamental.

Measuring the Tales

An impressionistic tale of the field (Van Maanen, 1988) is not simply any tale. If
it was otherwise, I could have told any other set of tales. By what standards
ought we judge the tales I do provide? Clearly the standards that are appropriate

to evaluating quantitative and positivist forms of data—reliability and the various canons of validity—are inappropriate to judging the quality of impressionistic tales and autobiographical/autoethnographical research. What standards might be more appropriate?

John Van Maanen, from whom I have borrowed the notion of impressionistic tales, describes the appropriate standards for judging such tales as follows:

Literary standards are of more interest to the impressionist than scientific ones. . . . In telling a tale, narrative rationality is of more concern than an argumentative kind. The audience cannot be concerned with the story's correctness, since they were not there and cannot know if it is correct. The standards are largely those of interest (does it attract?), coherence (does it hang together?), and fidelity (does it seem true?). Finally, since the standards are not disciplinary but literary ones, the main obligation of the impressionist is to keep the audience alert and interested. Unusual phrasings, fresh allusions, rich language, cognitive and emotional stimulation, puns and quick jolts to the imagination are all characteristic of the good tale. (Van Maanen, 1988, pp. 105–106)

Carolyn Ellis suggests a similar measure:

A story's "validity" can be judged by whether it evokes in readers a feeling that the experience described is authentic and lifelike, believable and possible; the story's generalizability can be judged by whether it speaks to readers about their experience.

Whoops! I slipped again into speaking in a generalized, abstracted mode that provides no concrete examples of what I'm talking about. (Ellis, 1997, p. 133)

These are essentially standards of verisimilitude (Denzin & Lincoln, 1994) and of utility. Does the account ring true to those who are in a position to know (those who have experience of classrooms from a teacher perspective)? And does it seem potentially fruitful for their practice?

Since my intention is to render clearly some of the actualities of classroom life, if what I write is recognized as having verisimilitude by those who actually live and work in classrooms, I view that as an important measure of the extent to which this recognition criterion has been met. Max Van Manen (1990) puts this criterion in more academic language:

The essence or nature of an experience has been adequately described in language if the description reawakens or shows us the lived quality and significance of the experience in a fuller or deeper manner. (p. 11)

In relation to utility, Elliott Eisner observes that "Qualitative research becomes believable because of its *coherence, insight* and *instrumental utility*" (Eisner, 1998, p. 39, emphases in the orginal). The criterion of *instrumental utility*—that is, the extent to which the research is seen as having value for practitioners and applicability to practice—was important to me in conducting the research project described in this chapter. In the years since I completed the research study and placed the dissertation on the Internet, that study has been shown to have instrumental utility for researchers conducting similar studies, but to have less utility for practicing teachers, partly because it has not been disseminated to them. Utility seems to me to be a key criterion for judging the quality of qualitative research projects, and one to which too little attention has been paid.

Reflections and the Moments of Ethnography

I chose a *narrative method* (Clandinin & Connelly, 1996) for the study, incorporating *impressionistic tales of the field* (van Maanen, 1988), because I felt that it was most able to capture the full richness, complexity and human quality of school life. Theories, however complex, must simplify life by abstracting some facets and ignoring others.

Stories, too, highlight some facets and hide others—a process of selection is involved. I believe, however, that stories, through allusion and shading and other fictional techniques, can capture facets, faces and voices in classrooms that are missed by theories and the practices of theory building. I argue that stories and impressionistic tales are valuable as planks of a research methodology for what they show us, but that their use must be accompanied by a critical consciousness of what they hide.

That's part of the role of the surrounding text and interpretation that embeds and reflects on the tales. Impressionistic tales are usually told from inside my own perspective, and therefore don't challenge my own assumptions and readings of events. By deconstructing the tales—applying Habermas' *emancipatory* interest to exploring my own reified notions—another layer of richness is added to the representation. And perhaps at least some of my personal biases are laid bare before the reader, in order that they might be taken into account when reading the tales.

This, too, is reflective action. My experiences in the school incorporated *reflection-in-action* (Schön, 1983) and writing the original impressionistic tales constitutes one level of *reflection-on-action*. Interpreting and commenting on the tales in writing my dissertation (Geelan, 1998) and adapting it as part of a book

(Geelan, 2004), and in this chapter, constitutes a second level of reflection-on-action and the pedagogically focused reflection that this text provokes within the reader is yet another layer of reflection. In a parallel set of descriptions provided by John van Maanen (1995) this last layer constitutes the *third moment of ethnography*. For Van Maanen, the first moment of ethnography corresponds to the fieldwork and the second to the writing. The third moment occurs when readers make their own meaning through a dynamic interaction of the text with their existing knowledge, beliefs and experiences.

I hope that these recollections and reflections of mine have provided evidence of a developing pedagogical thoughtfulness on my own part, and an occasion for reflection on your own pedagogical beliefs and practices. If so, I hope you'll consider writing some impressionistic autobiographical tales to capture and share *your* teaching/learning/research.

Notes

[1] This is a pseudonym, as are all names used in the body of this chapter except my own and that of my doctoral supervisor, Peter Taylor.

References

Clandinin, D. J., & Connelly, F. M. (1996). Teachers' professional knowledge landscapes: teacher stories—stories of teachers—school stories—stories of schools. *Educational Researcher, 25* (3), 24–30.

Davis, B. (1995). Why teach mathematics? Mathematics education and enactivist theory. *For the Learning of Mathematics, 15* (2), 2–9.

Denzin, N. K., & Lincoln, Y. S. (1994). *Handbook of qualitative research.* Thousand Oaks, CA: Sage.

Eisner, E. W. (1998). *The enlightened eye: Qualitative inquiry and the enhancement of educational practice.* Upper Saddle River, NJ: Merrill.

Ellis, C. (1997). Evocative autoethnography: Writing emotionally about our lives. In W. G. Tierney & Y. S. Lincoln (Eds.), *Representation and the text: Re-framing the narrative voice* (pp. 115–139). Albany: State University of New York Press.

Geelan, D. R. (1994). Learning to communicate: perspective transformations of a developing science teacher. Unpublished M.Ed. thesis, University of Melbourne.

Geelan, D. R. (1996). Learning to communicate: developing as a science teacher. *Australian Science Teachers Journal, 42* (1), 30–34.

Geelan, D. R. (1997). Epistemological anarchy and the many forms of constructivism. *Science & Education, 6,* 15–28.

Geelan, D. R (1998). *School stories: Weaving narrative nets to capture classrooms.* Unpublished Ph.D. thesis, Curtin University, Perth, Australia.

Geelan, D. R. (2004). *Weaving narrative nets to capture classrooms: Multimethod qualitative approaches for research in education.* Dordrecht, The Netherlands: Kluwer Academic Publishers.

Glasersfeld, E. von (1989). Cognition, construction of knowledge and teaching. *Synthese, 80,* 121–140.

Habermas, J. (1978). *Legitimation crisis.* Boston: Beacon Press.

Lincoln, Y. S., & Guba, E. G. (1985). *Naturalistic inquiry.* Beverly Hills, CA: Sage.

Schön, D. (1983). *The reflective practitioner.* New York: Basic Books.

Steier, F. (1995). From universing to conversing: An ecological constructivist approach to learning and multiple description. In L. P. Steffe & J. Gale (Eds.), *Constructivism in education* (pp. 67–84). Hillsdale, NJ: Lawrence Erlbaum Associates.

Taylor, P. C. (1997, March). *Telling tales that show the brushstrokes.* Paper presented at the annual meeting of the National Association for Research in Science Teaching, Chicago, IL.

Taylor, P. C., & Campbell-Williams, M. (1993). *Critical constructivism: Towards a balanced rationality in the high school mathematics classroom.* Paper presented at the annual meeting of the American Educational Research Association, Atlanta, GA.

Tobin. K. (1990). Social constructivist perspectives on the reform of science education. *Australian Science Teachers Journal, 36* (4), 29–35.

van Maanen, J. (1988). *Tales of the field: On writing ethnography.* Chicago: University of Chicago Press.

van Maanen, J. (Ed.). (1995). *Representation in ethnography.* Thousand Oaks, CA: Sage.

van Manen, M. (1990). *Researching lived experience: Human science for an action sensitive pedagogy.* New York: State University of New York Press.

van Manen, M. (1991). *The tact of teaching: The meaning of pedagogical thoughtfulness.* New York: State University of New York Press.

12 Transacting with Auto/Biography in the Teaching of Elementary Science

Judith A. McGonigal

In order to answer the question of what a form of behavior represents, [it is] necessary to discover its origin and the history of its development up to the present. (Vygotsky, 1981, p. 147)

School science has been viewed by many educators and researchers as a culture that competes with the worldview of learners in elementary classrooms in both Western and non-Western societies (Cobern & Aikenhead, 1998). This cultural difference often is identified as an underlying cause for students not embracing science. Inviting learners to engage in self-selected science inquiry can be a means to recontextualize the activities and objectives of school science with the real-life interests of learners. Coparticipating with learners in self-selected science investigations can be a medium that classroom teachers use to uncover the talents, beliefs, and resources for learning of individual students.

This auto/biographical study identifies how I deconstructed my prior concepts of science education as a transmission of facts and reconstructed science into an epistemological tool that has the potential to give voice and clarity to the worldview of learners. This auto/biography also identifies my personal experiences, which focused my professional inquiry on restructuring the science education in my elementary classroom into an occasion for students to engage in self-selected inquiries that are grounded in childhood curiosity and passion about a natural phenomenon. Finally, this auto/biography of an educator's self-reconstruction documents how I learned to listen to, and use the multiple perspectives of, other learners in my construction of knowledge about learning and teaching science.

Methodology

As I had become a reflective practitioner after participating in a research-based teacher certification program in the 1980s, I had acquired the habit of automatically generating and preserving student journals, correspondence archives, and the audiotapes of student and parent interviews as part of my teaching practice. I regularly recorded in my teacher's notebook when I was confronted with a disorienting dilemma that required me to change my teaching practices.

This auto/biographical study uses a five-year data source that I created while I participated in two summer science institutes and taught first and fourth grades in a small suburban elementary school. Reviewing this collection of saved journals, notebooks, correspondence, and transcriptions of audiotapes and selected resources helped me to identify experiences in my past that enabled me to create a new conceptualization of the role of science in the elementary classroom. Ongoing drafts of this text were shared with the participants whose interactions and feedback helped to shape my present understandings about doing and learning science through inquiry. However, it is important to note that, as Guba and Lincoln (1981) suggest, this interpretive narrative is a single translation of earlier events, which are filtered by my existing values and beliefs. Thus, this is not a record of what was, but rather a report of what I presently perceive as having occurred, or how I presently know my past (Gusdorf, 1980).

Composing my own Auto/Biography while Engaging in Science

My enthusiasm for doing, learning, and teaching science was born in a rural college laboratory school during a two-week summer science course designed to introduce teachers to an inquiry-based curriculum. Prior to my participation in this professional development opportunity, my inclination was to avoid the teaching of science to my elementary students, as is typical for many elementary school teachers (Roth, Tobin, & Ritchie, 2001). My personal experiences at that summer institute for fourth grade teachers revealed to me how worldviews can determine how learners approach a science activity.

My first invitation at the summer institute to be a scientist was offered as a challenge: without a prototype or directions, build an equal-arm balance scale from recyclable materials. This task, which took me more than ten hours to complete, introduced me to the motivating attraction "doing science" could have for

for learners. It also forced me to look at myself and begin to decompose my science auto/biography as I participated in a technology task.

Identifying My Problem-Solving Habits

Other participants completed their scales in less than an hour. However, coming with little prior understanding about how a balance scale worked, I needed to figure out so much. My most vociferous novice conception was that I ought to hang each weighing pan from the balance arm with two strings. I spent hours trying to find exactly where to attach the two strings to create balance. Even when my instructor suggested that I consider using three strings for each pan, I refused. I was determined to find a way to make it work with just two strings. Although every other completed balance scale made by the participants attached the weighing pans with three strings, I continued, as Watson and Kopenicek (1990) have documented that children do in elementary science classrooms, to hold on to my hardcore ideas, in the face of discrepant evidence. Finally, when I had manipulated every other variable on that scale without success, my instructor re-entered my zone of proximal development and reminded me that in geometry three points determine a plane. I added the third string to each weighing pan and constructed a working balance scale.

In this science engagement, I not only had discovered how to build a balance scale, but also I had come face to face with my auto/biography. How many times in how many previous situations had I held firm to a preconception, had I sought out solutions alone, had I been unwilling to acknowledge an ill-conceived plan of action unless no viable way of defending it existed? In addition, I had informally internalized the conditions that Strike and Posner (1985) identified were necessary for one science concept to be replaced by another. My initial way of thinking had been challenged by a discrepant event, a new understandable explanation for the phenomenon had unfolded, and an opportunity to test and confirm the new explanation had been provided. I had experienced science knowledge being individually constructed through social and material interaction, rather than transmitted.

Facing My Beliefs and Values

Another activity at that summer training session heightened my awareness of how our life experiences influence how we engage in a science investigation. I was asked to explore four different ways to start a fire. I refused to engage in this science activity. As a child, I had learned to fear fire. I had been coached not to touch matches. Someone else always lit the birthday candles on my cake and the gas pilot in the kitchen oven. As a teenager, my fear of fire was reinforced after watching, from my bedroom window, flames rage out of control and consume an entire apartment building.

This fire-making science assignment activated these memories, and I resisted using flint and steel, a hand lens, or a bow and drill to create a spark. My science education instructor, by providing a forum for me to compose my auto/biography, honored my worldview and then was able to lead me across the border to a new way of acting and knowing. After talking with me and discovering my fear of fire, he cautiously put my hands in his and together we used wooden spoons to connect the two electrodes of a dry cell battery with steel wool. We touched the glowing steel wool to small scraps of paper placed in an aluminum pie plate and started a fire. We put out the flames by emptying a small bucket of water into the pie plate. It was through this shared weaving of auto/biography and hands-on investigation of fire that my avoidance of teaching science began to fade. Later, in that summer science institute, I made a fire to cook the fish that I had dissected, to harden the clay earrings that I had made from soil collected on the roadside, and to brew the tea made from herbs that I had grown from seeds. As I participated in each activity, I watched my worldview start to value the customs and habits of scientists, as I began to internalize and use a discourse for science.

Reading Biographies to Uncover the Habits of Scientists

In the fall, when I returned to my elementary school, I wanted to make the culture of my classroom more science-like. I searched with my students in biographies of famous scientists to uncover the social and language structures, beliefs, and attitudes that were the habits of mind of scientists (AAAS, 1993).

Passion for Birds

While the fourth graders built bird feeders and documented the birds that they sighted near our school, we participated in the shared reading of the biography of John James Audubon (Kendall, 1993). As a boy, Audubon would carry home to his mother a sparrow's egg or a finch's nest in his bulging pocket. His mother would encourage his self-selected interest by delighting in each treasure that he showed her. To further facilitate his childhood passion for birds, she gave him a flageolet, a musical whistle, which Audubon took to the woods and used to practice birdcalls. We also read about his continual questioning and focused ingenuity to study birds in adulthood. He developed a means of tracking a pair of phoebes that nested in a nearby cave, and he invented a way to use wires to hold up the birds that he had shot so that he could paint them in lifelike poses.

Fascination for Fish

When the fourth graders built an aquarium in the classroom and visited the local fish market to dissect large catfish, we read together the biography of Eugenie Clark (McGovern, 1978). We learned how Eugenie's mother regularly took her daughter on Saturdays to an aquarium where she carefully recorded her observations of the sharks. We discovered how her mother bought her fish for each holiday present to place in her home aquarium. We found out that she encouraged Eugenie to dialogue with other science experts by helping her become the youngest member to join the Queens County Aquarium Society.

Love for Flowers

When the fourth graders planted flower seeds and investigated plants, we read the biography of George Washington Carver (Epstein & Epstein, 1960). Again we noticed how, as a child, this scientist had a passion for a specific natural phenomenon, which was recognized and nurtured by others. George Washington Carver loved flowers. As a young boy, he dug up flowers and ferns in the woods and carried them home to plant in his own secret garden where he carried out numerous experiments, without a predictable outcome, to determine how best to make them grow. At a very young age, family and friends called Carver "plant doctor," asking him for advice and help with their gardens.

Discovering the Resilience of Childhood Interests

Although my students and I had uncovered in these biographical texts examples of the habits of scientists (thriving curiosity, constant questioning, focused ingenuity, careful observation, planned experimentation, and tolerance of ambiguity), we also identified one particular pattern of social interaction. For each scientist the individual interest of the successful researcher had been encouraged and actively supported by significant others in childhood.

I wondered what the implication of this finding was for elementary science education. Where was this type of individual nurturing of a child's self-selected inquiry in my existing science curriculum? During the following three school years (Fall 1994–Spring 1997), I read professional books and journal articles searching for a way to manage individual science inquiries. Unfortunately, I concluded that, even when I allocated classroom time for individual investigations, I did not know how to initiate or how to sustain individual inquiries.

Observing Auto/Biographies Composed in Science Inquiry

My desire to learn how to understand and nurture science inquiry led me to attend another summer science institute held in New York City, where teachers came to participate in a four-week exploration of science inquiry. There I observed auto/biography being composed while students cycled back and forth across the border between living and sciencing. My developing awareness of the significance of learning science through identifying the differing worldviews of teachers and students, based on life experiences, was enhanced by my participation in science engagements with three students:

- Jenny, a middle-aged Ecuadorian undergraduate, who taught me that experiences determine perception;
- Liz, an African American teacher of fourth grade, who helped me identify and verbalize my own problem-solving strategy by comparing it to her own;
- Lee Ann, a 19-year old Asian American college sophomore, whose family showed me the need of schools to tap the home resources of every student.

An Auto/Biography Illuminates how Experience Influences Perception

Jenny had worked many years in the New York City schools as an educational assistant. When asked to self-select a material to investigate for a two-week science inquiry, Jenny found an iron bell that she wanted to study. For two days, Jenny walked around the summer institute workshop ringing the bell and trying to think of a productive question that she wanted to answer. Several students brought bells made from different materials (glass, ceramic, aluminum, and pewter) for Jenny to include in her investigation.

Initial Way of Thinking

I make the iron bell sound and it sounds great. I did the glass and also this one was good. I made the ceramic sound and also it was good and, for the other two metal materials, the sound didn't sound as a treat at all. I talked about the bells to a couple of students. I asked them, "So you like it?" I'm not sure that they are impacted by the bells as I was. (Jenny's science notebook entry, July 1997)

Jenny later shared with her classmates at her science inquiry presentation that she had selected the iron bell to investigate because it was a treat to hear. It reminded her of the church bell that rang in her mountain village in Ecuador. Whenever her dad heard that bell toll, he called for his two daughters to dress in their best clothes and join him as they walked, hand-in-hand, down the mountainside together to worship. Handling the iron bell in the science classroom provided Jenny a forum to share her auto/biography, which eventually helped me to understand how I was not matching her zone of proximal development.

I did not know what to do with the bells. How was I to find science in the bells? I went to my adviser. She looked at the bells and then said, "What would happen if you moved the clapper higher or lower? Would it change the sound?" Bill, another student in the class, yelled to me, "Music is based on the *pitch*. See if the sound of each bell is high or low." *Pich*???? (Jenny's science notebook entry, July 1997)

As her advisor, I had imposed my own personal question on Jenny's investigation. I had not yet learned about the importance of trusting students to become self-reliant learners who sought to follow the trail of their own questions in a science inquiry. I had not yet discovered how life experiences intertwine and inform how one goes about doing science. As teachers and researchers often do (Duit, Treagust, & Mansfield, 1996), I was interpreting a student's responses through my own perspective. While trying to construct a concept of Jenny's conception of sound, I was giving my meaning to Jenny's investigation. Since my daughters played the hand bells in church each Sunday, I was aware of how the height and circumference of the base of the bell's opening determined its pitch. I was curious about whether the placement of the clapper would change the quality of the tone. Jenny had grown up listening to only the one bell ringing in the church tower. When she listened to music she attended to the feelings that the sounds elicited from her. In retrospect, I do not believe Jenny had ever been invited to hear the different pitches in music.

I was desperate. I was working on how to tie the clapper to the bell for two days. I go up to my adviser and say, "I still don't know what my question is?" She said, "What determines the pitch?" I say, "*Pich*." Inside me I am thinking that I hear that word before, because she is not talking about peach fruit for sure. She said, "The pitch." I respond, "Very little." (Jenny's science notebook entry, July 1997)

I initially believed that I was encountering a communication problem associated with English being a second language for Jenny. So I took Jenny over to the musical instruments and asked her to tell me what she heard when we played a xylophone. I was trying to discover her label for pitch:

My advisor made me play with musical instruments. She asked me to tell her how the sounds were different. Not knowing what to say, but to say something I said here is a dull sound. And here is a fine sound. (Jenny's science notebook entry, July 1997)

I thought I had discovered the labels Jenny used for low (dull) sounds and high (fine) pitches. But unfortunately, I was again imposing my understandings on her science investigation. When I reversed the position of the xylophone, Jenny told me that the dull sounds were now what I called the high pitches and the fine sounds were what I labeled as low. After a few more times of changing the position of the xylophone, it appeared to me that "dull" meant sounds that were made close to her and "fine" meant sounds that were made at a farther distance from her. She was still not attending to my construct for pitch.

New Understandable Explanation

I obtained a movable xylophone, which is composed of metal bars that are mounted on separate blocks of wood. Hoping to connect with her experiences, I spoke about how an opera singer would sing the Ave Maria. I exaggerated the high tones as I sang. I asked her to mimic my opera singing. Then I had her try to match her voice with the tone of each bar as it was repeatedly struck. Next I took a guitar from the musical instrument collection. I began plucking the same string but holding it down at different frets. As I plucked the string, I asked Jenny to tell me when the sound was the same pitch. Then Jenny took the guitar and she began plucking different strings and labeling the different pitches that she heard as higher or lower.

Opportunity to Test and Confirm the New Understanding

This was the learning of my life about pitch. Proudly after I learned, I consulted most of the students I could to show them the pitch! I asked to take the colored xylophone home for the weekend. I spent most of Sunday playing songs on the xylophone using a color-coded book. I now was able to understand what I was supposed to have learned last year when I had my music education class and was unable to play the recorder to please my instructor. Now I could hear the pitch. (Jenny's science notebook entry, July 1997)

I never perceived that students and teachers could hold a different meaning for a science concept until I had this interaction with Jenny and the bells. I had believed that, as Trumbull (1990) had noted about too many elementary educators, there was one correct answer that is transmitted from teachers to students when science is being taught. Spending so much time at the side of this bilingual scientist as she composed her auto/biography while we engaged in science inquiry allowed me to observe how individuals perceived a natural phenomenon differently, though it was labeled similarly. Our life stories served as a filtering lens that determined how and what we uncovered in our science explorations. As an anthropologist had reported while living immersed in foreign cultures, I likewise began to understand how "deeply perception is shaped by forces of memory, desire, and expectations, other then the messages of the senses" (Bateson, 1994, p. 55).

This intersection of life and science demonstrated to me that perception was not only constructed but also constricted by life experiences. It highlighted how important it is to honor my students' auto/biographies that are voiced while they participate in doing science. It made me aware that as a teacher I needed to encourage dialogue in the science classroom along with fluency in science discourse. I believe that this experience of colearning with Jenny caused me to make time the following year to gather close at the side of each first grader and listen carefully to what they were doing and learning as they engaged in their self-selected science inquiry.

An Auto/Biography Identifies Problem-Solving Strategies

Liz was a fourth grade teacher in the New York City public schools where recently simple machines had been added to the science curriculum. She decided to use the four-week summer institute to prepare herself for her teaching assignment in the fall. Liz found a box containing single and double pulleys, ropes, and weights, and she began her exploration of simple machines.

Initial Way of Thinking

As Liz started to engage in her investigation, it quickly became obvious that pulley systems were not part of her prior experience. She hung the pulleys on the ropes like Christmas tree ornaments. After another student tried to suggest a pulley system that she might try to construct, I watched Liz set to work.

Discrepant Event

Each time she encountered a problem with her system, when the string tangled or jumped off the wheel of the pulley, Liz, without ever trying to uncover the cause of the problem, would tear the entire system down and start anew. She never moved any closer to success, but always moved closer to increased dissatisfaction with herself. Once in a while, I could hear her murmur, as she tore her pulley system apart, "I hate science and especially working with these pulleys" (Instructor's observation notes, July 1997).

New Understandable Explanation

At lunch, I dialogued with Liz about our experiences teaching fourth grade and our lack of experience with pulley systems. I suggested to Liz that she might try using an alternative problem-solving strategy. Instead of starting from scratch each time she encountered a difficulty, she might want to stop and observe the situation in order to identify a possible underlying cause of the problem.

Opportunity to Test and Confirm the New Explanation

The next morning Liz asked if I would come and work with her when she encountered her first snag in her pulley system. Together we began untangling the ropes and constructing knowledge about effort, load, and resistance. As we worked together, building and refining several fixed and movable pulley systems, Liz began composing her auto/biography for me. She told me about growing up in the Bronx, where she always had tried to do things just right in school. She recalled how frustrated she felt when she made a mistake and how she would crumple her schoolwork up and start all over again. In Liz's childhood worldview, an error was evidence of ignorance, which must be hidden from others and not viewed by oneself as a starting point for discovery and learning.

Again I was seeing and hearing auto/biography being voiced as teacher and student co-participated in a science inquiry. This time it was not a story about a prior experience influencing perception, but rather it was a narrative about a ritualized problem-solving strategy. As Palmer (1998) has so clearly articulated, I was learning how the "knower and known are joined" and how "any claim about the nature of the known reflects the nature of the knower as well" (p. 92).

I also realized from this experience of interacting with a learner who was investigating a topic for which I had little prior knowledge, that it was possible for a teacher to co-construct knowledge of science concepts while facilitating a student's science investigation. This understanding gave me the freedom to allow my first graders to select any topic to investigate, regardless of my own expertise.

An Auto/Biography Constructs Respect for the Culture of Students' Homes

The final student at the institute who informed my teaching practice was Lee Ann, a first generation Chinese student who had been raised with her six brothers and sisters in a two-bedroom apartment in a high-rise housing project at the foot of the Brooklyn Bridge. At the summer institute, Lee Ann studied the structure of a eucalyptus plant. Carefully she made slides of cross-sections of the plant. As her science notebook steadily filled with detailed drawings and reflective comments, Lee Ann also began mentoring another student, Juanita, who was unsuccessfully trying to dissect fish. Lee Ann invited Juanita to come with her to the fish market in Chinatown where they could witness and learn how to observe and to identify the inside organs of a fish.

I joined these two students as they tried to coax shop owners in Chinatown to be their science instructors. However, we soon realized that we were not going to be informed unless we made a purchase. So we bought a large bluefish and were shown how to enter the body cavity through the anus. At the conclusion of our science lesson in the market place, we were left holding a large freshly gutted bluefish. Lee Ann suggested that we take it home to her mom to cook.

Initial Way of Thinking Deconstructed by Discrepant Event

Many of my stereotypes about the housing and the culture of the urban poor were deconstructed, when I entered Lee Ann's immaculate two-bedroom apartment in a high-rise public housing complex. I did not expect to see windowsills covered with eucalyptus plants tended by her mother and the living room wall hidden by her dad's aquariums, including a hospital tank for unhealthy fish and a nursery for the newly hatched.

New Understandable Explanation

While we ate dinner with the family, Lee Ann's father, a watch repairman who took extra work home to pay for equipment that he needed to maintain his fish, spent fifty minutes teaching Juanita about how to set up an aquarium. He gave Juanita chemicals and tools to take back to our science classroom to help her to establish a tank for thriving fish.

As Juanita (from the Dominican Republic where Spanish was her first language) and Lee Ann's dad (from China where Mandarin Chinese was his first language) shared in science discourse with me (from New Jersey where English was my first language), I realized that doing science was multi-lingual and multi-ethnic. I was confronted with the reality that each of us had much science to learn from the life experiences of others. Here, in a crowded apartment in a housing project, was a family that knew how to observe nature and nurture life. Here were parents who knew how to engage in science discourse at the dinner table with their children. Here was a home that was rich with science resources for our classroom. This experience of instructor, student, and family members talking science together in the home etched a memory which later served as a foundation of how I interacted with the families of first graders when I went to their homes to uncover how their self-selected science investigations were progressing.

Opportunity to Test and Confirm New Understanding

While co-participating in doing science inquiry with these college students, I discovered how auto/biography not only was composed as one engaged in science exploration, but also framed the shape of the investigation. I saw in that science classroom that "the realities of self and world are relative, dependent on context and point of view" (Bateson, 1994, p. 12). I began to be able to see how science was a way of observing and knowing, a tool that gave richer meaning to life's experiences in any culture.

Embracing Multiplicity in the Elementary Classroom

When I returned to my suburban elementary school, I was determined to uncover a way to replicate the learning interactions that I had experienced at the Science Inquiry Summer Institute. Because I had experienced learning on the periphery while encouraging others in their self-selected inquires, I had an intuitive, but not yet actualized, understanding of how to initiate and sustain science inquiry. I also had a new belief system that supported my intention for finding a way to have students engage in self-selected science inquiries. I now viewed self-selected science inquiries not only as a means to make science education more meaningful for the individual learner, but also as a way to embrace multiplicity in my classroom.

Giving Voice to Children through Self-selected Science Inquiry

Three months into the school year, I invited the twenty students in my first grade classroom to self-select a science topic to investigate at home. Each topic had to be one that could be explored by handling materials, not reading texts. With support from parents and the classroom teacher, each of these twenty students did become science experts, who shared in oral reports surrounded by a whiteboard and hands-on evidence, their science news from their self-selected inquiry with their teacher, their peers, and their classmates' families. Even though I had visited each home once, to replicate the science talk I had experienced at Lee Ann's dining room table in New York City, I still had few opportunities to see and hear the auto/biographies that were composed as the six-year old scientists engaged in their research. Therefore, I asked the parents of the first graders to write the earlier history that they believed surrounded their child's choice of topic. Perhaps because parents enjoy looking backwards and finding meaning in the ordinary interactions with their child, their written responses were rich with detail. Two first graders' histories document how, when given the option to self-select a topic for science inquiry, young learners seem naturally to connect doing science to a real-life personal passion or puzzlement.

Identifying the Roots of Engagement: The Flower Expert

I first met Danielle, a new student assigned to my first grade classroom, a week before school when I visited her home to introduce myself to her family. When I asked to take a photograph of Danielle in her favorite spot in her home, this spunky red-headed lass ran out the front door, across the street, and sat herself in the middle of her neighbors' flower bed which was abloom with red, pink, and white petunias. It was no surprise to me that, three months later, Danielle selected flowers as her topic to investigate. However, it was not until more than a year later, when reading a reflection written by her mother, that I learned about the meaning of flowers in Danielle's life:

At age two: Danielle always seemed to pick flowers. She would pick them without the stems and give them to me as a gift.

At age two years, six months: Danielle loved smelling different flowers that drew her to them. I can remember when she was two and a half years old smelling all the lilies in my garden. I even have a picture of it.

At age four: But I believe it was her grandfather who influenced her even more about flowers. He showed her how to remove the seeds from pods and save them in bags to plant for the next year. He showed her how to rub pollen from one flower to pollinate another one to create a new flower. He had her planting seeds and watering them each visit to his house.

At age five: Danielle continued to be attracted to flowers because of their fragrance. She found comfort in touching, controlling, smelling, and experiencing flowers.

At age six: For her science inquiry Danielle studied flowers. She picked flowers out at the supermarket and from our garden. She dissected a lily. She opened up several stems to see if they were wet, hard, dry, hollow, or soft. She smelled the flowers and discovered that flowers that had hard stems were more likely not to have a fragrance. She took various flowers and sat them outside in the cold, in water, to see what would happen. She got seeds and planted them in the kitchen. She dried flowers and noticed how they changed colors. (Danielle's mother, written response, November 15, 1998)

When Danielle did her science presentation and taught her classmates what she had learned about flowers (see Figure 12.1), I didn't know to question and

Figure 12.1. Danielle shared her knowledge and love of flowers with her peers.

listen for the auto/biography that surrounded her investigation. In looking back at both the words that she verbalized and the words that her mother penned, I now realize how significant was her personal theory about the correlation of the hardness of a stem with strength of a flower's fragrance. The study of flowers was full of personal meaning and significance for Danielle. Science was a tool for Danielle to make more meaning of the world she valued.

Connecting with a Childhood Passion: The Frog Expert

Another first grader whose auto/biography was silently composed as he did his science inquiry was Steven. I was first introduced to Steven when I visited his home before school started in the fall. Steven was a petite, quiet child whose eyes scanned my every move and whose ears captured every word I uttered. The photograph that I took to document our first interaction shows Steven kneeling at a coffee table in his living room while playing with small plastic toy reptiles and amphibians. Here in the safety of the culture of home, Steven was able to signify to his new teacher his personal interests and passion.

When later provided an opportunity to self-select a topic to investigate for two months during first grade, Steven decided to observe live tadpoles and frogs. At the conclusion of his study, he presented his science news about these amphibians to his classmates with confidence and pride.

Steven's science inquiry oral presentation was uncharacteristic of Steven's classroom persona. Five months prior to his science talk, he had asked to be the director of a class play because he did not want to perform in front of an audience. One month prior to his science presentation, Steven had asked his classmates to move away from him while he read a favorite book to them because he got very scared when he had to perform for anyone.

But sharing what Steven had done and what he had learned about frogs was not a performance for Steven; rather he was being himself, a frog expert who had been allowed to use his childhood passion to frame his science inquiry. After teaching his classmates about frogs, Steven begged to be given an opportunity to share his frog presentation with another audience. His mother recorded the history of Steven's unfolding interest and expertise:

At age eight months: I just found a five-minute-plus segment on videotape that shows Steven crawling around with his grandmother's friendly dog, Bandit. His dad and I are throwing Bandit's favorite toy around the room and baby Steven and the dog repeatedly bound off together in a mock race for a toy frog. Bandit, being the gentlemen he was back then, allowed Steven to get to the frog before him, or they would engage in a gentle game of tug-of-war with the frog. All the while, the grownups in the video kept encouraging Steven to "get the FROG" and verbally exulting him, "Steven got the FROG!" each time that he successfully retrieved the toy. Watching the video, you can see how Steven loved the attention. I can't even count how many times the word 'frog' is spoken so dramatically in the video segment.

At age one: First by baby coach and then by foot, Steven always adored a good spin around the block searching for life in the form of little toads. He would insist the grownups catch them so that he could gently stroke their skin before releasing them safely home to their awaiting families.

At age two: Steven's world blossomed when weekly visits all year round became routine once we discovered the Cape May Zoo. The zoo park system included a fresh water lake where Steven's dad took him on his first fishing expedition when he was two years old. That day Steven watched some older boys pull some frogs out of the lake's feeder stream. Each return visit to the lake brought with it the inevitable search for frogs; we never did catch any there for him to hold or touch. It became an obsession – catching a frog from that lake. The fishing was a necessary ruse to get Dad to drive him to the zoo.

At age three: Steven's passion for collecting and organizing little animal toys expanded beyond his hundreds of frogs, snakes, lizards, turtles that he had collected since he turned one (and still is intact today). He also began collecting a full range of amphibian and reptile books, posters, and costumes.

Figure 12.2. Steven shared his passion for frogs with his peers and his fourth grade mentors.

At age four: Since Steven's dad had kept an aquarium as a youngster, he made special trips to pet stores and the public aquarium with Steven to expose him to different types of fish. Steven loved the fish and never missed an opportunity during those trips to check out the amphibians and reptiles that he saw in those places.

At age six: Steven's self-confidence and willingness to take risks soared on the wings of his self-driven investigation into frogs. His inquiry was a window for Steven's school family to see what we have seen all along, a person who is thrilled by the prospect of learning more about the world around him, a person who is driven and focused when his curiosity is ignited, a person who loves to learn and share what he has learned with others. We could never have imagined our six-year old son standing in front of first graders, fourth-graders, teachers, parents, and a video camera to speak about what and how he learned about frogs (see Figure 12.2). He didn't have a performance issue because he was the expert. He was empowered already before he even began to speak. He knew his stuff about frogs; he had no fear about performing, because he was teaching, and in his mind no person in the room knew more about frogs than he did. (Steven's mother, written response, October 10, 1998)

As Steven investigated frogs for his self-selected first grade science inquiry, he was looking back and giving past experiences new meaning. The frog expert was discovering for himself the patterns in the behavior of the amphibians that he now kept in a plastic terrarium in his bathroom and exercised in his bathtub. He also was teaching me how an elementary student will grasp science with delight when it is viewed as a tool that allows a child to better see and describe the small creatures that he had a history of trying to catch and view as a toddler.

Conclusions

Building the balance scale as a learner and exploring the sound of bells as an instructor helped me to stop viewing schooling as the transmission of facts or labels from teacher to student. I began to envision learning as the co-construction of understanding as participants in an activity mediate meaning while relating the present experience to past experiences.

Recognizing that initially I was unaware that my own auto/biography was fuelling my resistance to participate in the fire-making task encouraged me to help learners identify the concerns and fears that they bring to a science activity.

Reading about the childhood science activities of Audubon, Clark, and Carver challenged me to find a way to invite the children in my classroom to identify an interest to use as a focus for their own science research. Engaging children to carry out a self-selected investigation taps the natural curiosity and motivation of learners, provides an authentic way to honor life experiences, and creates an occasion for each child to be supported in his/her own individual interest by significant others.

Visiting with Lee Ann's family in New York City made me aware of the many resources for learning science that exist in each student's home. Dialoguing at the dinner table with Lee Ann, her parents, and Juanita about the care of fish in an aquarium helped me to embrace multiplicity and begin to develop an understanding and respect for the social construction of knowledge.

Acknowledging the existence of multiple perspectives and recognizing the benefit of giving voice to others enabled me to grow and to develop as a learner of science and science education. I realized the need for a time and place in my classroom for students and myself to construct science knowledge by rubbing our existing constructs up against the perspectives of others. I later extended this understanding to include the importance of shaping my classroom practices with the input of students and their parents.

Listening to the life stories of Danielle and Steven helped me to realize how rich are the life experiences that first graders bring to a classroom. I learned to view doing science as an epistemological tool that amplifies the authority of each individual learner.

References

American Association for the Advancement of Science (AAAS). (1993). *Benchmarks for science literacy.* New York: Oxford University Press.

Bateson, M. C. (1994). *Peripheral visions: Learning along the way.* New York: Harper Collins.

Cobern, W. A., & Aikenhead, G. S. (1998). Cultural aspects of learning science. In B. J. Fraser & K. G. Tobin (Eds.), *International handbook of science education* (pp. 39–52). Boston: Kluwer Academic Press.

Duit, R., & Treagust, D. (1998). Learning science: From behavourism towards social constructivism and beyond. In B. J. Fraser & K. G. Tobin (Eds.), *International handbook of science education* (pp. 3–25). Boston: Kluwer Academic Press.

Epstein, S., & Epstein B. (1960). *George Washington Carver: Agricultural scientist.* New York: Dell.

Guba, E. G., & Lincoln, Y. S. (1981). *Effective evaluation: Improving the usefulness of evaluation results through responsive and naturalistic approaches.* San Francisco: Jossey-Bass.

Gusdorf, G. (1980). Conditions and limits of auto/biography. In J. Olney (Ed.), *Auto/biography: Essays theoretical and critical* (pp. 28–48). Princeton, NJ: Princeton University Press.

Kendall, M. (1993). *John James Audubon: Artist of the wild.* Brookfield, CT: The Milbrook Press.

McGovern, A. (1978). *Shark lady: True adventures of Eugenie Clark.* New York: Four Winds Press.

Palmer, P. (1998). *The courage to teach.* San Francisco: Jossey-Bass.

Strike, K., & Posner, G. (1985). A conceptual change view of learning and understanding. In L. West & A. Pines (Eds.), *Cognitive structure and conceptual change* (pp. 45–67). Orlando, FL: Academic Press.

Roth, W.-M., Tobin, K., & Ritchie, S. (2001). *Re/constructing elementary science.* New York: Peter Lang.

Trumball, D. (1990). Introduction. In E. Duckworth, J. Easley, D. Hawkins, & A. Henriques (Eds.), *Science education: A minds-on approach for the elementary years* (pp. 1–20). Hillsdale, NJ: Lawrence Erlbaum Associates.

Vygotsky, L. S. (1981). The genesis of higher mental functions. In J. V. Wertsch (Ed.), *The concept of activity in Soviet psychology* (pp. 144–188). Armonk, NY: Sharpe.

Watson, B., & Kopnicek, R. (1990). Teaching for conceptual change: Confronting children's experience. *Phi Delta Kappan, 71,* 680–684.

13   Biomythography in Teacher Education

Sherry Nichols and Deborah J. Tippins

In this chapter we report on using photo essays as tools for critical reflection and for creating an outlaw genre: biomythography. Our reference to tool does not imply using an intrusive approach to manipulate or analyze prospective science teachers' learning for the purposes of research. Rather, our notion of a tool "allows group and contextual differences in mediated action to be understood in terms of the array of mediational means to which people have access and the patterns of choice they manifest in selecting a particular means for particular occasion" (Wertsch, 1991, p. 94). Accordingly, photo essays were intended to serve as tools that would allow us to negotiate our experiences and ideas about science teaching in our science methods courses.

Biomythography: An Outlaw Genre of Auto/Biography

Others in this volume present approaches and rationales for using autobiographical research in education. Our study explores an alternative framework and approach to auto/biography referred to as outlaw genres of auto/biography. Outlaw genres of auto/biography resist the tendency of western auto/biography to craft narratives that will ultimately link the life of an individual to a universalized person—someone to whom all readers can relate (Smith, 1998). Kaplan (1998) writes that the

homogenizing influence of auto/biography genres identifies similarities; reading an auto/biography involves assimilating or consenting to the values and worldview of the writer (p. 212) . . . outlaw genres [enable] a deconstruction of the master genres, revealing the power dynamics embedded in literary production, distribution, and reception. (p. 208)

The works of bell hooks (e.g., 1996) are examples of outlaw genres as she writes to preserve and transmit the life experiences of black southern life. Hooks' concern is that since most published biographical and autobiographical work documents the lives of white, middle and upper class writers, auto/biography as a literary archive has fallen short of its potential to render invisible the alternative life experiences of those persons whose lives are lived outside the dominant class. Outlaw genres renegotiate the relationship between personal identity and the world, between personal and social history. Personal histories, which traditionally have been written as "I," are deconstructed to recognize the social composition of individuals. In effect, mythologies that perpetuate the censorship of certain individuals can be re-examined as hegemonies working to confer inequitable identities in social contexts (Smith, 1998).

Roland Barthes (1985) describes myths as codified language that serve to notify us of cultural values, and simultaneously impose on us the sense that we should adopt these as values without question. Catherine Milne (1998) demonstrates how mythologies have shaped how science becomes texts to be taught in school. In the process of creating texts for science teaching, it is not possible to represent all events, thus a selective process is undertaken to communicate science events and ideas into coherent texts—or stories. Milne points out that all stories have in common their relation to culture via codes that are agreed-upon sets of rules or social norms or myths. Metacodes deeply embedded in science texts communicate and structure our interpretations of how things are in science and society. Texts that limit science history to descriptions of how European white males is an example of a metacode that communicates a myth that females and non-Europeans have not contributed to science. Mythologies similarly work toward establishing norms that shape how teachers come to make sense of teaching (Britzman, 1991).

We extend the notion of myths to consider the nature of mythologies in elementary science teacher preparation. However, as we resist seeing ourselves and our students as having unitary histories, we want to consider the possibilities that *multiple* mythologies mediate learning in the classes we teach. Biomythography, a genre of outlaw auto/biography, was a concept introduced by Audre Lorde that addresses the idea of multiple mythologies. Lorde's work was a strategic approach toward representing the politics of personal and social identity. King (cited in Kaplan, 1998) writes: "[Biomythography] as outlaw genre requires a recognition of layers of meanings, layers of histories, layers of reading and rereading through webs of power-charged codes" (p. 212). Kaplan describes the "text" of biomythography as the construction of maps that represent changing affiliations and coalitions that create a constant sense of flux in identities for persons whose personal sense of "identity" does not neatly resemble mainstream identity kits.

These ideas are important to our thinking about the nexus of identities and philosophies that come together in our elementary science methods courses. Our students, mostly females, each have a unique personal history. In the processes of becoming a teacher" however, mythologies work to censor and unify their images of what it means to be a teacher (Britzman, 1991). In effect, they lose their personal sense of agency thus undermining their potentials as critics and agents of change. Our own teaching, influenced by notions of critical and feminist pedagogy, creates tensions as we strive to contest myths associated with becoming teachers of science (Tippins, Nichols & Dana, 1999). While we are aware of affiliations that influence our activities as instructors, we are striving to find ways that help our students become aware of affiliations that shape their past and emergent identities as science learners and of teachers. Such awareness, we believe, will provide a basis for us to critique and negotiate identities and activities of teachers of science. In the process, we will be better able to censor myths that have historically alienated learners and teachers from science.

A characteristic of outlaw genre is there is no insistence on adhering to any one rule or form. Unlike the linear constraints of written or spoken auto/biographies, the graphic form of photo essay was intended to permit individuals to represent diverse referents they associate with science education as these are embedded in their life histories as science learners. Pauline Chinn (cited in Hatch & Wisniewski, 1995) defines life history as "self-referential stories through which the author-narrator constructs the identity and point(s) of view of a unique individual historically situated in culture, time, and place" (p. 115). Personal referents represent how teachers contextually think about and enact their science teaching practices (McRobbie & Tobin, 1995). We anticipated that photo essays, as alternative approach to auto/biography, would expand how prospective teachers reflect on their experiences and ideas of teaching and learning science.

In this study, we used a photo essay assignment as a way to facilitate student reflection on their views of science and science teaching and learning. We anticipated that their referents for science and learning would reflect various mythologies (i.e., Milne, 1998). The photo essay would create an opportunity for us to negotiate with our students diverse myths we hold about science, and science teaching and learning and implications our views might have in our science teaching practices. The notion of biomythography as a layered critique served us, as teachers and researchers, to look at multiple situations mediating teaching and learning in our courses. The nexus of our histories as students, science learners, and teachers, interacting with our diverse vantage points as critics of our experiences represented multiple layers that challenged our study. Accordingly, questions guiding our research included:

- What sorts of images mediate prospective elementary teachers' perspectives of learning to teach elementary science?
- What personal referents mediate their views of science, science teaching and, learning?
- In what ways do mythologies shape learning in our teacher education courses?
- What are the implications of using alternative frameworks to inform reform in science teacher education?

Biomythographies through the Production of Photo Essays

This study was a collaboration we (the authors) undertook to further inform our teaching and research using tools for reflection. Study participants involved prospective elementary teachers enrolled in science methods courses taught at our respective institutions. At the start of the semester, we engaged our students in the Draw a Scientist Test activity to initiate building a culture where outlaw dialogue was seen as acceptable. Science was not presumed to be a privileged way of knowing, or that we assumed an a priori definition of what counts as science. Rather, we wanted to engage our students in critiquing science and learning as personally socially constructed ideas and activities. With this agenda in mind, students were given an assignment we referred to as the Personal Science Inquiry Project. Students could use any approach they might like—experiments, collections, writings, drawings—to explore their ideas about science learning. We suggested the photo essay as one approach they might use. Our idea was that artifacts of their work would in effect create a community archive that would help us question mythologies and legacies of our science learning. We focused this study on results of the photo essay as this particular approach was an attempt to incorporate auto/biography into this archive-building endeavor.

Heeding the advice of others who have similarly attempted pedagogical approaches involving auto/biography (Richmond, Howes, Kurth, & Hazelwood, 1998), we tried to avoid describing this assignment to our students as an autobiographical writing assignment. Guidelines for the photo essay were designed, instead, to focus students' reflections on their ideas of science, and science teaching and learning. We encouraged students to frame their essay as a "story" or stories that reflect how they constructed their understanding in their personal experiences of science learning—in and out of school. To do the essay, students needed the following items: one roll of black and white film; one camera, one tape recorder, and one cassette tape. The assignment was given as follows: You are to take pictures that tell stories about your understandings of science, science teaching, and science learning. You will share your photo essay as your five-minute Personal Science Inquiry Project presentation in class. Fifteen students completed the photo essay assignment.

As an interpretive study, several data sources were used including: photos presented in essays, transcripts of students' oral essays taped during their class presentations, and narratives we developed to capture our reflections about this assignment. While it may have been desirable for the purposes of research to conduct interviews with students about their essays, we decided against this for several reasons. One, the Personal Science Inquiry Project was one of several approaches being used for this assignment, thus we felt others might feel neglected if their projects were not followed up with individual interviews. Second, we did not have sufficient time for individual interviewing as we had many other teaching responsibilities at the time. We, served as peer debriefers to each other throughout the semester, holding phone conferences to reflect on our experiences. As we reviewed data and reflected on our impressions, we wrote brief narratives to capture our thoughts. Writing the narratives helped us maintain a more holistic interpretation of the essays (as opposed to coding which would fragment ideas) and reflexively allowed us to incorporate our own interpretations in light of our specific research questions.

As a beginning point, we generally looked over the essays comparing and contrasting their general forms and expressions. We readily noted that few essays were communicated as reflections embedded in their life history. We also reviewed our own narrative notes to reflexively help us recall unique aspects of the presentations. Through multiple conversations and writings, we developed the following Results narrative to report outcomes of our collaborative study.

Archive of the Majority

While we were most interested to look at essays that were autobiographic in their construction, we also wanted to learn from the overall types of essays students submitted. Thus, we begin this section with a description of the majority of essays presented.

As we looked over the essays, we created two categories that described essays we called: *snapshots* and *slideshow*. A quality that distinguished these essays was an underlying rhetorical voice.

Snapshots

Photo essays in the "snapshot" category refer to essays having a single picture accompanied by brief commentary. One snapshot essay, for example, was entitled: "Leading Students to be Responsible, Aware, and Interactive Adults." The participant's photo depicted a group of adults standing outdoors watching birds. In the presentation of this essay, we heard an urgent storyline about the responsibility of the teacher to prepare students for their science future:

Teaching science in the younger grades prepares students for a lifetime of science. If they are not taught how to question, apply, and love the science they see around them they will never truly experience their world. We, as teachers, must instill in them a basis for a lifetime of learning. It is our responsibility to make science fun and engaging—for if we do not, we could loose out on the adults that we create. I never realized what an awesome responsibility has been laid at our feet as teachers and especially as teachers of science.

Another student's essay also articulated urgency for teachers to teach science, and for students to learn science. This student's snapshot was a picture of an outdoor carnival ride, and was entitled: "Making Students Aware of Science Around Them." Her story was punctuated with "musts" for both teachers and students:

Students *must* see how science applies to them personally for them to "buy" into learning. They *must* see that science surrounds us daily. Without it [science] the world would have no order and things we cherish would cease to exit. They *must* also be given the real life implication of learning science and why it is important. For students to see this, teachers of science *must* look for teachable moments all around them.

Underpinning these stories are mythical views that the teacher can empower students to become questioners, and that teacher can coerce students to "buy" into science. The narratives have a dogmatic tone. Participants' stories convey themes of conviction and commitment about the necessary importance of teaching science to children. Despite the fact that the majority of participants indicated a personal discomfort with their own science learning, they insisted that science must be taught and learned.

Slide Shows

Some essays were supported by multiple images, involving at least five photos. Slide shows, like the snapshot essays, promoted the theme that science education is essential to children's future well being. Terry's essay, an example of a slide show, was presented as series of photos accompanied by one-liners about the "benefits of science ideas." Terry entitled her essay: "A Lens Full of Science." She presented slide 1—a picture of a casserole cooking on her kitchen stove. Terry stated: "Science is a mixture of new idea, theories, and new worlds waiting to be discovered." Slide 2— a picture of a beautiful garden area, and Terry explained, "We want our children to express their ideas and grow with science." Slide 3—a scene of a house being built: "Children should be allowed the freedom to construct new ideas of their own." Slide 4—a picture of a motorcycle: "Many of these ideas will help human kind race towards a new and bright future." Slide 5—looking up through trees showing the sky above: "Many of these ideas will lead to advancements in space or," and Terry continued this thought with Slide 6—a picture of a cat," new ideas to help the animal kingdom on Earth." Slide 7—a picture of a box: "Instead of boxing children into the same way of thinking," Terry continued, finishing with Slide 8—a picture of yard gates, "science can open gates towards higher levels of understanding."

Terry is selling an irresistible package of science. Science is empowering in all senses. It frees our minds, takes us places, and opens up new visions for us. Interestingly, like many others' essays, Terry's photo essay is devoid of any human images. Science is simply out there, around us, available for anyone to use. Few essays explicitly dealt with the activities of science teachers, rather teachers were implicated as ideological vehicles. Without question, they promote the message that science is necessary and good for all.

These essays, albeit brief, provided a glimpse of referents prospective teachers' associated with science learning and teaching. Feelings of conviction, responsibility to promote science, and nervousness about being able to carry out science teaching revolve around mythologies of becoming a teacher of science. The dogmatic rhetoric prospective teachers used to communicate their ideas about science teaching perplexed us. Our students appeared firmly grounded in the belief that science learning is critically important for children. However, given that research has well documented that elementary science teachers infrequently teach science, we anticipate that few of these teachers will teach science with the sense of fervor communicated through their essays. The snapshot and slideshow essays raised many questions for us: Why did prospective teachers construct the types of essays they presented in class? What purposes are their products of reflection serving? Were their images and language being used to convince us or themselves that they were becoming prepared to teach science? Did we insufficiently create an environment where "outlaw" feelings and ideas about science learning and teaching could be expressed? Is the non-autobiographical construction of their essays perhaps signifying a metacode we should take note of?

Alternative Archives: Memory Boxes

Four out of the fifteen essays presented had a personal story underpinning their representations. We referred to the essays as being like "memory boxes," that is, a kind of container where people often use to keep photos of significant people, places and experiences. The personal level of insights conveyed through memory box essays distinguished these presentations from the majority of essays presented.

Katrice, an African American in her early thirties, presented one memory box essay. Katrice was born and raised in New Jersey. She shared with the class that she had enrolled in the Navy after graduating from high school, and later moved to North Carolina to join family members living in the area. She presented several photos of trees located beside her trailer home, and a couple of photos taken in science methods class. Katrice explained the images:

I took these pictures because I wanted pictures of learning centers being used to teach science. These [learning centers] were really important to me. They totally changed my view of science teaching. I always thought science was taking notes about some thing. That science is not like how we have learned science in here. Through the centers, we use many ways to look at many things all at once. I took the tree pictures because I didn't know you could do science looking at something like trees. I mean, when we look at trees you can study why some are tall, and why some are short. Before this I would have thought studying trees for science meant looking at a book. It was chemistry, earth science, and biology—individual subjects we studied. Now I realize, science is all around us. I can just walk out of my trailer and ask questions about the trees. I could plant a tree. We could watch it grow over time. That's science. Science is everywhere, and see, we can ask questions. I just didn't know.

Katrice saw approaches used in the science methods class as alternatives to learning science that contrasted her prior memories of science learning in school. The photo of students at learning centers prompted Katrice to rethink her notions of what it means to learn science. She began to challenge the myth that science is a body of knowledge she "should have" obtained through her years of schooling; she decided that science was more a process of questioning and investigating, and that she could play a legitimate role being a resource to her own science learning. Her essay, albeit brief, represented to her significant shifts in her thinking about her role as a learner of science.

Terrell presented another example of a "memory box" essay. Terrell, an African American in his late twenties, lives in a small rural town nearly two hours from the university. Last year, he obtained a job as a teaching assistant in charter middle school. Initially, the photo essay assignment appealed to him as he had experience as a "semi professional" photographer. He felt quite assured that his photographic strategy would capture his view of science as: "nature all around us." He began trying to photograph nature as science but found it problematic to think of science as objects. While his photo essay showed snapshots of nature (i.e., trees, a river, dead cat, garden), his narrative shared in class evidenced his development of much broader notions of science and science learning:

Before doing this project, I'd never given thought to this matter: "What is science?" I basically went around my town, taking photographs of things I deemed to be scientific. At first, I had difficulty—Where do I start? Where do I begin? But as I began combing the area, and put myself in a position of being more observant, I came to realize that everything is scientific. The question is, how can we take our daily experiences that are scientific and help relate them to kids we try to educate? Science, to be appreciated, must be hands-on, must be inclusive, and must allow persons to find out for themselves. Give them a way they can take their knowledge and explore what the possibilities are. I found out that science can be fun if the person taking part in this educational process can be included—allowed to ask questions, allowed to take away things and figure out by myself, how does it work?

My experience as a science student growing up was basically: teacher gives notes, teacher assigns reading passage, teacher gives quiz and test; not much room for experiment or observation. I attributed this to me not being interested in science at all. But, as I got older, and as my quest to know about things grew, I myself had to become my own scientist. Asking questions. Making observations. I figured out through personal involvement and re-working my way of thought as to how science should be studied, and how science is studied—being that it's not necessarily the way that it has to be, or necessarily the best way that it has to be. So with me, beginning with this field of education, and trying to be the best teacher I can be, and trying to instill a passion to help students to be the best they can be—I've come to the conclusion that it's up to me to help them see what they're actually taking part in, and that what's going on can deeply instill in them a passion to learn. That there's no real structure in the way things have to be studied. As long as they study with an enthusiasm and feeling that, "Yes, I feel like I'm involved," and, "Yes, I feel like I'm a part of this", that's what we all want when we get to the bottom line of things. We all like to feel involved. We all like to feel like we have some say in why this is the way it is. And with that in mind, it helps us have a better understanding of certain things.

So, my quest now is to try to help students realize their potential, and realize that science can be- not just a subject for those who seem serious, and not to have the opinion I once had that I, or they, can't possibly be a scientist. I mean that couldn't possibly be further from the truth! In our everyday lives, there are things we do, and things we are that make us scientists. And as a new teacher, and a possible teacher of science, it is my duty to help those students realize this objective. And to help them see that science is something that is fun and to have a feeling of goodness about what they are involved in. Scientists are not just the guys in the white coats. We all are scientists in our own way. And it's our duty to make sure that we investigate, observe, and infer about things that are questionable to us. We are inquisitive by nature. If we can instill in our students that being inquisitive by nature, and that being inquisitive is a good thing. And when being scientific can be a fun thing, then we as a society, and more so as our education goes, will be a success. And with reform going on in the field of education—it's up to us to open up new doors for students so that they can broaden their horizons and be the best they can be.

Terrell's presentation evidenced serious thought about his experiences as a science learner and his general view of science. He explicitly associated his disenfranchisement from science due to school science. The inflections of his voice on being allowed to ask questions, and being allowed to use materials suggest constraints he experienced as a learner. As teacher of science, he wants to give priority toward helping children experience "goodness" and broadening of life opportunities through his science teaching practices. School science is a site for connecting children's academic and ethical development in school. He also describes becoming aware of his mythical views of how science is done, and who does science; he has a broader view of science that allows him to be a scientist in his daily life. Like Katrice, he finds new possibilities to experience science beyond the school walls. He challenged the myth that schools are privileged to serve dispensers of science. He beamed in class as he made the point that he could appreciate learning science wherever he might choose to do so. It is not possible here, in written text, to convey the significant shift of spirit Terrell shared with us in class; his transformation as a learner of science was inspiring to us all. (Participants in class clapped when he finished!)

We present one final example of an essay presentation that has particularly provoked our thinking. Heather developed her photo essay on the topic of "Cloud Study." Her essay featured snapshots of clouds and included a demonstration of "making a cloud in a jar." Heather presented her "new scientific understandings about clouds" and proudly conducted her demonstration for us. But in her closing comments, she stated that her study made her "realize how stupid I am." She explained that she remembered studying the water cycle and cloud formation many times in school, but didn't seem to recall any of the information. In the process of making her essay, she became aware that she "knew little or nothing about how clouds formed, how it was possible for raindrops to hang up in the air as clouds, or why some clouds are big while others are not." Several times, she restated, "I just feel so dumb. I need to start learning science for real." As with all presentations, a few minutes were taken to respond to Heather's presentation. Sherry later reflected in her own narrative:

The conversation seemed to involve only myself and the student. I was not certain, but I felt other students were bothered by my evidently heightened interest to talk about Heather's presentation. No one else seemed too interested to explore Heather's feelings, they wanted to move on. (I later talked with Heather after class about her presentation.) We really needed more time to reflect on these important issues, but I'd only been able to squeeze these presentations into one day of our schedule. Most of our course had been devoted to making units and leaving campus to do practicum teaching—these are the activities students really invest their ideas and energies toward. The activities of reflection seemed of little value.

Our reflections on Heather's essay presentation raised multiple concerns for us. Unlike Katrice and Terrell, who seemed to dispel a school-imposed myth that knowledge must be given, Heather was blaming herself for not being a constructor of her own knowledge. A rather unethical situation had been created. Did Heather need further support to help move her beyond the myths of self-blame? The semester was ending, and both Heather and Sherry would be leaving town for the summer. Should Sherry try to establish follow-up meetings with Heather? If, so how and when should she do it? What if further explorations with Heather led into a personal history that extended beyond her auto/biography as a science learner? What sort of preparation did Sherry have that would qualify her to help Heather?

Katrice and Terrell's reflections seemed to help them resolve past histories of disempowerment as science knowers. Terrell's construction of alternative science learning referents for science learning contributed toward his construction of alternative referent for his future science teaching practices. What would happen to Terrell as he approached teaching with these alternative referents? What basis did we have for presuming that critical reflection would better prepare teachers to teach?

Discussion

This study was an attempt to further our understandings about prospective elementary teachers' referents for science, and science teaching and learning. In addition, it provided an opportunity for us to examine the use of a critical reflection tool in our teaching. The study raised problematic issues for us.

On a minor level, there were technological dilemmas with using the photo essay to learn about our students' views. The study was limited to some extent by the use of camera technology. Nearly all participants' were concerned about their ability to take "good" pictures. Many of the images produced were of low quality in terms of their visual technique. Most pictures had blurred images, or the subject of interest was not being clearly evident in the picture (e.g. a dead animal in the road too small to see). One participant, however, took advantage of an underexposed photo to reflect further on her notions of science teaching (i.e., mistakes are a part of learning science). Participants were hesitant to share their visual products with others, often making apologies for their "poor pictures." In one case, a participant abandoned use of the camera and simply drew a "Big Book" to share her ideas. In some sense, her drawings permitted greater exploration of images as she was not temporally or spatially constrained by the technology. She could produce images of her past and future, and was free to construct images that fit her perceptions of experience. Given the nature of our research interests, we see the need to explore alternative ways for participants to be able to generate images. It may be that using technologies (i.e., crayons and paper) that participants are already familiar with could better support their processes of critical reflection and image production.

In thinking about our research questions, we learned most about participants' science referents. Most of the participants' essays focused on their views of science, thus we learned less about referents they personally associated with being learners, and becoming teachers of science. Although we verbally encouraged students to develop the essays as stories, perhaps the task directions given did not prompt them to frame their essays as personally embedded stories. Or, perhaps their impersonal essays were indeed reflecting their personal disconnections from science. Their statements that "science must be taught" were perhaps delivered sincerely, however, the extensive archive of research indicating that elementary teachers do not teach science on a regular basis led us to wonder why our students would express such views in their essay presentations? The essays may have been constructed as rhetorical devices being used to convince us, as well as students themselves, that they were indeed prepared to teach science.

The results of the essays encouraged us to consider deeper issues about the context of learning in our science methods classes. While the assignment was intended to help our participants challenge mythologies of science learning and teaching, we did not extend this to consider myths of our teacher education culture. Biomythography, with its emphasis on the nature of changing affiliations and coalitions that challenge our identities, led us to wonder about the new layer of identity they were developing as prospective teacher. Were the essays glimpses of their emergent auto/biographies as learners in teacher education? Preliminary efforts were made in class to create a culture where any ideas and positions of status (e.g., who was "teacher", who was "student", what is "science") were open to critique. The essays, particularly the memory boxes, indicated that our students' auto/biographies were permeated with myths that have disempowered them as learners. A few students began to resist mythologies that had undermined their science learning, but this entitled them to join us as a marginalized group of critics from the rest of our class community. We wondered about our own role as practitioners of "critical" reflection. What justifies our pedagogy that has been influenced by critical and feminist theories?

In terms of the cultural creating a culture where alternative views could be exchanged, teacher education presents new mythologies that complicate this process. Predominantly, our teacher education programs contend with the hegemonic charge to "train" teachers. Students attend methods classes with an expectation that they will, in the end, become finalized products—teachers generically prepared to teach (Kincheloe, 1993). In the process of becoming prepared, they will likely have adopted the mythology of standardized pedagogy that denies the non-unitary identities of students they will teach. We do believe that critical reflection can play an important role toward creating a culture of diverse teacher learners as evidenced by the work of Katrice, Terrell, and Heather.

While well-intended as an assignment that might free our students from myths of science education that have alienated them from participation in science learning, soon they will be required to negotiate their ideas in the political and moral contexts of being teachers in schools. As teachers, they will find themselves in a profession challenged by policies of curriculum alignment, standardized evaluation, and teacher accountability. We are asking ourselves—to what extent does critique about science ideology and self contribute to prospective teachers' thinking as they make sense of their pedagogical practices within the contexts of elementary teaching? Research has indicated that their socialization into professional elementary teaching cultures is likely to make it problematic for them to enact science teaching practices that diverge from mainstream traditions of elementary science teaching practices (Nichols & Tobin, 2000)? In addition to local teacher cultures, how might educational myths related to policies influence their thinking about teaching elementary science?

Through this initial exploration involving photo essays and biomythography, we have developed results and questions that warrant further exploration into uses of auto/biography in science teacher education. We conclude our study with implications for science teacher education reform and research.

Implications for Teaching and Research

It is important that we develop ways to better understand the relationship of prospective teachers' identities to science, the political contexts of being students in teacher education, and ways mythologies work to regulate teachers' science teaching practices. We thought by asking our students to develop stories about science and science teaching and learning using photographic essays and oral narratives, it might help them critically identify and examine their assumptions. The majority of essays however presented reified views of science, and rhetoric about the need to teach science. For a few of our students, we felt they had constructed alternative views of science that excited them about becoming learners and teachers of science. These results encourage us to continue exploring autobiographical tools to promote critical reflection about science, and science teaching and learning in our classes.

The problems creating a culture where prospective teachers can be critics and change agents poses complex problems we need to further consider. This study challenges us to think about how our students come to see themselves as learners, and how they make sense of their roles as teachers in our classes. Many teacher educators are working to help prospective teachers reconstruct their personal views of themselves as learners and their views of content areas (i.e., science). Using the reflection tools such as auto/biographies or photo essays provides micro contexts that serve this purpose. We are less sure about how our activities of critical reflection contribute to teaching and learning in the larger systems of education. Long-term research is needed to follow up on the learning of students, such as Terrell and Katrice, who construct alternative ideas for science teaching via science methods courses. As well, we are compelled to look at how, and if, critical reflection is used in other sectors of our teacher education program. If we are committed to encouraging our students to be critically reflecting, knowing that Heather's type of dilemma is to be expected, we may need to be willing to extend our interactions with students beyond the brief period of time of our scheduled semester of instruction. We could perhaps create virtual communities where marginalized students and teachers can build an archive (i.e., case writing) where their experiences of change can be read and remembered and used to inform instructors and future prospective teachers.

Finally, we want to address using alternative approaches in research. Science education research has predominantly focused on text-based representations of knowledge. The preoccupation with text-based forms in research has been driven by cognitive psychology which, when grounded in positivistic tradition, treats knowledge as an object of study. Constructivist notions of epistemology introduced science education researchers to alternative ways of thinking about science learning, and accordingly science teaching. In the wake of interest in constructivist learning and teaching, science education researchers have begun to explore ways to research individual and group meaning making. Researchers have explored various sociocultural and epistemological borders that mediate diverse learners perspectives of science, at times working to disenfranchise them from science education. Cobern's (1999) use of elicitation devices to explore students' perspectives of nature demonstrates the potential for research to be enhanced through the use of visual mediums and story telling. We would argue, however, that text-based forms, whether produced in written or oral form, are limited in their potential to represent complex social situations, and to serve as mediators of our interpretive activities. One need only think of the proverb "A picture says a thousand words" to appreciate the possibilities for image-based genres and other "outlaw" approaches to extend our insights in science education research.

Notes

A previous, considerably revised version of this text had been published as Nichols, S. E., & Tippins, D. J. (2000). Prospective elementary science teachers and biomythographies: An exploratory approach to autobiographical research. *Research in Science Education, 30*, 141–153.

References

Barthes, R. (1985). *Mythologies*. New York: Hill and Wang.

Britzman, D. (1991). *Practice makes practice: A critical study of learning to teach*. Albany: State University of New York Press.

Cobern, W. W. (1993). College students' conceptualizations of nature: An interpretive world view analysis. *Journal of Research in Science Teaching, 30*, 935–951.

Hatch, J., & Wisniewski, R. (1995). Life history and narrative: Questions, issues, and exemplary works. In J. Hatch & R. Wisniewski (Eds.), *Life history and narrative* (pp.
113–136). Washington, D.C.: Falmer.

hooks, b. (1996). *Bone black : Memories of girlhood*. New York: Henry Holt.

Kaplan, C. (1998). Resisting auto/biography: Outlaw genres and transnational feminist
subjects. In S. Smith & J. Watson (Eds.), *Women, auto/biography, theory: A reader*
(pp. 208–216). Madison: University of Wisconsin Press.

Kincheloe, J. L. (1993). *Toward a critical polities of teaching thinking: Mapping the
postmodern*. Westport, CT: Bergin and Garvey.

Milne, C. (1998). Philosophically correct science stories? Examining the implications of
heroic science stories for school science. *Journal of Research in Science Teaching,
35*, 175–188.

Nichols, S., & Tobin, K. (2000). Discursive practice among teachers co-learning during
field-based teacher preparation experiences. *Action in Teacher Education, 22*, 45–
54.

Richmond, G., Howes, E., Kurth, L., & Hazelwood, C. (1998). Connections and critique:
Feminist pedagogy and science teacher education. *Journal of Research in Science
Teaching, 35*, 897–918.

Smith, S. (1998). Performativity, autobiographical practice, resistance. In S. Smith & J.
Watson (Eds.), *Women, auto/biography, theory: A reader* (pp. 108–115). Madison:
University of Wisconsin Press.

Tippins, D., Nichols, S., & Dana, T. M. (1999). Exploring novice and experienced elementary teachers' science teaching and learning referents through videocases. *Research in Science Education, 29*, 331–352.

Wertsch, J. (1991). *Voices of the mind: A sociocultural approach to mediated action*.
Cambridge, MA: Harvard University Press.

IV

Writing
Institutional Critique

As teachers, we do not exist in a vacuum, neither as individuals nor in the dialectical relation with our classroom settings. We are constitutive part of institutions. Constitutive here means that the institutions are what they are because of our actions. That is, with each and every action, we produce|reproduce the institution. Many of our colleagues—both schools and ivory towers—tend to emphasize that they are constraint in their actions. Many of my colleagues in middle and high schools taught curriculum in a very inflexible way or taught to tests because they felt that the institution made them do so. Similarly, many of my university colleagues tell me that they are "expected" to do this or that. Yet if I consider myself as a constitutive member of the institution, I begin to realize that if I personally change, so does the institution, which only exists in and through my actions. Thus, agency means that I not only reproduce the institution but also produce it anew and in new ways. But how do I act to bring about change? This requires that we begin doing and writing institutional critiques. Auto/biography and auto/ethnography constitute important means for educators to investigate *our* institutions and write institutional critiques, for example, analyzing peer review processes (Roth, 2002), the review process of research ethics involving human beings (Coupal, 2004), or the vagaries of doing a Ph.D. (Birck, 2005).

In this section, three different institutions are critiqued through the lenses of auto/biography and auto/ethnography. Margaret Eisenhart describes the challenges involved in publishing a book manuscript because one of its chapters dealt with a contentious issue in U.S. society, abortion; more specifically, the chapter dealt with the ways in which pro- and anti-abortion groups used scientific language as a resource for promoting their causes and interests. Using phrases such as "this chapter does not add anything" as discursive resources, reviewers and publisher argued that Eisenhart's book should be accepted but without the contentious chapter. Eisenhart describes the personal conflicts that led her to ultimately sacrifice the chapter and her commitments to the student responsible for the research it contained.[1]

In my chapter, I attempt to do a critical anthropology of research funding at one national council, the Social Sciences and Humanities Research Council of Canada. In this, I follow its own paradigmatic inscription on the cover of the "Manual for Adjudication Committee Members" (which regulates funding related evaluation and adjudication at the Social Sciences Research Council of Canada) and take "a closer look," an inspection de plus près, at its process, the vagaries and politics included. To guide my anthropological investigation, I draw on different social science theories, which I articulate in terms of the topologies they provide for structuring the social. I draw on a form of writing that integrates third- and first-person perspectives on the social processes of funding and the auto/biographical experiences of being and not being funded.

In the final chapter of this section, Kathryn Scantlebury analyses the tenure and promotion processes at her university, where she holds a position as a science educator. Other than similar individuals in her institution and across the US, Scantlebury is associated with a chemistry department, where the standards for tenure and promotion are very different than in education departments or schools of education (e.g., amount of external funding brought to the institution or publication in ranked journals). In addition, Scantlebury is a female and feminist educator in a traditional male discipline and context. Her auto/biographical and auto/ethnographical text provides insights on the struggles that a scholar significantly different from others in her department experiences in the tenure and promotion process.

Notes

[1] The chapter was subsequently published as part of an edited book (Lawrence & Eisenhart, 2002) in which the contributors argued that science education ought to be an education as and for sociopolitical practice (Roth & Désautels, 2002).

References

Birck, A. (2005, February). Laura gets her PhD. A satire in seven acts [289 paragraphs]. *Forum Qualitative Sozialforschung / Forum: Qualitative Social Research* [On-line Journal], *4* (2), Art. 17. Available at: http://www.qualitative-research.net/fqs-texte/2-03/2-03birck-e.htm [Date of Access: March 10, 2005].

Coupal, L. (2004, October). Practitioner-research and the regulation of research ethics: The challenge of individual, organizational, and social interests. *Forum Qualitative*

Sozialforschung / Forum: Qualitative Social Research [On-line Journal], *6* (1), Art. 6. Available at: http://www.qualitative-research.net/fqs-texte/1-05/05-1-6-e.htm [Date of Access: March 10, 2005].

Lawrence, N., & Eisenhart, M. (2002). The language of science and the meaning of abortion. In W.-M. Roth & J. Désautels (Eds.), *Science education as/for sociopolitical action* (pp. 185–206). New York: Peter Lang.

Roth, W.-M. (2002). Editorial power/authorial suffering. *Research in Science Education, 32,* 215–240.

Roth, W.-M., & Désautels, J. (Eds.). (2002). *Science education as/for sociopolitical action.* New York: Peter Lang.

14   Boundaries and Selves in the Making of "Science"

Margaret Eisenhart

This chapter is about some practices of people actively engaged in what they call "science." The groups and actors described here, including myself, mean different things by "science," and we do different things with it. Yet, in one way or another, all of us are at work regulating a normative boundary—determining what counts as science and science education in contemporary U.S. society.

Introduction

The main story line is mine. It is a story about trying to publish a book whose contents are in some ways marginal to what is normally considered science or science education. The book, *Women's Science: Learning and Succeeding from the Margins* (Eisenhart & Finkel, 1998), was published and is selling well but not without some hard feelings and loss of content. During the publishing process, what counts as science got tangled up with what counts as "credible" science and "marketable" literature. As a result, a book dedicated to a broad view of science and science education also became a contributor to the very same boundaries its authors intended to expand.

   I offer this story not as "the truth" about what happened, but as a personally constructed narrative about my experience of boundary making in science and science education. I tell my "own" story, but in the tradition of critical auto/biography (Behar, 1993; Gilmore, 1994), I attempt to reveal how the story is a product of both power relations (so-called "outside" or "larger" influences) and my subject position (my identities-in-context).

   The story I tell and my way of understanding it also were informed by my recent attempt to apply practice theory (also referred to as activity theory or sociohistorical constructivism in earlier works) to research on science and science education. In that work (Eisenhart, 1996; Eisenhart & Finkel, 1998; Eisenhart, Finkel, & Marion, 1996), I use practice theory as a way to consider together the insights of constructivists and sociologists of science. Generally speaking, constructivists view science as a socially and experientially produced set of useful ideas about how the natural world works. As such, science is not a fixed body of facts and theories but a set of ideas that changes over time as people produce new and more productive ways to observe and think about their experiences in the world. From this perspective, science pedagogy is an exciting process of introducing students to natural phenomena, to ways of empirically observing and testing them, and to theory building about them. Students are encouraged to "construct" their own ideas about the natural world based on their experiences and then to defend or modify the ideas in light of questions and challenges from others and their ideas. When science education reform is premised on constructivism, the preceding principles guide reform efforts. When science education research is based on constructivism, case studies of individuals, short biographies, and occasionally auto/biographies have become popular methods of investigating what learners construct, how they use their constructions, and how they revise them over time.

In contrast, sociologists of science, along with some feminists and anthropologists of science, view science as a set of historically and politically *compelled* ideas about how the natural world works. As such, science is neither a fixed body of knowledge nor an empirically tested set of good ideas but a "technology" that tends to advance the interests of the historically powerful (Haraway, 1989; Harding, 1991; Keller, 1982; Lave, 1993; Minick, 1993). From this perspective, the crux of science education is to introduce students to the body of knowledge called "science" (cf. history) and to social critiques of it: what is included, what is not, why certain things are left out or ignored, what might be different ways of thinking about science and conducting it, and so forth. Science education reform premised on the sociology of science promotes this goal. Science research informed by this perspective tends to rely on methods of participant observation along with social, political, or literary critique.

Practice theory orients researchers to consider together the things that separately concern constructivists and critical sociologists, feminists, or anthropologists (Eisenhart, 1996; Eisenhart & Finkel, 1998; Holland, Lachicotte, Skinner & Cain, 1998; Lave, 1993; Levinson & Holland, 1996). Practice theory "locates persons in history and history in persons, focusing on the ways in which individuals and groups fashion and are fashioned by social, political, and cultural discourses and practices in historically specific times and places" (Skinner,

Pach, & Holland 1998, p. 3). This perspective reminds us that social constructions "should not be romantically portrayed as unleashed creativity and agency,
but rather [they consist] of ambiguous activities still subject to domination and
tied to identity struggles" (Skinner et al., 1998, p. 13). My application of practice theory to the study of science and science education has focused on "the
ways in which individuals and groups fashion (the social constructivist part) and
are fashioned by (the sociology of science part) social, political, and cultural
discourses and practices." In *Women's Science*, we relied on methods of participant observation, interviewing, and case study analysis to show how small
groups of women made sense of their work in science, and how they pushed
against, as well as were constrained by, larger discourses and practices of science. In this paper, I use the same perspective to consider how I fashioned a
story of one of my experiences during the *Women's Science* study and how this
story has itself been affected by larger discourses and practices in which I participate.

A Word about Auto/biography as Method

Auto/biography is presumed to be an authentic way for someone to tell what
happened to her, from her point of view. In its traditional sense, the genre of
auto/biography is based on a proprietary claim to a narrative and an identity
("this is *the* story of *my* life") that is expected to conform to the requirements of
realist narrative and non-fiction reporting (i.e., an auto/biography is expected to
be the truth about what happened with historical reference [Gilmore, 1994]). Put
another way, the conventional understanding of an auto/biographical text is that
it "makes public that which has been private, typically claiming to avoid filtering mechanisms of objectivity and detachment in its pursuit of the truth of subjective experience" (Felski, 1989, pp. 87–88).

Many have suggested that the tenets of auto/biography–to be authentic, true,
and real–give it especially high status as a literary genre in the US. In colonial
days, for example, "in accordance with the Puritan precept that literature is useful . . . authentic personal experience had greater prestige than poetry or any variety of fiction" (Sayre, 1988, p. 35). Today, auto/biographies are especially
popular because they give outsiders access to information ("private landscapes")
that only the authors know (Simon, 1999). Their popularity makes them an attractive genre for writers and makes them easy for publishers to sell. In fact, to
gain attention and market share, some stories are advertised as "auto/-
biographies," when they may not be, at least in the conventional sense (cf. *I,
Rigoberta Menchu*).

Although seemingly valuable and straightforward as a method for obtaining an authentic story, auto/biographies also have been critiqued for their authors' naiveté in suggesting that their accounts are unfiltered or unbiased. Intended audiences, authors' purposes and vanities, historical context, and publishers' interests have all been implicated in the production of auto/biographical accounts (Behar, 1993; Felski, 1989; Gilmore, 1994; Gray, 1997; Payne, 1992). For example, in discussing the auto/biography of Elizabeth Keckley who was Mary Todd Lincoln's attendant and confidant in the White House, Frances Foster (1992) reveals how Keckley tried to tell her story so as to portray Mrs. Lincoln positively, while publishers later edited Keckley's work to cast Mary Lincoln in a more negative light, consistent with prevailing public opinion at the time. Keith Byerman (1993) describes W.E.B. DuBois' auto/biography as his attempt to rehabilitate his image in the eyes of the American public near the end of his life. Ruth Behar, in recounting the auto/biography of Esperanza, a poor Mexican working woman, suggests that the story Esperanza told (of private suffering and struggle) would not be believed in her hometown because the townspeople considered her a combative woman who did not know her place. However, Behar knows that Esperanza's story will be believed across the border in the US, because it fits American readers' image of what life is like for poor women in Mexico.

These considerations mean that the story I tell next must be understood as "what happened" in a very qualified way. My story is not a neutral, transparent, or decontextualized account of what happened or what kind of person I am. It is positioned—presented from the perspective of someone with certain intentions at a specific moment in historical time. It also is situated—made to fit with my expectations about who will be in my audience and what they will expect from someone like me and the other "characters" in my story. It is a literary genre actively constructed, by a person in a social and cultural space, so as to be believed (as something that actually happened to me, the teller) and so as to be taken seriously (as something that is meaningful for those I expect to read this account).

My Story–Part 1

The first part of my story concerns the "fashioning" of *Women's Science* by my co-authors and me. On one level, we wrote the book to report the findings of a research study we conducted about women successfully engaged in various forms of science. In telling this part of the story, I position myself as an academic writing mostly for other researchers and policy makers. Consistent with this identity, I produce (below) a standard expository account of the research process and its results.

The study itself began in 1991, when the five of us—Eisenhart, anthropologist and educational researcher; Finkel, geologist and university science educator; Behm, middle school science educator; Lawrence, political activist and educational researcher; and Tonso, engineer and educational researcher—decided to do participant observations and ethnographic interviews in sites of science-related activities. Initially, we chose four sites where women were present and apparently successful in more than token numbers. The sites were a high school genetics classroom (40 percent girls), an internship for college students preparing to be engineers (26 percent women), an environmental action group (50 percent women), and a conservation corporation (46 percent of scientists were women). We were especially interested in these sites because they seemed to offer a striking contrast to the many reported examples of women's small numbers and special difficulties in science. We hoped to learn—through in-depth, first-hand data collection and analysis—why women's experiences in these sites appeared to be so much better than what has typically been reported for women actively pursuing science.

As Behm, Tonso, Finkel and I began our work in these four sites, Nancy Lawrence was investigating two abortion activist groups–one pro-life group ("PL") and one pro-choice group ("PC")—for her dissertation on the meanings of "choice" in contemporary U.S. society. In my capacity as her dissertation advisor, I read over her fieldnotes of the meetings she attended. I was surprised to find that discussions in the meetings of both groups focused on the biology and technology of reproduction. I also was surprised to learn that when members of the two groups were asked in interviews why they joined, many mentioned the opportunity to learn more about reproductive biology. Given that women comprised nearly ninety percent of the members in both groups, given that a large number of the women members had advanced degrees, including some in science or engineering, and given my interest in women engaged in science broadly construed, I was fascinated with this discovery. I thought of it as something special–something that marks good ethnographic studies and makes them exciting to do. I saw the opportunity to learn something new and unexpected by watching and listening to how women used science in these groups. In my mind, Nancy had found something wonderful–an unexpected interest in science among groups comprised almost entirely of women. We decided to add the abortion groups to the science study.

The first complete version of the resulting book manuscript had ten chapters. Five of them—the book's heart—consisted of case studies of each group.

One chapter was devoted to each of the first four sites in turn; then the two abortion groups were discussed together in the final case study chapter. As each case was told, their distinctive features, as well as patterns across them, were revealed. We found that science certainly was different in each site, but we also found clear patterns in the way women thought about science and in their experiences relative to men's.

The story we tell in the book is based on well-established social science methods of data collection and analysis. The story also is perverse, or counter to popular expectations, in two important ways. First, the book challenges the commonly held idea that "to work in science" means producing facts or theories about natural or physical phenomena. For example, we call political action work "science" when it involves the use of scientific information to promote environmental causes, just as we call schoolwork "science" when it focuses on the genetics of fruit flies. We do *not* argue that these activities are identical, but rather that together they constitute an arena of practices that are thought of as "science" by their participants and that depend on each other for their meaning and status in contemporary U.S. society. We knew that such a broad view of science would chafe at conventional expectations—both academic and popular—about what constitutes science.

Second, because the book tells about women who are successful and enjoy their work in science-related activities, it contrasts with the three most widely accepted "truths" about women and science: (a) that women are not inclined (by nature or culture) toward science (the conservative position); (b) that science does not appeal to women because of its assumptions, content and procedures (the feminist position); and (c) that success for women in science is blocked by discrimination (the liberal position). None of these positions sufficed to explain the experiences of the women we were studying.

At the time, this perversity meant two different things to me: The book might become well-known because it was unconventional in a provocative sense; or, it might be disregarded because its unconventionality placed it outside the boundaries of what most people would expect (cf. Esperanza in her hometown). No one who writes a book wants it to be ignored, so this ambiguous situation made me nervous.

In the preceding account, I portrayed myself as an academic justifying her actions primarily in terms of social science research standards (the credentials, the methods, the sample, the systematic comparisons, and so forth). But when the results turned out to be unconventional, I worried that my careful scholarship might be ignored or worse: that my identity as a credible academic might be challenged. As it turned out, something like this did happen, although I am hard-pressed to admit it!

My Story–Part 2

As the book took shape, Finkel and I began talking to the funding sponsors about the results and to book editors about publishing them. In the process, we experienced how social pressures, historical precedent, and economic power can work to constrain authors' liberty (or agency) to publish their findings. This is the second part of my story.

On September 10, 1996, I finished a complete draft of the manuscript that would eventually become *Women's Science*. On that September day, I sent the manuscript off to the University of Chicago Press with a great sense of accomplishment and relief. To have it finished, off my desk, and out of my mind (almost) was wonderful! I was particularly satisfied with the way the chapter on the abortion groups was integrated with the rest. From early on, some important people questioned their inclusion or complained about it. But now I was impressed with how well they fit, and I thought they were crucial to underscore some important points. Nonetheless, earlier complaints came back to haunt me, and inclusion of the abortion groups later came to threaten the book's publication.

Lawrence first wrote about the abortion groups in "The Language of Science and the Meaning of Abortion," a paper she presented at a national conference in 1994. Here are a few of the examples she included to illustrate the use of science in the abortion groups.

From literature discussed in the groups:

When a human life begins is not a religious, moral, or philosophical issue; it is a scientific and biological one.

The Nobel Committee noted that life begins with the activation of ion channels as the sperm merges with the egg in fertilization. All cells have electrical charges within and outside the cell and the difference is known as the membrane potential. Fertilization changes the potential to prevent other sperm from joining the fertilized egg.

From fieldnotes taken at a pro-life meeting:

We were advised to "begin with research" and "know absolutely all about fetal development, abortion procedures, and local abortionists." We were encouraged to "be conservative with facts and statistics" so as not to be falsely accused of magnifying favorable numbers. "Know your history," we were instructed.

From interviews with group members commenting on what the group does:

We describe the nature of the unborn child, development in the womb, the scientific facts of reproduction, when conception has occurred, when reproduction has occurred.

My knowledge of reproductive health care has increased considerably. I've learned things about my body in the past two years [while in the group] that I didn't know and I'm twenty-five, and it's really pathetic. . . . I don't understand why I didn't actively seek out this information before, and I also don't understand why it wasn't more readily available to me."

I first wrote about the abortion groups in an interim report to one of our funding sponsors in 1994. Here is an excerpt from that report:

This [section] focuses on the way in which the language of science has been appropriated by [the pro-life (PL) and pro-choice (PC) groups] and used as a vehicle of "empowerment" for members of the groups, most of whom are women. We find that both groups draw on the . . . discourse of the hard sciences. In so doing, they accomplish two things. First, they turn woman-centered and locally *shared* concerns into two opposing positions, each supported by different scientific "facts." Second, by repeated reference to the scientific facts supporting their positions, they suggest that their causes are unbiased, apolitical, and "serious." Both groups purposefully simplify, distort and manipulate science, but they also succeed in leading members to take an interest in science, to believe that they can understand the science behind the issues, and to take personal pride in that understanding. By means similar to the processes . . . in our other outside-of-school sites, the social arrangements in PL and PC make scientific knowledge worth having, especially for its use in public discussion and debate. As in the other sites, women are motivated to learn and use science. However, in these two most politically active, woman-centered, and female-dominated groups, the science available was the worst, i.e., it was weak, unsophisticated, distorted, and divisive.

My first clue that inclusion of the abortion groups could be problematic came when a reader from the funding sponsor called to talk to me about the report and our progress. She told me that she did not see the connection between the abortion groups and the other four. She wondered whether we really needed to include the abortion groups. I argued that they were relevant because many of the patterns we found in PL and PC supported findings from the other groups, yet the situation in PL and PC made clear that we would have to face the distinction between sites where science was credible from those where it was not. At the time, I was not sure the reader agreed with my assessment of the group's relevance, but I never thought seriously about omitting them (and she did not ask me to). What I did think about was the need to make a stronger case for their inclusion.

A year or so later (in 1995), when I reported our findings at a conference (using similar language to that in the interim report excerpt), the question about the need to include the abortion groups came up a second time. This time, it was raised by several women in the audience who felt that the groups' inclusion "distracted" from the importance of our findings about the other four sites. Again, I attributed the question to my inability to articulate the special importance of the abortion groups.

The next piece of this story did not occur until many months later after drafts of most of the book chapters were completed, and I wrote a long book prospectus to show to publishers. (Often authors will write a book prospectus and hope to get a publishing contract before anything of the book is actually written. In this case, I was concerned that the contents were unconventional, even without the abortion groups. I had decided that I would have a better chance getting a contract with a publisher who would take the book seriously if my points and arguments were well-thought out and clearly written in advance. Thus, I did not "shop the book around" until I was sure what would be in it.)[1]

After brief face-to-face meetings with me at a conference, two publishers expressed interest in seeing the prospectus. (Getting publishers interested in your book manuscript among the many they receive and hear about is itself a difficulty task. In my experience, personal contacts—friends, colleagues, or mentors who know a publisher and can recommend your work—are the best means of introducing yourself to publishers. In this particular case, I had some advantages over the first-time book author because I had already published two books, already knew some publishers, and had many close colleagues who had published books.)

Within twenty-four hours of enthusiastically receiving the prospectus, one book publisher told me in no uncertain terms that she could not publish the book with the abortion groups included.

At first, I thought I could persuade her to reconsider, but I was wrong. She was adamant. The second publisher was still interested but noncommittal. He wanted to see the complete manuscript. When I met with him to discuss a time line, I told him about my experience with the other publisher and asked whether he was comfortable including the abortion groups. Unfortunately, I do not remember his immediate response, but I am sure he did not say that I should omit them. In his later written comments on my prospectus, he suggested that I add more discussion to clarify the points about the abortion groups.

With this security, I went back to work on the manuscript. In the meantime, the publisher sent my prospectus out to two anonymous reviewers. Ten months later, I received the reviewers' comments. They were generally positive and made a number of important suggestions that I later incorporated. However, one raised the question of whether the discussion of PL (the pro-life group) and PC (the pro-choice group) contributed anything different than was already evident in the earlier chapters about the conservation corporation and the environmental action group. When discussing this question with the publisher, I argued for a chance to address it and make the case for the abortion groups in the complete manuscript. He agreed to my request. Several months later (September, 1996), I sent him the complete draft, which he in turn sent back to the same two reviewers for comments. These reviews also were generally positive and constructive, but this time, both suggested possibly omitting the chapter on the abortion groups because it added too little (new) to the story and too much to the book's length. The publisher concurred, adding that a shorter book could be more attractively priced.

For several months after that, I tried to figure out new ways to argue for the groups' inclusion. For example, I talked to a copy editor and showed him the manuscript. He thought that fifty pages (the length of the chapter on the abortion groups) could quite easily be cut from the overall text, thus leaving space for the abortion chapter. I suggested this to the publisher, and finally, he made clear that he did not think he could make a strong case for publishing the book to his editorial board unless the chapter about the abortion groups was removed. At this point, I had completed the manuscript, had already undertaken two revisions, and now felt threatened with a rejection. Reluctantly, I agreed. The decision of the editorial board was positive, the necessary revisions were made, the chapter on the abortion groups was removed, and the book was scheduled for publication.

Thinking back now about these events, I know I wondered from the beginning: What did it really mean when the reviewers said that the inclusion of the abortion groups did not *add anything* to the overall argument? One possibility is that there were no new data about science or women in the chapter about the abortion groups once the environmental action group and the conservation corporation had been presented.

I did not think this was the case. For example, the science available to the women in PL and PC was more superficial and selective than in any of the other groups. Nonetheless, the women—many of whom were very highly educated—were eager to learn more science in the group and felt politically emboldened by the scientific information they got there. For anyone seriously interested in opportunities for "teachable moments" in science, or for promoting scientific literacy in locally relevant contexts, or for increasing the involvement of women in science, PL and PC looked like good candidates. They were places where these opportunities seemed to exist but were being missed.

In addition, women in the pro-life and pro-choice groups were considerably more active in educating themselves about science than women in the other groups. The pro-life and pro-choice group members voluntarily joined the groups in part to learn more science and be able to use it in public debates about abortion. Like members of the two environmental groups, pro-life and pro-choice group members drew on science in an effort to improve their arguments with the public, but unlike in the other two groups, pro-life and pro-choice women did this for themselves, their families, and friends, and not as employees. They received no salary, no raises, no titles, and no promotions for their effort. Like many other groups that have been started by one or two women sitting around a kitchen table and talking about immediate family or local problems (e.g., hazardous wastes, undiagnosed illnesses, drunk drivers), the pro-life and pro-choice groups consisted of people who came together primarily so they could learn what they needed to know to be more effective citizens in a public debate they cared deeply about. In my mind, their participation in trying to learn more about science—however selective or unsophisticated—as a means of strengthening citizen activism is a legitimate and important activity for scholars of contemporary science practice to consider, and it is a type of activity not as clearly illustrated in the other sites of our study.

Finally, *even if* the abortion group chapter made the exact same points as the chapters on the conservation corporation and the environmental action group, why was the suggestion made to omit the abortion groups rather than one of the other two? Why were there no suggestions to incorporate the findings from the abortion groups into one of the other chapters that made similar points? If the abortion group chapter did not make the same points, why should it have been omitted?

I can only speculate about answers, but something was going on. Was the *possibility* of any important "science content" in abortion groups just too extreme for the likely audience—mainly academics—of our book? Why was the possibility of "real" science in a conservation agency and even an environmental action group (and of course in the high school class and the college internship) plausible in a way that it was not in the context of the US abortion debate, *even though* we could document the presence of some science-related activities and women's interest in science there? Was one chapter about science in abortion groups so controversial that it could compromise the credibility of the whole book? Why would these possibilities be so hard to accept?

In the chapter on the abortion groups, we made very clear that, although the women were there in part to learn science and more about it, the "science" they received was highly selective, incomplete, and inaccurate. We were not celebrating the science there, only the context that motivated women to be interested in learning more about science—a context often said to be missing in school and workplace science. Why was it not important that our readers consider a motivating context that, much more than any of our other sites, constructed pretty poor science and relied on it as a lever for political activism? If poor science is being produced in sites that are of special interest to women, why is it not important to know what these sites are and what their characteristics are?

Finally, if length were a real issue for marketing purposes, why was there no interest in finding other ways to shorten the manuscript? Why, when all the chapters were roughly the same length, was the abortion chapter singled out as the way to cut down on the book's size and to broaden its market?

Could it be that the idea of science in the abortion groups was just too inconsistent with the whole category of taken-for-granted ideas about what science is, who does it, and how? Could it be that groups of women who care deeply about an issue that affects them directly are *never* considered scientists or legitimately engaged in some kind of science? If so, in Donna Haraway's terms (1989), the possibility of science in abortion groups would be an especially perverse (counterstereotypic) reading of what science is: It would be a reading of science that makes its boundary much wider (more inclusive) than normally accepted, much wider than either the conservation corporation or the environmental group would require. Like Behar's *Esperanza* whose auto/biography would not be believed in her hometown because it was too inconsistent with how townspeople viewed her, was there something about the "story of science" in pro-life and pro-choice groups that was simply too inconsistent to be taken seriously? Although I can't definitively answer these questions, it seems to me that ideas and pressures around what constitutes "real science" and attractive marketing were used to block the publication of the material about the abortion groups.

Discussion and Critique

Authors of critical auto/biographies are supposed to analyze (or deconstruct) their accounts in at least four ways: in terms of their intended audiences, their purposes for telling the story, the identities motivating their portrayal of self, and some form of social critique. As I think now about the audiences I hope to reach with this article, three are salient: science education researchers, science education policy makers, and academic book publishers. With these groups as audiences, my story—both parts of what I constructed above—was affected in some specific ways. First, because I think most people in my audience consider themselves "academics," I wrote my story so it would be believed and taken seriously by academics. Because I consider myself an academic too, I thought I knew the best way to tell them a believable story: I should tell what happened in the most "objective," "true-to-life" way I could. That is, the story should be non-fiction, it should be about things that really happened to me, and these things should have happened in the way I said they did. My audiences would not expect imaginative details, selective omissions, or revised endings here.

I trade on my academic credentials to enhance the chances that my audiences will believe the story (that it happened to me) and will take it seriously (consider it meaningful to them). I already have an identity as an established educational researcher—someone whose stories *should* be believed and taken seriously by others who consider themselves academics. I already have a book published, by a very reputable press, on the work my story is about. I do not expect to have trouble convincing my audiences that the story is both authentic and worth listening to.

As I think about it now, I am struck by the selfish reasons I have for writing this story. One is to bolster my identity as a good educational researcher and scholar: The academic contents of my book, over which I expected to have full control, were abridged, even in the face of my arguments. How could such a thing happen to me? I am a full professor. I have been doing well-regarded educational research for more than twenty years. I have a track record in book publishing. Why couldn't I publish the book I wanted to publish?

One interpretation, suggested (at least) by both reviewers and editors, is that I failed to make a good enough case for including the abortion groups. This answer fills me with fear: Maybe I do not have the high academic identity I thought I had. Maybe it was just my ethnographic imagination or my eagerness to bust the boundaries of "science" that led me to see science in the abortion groups. This is neither the interpretation I want for myself nor the one that I want for my audiences. Interestingly, my telling of the story now attributes the suggestion that I was not smart or persuasive enough to *me* (not the reviewers) and to my naiveté about what was going on *early* in the chronology of events.

In my story, I overcome the suspicion of inadequacy by implicitly placing the blame for what happened somewhere else—on the reviewers and publishers who, constrained by larger, more powerful external forces, restricted my academic freedom. This is a favorite interpretation among confessing academics (cf. Atkinson, 1990): We pride ourselves in being careful investigators, accurate recorders, systematic analysts, and sure of our results, but sometimes we just are not powerful enough to beat larger, more compromising forces. This interpretation not only preserves the status of an academic but can enhance it: When powerful forces exert influences beyond one's control, one can still come across as doing good research in a difficult situation, smart enough to recognize external influences, and concerned enough to write about them so others can fight back in the future. As it turned out, this was the way I constructed my story of "what happened."

My identity as a good advisor and friend to graduate students also was put at risk in this episode. I felt guilty about the outcome, particularly its effects on Nancy Lawrence, who studied the abortion groups. Although Nancy remained a co-author of the book (and rightly so), her case study chapter was no longer included in the book. In other words, unlike me and the other co-authors, she was not able to show off her particular contribution to our study and our thinking.

From the beginning, Nancy had trusted my intuition that finding evidence of science in the abortion groups was significant (recall that her dissertation study of the groups focused on another topic). From the start, she was more skeptical than I; but I pushed her to explore the issue and she did. Many long hours of her time were devoted to analyzing her data and to writing and revising her case study chapter. Despite the various objections, I assured her that her chapter would remain a part of the book. This was a promise I did not keep. I knew there was a sense in which I had sold out in order to get the book published, and she had been the price. It was a high price to pay. Writing the story as if powerful forces prevented me from doing what was right by Nancy pushed back my sorrow at disappointing her and made me feel better about myself, at least momentarily.

In standard research practice, a critique of my subjectivity (if it were included at all) could be used to strengthen the validity of my account (Eisenhart & Howe, 1992; Howe & Eisenhart, 1990; Peshkin, 1988). This might occur in one of two ways. First, I might use my announced biases to account for (in part) the things I paid attention to or cared about in my story (see especially Peshkin, 1988). Second, by providing information about myself as a person and about my motives, I could give readers information to judge for themselves the biases assumed in my account (Howe & Eisenhart, 1990).

In what I am calling "critical auto/biography" though, this critique has a different purpose—to show the author's vulnerability to the same kinds of motives, concerns, and partiality that influence the so-called "subjects" or "participants" in social science research. Just as I depicted the reviewers and editors as worried about credibility and marketability, I was too. Just like I worried about making a strong case for the content and argument of the book, they did too. It is not as if they and I live in different worlds—me as the innocent, dispassionate raconteur, they as pawns of some larger pressures. I am not immune from their concerns, issues, or pressures, nor are they from mine. We are all in this story together— negotiating identities, testing boundaries, considering options, and trying to make a mark somehow on this product that I thought of as "my" book.

Conclusion

In the end, it seems that we could push the boundary of science only so far. In *Women's Science*, we were able to demonstrate multiple and alternative ways of practicing "science." We were able to present stories of women who were interested in science and in learning more about it, and who were successful in a variety of different capacities. Yet, we could argue for science in an environmental action group and have the argument accepted, but not in the abortion action groups. Science-related work done by women championing environmental causes was plausible; science-related work done by women arguing the pros and cons of abortion was not. In our case, funding agencies, reviewers, and publishers served as guardians of the boundary. Using our data, our findings, and my credentials, I negotiated with these guardians for more space inside what is considered legitimate science for discussion and debate in schools and other public settings

I think we did gain (or reinforce the importance of) some unconventional space for science. As a result of reading the published version of *Women's Science*, perhaps more science educators will consider using the forms of science– ecology in the service of state legislation, cartography in the service of raising public awareness, mechanical engineering in the service of disabled access— that appeared in our sites as models for some of their science projects or curriculum units. Perhaps more people will consider the possibilities for scientific literacy that exist in community-oriented science activities (activities defined by participants as "science-related" such as PL and PC) and after-school programs.

But we did not gain all that we might have. In the face of pressure to conform, I colluded with the other boundary guards to omit the abortion groups. Whether this was due more to my intellectual limitations; to social history (expectations) about science, women or abortion; or to economics (marketing strategies) is not as important to me as the fact that the outcome limited the purview of "science" more than I think it should–more than is necessary to think broadly about the kinds of science that are relevant, interesting, and important in contemporary public life and thus important for schools and young people to consider. That I might have pushed the boundaries farther (but could or did not) is a chance I hope will come again.

Notes

A previous version of this chapter was published as Eisenhart, M. (2000). Boundaries and Selves in the Making of "Science." *Research in Science Education, 30,* 43–55. Nancy Lawrence and John Tryneski, participants in the events I describe here, read a draft of the article and commented on it. They gave me their own views of what happened and why. I changed a few things to better represent their positions, but they will not agree with everything I have written here. Nonetheless, they generously offered me their comments and support, for which I am very grateful. I also want to thank Joe Harding and Leslie Edwards for their comments on the earlier draft of this paper.
[1] I included these details because they may be unfamiliar to readers who have never published a book; however, I placed them in parentheses because they are not part of the main story line of this article.

References

Atkinson, P. (1990). *The ethnographic imagination: Textual constructions of reality.* London: Routledge.

Behar, R. (1993). *Translated woman: Crossing the border with Esperanza's story.* Boston, MA: Beacon Press.

Byerman, K. (1992). The children ceased to hear my name: Recovering the self in the auto/biography of W.E.B. Du Bois. In R. Payne (Ed.), *Multicultural auto/biography: American lives* (pp. 64–93). Knoxville: University of Tennessee Press.

Eisenhart, M. (1996). The production of biologists at school and work: Making scientists, conservationists, or flowery bone-heads? In B. Levinson, D. Foley, & D. Holland (Eds.), *The cultural production of the educated person* (pp. 169–185). Albany: State University of New York Press.

Eisenhart, M., & Finkel, E. (1998). *Women's science: Learning and succeeding from the margins.* Chicago: University of Chicago Press.

Eisenhart, M., Finkel, E., & Marion, S. (1996). Creating the conditions for scientific literacy: A re-examination. *American Educational Research Journal, 33,* 261–295.

Eisenhart, M., & Howe, K. (1992). Validity in educational research. In M. LeCompte, W. Millroy, & J. Preissle (Eds.), *The handbook of qualitative research in education* (pp. 643–680). San Diego: Academic Press.

Felski, R. (1989). *Beyond feminist aesthetics: Feminist literature and social change.* Cambridge, MA: Harvard University Press.

Foster, F. (1992). Auto/biography after emancipation: The example of Elizabeth Keckley. In R. Payne (Ed.), *Multicultural auto/biography: American lives* (pp. 32–63). Knoxville: University of Tennessee Press.

Gilmore, L. (1994). *Autobiographics: A feminist theory of women's self-representation.* Ithaca, NY: Cornell University Press.

Gray, A. (1997). Learning from experience: Cultural studies and feminism. In J. McGuigan (Ed.), *Cultural methodologies* (pp. 87–105). Thousand Oaks, CA: Sage Publications.

Haraway, D. (1989). *Primate visions: Gender, race, and nature in the world of modern science.* New York: Routledge.

Harding, S. (1991). *Whose science? Whose knowledge? Thinking from women's lives.* Ithaca, NY: Cornell University Press.

Holland, D., Lachicotte, W., Skinner, D., & Cain, C. (1998). *Identity and agency in cultural worlds.* Cambridge, MA: Harvard University Press.

Howe, K., & Eisenhart, M. (1990). Standards for qualitative (and quantitative) research: A prolegomenon. *Educational Researcher, 19* (4), 2–9.

Keller, E. (1982). Feminism in science. *Signs, 7,* 589–602.

Lave, J. (1993). The practice of learning. In S. Chaiklin & J. Lave (Eds.), *Understanding practice: Perspectives on activity and context* (pp. 3–32). Cambridge: Cambridge University Press.

Levinson, B., & Holland, D. (1996). The cultural production of the educated person: An introduction. In B. Levinson, D. Foley, & D. Holland (Eds.), *The cultural production of the educated person* (pp. 1–54). Albany: State University of New York Press.

Minick, N. (1993). Teacher's directives: The social construction of "literal meanings" and "real worlds" in classroom discourse. In S. Chaiklin & J. Lave (Eds.), *Understanding practice: Perspectives on activity and context* (pp. 343–374). Cambridge: Cambridge University Press.

Payne, R. (1992). Introduction. In R. Payne (Ed.), *Multicultural auto/biography: American lives* (pp. xi–xxxiii). Knoxville: University of Tennessee Press.

Peshkin, A. (1988). In search of subjectivity–one's own. *Educational Researcher, 17* (7), 17–22.

Sayre, R. (1988). *The examined self: Benjamin Franklin, Henry Adams, Henry James.* Madison: University of Wisconsin Press.

Simon, L. (1999). Witness protection. *The New York Times Book Review,* June 27, p. 14.

Skinner, D., Pach, A., & Holland, D. (1998). *Selves in time and place: Identities, experience, and history in Nepal.* Lanham, MD: Rowman and Littlefield.

15 Vagaries and Politics of Funding Educational Research

Wolff-Michael Roth

In this chapter, I write a critical auto/ethnographic study of research funding at one national council, the *Social Sciences and Humanities Research Council of Canada* (SSHRC). In this, I follow its own paradigmatic inscription on the cover of the "Manual for Adjudication Committee Members" (which regulates funding related evaluation and adjudication at SSHRC) and take "a closer look," an inspection *de plus près*, at its processes, the vagaries and politics included. To guide my auto/ethnographic investigation, I draw on different social science theories, which I articulate in terms of the topologies they provide for structuring the social. I draw on a form of writing that integrates third- and first-person perspectives on the social processes of funding and the auto/biographical experiences of being and not being funded. This approach, in my view, justifies the use of the slash in auto/-ethnography, because it simultaneously investigates the self and the generalized other, the generalized other through the self, the self through the generalized other. Auto/-

How do you write about something that you really seem to understand only when you have experienced it? How do you write about something that you understood only through inflicted pain without sounding apologetic or accusatory? How do you write "objectively" about the politics of funding without having experienced the rejection of a grant proposal however unjustified the decision may have been or appeared? Does it matter that I am actually not too concerned with the rejection? Does it matter that the rejection provides me with time to do and complete other dear-to-my-heart projects rather than running around seeking, recruiting, and training suitable graduate students? Finally, does it matter that I had already planed to write an analysis of the process of funding?

ethnography is therefore also a technique to do sociology from a position, enact a sociology of positioning that interrogates the conceptual practices of power (Smith, 1990), and to write a positioned sociology (e.g., Smith, 1999).

This is a critical investigation of the vagaries and politics of research funding; my observations derive from my participation as applicant, assessor, committee member, and committee chair in funding-related evaluations and adjudications of four councils, the *Australian Research Council* (ARC), the *Canadian Social Sciences and Humanities Research Council* (SSHRC), the *U.S. National Science Foundation* (NSF), and the *Fonds FCAR* (Quebec). I concentrate my investigation on SSHRC, with which I have extensive experience in all roles.[1]

A Third-Person Perspective on Funding . . .

An important question in scholarly debate over the past two decades has been about the nature of truth and scientific revolutions, based on historical studies of published research. More recently, research in the emerging field of the social studies of science focused on science in the making rather than science as ready-made product. Studies from the latter perspective have shown how the nature of scientific knowledge cannot be understood independent of politics, economics, and other social processes. That is, what we encounter as new facts, depending on our familiarity with the particular field through the daily news, popularizing media, or specialized, academic literature is a function, among others, of the nature of the projects that get funded. A particularly nice case in point is the history of artificial intelligence research in the United States, which, after what turned out to be an influential academic paper, shifted from a symmetrical approach to funding neural network and von Neumann architectures (which had led to tradi-

For an entire week, I am chairing a committee that ranked research proposals in the field of educational psychology and areas of education to determine those approximately thirty to forty percent that would receive financial support by the national funding agency. Although being the only one who had read all proposals, I am not able to predict with certainty whether a particular proposal, though it is ranked highly by the two readers, would actually be funded. It only takes the opinion of one reader who also makes his or her point very forcefully, to change a proposal rating from high into not fundable. Having submitted my own proposal to another committee, I begin to have anxiety attacks—will my proposal be receiving a score that makes it not fundable? What makes it worse, I see the members of the committee during the breaks and lunch periods, continuously reminding me that what is happening to proposals in my committee could also happen to mine.

tional, symbolic artificial intelligence and cognitive science) to the almost complete abandonment of the former approach (Olazaran, 1996). Following the predilections of their directors and program officers, the U.S. Advanced Research Projects Agency through its Information Processing Techniques Office, for example, directed its funding exclusively to symbolic artificial intelligence (AI), so that the history of AI really "is a paradigm of massive and effective state intervention in science and technology" (Guice, 1998, p. 107). In many countries, though, program directors and officers have less influence than they have in U.S. agencies, rhetorically constructing their fairness through reliance on the peer review system.

There are differences in the structure of funding and the way funding agencies operate across nations. I am most familiar with funding in Canada, though I have participated in evaluating proposals in Australia and the USA, too. In Canada, there are three major federal funding agencies, SSHRC, the *Natural Sciences and Engineering Research Council* and the *Medical Research Council*. Differences in the way evaluations and adjudications are handled by the agencies and the participating scholars also exist across different funding councils. Here, I analyze the processes involving the social sciences and humanities; in particular, I focus on the standard research grants program, not only the largest programs but also the most commonly known by the researchers. The Canadian minister for industry summarized the program in this way:

Standard Research Grants (SRG) is SSHRC's largest program, with a 2000-2001 budget of $39.3 million. This program provides three-year grants to individual researchers and to small research teams. In 2000–2001, the program supported 642 new research projects in all disciplines of the social sciences and humanities. This represents a 41.6% success rate, a slight decrease from the 43% funded in 1999–2000. (Tobin, 2001, p. 10)

The standards research grants program accepts applications in seventeen different categories that cover the various social sciences and humanities disciplines, including one category for interdisciplinary/multidisciplinary research. Neglecting for the moment that the success rates differ across the committees, the very articulation of success co-articulates failure, though the latter remains normally unmarked. Not receiving funding is a failure, even if it was the result of injustice, sloppy work, or bias and prejudice. On *this* side, only the successes are marked and remarked.

Does the peer review system guarantee that every proposal is fairly evaluated? What are some of the potential problems in the peer review system, which crucially selects between research projects being done versus research projects not being done and ultimately, what will be published as outcome of the research? But there are other questions, too, which we could raise—these questions come particularly salient when we look at the effect that the proposal adjudication and, with it, the peer review (evaluation) process has on the individual researcher. How do individuals experience the process of seeking research funding, particularly the moments associated with the process outcomes? What is the impact of a particular result when there appears to be, from the perspective of the researcher, clear evidence of misconduct, bias, prejudice, or carelessness?

... and a First-Person Perspective

On the other side lies the experience of success or failure in the grant-seeking process. Writing and submitting applications for research funding has a very personal side, even for those who normally are successful and who do not feel pressured by their heads of department, deans, or other parts of the university structure. As individual researchers, we are not only celebrating successes but also cope with the presumed shortcomings especially when we detect injustice and prejudice.

For months I have been wondering about how my proposal would fare in this committee for interdisciplinary research, where I have not submitted an application before. There are moments when I think that my proposal could experience the same fate that the proposal of another well-known researcher has had in my own committee: my proposed research program could be rated 5.9 (out of 10), thereby failing the minimum score required, and even a high score on my past record would not help me. At other moments I feel much more positive figuring that even if I was given the lowest passing score, 6.0, a rating of nine on my scholarly record, the score that I have received three years before, would give me a combined score of seventy-eight percent, where the weighting is sixty–forty for previous record and research program, respectively. The weeks before I find out the results, I am going through a roller coaster, moments of high when I feel that I would surely be funded and moments of low, when I feel that the vagaries of the committee process might lead to a not-funded decision.

As I am attending a particular conference, I meet many colleagues who already have received their results. (Despite the confidentiality agreement to which committee members and SSHRC personnel are committed, there are always researchers who know the results prior to the official notification!) The week before returning home is the worse of all during this period of waiting: highs are following lows and lows are following highs. Upon returning, I find the email from my dean—I have not received the funding sought. My combined score is so low that it falls into *Category 4A*, recommended for funding but there was not enough money to actually receive funds from the agency. I cannot not understand—have

I not figured that under the worse circumstances, I will get a score that ought to have been sufficient. But I have to wait for another several weeks before I receive the official notification including the scores and the justification of the committee recommendation, which I expect to provide me with some insights about what has gone awry, from my perspective. The justification contains the following information:

Record of research achievement:
"Members found the candidate's record quite respectable, though it noted assessor 8's concern that some of his research papers appeared to be somewhat repetitive. The committee found the supporting document of good quality." (Notification from funding agency, p. 1)
As evident in the bibliography and in Roth's vitae, he is an unusually prolific writer and his research interests are broad. . . . The quality of Roth's writing and his contributions to the field of science education are good, in my estimation. Many of his papers are repetitive, and he borrows extensively from others' more original contributions . . . (Assessor 8, p. 2)

Assessor 8 had made his comment without providing supporting evidence or pointing the committee to the particular place in the document where he found repetitiveness and borrowing "from other's more original contributions." The meeting justification not only noted the "concern that some of [Roth's] research papers appeared to be somewhat repetitive" but also omitted what can be read as a qualifier—"his contributions to the field of science education" directly precedes the comment about repetitiveness so that the repetitiveness is likely to pertain to that field. There is no indication that the committee actually cared to check that only three of the forty publications on the limited two-page list pertained to journals in science education, the others being books and journals in social studies of science, applied linguistics, educational psychology, education, and cybernetics.

In my initial response to the program officer responsible for my file and following "proper" appeals procedures, I write:

I just received the evaluation of my proposal. I have some very grave concerns about the score that I have received on my research record.
I am writing to you following the procedures for appeal listed on the SSHRC website. My submitted record shows:

Refereed		Other refereed		Non–refereed	
Articles	Proceedings	Papers	Professional	Reviews	Lectures
118	20	149	5	5	49

During my work on SSHRC committees (I chaired Committee 12 this year), I have not seen a single application with such a record for a single scholar.
It is incomprehensible to me and seems to smack bias (on reviewer 8's part, perhaps) that I would receive 7.45.

My articles listed have appeared in the highest rated (SSCI) journals of several fields, and I have had 7 awards for the quality of my scholarship. (My initial reaction to the program officer, May 14, 2002)

In this initial contact, I communicate grave concerns; I feel that there has been bias, perhaps on the part of one of the assessors and perhaps there has been a lack of diligence on the part of a adjudicating committee member—which would not be, according to the information I am provided by insiders, the first time. If my case is singular, one could go on though hurtful to me and trust in the justice of the system in general. But I am not the only scholar who has serious concerns with the process. Another, world-renowned Canadian scholar recently provided me with access of a letter written to the granting council that states:
    I write to express severe dissatisfaction with [the committee's] conduct in evaluating my application . . . and lay serious charges that the [committee]:

1. failed to apply due diligence that is obliged by the high standards of scholarly review to which I am certain SSHRC subscribes, namely, to be open and clear about reasons for judgments, and to be consistent and fair in adjudicating applications.
    1. acted with prejudice. By the word prejudice, I mean exactly and only this:
    2. a preformed opinion, usually an unfavorable one, based on insufficient knowledge, irrational feelings, or inaccurate stereotypes
4. disadvantage or harm caused to somebody or something (Encarta World English Dictionary © 1999 Microsoft Corporation)

Social Topologies

First person perspectives, though providing an articulation of why we do what we do, can be limiting because they do not reveal determinations that come from the outside of our lifeworlds (Holzkamp, 1984). My personal life conditions are always mediated by society as a whole, so that the resources for my actions embody ideologies that are not immediately apparent to me (Smith, 1990). To explicate why I have the experiences I have, I need more general insights than those that can be gained from the way in which the world appears to me, though these insights always need to be concretized with respect to my general life conditions and possibilities. In my research, I therefore contrast my first-person perspectives with third-person analyses that use social theories and concepts as their tools.

Social topologies come in different forms—in the sociological literature one can find theorizing efforts in terms of regions, networks, and fluids (Mol & Law, 1994). First, in a regional topology, social objects are clustered together and defined by relatively clean boundaries; Erving Goffman (1959) articulates social space into region, such as "front," "back," "in the wings of," and "outside" the stage, depending on the relationship of the audience to the performance. While the "official stance" of the performers is visible on front stage, the impression fostered by the presentation is knowingly contradicted as a matter of course backstage, indicating a more "truthful" type of performance. In the adjudication process, "objectivity" and "objective evaluation" are on the front stage; on the backstage, things are being said that clearly smack bias. On the backstage, the conflict and difference inherent to familiarity is more fully explored, often evolving into a secondary type of presentation, contingent upon the absence of the responsibilities of the public performance. To be outside the stage involves the inability to gain access to the performance of the team, described as an "audience segregation" in which specific performances are given to specific audiences, allowing the team to contrive the proper front for the demands of each audience. This allows the team, individual actor, and audience to preserve proper relationships in interaction and the establishments to which the interactions belong.

Second, there are (actor) networks characterized by relations between rather heterogeneous elements (human, non-human); the nature of the relations constitutes socially relevant entities such as distance, difference, and power (e.g. Latour, 1987). In actor network theories, each individual, group, technology, company, belief, finance, raw material, or artifact counts as an actor. Actor networks do not a priori distinguish between human and non-human actors on a priori grounds, and therefore constitute "symmetric anthropologies" (Latour, 1993, p. 101). Any social process is modeled by including all the relevant actors as nodes in a network; methodologically, this means that researchers have to follow the various human and non-human actors that are present. Stability arises from "immutable mobiles" (e.g., inscriptions) that circulate in the network and thereby put different actors in relations. Changes necessarily ripple through the network and therefore have consequences not only to the individual actor but, reflexively so, to the network as a whole. Recently, I used actor network theory to articulate and explain the origins of editorial power, authorial suffering, and the stability of the "publish or perish" practices in North American academe (Roth, 2005).

Actor network theory was useful because it allowed me to represent publishing, reviewing articles, editing journals, and undergoing tenure and promotion review as a seamless web of activities and actors. This web is relatively stable (and therefore difficult to change) because of the stakes involved, documents exchanged, biographies, and the history of the community. Most importantly, actor network approaches emphasize that the "same" social process can be viewed from the perspective of any of the actors, the Nobel Prize winning physicist, his cleaning personnel that make work in the lab possible, or the graduate students who spent many overnighters to get the data on which the award was ultimately based. In fact, taking the perspective of the non-heroes provide different, less complimentary, and down-to-earth account of the events that others recount in terms of heroism and in the form of master narratives (Redfield, 1996).

Third, the metaphor of fluid has been used to theorize both social space and social (including non-human) actor (Mol & Law, 1994). In contrast to a regional topology, fluid spaces do not have clear boundaries, objects generated within them and the objects/actors that generate them are not well defined, and boundaries (separating, e.g., normal from pathological) are gradients (de Laet & Mol, 2000) rather than discontinuities characteristic of traditional ontologies and mereologies (e.g., Smith, 1997).[2] Fluid topologies and fluid objects are not easy to deal with, because the nature of their ambiguous boundaries makes them resist easy classification—their identities cannot be determined nice and neatly, once and for all. Inside, outside, and borderline, important to making distinctions in traditional ontology (e.g., what is the nature of a point on the boundary separating green and red surfaces) cannot easily be distinguished, nor can similarity and difference. They come "in varying shades and colours" (de Laet & Mol, 2000, p. 660). A fluid ontology gives rise to other interesting entities, such as *mixtures*, and properties, such as *robustness*. Finally, a fluid is inherently dialectical because it accepts the other two topologies as coexisting with itself. Thus, fluid spaces are not better than regions or networks:

Fluid objects absorb all kinds of elements that could only ever have come into being within the logic of other topologies. Doctors use numbers and observations. They mix them together happily. (Mol & Law, 1994, p. 663)

And thus I will happily mix discourse analyses of the contents of policy documents, reviewer comments, and minutes of meetings; observations made in meetings where decisions about funding were being made; and computer models of decisions that implement an actor network ontology. I will also happily mix first-person perspectives with third-person perspectives, which have been used by traditional ethnographers and are still the most acceptable to most journals of social science research.

Structure of Evaluation and Adjudication at SSHRC

Funding Agencies as Black Boxes

The peer review process has been implemented, as in other parts of academia, because it is often thought to be the best of all systems to assure fairness and quality. But, as I have argued elsewhere, the very structure of peer review, especially blind and double-blind review processes lends itself to heinous attacks on the part of reviewers (even editors) against which the author of the reviewed piece has no recourse; it also gives some individuals, those that are placed in special nodes of the network such as editors in journals, enormous power over what and who gets published and who does not (Roth, 2002).

In the field, funding agencies are referred to as if they were singular actors. Thus, when talking to academics, one can hear "SSHRC (Canada) did not fund my proposal," "In the DFG (Germany), there is a bias against qualitative research," or "I got a career grant from NSF (USA)." That is, such parlance divides the field into different regions, the agency, often associated with the city where it is located (In particular contexts, "I am going to Washington" means "I am going to NSF"), and the world beyond. The agency is treated like a single point in the topography of funding in the social sciences; it is also an actor, dispensing funds; and, as Latour (1987) taught us to think about such issues, it is a black box. To the outside, the infrastructure is invisible, but it can, under certain circumstances, be opened up—though, as I will show here, among others, it cannot be opened by the ordinary academic out there. A relationship of power is enacted at the very moment more researchers attempting to get funding from to the agency than there is money to fund; somehow a decision is being made to fund some but not others.[3] Because the agency dispenses a desirable good, the competition for this good stabilizes the agency and its infrastructure; it is thus that relations of power come about rather than existing a priori.[4] If there was no competition, a small office would suffice to dispense the available funds. In this way, those who are not funded, even those subject to a non-funding decision based on a biased process, support the funding agency and its infrastructure. This stability is based, to a considerable part, on the fact that the processes within the black box are invisible to most academic actors, who are therefore subject to, or shall I say, subjected to the decisions regarding their request without recourse.[5]

In the Canadian Social Sciences and Humanities Research Council, peer review is instantiated in two stages:

- SSHRC grant applicants submit detailed research proposals that are evaluated:
  o first, by a series of external assessors outside SSHRC who are experts in the research field in question;
  o second, by peer review committees composed of other experienced researchers.
- The review committees recommend to SSHRC which proposals to fund, based on the highest standards of academic excellence and other criteria, including the importance of the proposed work to advancing knowledge. (www.sshrc.ca/english/about/peerreview.html)

I have become quite disillusioned with the peer review process after an experience with one of the highest ranked journals in education (based on impact ratings by the Social Sciences Citation Index). I had submitted an article that was returned, after a lengthy period, with two recommendations for "rejection." I took the article, gave it a new title but changed nothing in the body of the text and then submitted it to the same journal. This time it came back highly rated with one "accept as is" and one "accept with minor changes."

Before articulating and theorizing the adjudication process, I describe some of the key actors and their duties in the process, program officer, committee members, and assessors and their assessments.

Program Officer

Without doubt, the program officer who selects assessors, committee members, and committee chair has a critical role. His or her acquaintance with and knowledge of the field is crucial for guaranteeing the fairness of the process. Unfortunately, at SSHRC, the program officers often do not know the field and thereby leave the process open to fail.

The program officer serves as both resource person to the committee and SSHRC's representative during the adjudication process. The officer is responsible for ensuring that the committee understands fully and applies consistently all relevant SSHRC policies and regulations in order that all applications receive equitable and fair treatment. The officer will intervene as necessary during the adjudication to guide and advise the committee and to interpret SSHRC policy. The Program officer also alerts the committee to any problems with specific applications or recommendations and suggests possible solutions or alternative recommendations. (SSHRC, 2000, p. 12)

At SSHRC, the program officers have or rather should have relatively little impact on the decision, though their choice of the reviewer and their assignment of the readers can make or break a proposal. The field of expertise of a program officer may not lie in the area that they are responsible for—someone trained in anthropology may be responsible for the process in educational psychology and areas of education. In this case, they are less familiar with the microstructure of the field, the relations that make friends and foes—they may select an assessor who has friendly or inimical relation to the proposing author without declaring the nature of the special relation. The officer is not an insider in the field and because of this ignorance, is likely to commit errors in the selection of assessors. In actor network terms, this potentially very powerful actor on the inside of the black box makes decisions that have an aleatory aspect, which, in this case, is not a way of eliminating bias (in contrast to the reigning paradigm in randomization in experimental designs). In addition to making these decisions, the program officer organizes the meeting, sending the files and returned assessments to committee members and chair.

The nature of the program officer differs significantly from, let's say, the U.S. National Science Foundation (NSF). Here, the program officer frequently is a specialist in the field, an academic him- or herself, who selects the four reviewer-panelists, whom they often know personally from conferences and other venues. Unlike in my Canadian context, I have experienced on many occasions NSF program officers intervene in discussions—attempting to put a better light on a particular proposal and proposing faculty, especially when there are several unfavorable reviews. In any event, the program officers often do, if they do not like the reviews, solicit more either during the meetings or subsequent to them to get reviews of the kind that support their funding or non-funding inclinations. Because of their knowledge of the field, they can select the reviewers such that they are likely to come up with the preferred assessment. (A friend serving as the editor of an international journal told me repeatedly that it is not difficult to get specific results in the review process. It all depends who he selects as reviewers to get a proposal rejected or accepted, and thereby bias the process in favor or against a particular article or proposal.)

Assessors and Assessment

Ideally, two sometimes three assessors external to the adjudication process assess each proposal intended to assist the committee, which may not have the required expertise, in evaluating a proposal.

[A]djudication committees depend on the advice of external experts since they do not always possess the range of expertise necessary to competently judge all applications. (SSHRC, 2000, p. 17)

In my experience, I observe the most scathing and biased attack on any proposal during an adjudication meeting at NSF in Washington. A nontraditional artificial neural network (ANN) proposal has received very good and excellent assessments by all four panelists. Although this would have been sufficient, the program officer decided to solicit another review, this time from a world-renowned scholar who publicly defended GOFAI (Good Old-fashioned AI) and hardwired linguistic competencies of humans. Within an hour, the scholar not only "reads" the fifteen-page ten-point font proposal but also writes a scathing two-page review: It has taken me, one of the assigned readers and familiar with several domains of the described interdisciplinary effort including ANN modeling, an entire afternoon to read.

If no suitable assessors can be found, "the committee is asked to give the application an in-depth review" (SSHRC, 2000, p. 7) and "must take special care to justify its recommendations [based solely on committee members' assessments] as fully as possible" (SSHRC, 2000, p. 18).

The assessors' reports are subsequently made available to the review panel, and in particular to the two readers assigned to each proposal.[6] Whether the two readers (and the committee) draw on the assessors cannot be determined a priori. Frequently, the readers and the committee as a whole judge the assessment as too complimentary, only infrequently as too critical or biased. Some assessor reports read as if there were ideological or personal differences between assessor and applicant, differences that are then played out in the review. Information that has no grounding in the proposal itself is used to provide a negative critique and worse, to slander an application. Personal or paradigmatic bias can also exist between the applicant and a committee member, without such bias is openly declared as such.

On occasion, the committee reviews an assessment which it judges to be biased, unfair, or personally hurtful to the applicant. In such a case, the committee may wish to use the committee comments to inform the applicant that it does not endorse the views of the assessor in question. (SSHRC, 2000, p. 18)

The committee discussion more often than not disregards the assessors' reports. On the other hand, readers who have not taken the time to carefully read the assigned files tend to draw on the reviews more heavily.

How does a committee that depends on the advice of external experts because it does not possess the expertise decide that an assessment is biased or unfair? If there had been conflicts within the field between the applicant and one or both assessors, how would anyone be able to uncover the apparent conflict and injustice, especially given that the program officers have little understanding of the field? How does a committee on

Program officers are telling me that readers sometimes barely know the files assigned to them. These are readers that are not asked to return. Such readers often base their comments entirely on the assessments.

which none of the members have expertise in the field of the application deal with an assessor statement such as "Many of his papers are repetitive, and he borrows extensively from others' more original contributions"? How does it deal with the statement when there is no evidence provided, just a claim, period! When there is no basis for such an assessment, it constitutes mere bias, opinion, which does not even find support outside the proposal.

Some fields are relatively small; consequently, all of the assessors know and are familiar with the applicant. The reviews point out all the strengths of a proposal and are therefore inherently excellent and recommend funding, often basing the recommendation on the applicants past record rather than on the details of the particular proposal.

Being fluent in both official languages, I have no difficulties following the deliberations in either one. In fact, as committee chair I insisted on each member's choice to speak in his or her preferred tongue. At the same time, I know that several individuals in the meeting cannot follow what is being said. At times, those of us fluent in both languages translate. At other times, the mere fact of having to adjudicate 140 files in four-and-one-half days militates against delayed translations as a permanent fact. So at any one point, some of the members neither understand nor contribute. In the end, we nevertheless note a collective, committee decision.

Given the diversity of committee members and given the program officer's lack of familiarity with a particular field, the door is wide open for acrimonious, biased, heinous, and personal attacks against an individual researcher. How can a well-functioning committee take unsupported claims such as "His papers are repetitive" and "he borrows extensively from others' more original contributions" as matters of fact for basing a decision?

Unfortunately, the evaluation and adjudication procedures and the guidelines governing appeals are such that they give slim chance to applicants to uncover bias and to trigger remedial actions.

Under the provision of the *Privacy Act*, the name of the external assessor or appraiser of an application for SSHRC funding constitutes personal information about the assessor, not the applicant. Applicants will have access to the full text of the external assessments in the research support programs, with the exception of the name of the assessor. (SSHRC, 2000, p. 5)

Committee and Adjudication

The program officer selects a committee whose size depends on the number of files submitted to a particular area; in the two education committees and the interdisciplinary committee, there can be between 120 and 140 files each year. The officer selects committee members according to a set of criteria intended to ensure (a) the overall competence and credibility of the committee; the scholarly stature of the individual nominees; (b) appropriate representation on the basis of areas of expertise, university, region, language and gender; and (c) an appropriate knowledge of both official languages. (In order to participate in bilingual discussions without simultaneous translation, members must have a reading knowledge and good aural comprehension of the second official language.)

Putting together a committee given the listed constraints—plus the additional constraint of actually finding a professor who not only fits a particular profile but also is willing to serve on the committee given the enormity of the task—is a complex problem. The problem is particularly complex because "appropriate representation" is not only a matter of fairness and representation, but also an issue of political correctness in a country with diverse regions, cultures, and universities and of gender equity. Officers feel quite constrained, as one of them once wrote, "we have a set

There are also observers, whose task it is to further assure fairness of the adjudication process. However, when the "observer" enters the room, the committee seems to be really behaved. None of the almost bitter discussions that oppose two members of the committee occur in the presence of the observer, nor do I observe those moments that I call "ganging up against a researcher or a research group" in the inner conversations with myself. Very successful researchers or groups with lots of funding are more likely associated with a negative bias in a committee conversation than less known and individual researchers. When we deal with the proposal of well-known researcher, one might hear comments such as "the researcher just repeats him/herself," "he/she has already gotten grants for this numerous times," "this is only a marginal increment over what he/she has done in the past." For a "grant-writing machine," that is, a group of researchers that write multiple grants, taking turns in being the lead researcher (PI or principal investigator), I can hear in addition comments such as "they don't need it" or "they already have another one." All of these comments negatively bias the conversation.

of criteria that we have to respect in the selection of persons that may sit on our committees. I need a person from the province of Quebec."[7] Appropriate linguistic representation of and competency in the two official languages (English, French) is content of two of the four bullets. It is not surprising that under the best of circumstances, equity along all dimensions is practically never achieved.

Some committees have a tremendous charge, having to adjudicate 140 odd proposals. In any event, each proposal is assigned to two committee members, Reader A and B. Readers have approximately six to eight weeks to read and rate on a scale from one to ten about thirty to forty files. The meeting is then convened in a special place, a particular region of the country (in Canada, we often talk about regional disparities), the nation's capital. During the meeting (on a stage inaccessible to most proposing authors), Reader A presents his or her considerations, ending with the presentation of the scores for past record and present proposal. Reader B makes an equivalent presentation. If the scores are close, and especially after a day or two of meetings, the two members quickly settle on a score, changes to the original scores being frequently proposed prior to making the comments. A discussion follows in case of discrepancies between the two assessments. When there are differences between the two readers, especially differences that they do not seem to be able to resolve, other members enter the conversation. The committee chair mediates the deliberations and summarizes the consensus that emerges.

During the first two days, the committees actually develop something like a personality—at least those that I have worked on seemed to develop one. Being cooped up for eight or nine hours in the same room (sometimes without windows), one comes to know arguments and argumentative styles, particular sensitivities, preferences with respect to particular research methods and theoretical frames; and one develops friendly inclinations towards particular others in the room.

We can look at the committee, although it looks like a singular agent to the outside, as a network of actors. Because of the connections, and the stipulation that any decision has to be consensual, the identity of each actor is not that he or she would enact in a different network. Rather, new identities never experienced before (and perhaps never after) may emerge as a result of the particular situation that brings together diverse individuals under specific conditions and principles (Roth et al., 2004).

Before modeling the decision-making process about how to interpret a proposal and ultimately, whether to fund or not (see below), I show how the proposal itself can be understood as an immutable mobile or as a fluid.

I have had repeatedly the curious experience that the committee almost acted as organism despite the often great diversity of the individual members. At times, this new organism is not dispassionate in the way objectivist philosophers displayed science, it could be vengeful when it feels offended, inflict punishment. I am not only unable to explain this emergent behavior but also how I have became a part—an organ, a member—of this organism myself. In this collective, my individual I—which I might have experienced reading a proposal in the isolation of my office—is mediated and has taken a new identity to support the functioning of the emergent organism. There is this strange dialectic that I have become part of and where I now support decisions that on my own, independent of the collective, I might not and generally do not support. For example, at times I come to a meeting with a high score on the program of a particular proposal and end up consenting with all others that the proposal lies below the funding threshold.

Proposal: Immutable Mobile or Fluid?

To understand social processes, different topologies have been proposed—my exposition thus far exhibited two such topologies: places and networks. "Ottawa" and "SSHRC" (funding agency) as opposed to the geographic location and researcher status of individual applicants implicitly uses "geography" to create distinctions. The expression "Going to the trough" to refer to seeking funding also embodies this topology of places. On the other hand, my description also articulated actors that stand in particular relations—applicants, program officers, program directors, assessors, and committee members. These actors form a network, an actor network; the applicants use their proposal to enroll assessors, individual committee members, the committee as a whole, and, ultimately, the president who acts for and represents the agency ("SSHRC staff submit recommendations for funding to the President of SSHRC for approval" [SSHRC, 2000, p. 19]). That is, each proposal travels in the network, which includes different geographical places, from the applicant (and his or her institution) to SSHRC (Ottawa), to applicants and committee members and their home institutions, and from the committee members back to Ottawa for the adjudication. As the proposal text does not change when it is copied and while it travels to different places and actors, it takes the aspect of an *immutable mobile*. It is the flow of these immutable mobiles in networks that stabilizes the network; it is the lifeblood of these networks. Without them, the network would not exist.

Although there is an aspect of immutability, there is also an aspect of flexibility, for the proposal means different things to the different actors and in different places. These differences can be used to identify boundaries in a topology of places, which has given rise to the notion of *boundary objects* (Star & Grie-semer, 1989) that are, as other material and technological objects, subject to *interpretive flexibility* (e.g. Bijker, 1995). The proposal, qua boundary object travels to different places where it is interpreted flexibly. The same research record as articulated in the proposal can therefore be both evidence for originality and copying, for distinction and ordinariness:

As a whole, it is evident that the researcher distinguishes himself by his research record, both in terms of its quantity as in its quality. His previous work both prove his originality and are of interest to more than one discipline . . . (Assessor 5, p. 1, my translation)

Many of his papers are repetitive, and he borrows extensively from others' more original contributions . . . (Assessor 8, p. 2)

The committee members, individually and as a collective, may agree with one of these assessments or interpret the record in yet another way. This is an ontology in which the *same* object, with a constant internal structure, is merely interpreted differently. But we can think of the proposal in a different, dialectical way, leading to a different ontology.

The proposal can be viewed as a fluid, changing (a part of) its identity, in the same way that human beings are characterized by different identities when they change their social location—they can be powerful (as father towards child) and powerless (as assembly line worker) at the same time, they can be, as history showed, both loving (as father towards their children) and demonic torturers (as guards in concentration camps, White police officers on duty beating up on Blacks [e.g. Rodney King affair]). In the same way, the proposal changes its identity, is something in its relation to different people and groups. At the same time, there is also something constant about it, some aspect of materiality that doesn't seem to change even if replaced by a copy. This is the dialectic aspect of identity, difference in the face of sameness, sameness in the face of difference.

Conceived as a fluid, the changing identity of the proposal is not surprising. Fluid spaces (e.g. academe and funding agencies) do not have clear boundaries and "the objects generated inside them—the objects that generate them—aren't well defined" (Mol & Law, 1994, p. 659). This makes it difficult to define boundaries; even those between the pathological (leading to a non-funding decision) and the normal (suitable for funding) are no longer stable and unambiguous. The same proposal that was highly rated by the assessors and both readers as meritorious for funding, may end up, after the committee meeting, having some pathology that makes it unfit for being recommended. That is, even if all a priori conditions were positively biased toward a particular identity of the proposal-fluid, the adjudication meeting may give it a different identity. In a fluid

space, it is not possible to nice and neatly establish boundaries (as this is attempted in ontology), and therefore identities, once and for all.

Vagaries and Politics of Adjudication

Looking at the entire process of adjudication any one file after the fact—in an
analysis not unlike the one Mehan (1993) made about the "social construction"
of a disability—we might easily come to the conclusion that the decision was
"socially constructed." Accordingly, each member contributed his or her pieces,
the building blocks from which the collective constructs the outcome.

* * *

During a recent adjudication meeting: I sit with nine other professors around a
table having to make decisions about funding or not funding a large number of
proposals. For each file, we come to a decision. Sometimes it takes a long time.
Sometimes a file that comes in with high scores retains high scores. At other
times, despite initial high scores, an application is scored so low as not to be eli-
gible for funding. As the chair, I attempt to predict the contributions of individual
members to a particular file. But more than once I am astonished how, for example, two individuals sometimes support the same file, whereas their input support
opposite decisions (funding, not funding). During some of the specific discussions, I am not in the position to make any accurate predictions as to its outcome. Some members speak in favor of funding, others provide arguments why
the project should not be funded, and still others do not speak out at all. At the
end of each discussion, however, the committee, through its chair, formulates a
consensus position representing the committee as a whole. The "committee consensus" is therefore a construction in more than one sense. First, it is socially
constructed because of the involvement of more than one person and the use of
language, a cultural tool, to make it what it is. Second, it is a construction, a front,
a lie, because many members of the committee actually never are in a position to
contribute.

    I experienced myself as taking on another person's position, being more or
less convinced by the argument he or she has been making. At other times, nothing that another person said seemed to be able to get me off my own position. In
a few cases, we seem to get stuck one or two insisting on supporting funding,
one or more others insisting on not funding. None seems to be willing to move.
As the committee chair, I ask those who have not yet contributed to the particular
conversation to declare and support their own preferences with regard to the assessment of a file. Going around the room, a sense usually emerges for the
group's predilection for one or the other solution and a decision can ultimately be
agreed upon unanimously. In isolated instances, we deliberate for a one- or one-
and-one-half-hour period before we get to that point. With one hundred and forty
files to be adjudicated in a four-and-one-half day period, however, simple arith-

metic shows that spending so much time with each proposal is not feasible; in fact, it is impossible.

* * *

When this occurred for the first time, images of some of my modeling efforts emerged; I had translated an actor network approach in which each statement made by a person in a meeting is modeled as a semiotic actor that stands in some relation to other statements (actors), supporting some of them while contradicting others.[8] My modeling efforts show that even minute new input may provide sufficient change to the overall constellation to get the decision-making process going again and bring it to one solution or another.

In the meeting: At times, I feel ridiculous. The entire discussion has been in English or French, while the respective non- or poorly-speaking members evidently had attended to other things or given the impression of dozing off. Yet I am to formulate the consensus position—consensus of how many individuals? How many knew sufficiently about the file to make judgments about the "quality and significance of the published work," the degree of originality and nature of expected contribution to the advancement of knowledge," or the "appropriateness of the theoretical approach or framework"? De facto, the decisions are based on the two readers' decision and consensus, whatever their own competencies vis-à-vis the application and the field. I nevertheless contribute in a way so that the occasional observer can note that the committee as a whole and I in particular have "followed the rules."[9]

Figure 15.1 shows the outcome of the decision-making process for different scenarios. Or, in terms of the fluid ontology, the committee attempted to arrive on its own understanding of the proposal's identity. I take each statement that is made in a conversation as describing an aspect of the proposal's identity as a node; some statements support one another and are therefore modeled as supporting (reinforcing) links between nodes. Some pairs of statements are contradictory, each supporting a different identity, which I model in terms of links between nodes that weaken each other. Some statements do not relate to other statements, which is characterized in the model by the absence of a link. The final model is therefore a network of statements about a proposal that mutually reinforce, weaken, or are neutral to each other. The outcome of the process is a solution with the least constraint in the network. (More details of this form of modeling, and a concrete case of modeling one concrete decision-making process can be found in Roth [2001].) The network relaxes. Mathematically, the system finds itself somewhere up on a mountainside in an n-dimensional landscape and is moving (could we say flowing?) down the steepest slope until it ends at some lowest place (lowest state).

a.

b.

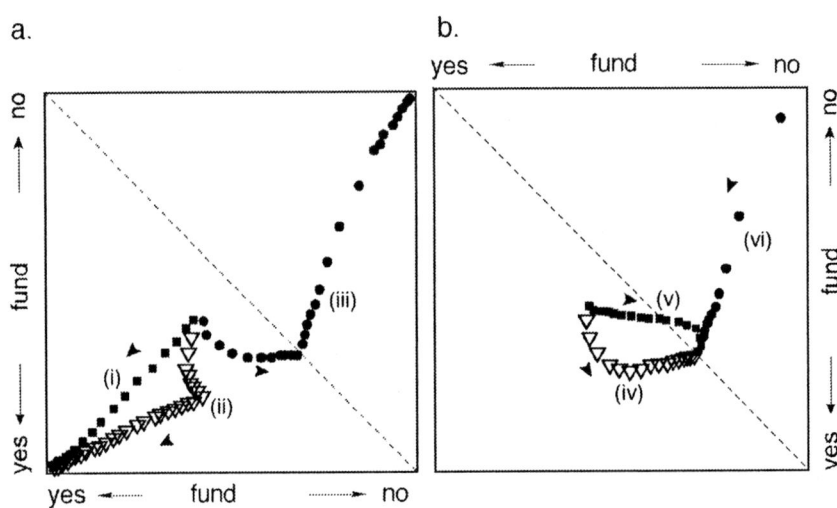

Figure 15.1. Modeling group decision making when some propositions favor funding and other propositions favor not funding. Propositions can be supportive of other propositions or contradictory. The "strength" of support or contradiction corresponds to how "emphatic" the statement is presented in the meeting. a. The three scenarios are based on the same set of propositions (semiotic actors), but which are related to one another more or less strongly because of different emphatic level with which they have been put forward. The committee begins without strong commitment to recommend funding or not funding. b. Despite very different starting positions, one strongly favoring not funding, the committee ends up in a stale mate. The three scenarios are based on the same set of propositions but which are put forward with different emphatic levels.

In Figure 15.1a, the committee starts mildly favoring a decision to fund. However, because of different ways in which the same propositions are affecting one another, the committee comes quickly to a supportive decision (Figure 15.1a.i), after initial consideration to the contrary supports funding (Figure 15.1a.ii), or during the considerations shifts to support not funding (Figure 15.1a.iii). The fluid seems to flow into one direction but then moves off to the other.

The model is somewhat simplistic in that it only models the changing strength of the propositions but not the relation between them; further, it models all statements given simultaneously rather than being added in time, continuously modifying the context in which future statements are made. Nevertheless, the model underscores that minor variations in initial conditions can lead to substantially different outcomes—one decision over another.

In this example of the committee meeting, it was not only the final product that emerged, indeterminately from the complex and ever changing interactions between the members of the committee; the trajectory of each discussion itself emerged indeterminately. The expression, "laying a garden path in walking" may be the best description for our experiences as members on the committee. The notion of "indeterminate" here means that even after doing 140 or so files, we could predict with any certainty either process or product of our conversations other than in rather encompassing and indistinct terms.

In this example of the committee meeting, it was not only the final product that emerged, indeterminately from the complex and ever-changing interactions between the members of the committee; the trajectory of each discussion itself emerged indeterminately. The expression, "laying a garden path in walking" may be the best description for our experiences as members on the committee. The notion of "indeterminate" here means that even after doing 140 odd files, we could predict with any certainty either process or product of our conversations other than in rather encompassing and indistinct terms.

An important "biasing" aspect of the direction a committee will take is the real or perceived expertise of the reader or committee member. In the case of real or perceived expertise, the committee decision will be close to the opinion and assessment of this reader. If real or perceived expertise lies with another committee member who was not the reader, this person, depending on the level of his or her engagement, can change the direction of the discussion to the point of getting a well-rated proposal into the category of un-fundable projects. In some situations, even proposals with high ratings by both readers and the two or three assessors might end up not being funded as a consequence of the influences within the committee. Thus, I found myself in situations where I had to assist the program officer drafting the committee summary that would become part of the notification letter, particularly when there was the perception that the applicant might complain and file an appeal.

Should the committee make a negative recommendation contrary to the generally favorable recommendations of the assessors, the committee must take particular care to provide a clear rationale for that recommendation. (SSHRC, 2000, p. 17)

A most important issue in funding is systemic and systematic bias within the committee structure that excludes particular types and styles of research.

While not apparent to me on the SSHRC committees on which I served, I have (a) noticed bias on the part of members of certain disciplines (psychology, cognitive science, computer science) for experimental designs and against qualitative research designs and ethnographic research. The same type of bias has been reported to me to occur, for example, on the SSHRC panel evaluating and adjudicating psychological research; according to my informant, qualitative research stood little to no chance of receiving funding because there was a systemic bias against this form of investigation. Finally, many German colleagues in science education (Didaktik der Naturwissenschaften) told me about the difficulties to get funding for research with qualitative designs, which they explained (we can take them as lay sociologists) by the predominance of experimental and quantitative psychologists on the DFG panels. One German psychologist at DFG—influential because tak-

Although my (i.e., Reader A's) recommendation as well as Reader B's recommendations have been high, we ultimately decide to give a score so low that the proposal is automatically excluded from funding, "to send a message to the researcher." More difficult to me, I am asked at times to articulate the "flaws" in the study and the committee consensus, although I have not been the chair at the time, but perhaps because I know the application very well and am perhaps the only one to fully understand its complexities. It is a strange feeling to write a committee consensus that is opposite to your own thinking prior to the considerations. It is even more difficult to construct a consensus when some comments made during the deliberations have to be interpreted as "off the record" even though they were not marked so while they were made and other comments pertained to information that was not available in the proposal itself but to the deliberations about another of the applicant's research programs.

ing key gatekeeper positions, i.e., he is sitting at an *obligatory points of passage* (Latour, 1987) for German researchers— has told me repeatedly that my own research program—though clearly successful on an international scale—would not be funded by his agency.

Shoring the Agency from Appeals

Justifying Committee Recommendations

In an attempt to maintain fairness in the peer review process, SSHRC established an appeal procedure that provides applicants an opportunity to seek reconsideration of a decision. The extent to which this procedure constitutes a true opportunity or whether it is simply a lip service to fairness is, of course, a matter of the appeal as a practical accomplishment rather than a matter that can be decided through theoretical considerations. The first step in dealing with potential appeals begins in the adjudication meeting, where the chair of the committee is asked to provide a summary that reflects the "committee decision."

Independently of the fact whether there is actually a chance for overturning a committee decision, and perhaps in order to veil and cover up for the insufficiencies of the process, the Council, at least on paper, attempts to provide researchers with information on which to ground the appeal.

It is essential for SSHRC to be able to provide the applicant with a clear, reasonable and sufficient explanation for the adjudication committee's recommendation and the Council's final decision. This is crucial for applications refused on merit and for applications that the committee judges meritorious but which cannot be funded. The recommendations also provide important feedback and encouragement to applicants, serving as a developmental instrument for future research proposals . . . (SSHRC, 2000, p. 19)

This was an interesting discursive move that the "Council" provides the feedback, whereas in other circumstances, it is the program officer. Perhaps this is useful on the inside. It is a Council decision as long as things go right, but it becomes the program officer decision when things go wrong—he or she can be fired. (The precariousness of the officers and the insecurities of their status because of constant renewal of contracts has been communicated to me by more than one program officer.)

In actual fact, the comments to the researchers are, in most instances, very brief. In my own case, the crucial assessment of my record of achievement was barely more than a two-liner: "Members found the candidate's record quite respectable, though it noted Assessor 8's concern that some of his research papers appeared to be somewhat repetitive. The committee found the supporting document of good quality." Do these two sentences constitute "clear, reasonable and sufficient explanation for the adjudication committee's recommendation"? In particular, does it provide sufficient grounds to decrease the assessment score of a researcher's record from 9 (out of 10) to 7.45, when he has published in the intervening period five books, forty-five articles, and fifteen chapters? The council guidelines for the adjudication process point out that that sufficient explanation is especially "crucial for applications refused on merit and for applications that the committee judges meritorious but which cannot be funded." Does such a brief statement really serve as the "developmental instrument for future research proposals"? How am I to develop if the assessors charge that my papers are repetitive was true? The previously quoted colleague had this to say:

The committee is especially obliged by the standards of scholarly peer review to provide open and clear reasons for why it recommended such a severe reduction. Instead, the Committee provided one, 18-word sentence: 'It judged that savings could be made in the proposed expenditures for personnel, travel, supplies, and equipment.'" (Scholar's Letter to SSHRC, p. 2)

On paper at least, the agency appears to have a process that can be appealed. The policy states that committees should provide sufficient feedback about its deliberations, which could be used in an appeals process. Whereas in my NSF experience, researchers received feedback of considerable length, written by the first (Reader A) of four readers, the actual feedback provided by SSHRC to Canadian researchers is (ridiculously?) short. Although the Council policy posits "clear, reasonable and sufficient explanation," in actual practice, the feedback often is neither clear, nor reasonable or sufficient.

My account thus far already articulated features of the adjudication that can be counted as mediating factors that lead to insufficient feedback from the agency. The program officer constructs this feedback during the month following the meeting from notes taken during the meeting and, particularly, on the basis of the chair's consensus statement at the end of a discussion. The officers are not a specialist in the adjudicated field and therefore does not necessarily understand the arguments put forward during the discussion. Their task is made more difficult by constructing notes with some delay (during the weeks after the meeting), not *during* the meeting pauses and at the end of each day as we had done on NSF panels—the notes were completed and ratified by the other readers before the meeting was adjourned. Finally, the shear quantity of feedback notes that officers have to construct further mediates the quality of the feedback.

Constraining and Limiting Appeals

In the appeals process, the program officer attempts to get as many committee members as possible to agree on a telephone conference. The original file and the letter in which an applicant files the appeal are mailed to the members that agreed to read the proposal and the appeal, and to contribute to the conference discussion.

The Council has constructed the appeals procedure such that it is very difficult if not impossible to get a decision revoked. These barriers are built (a) into the procedure and (b) into the fact that the committee deciding on the appeal is the same as the committee that took the original decision.

First, the SSHRC Manual (2000, p. 7) states, "Decisions may be appealed on the following grounds: where there has been an administrative or procedural error in the adjudication process; or where the decision is based on a factual error." The two types of errors are subsequently explained.

Procedural error includes any departure from the Council's policy regarding undeclared conflict of interest or a failure to provide prescribed information to the adjudication committee...

Factual error exists where there is compelling evidence that the committee based its decision not to recommend an award on a conclusion which is contrary to information clearly stated in the application. An example of such an error would be a committee statement that an application was not recommended due to the applicant's lack of any peer-reviewed publications, where in fact, the application lists several publications in media universally acknowledged to be peer-reviewed. (SSHRC, 2000, p. 7)

Pertaining to my own appeal, an officer offers the following advice: "I am suggesting to you to wait for the committee's comments and to resubmit your project next year to one of the two education committees. It doesn't help at all to appeal, because you won't have valid grounds to appeal. In any case, it won't help you." It doesn't help at all to appeal because I won't have valid grounds? Is it meant to tell me that the process is inherently designed to stabilize the initial decision that a committee had taken?

But the appeals document then continues

The Council will not accept appeals where the committee, though it could be in error in interpreting the proposal and any assessments, has made a reasonable attempt to judge fairly the merit of an application. Nor is the appeal process intended to deal with differences of scholarly opinion among applicants, adjudication committees and external assessors. (http://www.sshrc.ca/english/programinfo/policies/appeals_peer-review.html)

Thus, although there may be errors, the council—or rather, the small network of people making the relevant decision—does not have to accept appeals on the grounds of error. Here, again, the appeal is a fluid object and though there might be evidence that errors have been committed, the appeal is pathological itself, insufficient to bring about a change in the original decision. "Nor is the appeal process intended to deal with differences of scholarly opinion among applicants, adjudication committees and external assessors"—thus if an assessor's statement "Many of his papers are repetitive, and he borrows extensively from others' more original contributions" is interpreted as a matter of scholarly opinion, the applicant has no grounds for appeal.

Second, the process is inherently biased against the applicant because the very same committee (or parts of it) that made the original decision evaluates the appeal. Whereas the legal system has another level where appeals are considered by a different panel, and other aspects of society make use of an ombud-sperson, the funding agency takes appeals to the same committee, which then deliberates whether it erred in the first instance. Curiously, therefore, the committee deliberates whether it has erred though the Council states that it will not accept appeals, even if the committee had erred. This provides opportunities for rejecting appeals based on a factual error in initial deliberations, as long as the committee comes to the conclusion that it "has made a reasonable attempt to judge fairly the merit of an application."

Critiquing Institutions

Working on this text has made salient many questions in my mind, theoretical and empirical ones. In addition to the questions that opened this article, I am posing others in the following list without pre-supposing that the order is a statement about the importance of each question or set of questions.

First, from which or whose perspectives (proposal author, reviewer, evaluating committee member, committee chair, program officer, program chair, proposal author's superiors, lawyers, etc.) will we gain particular insights? Which or whose perspectives are of most practical relevance to the different actors in different parts of the network. What gains can be made if we take the perspectives of various non-human actors?

Second, if there are multiple suitable perspectives, how do these relate to one another? Are there dominant perspectives and if so, at the cost of which other perspectives? Can there by multiple incompatible perspectives or should we seek to triangulate a "common" perspective? What are some reasonable or interesting solutions to the incompatibility-of-perspectives problem?

Third, how should a social phenomenon such as funding be theorized? What advantages are there taking, for example, a grounded theory approach (Strauss & Corbin, 1990) versus making explicit one's ontology, such as I have done here?

Fourth, doing ethnography of one's own community, that is, doing auto/ethnography especially if it is of an agent that can withhold certain resources and therefore is in a power-over relation, comes both with risks (to the author) and opportunities (e.g., changes in praxis). What processes can be set in place so that such ethnographies are possible without punitive measures from those at obligatory passage points in power of withholding valued and desirable resources? Do we have to play the game, shut up, and thereby leave unjust practices intact so that we can cull the resources? What is/ought to be the roles of more prominent scholars in changing our practices and communities?

Finally, how similar/different are the funding-decision processes across different agencies? How similar/different are the processes across countries or continents?

Notes

This is a vastly modified version of an article originally published as Roth, W.-M. (2004). Vagaries and politics of funding: Beyond "I told you so." *Forum Qualitative Sozialfor-schung/Forum: Qualitative Social Research*, *5*(1). http://www.qualitative-research.net/fqs-texte/1-04/1-04roth-e.htm

[1] It is evident that ethics and professionalism prevent me from naming individuals (applicants, assessors, program officers, program directors) or particular files. It should also be evident that I put myself in difficult and dangerous waters—see the fluid analogy use below—by doing such an investigation that turns up the problems in the evaluation and adjudication process of the one agency that funds social science research in my area.

[2] Even mereology, the study of wholes and their parts, wrestles with difficult if not undecidable problems. What is the color of the boundary that runs precisely through the middle of a disk, symmetrically segmenting it into two segments one of which is red, the other green? Smith (1997) provides the beginning of an answer to this question.

[3] I have once served as the chair of a committee in which all proposals were funded. The committee meeting therefore was a farce, because it was evident from the way the program officer interfered with the meeting that normal peer review processes were not followed and all proposals would be funded.

[4] This is the content of Kafka's parable of the gatekeeper in the novel The Trial. A man from the countryside comes to the city gate (door of the Law) and yet is denied admittance by the gatekeeper. No reason is given for his denial, and seemingly the man has no reason to stay, and yet he sits down and waits. In this situation, the gatekeeper had no power whatsoever over the man until the main began waiting for the gatekeeper to let him in.

[5] I show below that the appeal structure is biased against the applicant who desires to appeal; people who work in the agency, as Kafka's gatekeeper, tell that it is not worth appealing because it does not get you anywhere.

[6] In my experiences on review panels at the U.S. National Science Foundation, the two levels were collapsed into one: four assessors read each proposal and subsequently participated as panelists.

[7] The issue of Quebec is particularly sensitive given the repeated attempts of large parts of its populations to secede from the rest of Canada, because of their sense that French culture and language are not sufficiently supported by federal politics.

[8] In *ARAMIS ou l'amour des techniques*, Latour (1992) presents an interesting case of the failed development of an urban transport system. Central to the story are the tensions between different constraints in the actor network. My constraint satisfaction models are explicitly based on finding the state of a network where the constraints are at a minimum.

[9] "Rule following" is much more complex than it appears from the traditional psychological or sociological literature. Interesting descriptions on the situated nature of actions and their relations to the rules that they can be said to have followed or disobeyed can be found in Suchman (1987).

References

Bijker, W. E. (1995). *Of bicycles, bakelites, and bulbs: Toward a theory of sociotechnical change*. Cambridge, MA: MIT Press.

de Laet, M., & Mol, A. (2000). The Zimbabwe bush pump: Mechanics of a fluid technology. *Social Studies of Science, 30*, 225–263.

Goffman, E. (1959). *The presentation of self in everyday life*. New York: Doubleday.

Guice, J. (1998). Controversy and the state: Lord ARPA and intelligent computing. *Social Studies of Science, 28*, 103–138.

Holzkamp, K. (1984, November). Die Menschen sitzen nicht im Kapitalismus wie in einem Käfig. *Psychologie Heute*, pp. 29–37

Latour, B. (1987). *Science in action: How to follow scientists and engineers through society*. Cambridge, MA: Harvard University Press.

Latour, B. (1992). *Aramis ou l'amour des techniques*. Paris: Éditions la Découverte.

Latour, B. (1993). *We have never been modern*. Cambridge, MA: Harvard University Press.

Mehan, H. (1993). Beneath the skin and between the ears: A case study in the politics of representation. In S. Chaiklin & J. Lave (Eds.), *Understanding practice: Perspectives on activity and context* (pp. 241–268). Cambridge: Cambridge University Press.

Mol, A., & Law, J. (1994). Regions, networks and fluids: Anemia and social topology. *Social Studies of Science, 24*, 641–671.

Olazaran, M. (1996). A sociological study of the official history of the perceptrons controversy. Social Studies of Science, 26, 611–659.

Redfield, P. (1996). Beneath a modern sky: Space technology and its place on the ground. *Science, Technology, & Human Values, 21*, 251–274.

Roth, W.-M. (2001). Designing as distributed process. *Learning and Instruction, 11*, 211–239.

Roth, W.-M. (2002). Editorial power/authorial suffering. *Research in Science Education, 32*, 215–240.

Roth, W.-M. (2005). Publish or stay behind and perhaps perish: Stability of publication practices in (some) social sciences. *Soziale Systeme, 11*.

Roth, W.-M., Tobin, K., Elmesky, R., Carambo, C., McKnight, Y., & Beers, J. (2004). Re/making identities in the praxis of urban schooling: A cultural historical perspective. *Mind, Culture, & Activity, 11*, 48–69.

Smith, B. (1997). Boundaries: An essay in mereotopology. In Lewis E. Hahn (ed.), *The philosophy of Roderick Chisholm* (pp. 534–561). Chicago: Open Court.

Smith, D. E. (1990). *Conceptual practices of power: A feminist sociology of knowledge.* Toronto: University of Toronto Press.

Smith, D. E. (1999). *Writing the social: Critique, theory, and investigations.* Toronto: University of Toronto Press.

Social Sciences and Humanities Research Council of Canada (SSHRC) (2000). *Standard research grants program: A manual for adjudication committee members.* Ottawa: Author.

Star, S. L., & Griesemer, J. (1989). Institutional Ecology, 'Translations,' and Boundary Objects: Amateurs and Professionals in Berkeley's Museum of Vertebrate Zoology, 1907–1939. *Social Studies of Science, 19,* 387–420.

Strauss, A. L., & Corbin, J. (1990). *Basics of qualitative research: Grounded theory procedures and techniques.* Thousand Oaks, CA: Sage.

Suchman, L. A. (1987). *Plans and situated actions: The problem of human-machine communication.* Cambridge: Cambridge University Press.

Tobin, B. (2001). *Social Sciences and Humanities Research Council of Canada: Performance report for the period ending March 31, 2001.* Ottawa: SSHRC.

16   A Snake in the Nest or In A Snake's Nest: Peer Review for a Female Science Educator

Kate Scantlebury

When I commenced my appointment, as an untenured, tenure-track, feminist science educator in a chemistry and biochemistry department, I was cognizant of the differences between departmental peers and myself. The ensuing years of working in my department but typically not with my colleagues, has sharpened my perspectives on the contradictions I experience as a female, feminist science educator in an academic science department. This chapter has three sections: In the first section, I share my tenure and promotion experiences as a feminist scholar in a content department by discussing whom my colleagues acknowledge as peers. In the second section, using the participation data of women in academic chemistry I highlight an ongoing concern that there are currently few women at the higher levels of "peer review" and the implications this has for junior faculty. In the third section, I reflect on how the use of auto/biography gives me special (sociological) insights in the life of academe.

Feminist Science Educator in a Chemistry Department

Take the fact of education. Your class has been educated at public schools and universities for five or six hundred years, ours for sixty . . . though we see the same world we see it through different senses. Any help we can give you must be different from that you can give yourselves, and perhaps the value of that help may lie in the fact of the difference. Therefore before we agree to sign your manifesto or join your society, it might well to discover where the difference lies, because then we may discover where the help lies also. (Woolf, 1938, p. 17)

I work in a unique environment for a feminist science educator. For the past thirteen years, I have had an appointment in a chemistry and biochemistry department. As an untenured, assistant professor, I accepted the position at the University of Delaware as the College of Arts and Sciences' secondary science education coordinator. At that time, the chemistry and biochemistry department had not tenured a faculty member whose research focused on education. The research interests of the other faculty who coordinated teacher education in the college focused did not focus on education.

This situation raised questions for my colleagues and myself on the criteria for promotion and tenure; peer review plays a critical role in that process. Prior to my appointment I engaged in a discussion with my future department chair and the college's senior associate dean regarding the "difference" in my role within the department compared to a research chemist. The concern of the chairman and other administrators was how the tenured faculty, that is my peers, would interpret the department's promotion and tenure guidelines. The guidelines stated, "The candidate must have established a quality research program. Quality in this sense denotes original research of significance to chemistry" (University of Delaware, n.d.). In my letter of hire, the chairman noted, "heretofore research in the Department of Chemistry and Biochemistry has focused on discovering and understanding properties of matters. The nature of scholarship in science education requires that this limited view be broadened."[1]

The decision as to how that view could be broadened was based upon a publication from the American Chemical Society (ACS). The previous year, the ACS's division of chemical education published a report called "Chemical Education Research" (ACS, 1992). Based upon Boyer's (1990) ideas, the report distinguished between research and scholarship by defining chemistry education scholarship into teaching, discovery, integration, and application. Further, the report noted that chemistry education research had a theoretical base, involved data collection, produced generalizable results, and stated that data could be either qualitative or quantitative. My departmental colleagues accepted the American Chemical Society as a group of *their* peers. This nationally and internationally recognized high status organization had defined chemistry education as a viable field of research. The guidelines provided authority for my departmental colleagues when, as my peers during the promotion and tenure process, they judged if I had established a "quality research program."

As a female science educator I needed to be cognizant of where the "difference lies" between whom my departmental colleagues would acknowledge as peers compared with who faculty in a college of education may label as a peer because the role of external peer review is critical on promotion and tenure decisions. The written external review of an untenured professor's promotion and tenure dossier by researchers outside of the university is a key piece of information that tenured faculty consider when voting on an untenured professor's promotion and tenure. In my department, a tenured faculty chairs the candidate's promotion and tenure committee that consists of all tenured faculty. The candidate and the committee submit a list of peers from other institutions who would review the dossier. The external reviewers' opinion of the candidate's research and scholarship is held in high regard within the department. The process of suggesting reviewers raised several questions and posed different dilemmas. Who were my peers? Are teacher educators in schools and colleges of education my peers with different demands and expectations of teaching, research, grantsmanship, and service my peers? Who would the department's tenured faculty consider as peers? Do they regard researchers in science education as their own and, by association, my peers? Would they value feminist scholars' opinions?

Proposing external reviewers was difficult because the majority of my colleagues did not know the leading researchers in science education. While some of them are interested in educational research and have been actively involved in reforming undergraduate chemistry curriculum, they do not attend or present at education research conferences such as the National Association of Research in Science Teaching or American Educational Research Association's. Several faculty members have participated in the American Chemical Society's chemical education division's national, regional, and biennial conferences and published articles in the *Journal of Chemical Education*. But none of my colleagues are involved in feminist research. Other than the *Journal of Chemical Education*, they did not typically read or contribute to the education research journals.

In consultation with my mentors, who consisted of a departmental colleague, my major professor and several colleagues from outside my university, the external peer reviewers I suggested, were either science education researchers in educational departments or chemistry faculty who had interests, and in some cases, did research in chemistry education. The usual practice is to include a cover letter and a copy of the department's promotion and tenure guidelines. The cover letter sent with my dossier to the external reviewers described my unique role and duties in the department and college. Further, the external reviewers received copies of my hire letter and the ACS Taskforce report on chemical education research. The department's tenure and promotion committee was not required to include the letter and taskforce report. However, the department expected my tenure and promotion application to be successful because I had attained external funds to support my research.

A primary method of accumulating cultural capital (Bourdieu, 1977) in a research chemistry department is attaining external research funding. While many faculty members relate to the academic slogan of "publish or perish," within my department this is modified to "funding and publish or perish." This external validation is another aspect of academe that relies on peer review. This external recognition and validation of my research provided me with social and cultural capital. All but one of the tenured faculty members voted positively to support my application for promotion and tenure. With strong departmental support, my application received unanimous support at the college and university committees. I had a positive experience with this aspect of peer review but I used my social capital to establish the necessary networks. For example, prior to my appointment at the University of Delaware I had not attended or presented at an ACS meeting. In participating at ACS I began to establish networks with faculty that my chemistry colleagues would acknowledge as peers. The culture of chemical education conferences is different from science educators' experience at international conferences. Fortunately, I was able to use my "cultural tool kit" (Swidler, 1986) to navigate the different cultures and establish the social capital I needed with those who would become my peer reviewers.

Changing the Climate for Female Faculty in Chemistry Departments

The influence of peer review on one's academic life is a constant, and at times difficult to negotiate. While being a science educator in a chemistry department poses unique and different challenges, there is also another added constraint of being a female in academe. As a feminist scholar I experience the alienation associated with my research, which is further exacerbated by being the only educational researcher in my department (Arpad, 1992). Negotiating peer review is in part being cognizant of "where the difference lies." For myself, the differences manifest themselves in several ways, as a science educator and my colleagues in a content department, as a feminist researcher, and as a female in academe. There is an underlying assumption that peer review is fair, equitable and based on merit. Because of my interest in feminist scholarship, I had read many studies regarding the different roles, expectations and experiences for women in academe compared to their male colleagues. Feminists have argued that equal treatment is not equitable and at universities the playing field is by no means the same women and men. Nearly twenty years ago, the academic climate for women was described as "chilly" and there is little to suggest that it has "warmed" very much since that time (Hall & Sandler, 1984).

Yet after several decades of discussion on the men and women the data show that there are significant differences between women and men in academic settings and consequently who are in positions to be considered as "peers" for external reviews of tenure dossiers, publication manuscripts, and grant applications. In the current academic climate, women faculty are less likely than their male colleagues to be employed at research institutions, be in tenure track positions, and if in those positions, attain tenure. This disparity between type of position, the prestige of the university and the attainment of tenure promulgates inequities for women in terms of salary, status, and power. For example, the report "A Study on the Status of Women Faculty in Science at MIT" (MIT, 1999) highlighted overt and subtle biases towards women faculty at one of the country's most prestigious universities. Those scientists found that they were isolated, "invisible," and marginalized. Their opinions were not valued and they had little or no power in departmental decision-making procedures. The depth of one's status and power influences a variety of situations for academics and in doing so establish who is identified and labeled as a peer. In academe, peer review is used in tenure decisions to evaluate faculty; and editors use it to guide their decisions about which manuscripts become publications. However, the phrase is a misnomer for assistant faculty because their peers—that is, other assistant faculty, rarely have the power to participate in these procedures. Although junior faculty review manuscripts for journals, the editors have the final decision-making power. At a minimum those editors are tenured associate professors. For associate professors, full professors are the gatekeepers for upper levels of academic influence such as department chairs, awards committees, journal editorships and other leadership roles, such as setting policy for the direction of chemical research. And even at the full professorial level women in academe have found an uneven playing field and peer review through informal and formal mechanisms contributes to that disparity. I will illustrate this point using an example from chemistry.

In 1993 there were eighty women (8 percent), who are full professors in American university, Ph.D. chemistry departments. Four years ago, a subset of those women gathered to discuss the status of women in academic chemistry. Most began their academic careers in the 70s, when about five percent of the full professors in chemistry were female. At that time, they were told "be patient' because it would take a generation for a substantive increase in the percentage of female full professors. The group has formed *COACh–The Committee for the Advancement of Women Chemists* (Richmond, 1999). They have begun to run mentoring workshops for women faculty, and at the present time they are focusing on women at the associate and full professor levels in chemistry and chemical engineering departments. COACh's programs focus on providing women the skills to obtain administrative positions at their home institutions and within the chemical and scientific community, receive external recognition for scientific and leadership accomplishments, and increase the number of women in chemistry. Why? Senior faculty are six times more likely to recommend a junior male colleague to chair conference sessions. "Peers" are more likely to identify male colleagues as candidates for promotion. Several recent studies report that these subtle practices, or informal peer reviews, consistently disadvantage women and the negative impact on their career is cumulative.

Auto/Biography and the Sociology of Academia

In this chapter, I used auto/biography to describe gender issues for women in academic science departments. But my account is more than auto/biographical, it is also a way of articulating how academia and academic relations are constructed. My auto/biography therefore also is an auto/biographically centered ethnography of the field, it is an auto/ethnography; more so, it is an account that takes feminist perspective for conducting social analysis. A feminist approach foregrounds gender and attempts to understand female perspectives (Reinharz, 1992). Women in science are caught in a paradox. They are rarely perceived as authorities in science and the producers of scientific knowledge. Often, women who are successful in science are viewed as "exceptional." Although tenured women in academe have achieved a high level of success, our research with female chemists and chemical engineers show that these women are still undervalued and disrespected by their male colleagues, administrators, and students. Senior women report their constant and ongoing efforts to maintain their status and position within the field. Moreover, they have a collaborative rather than competitive approach to conducting research that conflicts with the dominant culture (Fassinger, Scantlebury, & Richmond, 2005).

As a feminist researcher and educator in a chemistry department, my experience when engaging with my peers is less combative and confrontational than other women in the department because I do not compete with my male colleagues for human and material resources. There is no doctoral program in chemistry education within my department, so I do not court new graduate students to join my research group. Also my research does not rely on expensive material resources, such as laboratory space, analytical equipment, or chemical consumables. Further, the Dean's office provides the support and resources for my faculty line and the program that I coordinate. If I resigned, the department could not replace me with a "real" chemist. The department provides material resources for my work in the form of office space, access to technology and human resources, such as secretaries, staff that support faculty in grant-writing activities and computer support personnel. My responsibilities include coordinating and teaching students who plan to become high school science teachers. And my colleagues see value in my role within the department and for the university in terms of social networks and building social capital with schools from which we recruit undergraduate majors.

But my limited cultural and social capital within the department, in part because my research interest and expertise is outside of chemistry, has resulted in my colleagues attempting to dictate the direction and focus of my research using through formal and informal channels. For example, my five-year review after attaining tenure, the peer review committee suggested that I should focus my research within Delaware and that I should also consider conducting research studies within the department. This action is a direct infringement on my academic freedom. Further, none of my "peers" in this review conduct research in education, nor have they published in the field. I submitted a written rebuttal to the issues raised by the peer review committee. Informally, usually in social spaces such as department functions, colleagues will discuss gender differences they have observed in the teaching and learning of chemistry and suggest that I should conduct research on the topic. After attaining tenure, I had garnered sufficient social capital to use the opportunity to engage in dialogue on the gender research I was planning or had conducted,

Over a decade after accepting a position in a chemistry department, I continue to examine where the difference lies between feminist educators and research scientists. As a science educator, I have attained a higher symbolic capital with others, such as teachers and education policymakers, compared with my colleagues in the education. That status has provided me opportunities to foreground a feminist agenda in multiple ways.

When science educators act as peer reviewers, we should consider "where the difference lies" and that there is a "chilly" climate in academe for women and minority scholars. When we enact peer review assuming that the playing field is equal for all, we run the risk of marginalizing new scholars, ignoring the voices of those who have less power, and pushing peers who do not reflect our research views and opinions into invisibility.

Notes

This chapter is based on materials previously published in *Research in Science Education* (Scantlebury, 2002). The paper's title is taken from conversations with my departmental colleagues. After reading my two-year review dossier, a peer suggested that having someone like myself in the department whose research used the feminist critiques of science was akin to having a "snake in the nest." A friend in turn quipped that being female science educator in a predominately male department was comparable to being in a snake's nest. I use both analogies to describe my experiences.

[1] However, my departmental and college administrators verbally informed me that the letter of hire was not a legally binding document. If the situation arose were I challenged a tenure or promotion decision the department's approved promotion and tenure guidelines are the criteria used because those are ratified by the faculty Senate and approved by the university's Board of Trustees.

References

American Chemical Society (ACS). (1992). *Taskforce report on chemical education scholarship.* Washington, DC: Author.

Arpad, S. (1992). The personal cost of the feminist knowledge explosion. In C. Kramarae & D. Spender (Eds.), *The knowledge explosions: generations of feminist scholarship* (pp. 333–339). New York: Teachers College

Boyer, E. L. (1990). *Scholarship reconsidered: priorities of the professorate.* Princeton, NJ: Carnegie Foundation for the Advancement of Teaching.

Bourdieu, P. (1977). *An outline of a theory of practice.* Cambridge: Cambridge University Press.

Fassinger, R., Scantlebury, K., & Richmond, G. (2005). Career, family, and institutional influences on the work lives of academic women in the chemical sciences. *Journal of Women and Minorities in Science & Engineering, 10,* 297–316.

Hall, R., & Sandler, B. (1984). *The classroom climate: A chilly one for women?* Washington, DC: American Association of Colleges.

Massachusetts Institute of Technology (MIT). (1999). *A study on the status of women faculty in science at MIT.* URL: http://web.mit.edu/fnl/women/women.html#The Study. (Accessed February 20, 2005)

Reinharz, S. (1992). *Feminist methods in social research.* New York: Oxford University Press.

Richmond, G. (1999). *COACh—The committee for the advancement of women chemists.* Washington, DC: National Science Foundation, Grant # CHE-0078913.

Scantlebury, K. (2002). A snake in the nest or in a snake's nest: What counts as peer review for a female science education in a chemistry department. *Research in Science Education, 32,* 157–162.

Swidler, A. (1986). Culture in action: Symbols and strategies. *American Sociological Review, 51,* 273–286.

University of Delaware. (1988). *Promotion and tenure procedures and criteria.* Newark, DE: Department of Chemistry and Biochemistry.

Woolf, V. (1938). *Three guineas.* New York: Harcourt Brace Jovanovich.

V

Experiences
and Trajectories

In Section III, we find examples of how auto/biography and auto/ethnography constitute means for educators to generate teaching-related materials upon which they can subsequently reflect. But auto/biography and auto/ethnography have the potential to provide teachers with more than teaching-related materials. Teachers, teachers in training, administrators, teacher educators, and supervisors all have experiences away from their education-related aspects of everyday life. Auto/biography and auto/ethnography allow educators to explore other aspects of their lives, which can be seen as the background against which the work of education becomes figure. Too often educators and educational researchers attempt to understand the figure—teaching, supervision, and administration—as if it existed by itself. But this, inherently, is impossible. In all perceptual experience, what we hear, see, feel, or smell is noticed against a background; if this background no longer exists, we tend not to perceive. Thus, for example, we tend not to smell the characteristic odor of our homes, though we do perceive the smells of other peoples' homes. Thus, auto/biography and auto/ethnography are means and genres to bring the background back into the educational picture.

Students, too, do not only exist in and for school. They conduct their lives, sometimes in contexts similar to our own or in contexts similar to those in which we once lived. Thus, for example, both Canada and the USA have large numbers of immigrants, strangers coming to a strange land, which may or may not become their own. From colleagues in Toronto and Montreal I know that a researcher's or school administration's letter to parents might have to be composed in up to twenty languages; in Vancouver, less than forty-five percent of the families speak English at home. Yet these experiences are hardly ever found in many educational literatures, although they constitute much of the everyday life of the students once they leave school. The contributions in this section do some of the work educators ought to be doing to situate knowing, learning, and teaching in the everyday lives of their students.

Christiane Kraft Alsop (Chapter 20), as I in Chapter 4, deals with the double experience of emigration|immigration and the tensions that arise from it for the individual. Both contributions can be read not only for their content, as contributions that bring the foreign closer to ourselves, but also for their method of using auto/biography and auto/ethnography—with or without pairing with third-person methods—for better understanding just what it might mean to deal with alienation and re-familiarization that accompany the emigration|immigration dialectic.

Dealing with the experiences of emigration|immigration involves, as Alsop shows, a considerable amount of memory work—the new and old are continuously played out against one another. Memory work is also involved in grave tending, as Carolyn Ellis shows in her chapter. Such apparently simple events are also part of our students' lives, so that we can learn about ways of realizing cultural-historical possibilities that differ from our own through the auto/ethnographies and auto/biographies of others. They tend to be suppressed in the media, unless for this or that reason—a soldier fallen during a peace mission, a police officer killed while off-duty—they make it ground only to disappear from the picture altogether on the next day. Such events however do matter a lot in everyday life, from which auto/biography and auto/ethnography can rescue them and make them, for the moment, figure in their own right. Why and how such religiously and non-religiously motivated actions mediate the learning experiences of students most frequently eludes educators, and comes to the surface only sometimes, such as in a study of the interaction between (school-based) scientific and (home-based) religious discourses co-authored by one of the high school students featured in the article (Roth & Alexander, 1997).

Chaim Noy and Stuart Lee and I use auto/biography and auto/ethnography to deal with another experience of educators—engaging in graduate studies, particularly in doing and writing the research for which they are awarded a degree upon completion. Besides articulating for us the tensions and internal contradictions in these experiences, which in part consists of becoming in the community of researchers, both chapters also provide insights into the tensions and contradictions of writing social scientific research. Thus, Noy felt constrained in not being able to write with others the dissertation that would no longer have been his own; Lee and I play out the contradictions in collective writing, which, as all contradictions, give rise to change, here in the growth and development of both newcomer and old-timer in the research community.

An area that educators certainly would benefit from investigating in greater depth is the potential òf students as researchers conducting auto/biographical and auto/ethnographic studies both in school and at home. Such work could be of benefit both to the students themselves, who, by reflecting together with peers and teachers may learn about themselves and their cultural-historical patterns of actions, and to educators, who learn more about the lives of their students. In the latter case, a step would be taken towards viewing in students more than disembodied minds to be filled with the curriculum materials. Students, too, are embodied human beings, who act on grounds that are intelligible not only to them and their peers, but also to their teachers.

References

Roth, W.-M., & Alexander, T. (1997). The interaction of students' scientific and religious discourses: Two case studies. *International Journal of Science Education, 19*, 125–146.

17   Grave Tending: With Mom at the Cemetery

Carolyn Ellis

"Show me the manner in which a nation or community cares for its dead," William Gladstone, the Victorian-era British prime minister, once remarked, "and I will measure with mathematical exactness the tender mercies of its people, their respect for the laws of the land, and their loyalty to high ideals." (Quoted in Koerner, 2000, p. 52)

"Would you like to go by the cemetery?" I ask Mom, knowing she always is eager to go. It is July 2001 and I am visiting her in Luray, my hometown of 3,000 people in rural Virginia.

"Oh, yes. I don't get there like I used to when I could drive. I'd go by the cemetery every Friday after I got my hair done. Sometimes more than that."

"What did you do there?" I inquire, so she can tell the story.

"Fix the flowers. Sometimes they'd fall out of the vases. I'd check the flag on Rex's grave to see if it had blown down, and I'd replace it if it was worn. I've put many a flag on his grave. I look after all their graves—Daddy's, Rex's, and Florence's."

"I know you do," I say. "You've always been the grave caretaker."

* * *

I drive down the familiar gravel road, past the sign on a post that reads "Evergreen Memorial Gardens Perpetual Care," then past the small, eight-by-eight-foot guard house with most of its white paint peeled off. A yellow strip warning "Do not enter" wraps around the rickety front porch, making the shed look like a crime scene. Someone must be dead, I think, smiling at the joke inside my head.

"They need to fix this road," Mom says adamantly, her deep, southern accent strongest on the word "fix." I drive slowly, maneuvering not very successfully around the mud puddles fresh from the night's rain.

"They sure do," I say, as mud splashes on my mother's sparkling clean white Cadillac. We have this conversation every time we go to the cemetery. The road always has essentially the same potholes, more or less filled with water depending on the weather.

"See the tombstones on that side over there," my mother directs, pointing to the left. When I utter uh-huh, she continues, "We wanted one for Rex, but they don't let you have no tombstones on our side, just the flat stones, and they're hardly big enough to write anything on except the name and date."

Though I know the answer, I ask, "Why not?" as much to make conversation as anything.

"They say they're too hard to mow around," Mom replies.

"Is that also why they make you put the flowers and flags in the urns on the stones?"

"Yes," she nods. "They remove any flowers you put anywhere else on the graves." I think about how the owners privilege convenience of maintenance rather than families' wishes.

"Look how our side has filled up," she says, as we turn to the right. "When we got this plot for Rex, he was the only one in this area. Now look, graves everywhere. I swear, more people are dying now than ever." She shakes her head.

Only one death per person, I think, but out of respect, don't say. "It just seems that way because you're older, so more people you know are dying," I do say.

"I don't know. I think more people are dying, period," she responds.

I look around. Red, white, and blue flags wave from vases; bunches of pink, red, white, and yellow plastic flowers predominate, broken up by an occasional blue or purple cluster. "Yeah, seems like a lot more," I relent.

Mom retells the story of getting the plot for my younger brother Rex, after he died in a commercial airplane crash in 1982 at the age of twenty-nine (see Ellis, 1993). "In the beginning, we had two plots, one for Daddy and one for me. Right there in the middle on that hill," she says, pointing to the highest part of the cemetery. "Then when Rex died, we needed three plots, so we moved down here nearer the road."

"What about Aunt Florence's plot?" I ask, trying to remember how they had acquired the fourth site.

"We bought that later. We were able to trade our old plots to someone who had another plot right beside Rex. So then all four of us could be buried together."

"Guess Art and I should get plots or figure out what we're going to do," I say, feeling a slight chill as I speak, contained by the normalcy with which Mom treats the subject of burial. "We'll probably be buried in Tampa." Actually I've assumed I would be cremated. It's easier, cheaper, and doesn't take up space. What difference does it make anyway? I don't say any of this.

"Well, Tampa is your home," Mom replies, "so it makes sense you'd be buried there." I think of how far away Tampa is from Luray. Surprisingly, I feel left out of my mother's plans, out of the family plot. I know she assumes that her other three children, myself included, will be buried with our spouses.

Maybe I will want to be buried instead of cremated, I think, in a place where someone might come and remember me, as we do now for my brother Rex, Daddy, and Aunt Florence. I realize I've never thought seriously about this before. My husband Art and I don't even have a will, I think, much less a cemetery plot. Even though he is fifty-four and I'm forty-nine, we still react scornfully when telephone salesmen call to try to sell us cemetery plots. So much for being educated and prepared.

* * *

When I get back to Tampa, I talk these matters over with Art, who is Jewish. "I'd like to have a Jewish funeral," he says hesitantly. "It's our custom to be buried rather than cremated."

"It's okay with me," I respond, since I've not practiced my Lutheran religion since leaving Luray. "But you have to make the arrangements. You should get in touch with a Rabbi and we should have some connection with a synagogue." Delighted, Art agrees, though two years later, he still has not followed up, and I have not reminded him. We did, however, make a will and trust after his mother died in September 2001.

"We built that," Mom says about the stone mausoleum we drive by.

"Daddy did?" I ask, and she nods. "Of course, he couldn't have done it without you," I amend, remembering how, as secretary, Mom organized the family's small construction company.

"Ain't that the truth?" Mom responds.

Since there are only two names on the front of the mausoleum and ten vacant spaces, I ask her why more people weren't buried there. She says she doesn't know.

"That's where Clare is buried," she says, her attention now directed to her sister's plot farther along the road. "She don't have any flowers." She sighs, as we drive slowly past the unadorned grave. "When I could walk, I used to always pick hers up and put them in the vase if they had blowed out. Nobody takes care of her grave. Not like I take care of ours."

Thinking we've arrived at my family's graves, I press on the brake to stop just after passing Aunt Clare's grave. "No, up there," Mom says, "past the tree."

"Where you going?" she asks, when I apply the brake a second time. "Not this tree, the next one."

"Oh, yes," I say, feeling ashamed I don't remember where the family graves are. It's as though I block out the memory, like I block out the pain of loss. Perhaps I assume Mom will always know the way. Perhaps I don't really want to be here.

I recognize the three familiar graves in the distance decorated with some of the largest bunches of flowers in the cemetery.

It's clear someone takes care of these graves. A small American flag waves in the wind. "I see the flag," I say.

"I'd like a bigger flag, but they won't let you have one," my Mom says.

When I ask her if she wants to get out, she replies, "No, I can't walk on the grass anymore and it's uphill. I'll stay in the car. You go." Mom suffers with osteoarthritis and now can walk only with the aid of a walker. Yet it is still important to her to visit the graves, even if she can't get to them. I think how her deteriorating health has redefined and limited so many of her experiences, and how she still manages to find meaning in them. I hope I'm like that when I'm her age.

I breathe deeply as I get out of the car. I remember walking this same path at all three funerals: first, we buried my brother in 1982, then my dad in 1987, and finally my aunt in 1991. Each time I was in shock, somewhat removed, as

Figure 17.1. Mom tends the family graves.

though I were watching a movie, afraid that if I lost control, it would be gone for good. Today, this twenty-yard walk continues to be a sobering experience, not something I enjoy. At the graves, as always when I visit, I wonder what I'm supposed to do. This is the first time Mom hasn't walked here with me. With her at my side, I'd stare at the grave markers and watch her pull weeds, arrange flowers, and tidy up the graves.

Suddenly, I notice that I'm standing on my brother's grave, and I move quickly to the side. Mom always said standing on a grave was bad luck. As kids, my siblings and I would dance around the graves we visited, touching them quickly with one foot when no adult was looking to see what would happen. It doesn't matter now, I tell myself. Mom has not said anything about this in years; anyway, I've seen her walk on the graves. Maybe that tale applies only to children. Or maybe it's okay to walk on the graves if you have a purpose, such as fixing the flowers.

I move back onto the ground over the grave where it is easier to tend the flowers. Noting the freshly planted grass just starting to peek up through the straw, I recall my sister-in-law saying the graves were a mess, because the owners had covered the sinking graves with fresh dirt. She had said not to tell Mom because it might upset her to know the sites didn't look their best. I'm glad to see someone has planted grass now. I quickly and half-heartedly adjust the plastic flowers—artificial flowers are so ugly, I think—and walk back. "Bye," I say as visions of my father, brother, and aunt flash into my head. They don't stay long. As usual, when I am at the graves, I push these memories away. Too many reminders here that they are gone, their bodies decayed.

Mom watches me walk back to the car. "I don't like those yellow flowers in Rex's vase," she says. "They don't go with the red ones."

"They look okay," I say, wanting her to feel satisfied. What difference does it make? They're only plastic flowers, I think to myself.

"They should fix this road," she says as we drive away. "That side," she says, "it's older. See the tombstones."

* * *

The next day I tell my mother that I saw some plastic flowers when I went to the new Wal-Mart. The store has been opened for several months, but its existence is still big news in town. "What about that Wal-Mart?" you can hear people saying to each other as they pass on the street or do business at the local bank. Mom has not yet been to Wal-Mart's because of her inability to walk more than a few steps. She got a wheelchair recently, and I am anxious for her to try it out, so I hold out the temptation of the plastic flowers to entice her to go for a ride.

"Were they nice ones?" she asks, and I know I've piqued her interest.

"Yes, and you can go with me to Wal-Mart's to get them," I say.

"How am I going to do that? I can't walk."

"I'll take you in your wheelchair."

"That's too heavy for you to get into the car."

"That's why we got the portable one," I respond, excitedly, dancing around as I speak, determined to break through Mom's tendency to say no to trying anything new.

"I'll be too heavy to push."

"That's why I work out with weights." I flex my arm muscles. "Come on, Mom. We'll have a blast. You can look around the store and buy what you need, instead of having to rely on someone else to get things for you. Remember how we used to shop together. You haven't shopped for six months."

"We'll see," she says, and I know I have her hooked.

* * *

Next day we go into Wal-Mart. I lift the chair out of the trunk and bring it to the passenger side. When she stands, I slide it under her and she plops down, winded by the effort. Still she reaches down to unfold the footrests. "See, I told you it would be easy," I say, as I wheel her into the store. She greets several people as we enter and I can see her relaxing into the persona of a person in a wheel chair.

We locate the artificial flowers in the back of the store. The half-dozen bunches Mom picks out quickly fill the small basket I've placed on her lap. "Guess that's it," she says, stretching her neck to see what she's missing down the long aisle.

"Don't you want to shop some more?" I ask.

"The basket's full."

"I'll be back in a moment. Don't go anywhere."

She laughs a belly laugh. "Now just where do you think I'm going? I can't walk."

"I thought some good-looking man might try to pick you up and wheel you right out of here," I say, and she giggles.

"I ain't interested in no man," she says seriously.

I take the basket to the Courtesy Counter and ask the clerk if she will hold onto it for my mom who is in a wheelchair. "Certainly," she says. I pick up another empty basket. Six baskets and several hundred dollars of merchandise later, two very happy shoppers head for home.

* * *

The next day, I ask Mom if she wants to put the new flowers on the grave. She agrees, then says, "Oh, but Mr. Atkins is being buried today and I think it is at eleven o'clock. We shouldn't go during the funeral." Mom always knows who is being buried and when, compliments of small town news casting and the obituaries in the local weekly newspaper.

"We'll be there before that," I say, looking at my watch. "It's only nine thirty. On the way in, she again comments on the road and the mausoleum. When I again stop at the wrong tree, she gently says, "No the next one." This time we've not only brought new flowers, we also have a new flag for Rex's grave—another Wal-Mart find. "Look they're digging a grave," I say.

"That must be for Mr. Atkins," she says, turning to see. Two people are sitting under the tent; two others are bringing in the frame for the casket. Two are black; two are white; one woman and three men. I wonder what it is like to be a gravedigger. Do you become immune to death? What happens when you are the gravedigger and one of your relatives dies? I recall that a black man who worked for my father used my father's backhoe to dig graves. I doubt there are any black people buried in this cemetery. I wonder where they are buried. Maybe there are cemeteries on the other side of town, at churches on what is known locally as "Colored Hill."

"Put them on Rex's grave," she says, as I reach for the two bunches of multi-shaded purple flowers we have bought. "I guess you should take out the faded yellow and red ones?" she says questioningly. I nod and tenderly pull the new flowers out of the plastic bag. I recall the checkout clerk commenting on how pretty they were. I unroll and separate the two American flags. Mom takes one and I roll up the other. As I re-roll and place mine back into its plastic wrapper, I see Mom has re-rolled the one I gave her. "Oh, you want this one," she says. I gingerly take it from her.

I think about how much she wants to help even though she is almost eighty-five and can't walk more than a few steps. I remember how she hands me items from the table to put back into the refrigerator after we eat, how she fixed my coffee the first day I was home. Since standing is so difficult for her, I'll bet it took twenty minutes to fill the pot, get the coffee, and measure it just right. I try to let her help, but it is easy to fall into doing everything for her. "I want to do for myself," she say sometimes when I reprimand her for doing too much. "As long as I can."

"How do you want the flowers?" I ask.

"Just so they're spread out," she says, "in the vase." She pulls her hands close then wide apart to demonstrate.

I walk to the graves, this time with a purpose. I feel the responsibility of placing the flowers correctly, which means doing it so that my mother is pleased. I take the red carnations out of my brother's urn, and shake off the pieces of foam on the bottom. Then I remove some pink ones slightly faded from the sun, and the yellow orchids. I place the two large bunches of purple flowers into the vase. I replace the tattered flag, making sure the new one stands tall above the flowers. What else do I do? She said to spread out the flowers, so I push them carefully with my hands, making sure not to put too much pressure on the stems, just as I would arrange fresh flowers. It's not easy in the small, narrow, fake gold vase with the rounded bottom. I worry I have spread the flowers so much they will fall out. I remove them and start over, this time inserting the stems in the Styrofoam pieces in the bottom of the vase, the kind you get when you buy flowers from a florist. That will keep the flowers from blowing out of the vase. Finally, I again spread the flowers wide so they look plentiful.

I admire my work, then insert one stem of the discarded yellow flowers in the back of the vase, for depth and contrast. Not bad, I say, as I stand back. I will go to the car and ask Mom if she thinks the yellow flowers go with the purple. I'll let her choose.

No, I want to make the decision. I bet she'll like that I care enough to decide. She has had to decide all the time. I like them, I say out loud, then move to my father's grave. I remove the discolored flowers and then the yellow ones, which don't match the red ones already there. I place the pinkish-red carnations from my brother's vase in with my father's flowers. Now all of his are shades of pink. I stand back, then add some new white ones for contrast. Then I move to

Figure 17.2. Carolyn tends her brother Rex's grave.

my aunt's grave. I spread the flowers wide and remove the badly discolored ones, replacing them with new flowers from Wal-Mart. Her color scheme is pink, white, and yellow.

Always before, I've tried to be neutral about the cemetery, going *for* my mother. Today, tending the graves, I feel more fully *with* my mother, even though she is in the car. I feel more fully connected to my deceased relatives, the pain of loss, and my memories. Perhaps this is what my mother feels here.

In that mood, I read the small flat stones in the ground. Starting on the left, nearest the road: "Florence Good, Born 1912, Died 1991." This time instead of hurrying off, I stop and think of my dear Aunt Florence, my mother's sister, who lived with us and helped take care of all four of us children as we grew up. I always thought she looked and acted like Grandma on the Beverley Hillbillies—feisty, energetic, hardworking yet playful, quick to temper, shy with strangers yet blunt, seemingly from an earlier era. I think of how she limped after her stroke, her leg bending backward instead of forward. Then visiting her in the nursing home, where she lay naked and, when told by a nurse to cover up, she said abruptly, just like Grandma would have, "I came into the world this way, and this is the way I'm going out." No modesty. Case closed. Then she looked at me and said, "He's the one," and pointed to Art, who I had taken home to meet the family for the first time. Aunt Florence died two months after her foreshadowing proclamation.

I move to the right. "Arthur C. Ellis, Sr., Born 1915, Died 1987. I remember the call from my sister-in-law Barbara that fateful Valentine's day. "Your father had a heart attack. He's dead." "Are you sure?" I had responded, and when she said, "Yes, I'm sure," I replied, "I have to hang up. I'll call you right back." I sobbed and sobbed and it was a good half hour before I could talk to anyone. I was supposed to have gone home to see my parents that December, but I postponed my reservation until March, to help with recruitment in the department where I worked at the university. I never got to see Daddy again. I learned from that experience to do better at making decisions that would not lead to regrets. That strategy often brings the fear of death—my own and others—to my consciousness, but makes me feel peaceful at the same time.

I skip over the empty grave next to Daddy's, the one reserved for Mom, and move to my brother's. "Rex Allen Ellis, October 25, 1952–January 13, 1982." This one is the hardest. I think of what Rex was like as a kid—full of life, playing jokes, kind, and loving. We were best friends. I shudder when I read the date of his death; the tragedy comes into full focus. I imagine his head hitting the front seat as his plane dives on take off into the Potomac River in Washington

D.C. I remember vividly the day of his funeral. It was a blizzard-cold and snowy day, not warm and sunny like today. My body shook and I was numbed by the unreality of our loss, the cold, and the Valium I took to get me though the funeral. Will I ever get over this loss? Of course not. But I will continue learning how to live with it. I let the feelings of grief move through me. "Rex, I love you and miss you," I say out loud, my voice choking.

I move back to the plot that sits between my brother and father. "Mary Katherine Ellis," it says, "Born 1914, Died"—there is a blank space. Seeing my mother's name on the plaque troubles me, and I wonder how she stands it. "It don't bother me," she said when I asked her once. "We're all going to die." I glance back at my mom, who is watching me from the car.

I gather the discarded flowers and take them to the car, looking back over my shoulder as I walk. Looks good, I think. Having gotten so involved in the flowers, I find myself wondering who will tend the flowers on my grave, if I have a grave that is.

"What do you think?" I ask, getting into the car and waiting for approval. I place the tattered flag and discolored flowers on the back floor.

"You did a good job," she nods, and I smile.

"What do you think of the yellow ones with the purples ones?" I ask, wanting a more specific response.

"They're okay."

"Are you sure?"

"Oh, yes, they put any colors together nowadays." As we drive off, I look around the cemetery at the multi-colored clusters and think she is right. My eyes are pulled to the large stone statue of Jesus praying that stands in the center of the cemetery at the top of the hill.

We drive past the newly dug grave. Now the hole is covered with a green, grass-colored blanket, showing only the vault frame. Six chairs, draped in matching green cloth, are lined up beside the casket. The three men and one woman are gathering up their tools. "That must be for Mr. Atkins," my Mom says again.

"Hey, you want to put these flowers on Aunt Clare's grave?" I ask, pointing to the discarded ones in the back of our car. "They're not great, but they're better than none."

"Oh, yes," she says and smiles a big smile.

"We'll drive around the cemetery again," I say. "We're driving in circles." Again she smiles.

"It's that one," she says, pointing to a grave with no flowers.

Figure 17.3. Sister Judi, Sister-in-law Barbara, and Carolyn tend Mom's grave.

I get out and carefully arrange the flowers in the vase. "Her vase doesn't have any Styrofoam," I say when I get back into the car.

"I've got some at home," she says. "I'll bring it next time I come, whenever that is. Whenever someone can bring me."

"Won't Art bring you?" I ask, knowing my brother will take Mom to the cemetery any time she asks.

"Yes, but he doesn't like to come to the cemetery," she acknowledges. "He won't come by himself, only when he brings me."

On the way out, we once again drive by my family's graves. I think how well cared for they are. "Our graves look the best," I say, "of any in the whole cemetery."

She nods. "I always look after them."

Figure 17.4. Sister Judi continues the tradition of tending the family graves

Who will tend the plastic flowers on my mother's grave? I wonder. I hold her hand, feeling intense love as we drive home.

* * *

September 10, 2002. Mom died yesterday after being bedridden for a year. My sister Judi moved from Mississippi to take care of her. My brother Art and sister-in-law Barbara helped out whenever needed, and I visited often during the year to spend time with Mom and relieve my sister. The whole family was with Mom when she died. As much as we hated to see her go, we told her we loved her and then cheered her on her journey. For days before her death, Mom had dreams, fantasies, hallucinations, and premonitions of the trip she was about to take. When she asked us to go with her, we told her we couldn't, but that we were sure Rex, Daddy, and Florence would be there waiting for her. That thought calmed her, since she had recurring visions of being with them already.

As part of the funeral arrangements, Judi, Barbara, and I go to Wal-Mart's. Our mission is to buy new plastic flowers for our family's graves. Mom will be buried in two days and we want all the graves to look nice during her graveside ceremony. (It will not matter that nobody actually sees the flowers at her funeral since the green grave cloth covers all the family graves. Judi, Barbara, and I know the graves have been properly tended.) We take our time picking out flowers, going back and forth down the thirty-foot long aisle filled on both sides with plastic flowers. Flowers also are stacked at the head and to the sides of the aisle. Plastic flowers are big business in this small town. We get very serious about choosing the best.

"The fuchsia-colored ones are my favorites," I tell my sister, and she adds a few more stems to her selection.

"I like a little white mixed in," says Barbara, picking up some baby's breath.

"What do you think about these calla lilies?" I ask.

"Nice," says Judi. "I like calla lilies. They're different from what you usually see in cemeteries."

"We need these for bulk," Barbara says of her selection of tight bunches of plum and white star-shaped flowers.

When we drive to the cemetery, I point out where the graves are. Approaching, we admire the flowers that Barbara last put on the sites. She's been tending the graves since Mom became bedridden. We put the fuchsia colored flowers and white calla lilies on Mom's grave. Then we rearrange the other vases, taking out faded stems and replacing with new plum and white flowers.

We talk about Mom and how she used to take care of the graves. It feels good to be working together on Mom's behalf, knowing how important tending the graves was to her. It feels good to be with women who loved her as I loved her. Tending graves seems to be women's work. Odd, how good it feels to be at the cemetery this time.

On September 24, Mom's birthday, Judi adds real, fresh pink carnations and white baby's breath to Mom's vase and sends a photograph to me in Tampa.

Near Christmas, Barbara changes the flowers to poinsettias for the holiday season. Judi and I talk on the phone about how she and Barbara will put lit candles in glass on the graves, as Mom did every Christmas, no matter the weather. When I see the pictures my brother-in-law Ron sends me, Art and I decide to visit his mother's and my mother's graves in the summer. I find myself eagerly looking forward to returning to Luray, making a trip to Wal-Mart, visiting the cemetery, and rearranging the beautiful plastic flowers.

* * *

I had always thought there would be no connection for me with Sullivan, Indiana after our parents died. But now I hope one day to visit the graveyard where we released them. It is part of a ritual pilgrimage that heals the loss. This task is more important than words; it is more than I can say. The iconic gestures of ritual practice move us through these life transitions. (Russell, 2002, p. 9)

The word cemetery derives from the Greek, *koimeterion*, meaning "to lie down and rest." Perhaps this is why these spaces are so tantalizing. . . . Often located on high ground or within shady groves, they offer the gift of a spectacular view and a quiet space. . . . Whether a cross, a tablet or block, a carved image of the sepia fading of a photo daguerreotype, the grave site is a story, a gestural act of remembrance and connection. A cemetery is a version of a library, each grave serving as a unique bookend. (van Herk, 1998, p. 54)

Notes

An earlier version of this manuscript was published as part of a special issue on subjectivity and reflexivity of *FQS: Forum Qualitative Sozialforschung/ Forum Qualitative Social Research, 4*(2). Available at URL: http://www.qualitative-research.net/fqs-texte/2-03/2-03ellis-e.htm. Thanks to my family for tending the graves and to Arthur Bochner for going with me.

References

Ellis, C. (1993). "There are survivors": Telling a story of sudden death. *The Sociological Quarterly, 34*, 711–730.

Koerner, B. (2000). A matter of grave import. *U.S. News $ World Report, 128* (June 12), 52–53.

Russell, L. (2002). *Stopping by a cemetery on a snowy morning: A narrative argument for ritual healing.* Paper presented at National Communication Association, New Orleans, November.

Van Herk, A. (1998, September/October). Grave thoughts. *Canadian Geographic, 118,* 54.

18   The Write of Passage: Reflections on Writing a Dissertation in Narrative Methodology

Chaim Noy

> I can see by my watch, without taking my hand from the left grip of the cycle,
> that it is eight-thirty in the morning
> —Robert Pirsig, *Zen and the Art of Motorcycle Maintenance*

Where does a journey begin?
With a Quest(tion)?
As this one?
With its Writing?
Narrative as a journey.

When you come to think of it, it is difficult to pinpoint when or where a journey begins. Do the backpackers, who I researched in my dissertation, begin their journey upon their arrival in Cuzco or in Kathmandu? Or when, on their way there, they make a stop in New York or Tokyo for a few months in order to work and earn additional funding for the extended trip? Or, maybe when they embark on the plane leaving their homeland; or maybe before that, when they typically gather to hear adventure and travel stories of veteran backpackers, and thus are inscribed in the inner circle of backpackers-to-be, as their stories of identity are cast into a communal travel?

And when does the journey of the dissertation begin?[1] When one travels, "ethnographically speaking" (Bochner & Ellis, 2002), and enters the "field"? Or prior to that, when one's dissertation proposal is "accepted" (a minute rite of passage) and the way to travel is charted? Or when one is accepted to a graduate program? Or before that, when one embarks on his academic journey and enrolls as an undergraduate? Or even earlier, when one's father is a professor of Jewish folklore and one's mother an archeologist? Or maybe when some nebulous and vague narrative dream is crafted during latency years, to be awakened and pursued years later?

* * *

I'm remembering myself playing with my father's endless stacks of draft papers, rough, worn, on their blank, clear side. All retrieved from a large and dark space that laid between two platforms of thick, dark wood, that formed my father's timeless desk.

I was always generously permitted access to this abundant supply of draft papers. I don't remember what specifically I wrote, nor what were the many words written on the back of the used papers (probably correspondences in Yiddish, drafts of publications hammered into the paper by a typewriter, corrected papers his students' handed in, and the like). I just remember it was there, on the backside, a presence. Signifying something else. Raising my head I would see a fading picture on the windowsill. His parents. Overlooking the writing desk. Overlooking the writing. The background is not clear (in my memory?) Kolomia, Galicia. The twenties or thirties.[2]

* * *

With narrative, wondering where does it all begin is intelligible.

But how to start writing? That is, how to write—and how to read—one's reflections on oneself in a theoretically rich and informed fashion. Auto/ethnography is a genre that suggests innovatively that in some cases, writing about and through oneself, is scholarly illuminating. The writer addresses herself or himself ("auto"), as a subject of a larger social or cultural inquiry ("ethno"), vis-à-vis evocative and revealing writing ("graphy") (Ellis, 1999). The work tells of those constitutive dimensions that in ordinary, conventional scientific language are erased or play a backstage role. These include personal, lived experience and voice, relationship between researchers and their work, processes (rather than results or products), etc. (Richardson, 1997).

There is no recipe, no one correct way of writing an auto/ethnography. For example, in a few of the works in the field theoretical issues are either entirely implicit, or they are referred to scarcely (Dent, 2002). In such cases the contribution revolves around the writer's intimate knowledge of the subject matter, and the text's complex articulation of it and its innovativeness. In other cases the theoretical and the personal perspectives or voices are both explicitly presented, sometimes separately (Ellis, 1993), and sometimes in an intertwined way, where they are in dialogue throughout the text, and where this dialogue is what weaves the fabric of the text (Jones, 1998). Presently, I found the latter to be the most suitable possibility, conveying my own struggles throughout my work. In all cases, and in this one as well, the text articulates an evocative personal *narrative*, as it wishes to touch and move its readers in ways that are not only metaphorical; it is indeed, a he*art*full writing (Ellis, 1999).

And it is precisely from the perspective of narrative research that I wish to touch on and to problematize a few mainstream notions about narrative. According to some scholars people's lived experiences and life stories are conceived as carrying such qualities as, "unity," "purpose," "direction," "followability" and etc., as they "convey" an inner psychic reality (McAdams, 1997). While writing this chapter it become clear to me that it might be modern scientific research that frames stories of lives and lived experiences in terms of coherency and progression, while a post-modern narrative may be perceived as a less coherent and more fractured genre, and as a genre that does not only convey or reflect upon one's identity, as it evokes, performs and constitutes it in the event of narration. In stressing a text's polysemy and multiplicity, I am inspired by Umberto Eco's work, and particularly by ideas proposed in the *Open Work* (Eco 1962/1989). The complementary notions of "ambiguity," on the one hand, and "openness," on the other hand, suggest quite a different hermeneutic frame for narrative inquiry: a combination or contamination of genres that continuously evolve, and inspire new meanings, between writer and reader, teller and interlocutor.

The Journey from Proposal to Dissertation: How the Doctorate "Broke Free"

> It is by now something of commonplace within the theory of travel writing to acknowledge the ways in which travel is a form of writing and writing is a form of travel.
> —Susan Stewart, *Crimes of Writing*

The Proposal

Looking back now at my doctorate proposal, dated July 22, 1997, I find that, interestingly enough, its title has nothing to do with my proposed research. It is rather a statement concerning the formal status of the document, signed five years ago: "A research program submitted for approval as a dissertation plan." The title if followed by strings of little letters, to which I never seem to pay any real attention, running my eyes across them quickly, dismissing their potential trouble as "mere bureaucracy." Towards the bottom of the page the title of my work is printed: "The Great Journey: Narrative Analysis of Israeli Trekking Stories." And by its side are my advisors' and my own printed names, accompanied by *handwritten signatures*: lively blue and pink—Amia's pen—ink, conventionally signifying authenticity/singularity (Derrida, 1988). The next occasion anyone would be signing anything will be four years later, on the cover of the bound dissertation monograph. Regrettably, these are the only two occasions of handwriting, of that "track of the body" (Stewart, 1993, p. 14). Atop the proposal and the submitted dissertation, atop the outsides and bounds of the work, seals confirming authenticity. Rather than inside, within, embodying the text, breaking, even slightly, with printing conventions.

* * *

The dissertation's *pro*posal, I realize, is written *as a contract, as a legal binding document*. It describes what task the researcher takes on her/himself, and how s/he is going to carry it out. The language is authoritative, conveying the author's supposed knowledge of the field and of the genres constituting it. As the italicized "*pro*posal" suggests, it is a contract which is written in *future tense*—it is a *pro*spective *pro*gram depicting a trajectory of the "theorology" (theory-and-methodology) along which the researcher will travel in order to reach the sought after "scientific" destinations. The theoretical discussion should rationally lead to the methodological procedures, and these should systematically lead to the presumed "findings." While in positivistic and post-positivistic research some room is left for what the results might be, the structure leading to the outcome—i.e., the journey, the narrative—is not negotiable. It is a convention, not a conversation; and the *pro*posal is the journey's schedule or itinerary, which is agreed upon at the outset.

In discussing a new and more creative framework for writing proposals for narrative dissertations in psychology, Josselson and Lieblich (2002) offer what seems something more general and applicable to a variety of qualitative fields:

> In that narrative research is a voyage of discovery—a discovery of meanings that both constitute the individual participant and are co-constructed in the research process—the researcher can not know at the onset what s/he will find. . . . In most psychology graduate programs, the structure of thesis/dissertation proposals is dictated by the paradigm of quantitative, positivist research. Hypotheses to be tested are set out and located within the research tradition or theory from which they emerge. Methods are employed to test the defined hypotheses. Statistical analyses that will be conducted are specified. . . . Introduction, Method, Results and Discussion.

* * *

In my dissertation journey I set out to inquire into a collective social phenomenon in Israel, that of an extended backpacking trip to faraway destinations normatively undertaken by young, Jewish, middle class, Israelis, soon after they complete mandatory service in the military. The main body of the proposal, the "theoretical background," included three parts addressing three discrete, yet converging conceptual perspectives: the backpackers as pilgrims, as tourists, and the specific cohort of backpackers.

When I submitted the *pro*posal for approval, in late July of, 1997, I honestly thought these were the main theoretical issues I would and should be concerned with and researching in the following years. A comprehensive, systematic and tiered research was suggested, approaching the field of backpacking tourism through broad inquiry drawing upon the three different theoretical viewpoints.

Such was my idea at the outset.

However, following Josselson and Lieblich (2002), and considering that in a field where process and hermeneutics are part and parcel of our work—a field defined by "a series of tensions, contradictions and hesitations," (Denzin & Lincoln, 1994, p. ix)—it can hardly be imagined that such a work would (or should) develop precisely or even approximately along the *pro*posed lines. *And so, slowly but surely, the dissertation began drifting away from its proposal.* To my protests and growing anxiety I realized that if someone would have looked at these two documents—the earlier, preceding and binding one (the *pro*posal) and its consequence or result—only a loose connection, if any, could be found linking the two.

The dissertation consisted of two large chapters that, again, as if against my will, were each some two hundred pages long. Not something that I planned for, nor that I would have wished for, and *neither of which* dealt with the three topics I had described and committed to in the *pro*posal.

The first chapter reviewed the voices in the stories backpackers repeatedly tell and hear. "Where did that come from?" I continually asked myself. From semiotics to conversation analysis, and from sociolinguistics to narrative analysis I unintentionally wrote an essay about how backpackers construct an intertextual canon and how they quote and voice it in their narratives. The second chapter was an inquiry into the body as a social site and was informed by feminist and by sociological theories. The embodied narratives I found unfolding were presented mainly by women backpackers—women engaged in an activity culturally constructed as masculine and macho—demanded different reading, interpretation and presentation, one that was itself embodied.

"Up in my head" I knew that such narratives of personal experience suggest and open a nearly endless variety of readings which creatively envelop, as a result of the encounter between the material and the researcher, the literature and ideas he is exposed to, and so on. This composes the researcher's journey. But this knowing did not ease my emotional unrest. I was trapped. I felt quite bad about the directions things took. I felt, and I must admit it sounds harsh, that I was *deceiving* and not being *reliable* (but whom to?). I felt I was doing something *wrong*. In addition, and as a consequence, I also felt I was letting someone down, someone important, perhaps an imagined "anonymous reviewer" of my work. I had *pro*mised something that I failed to deliver, and I delivered something that was not asked for (and might have not received approval to begin with). It is not that I compromised one *pro*posed perspective or another, but that I simply took an entirely different direction (or it took me). Looked at narrowly, one large conceptual step or phase was missing between the initial proposal and the final dissertation; seen more broadly, what evolved was simply a different work altogether.

As I write these lines now I ponder: Doesn't a "different work" amount to a "different researcher?" Isn't writing a becoming?[3] Are we not in writing ourselves changing, transforming? Could we understand the dissertation as a journal, as a scholarly diary of sorts? If so, was I different? Did the Chaim of '97 differ from the Chaim of '01? Did Chaim of '01 adhere to the expectations, *pro*grams and *pro*mises of the former Chaim?

Should have I done so? Did I go astray?

But somewhere in my body it was clear: The further the better. The further the dissertation breaks free and drifts away, the further it journeys, the more generative and creative the processes that occur. The further the better.

* * *

I practice a pacifist form of a martial art called Aikido, a relational social practice. I have learned much about my work and myself through the Oriental concept of Tao, the Way, or the Japanese Do—as in JuDo, Karate-Do, and flower arrangement kaDo (ikebana). Interestingly, Do is translated as either "The Way of . . ." or "The Art of . . ." In my practice I conceive of the "Way" as referring to the systematic, arduous, and painstaking dimensions. It involves the whole of the living person and is not confined to the mental or intellectual life. At the same time, Do is also an "Art." In this sense it conveys the creative, that which is not planned, linear, and progressive. It has to do with generativity, innovativeness, and spontaneity.

During the years of researching and writing the dissertation, I have humorously referred to myself as a Do-ctorate student. The dissertation was for me both a "Way" of practicing and at the same time an "Art" of exploring, each complementing the other.

* * *

It dawned on me only later, in hindsight, that the change and development of my interests and research was closely related to other work I was doing at the same time, other theoretical investigations that I pursued intensely. That change, or shift, I began to see, was a natural consequence of intellectual and scholarly growth, and it unfolded within social, organizational and research contexts (Richardson, 1997). But at the time of writing I could not validate or justify what was happening. I was more than *bewildered* with my intense interest in voices and bodies in the backpackers' narratives, and with the shape and size it assumed in my work. The shape and size, and the fact it had not even been mentioned in the proposal, suggested to me that it might be too idiosyncratic. Too much a reflection of "my own" interests, of "my own" agenda, I thought.

Rethinking the Pro*posal*

Thinking about the *pro*posal retrospectively and more theoretically, I have come to feel that the *pro*posal had exhausted the theoretical fields it dealt with at the time it was written. I gradually came to conceive of it not in terms of a legal *pro*spective document, but as a more *personal and reflexive chapter in a continuous journal, the journal of my research journey.* Rather than excluding it from the body of the work, and defining as contractual the tensions that arise from such exclusion, I wish to think of it more inclusively. The proposal thus might not *pro*pose what is ahead, but instead *reflect* on and convey the current position and state of the researcher in relation to theoretical, methodological and presentational matters. Instead of a binding *pro*spective document, we would arrive at an "academic journal," serving as a significant point of reference for the researcher him/herself, as well as for other readers, such as committee members, allowing all an impression of the researcher's current "place." The proposal in this sense is an "introduction," a "first-step," an open reflexive chapter in a longer track, which it both referentially marks and performatively presents. It is not an obligating, binding *pro*gram that negates the possibility of surprise, or the open-ended ways in which the research and the researcher could develop. A posing rather than a *pro*posing.

Indeed, I regret not making more use of the proposal as means to probe inside myself and inquire where I am *now*, or where I am at *currently* in regards to the material I am working with. Such inquiry would generate a reflexive, hermeneutic document rather than a positivist one, a document that describes rather than prescribes. This is not to suggest that we omit discussion of theory and literature in the proposal altogether, but that these discussions should not be directed towards the future; instead, they should reflect on the present and the inner.[4]

This implicates the dissertation. I do not view it now as a product, an end product located at the end of a stressful manufacturing line, but as a reflection of its own becoming. A reflection of the numerous hesitations, challenges, fallbacks, breakthroughs, frustrations, illuminations, satisfactions, and insecurities that we encounter and which comprise the silent, or silenced, fabric of our work.

* * *

A Yiddish proverb comes to mind, "Men tracht un Got lacht" (Lit. "men plan and god laughs"). It points to the complicated tensions inherent in perceiving the flow of time and in the primordial human wish to plan what is "yet-to-be," that is, to grant it "intelligibility or interpretability" (Derrida, 1990, p. 993). God, so it seems here, does not laugh at humans for no reason, nor does he laugh over our troubles or misfortunes. He does have a laugh, though, at our attempts to tame time and to control it. Science, as a primarily modern and masculine endeavor of *pre*diction, is embodingly funny for Him or Her.

Dissertation Writing

While so far I have reflected on the space inscribed between what is *pro*posed and what later materializes, I now discuss some issues concerning writing itself. The first concerns my unfulfilled wish for shared writing, the second stylistic matters of presentation with which I grappled in the dissertation.

Authorship Issues: Why not Write the Dissertation with a Little Help from My Friends?

Individualism and enlightenment, and specifically scholasticism, developed side by side during the same era not by coincidence. In *Crimes of Writing*, Stewart (1991) points to the initial perception of authorship and the right of intellectual assets, such as ideas, as well as the socio-historical circumstances that bred such notions in the eighteenth century. Following Foucault's discussion of Hobbes, Stewart refers to the "conventions of attribution" (p. 9), and points out:

These concepts set the stage for the seventeenth-century development of the classical liberal principles of intellectual property. . . . The idea that no one is so much the master of his goods as a man is the master of the products and of the labor of his mind would emerge in a complex figuration regarding the nature of work, materiality and ownership, and, eventually, the relation of these concepts to mental labor and originality . . . the idea of personal ownership of words, or certainly personal ownership of the order of words, was not available. (pp. 9–10)

Now, there is surely an inclination in academic circles towards single authorship (co-produced publications being exception to the rule), *but there is no place in this writing scene where single authorship is so vehemently and orthodoxly observed as in the case of dissertations.* Of any other legitimate co-produced kind of work (from a seminar paper to an encyclopedia), the dissertation can hardly be even imagined as co-authored or co-composed. Located at the heart of the academia writing a dissertation and graduating is a form of an institutionalized rite of passage or, better, rite of institution. This rite, which is historically embedded in the age of enlightenment, constitutes an inherently modern and individualistic rite of passage; it constitutes a modern scholar in a modern institution.

My encounter with the implicit restrictions surrounding single authorship was powerful, since I had both a need and desire to share my ideas and to discuss them with fellow young researchers who have researched Israeli backpackers and written thesis and dissertations (or were researching/writing) on the subject in the last few years.[5] That is, I did not want only to discuss these matters and then confine myself to my own solitary, or simply mention my colleagues in the references dubbing them "personal communication." Instead, I thought these discussions had the potential to inject original ideas, ideas at least as worthy as my own "intellectual products" (Stewart, 1991).

Where does it say, I thought; where is the proof that collecting data, analyzing and interpreting it, and presenting knowledge in a solitary manner is preferable to doing so in collaboration? If I was anyhow daydreaming of having conversations with my colleagues, I wondered why not really (*literally*) discuss it with them and include these conversations it as an integral part of my piece.

Ellis and Bochner (1996) suggest, and demonstrate, a dialogic genre in which social knowledge is both created and presented at the same time. Relational social constructivism suggests that this is how knowledge is in fact created (Gergen, 1999). So why was there no room for this in the dissertation? Furthermore, the work of Handelman (1993) and Richardson (1997) suggest that it is the institutional structure of our individualistic "careers," and not something else, something "natural" or "essential," that leads us to neglect the voices of those colleagues who we engage. Absent from our work are the voices of fellow scholars, colleague-friends, and close members of our community—the very community that shares with us echoing, citing, resonating, amplifying ideas.

Originally my idea was to send the chapters I wrote to my colleagues and ask for comments and elaboration on my ideas to whatever extent they found suitable. Since those chapters included discussion of their work I wished for a conversation, a mini symposium to take place within the boundaries of my dissertation. That conversation would undoubtedly illuminate the common subject of our research in a valuable way. This way, I thought (and I still do), readers of the work would be exposed to more than one perspective or voice (mine), and would be able to read in the same compendium comments and reflections, even critiques, on both my ideas and the contributors' own previous work. Such a move promised to enrich the piece, to make it polyphonic, even.

But the more excited I grew, the stronger were my hesitations.

My early enthusiasm led me to believe that this debate would take place inside the work itself, forming an integral part of it. Gradually, as I came to see that a collaborative doctoral dissertation would by no means be accepted, I considered moving—downgrading—the discussions and conversations to the appendix, that area that lies somewhere at the fringes of personal authorship (where questionnaires are attached, whole transcriptions found, and so on).

However, I must admit that these ideas were not put to the test, and for a few reasons. First, the message I received from my immediate academic surroundings, though subtle, did not convey the usual enthusiasm I enjoyed. By no means was there any outright opposition to the ideas, but rather, they were viewed as a curiosity, an anecdote, a questionable addition that might or might not do any good. One of my mentors actually said, "that's a nice idea, Chaim, but now get on with your work." My enthusiasm over the new venues of knowledge was not shared, and since I constantly felt I was late anyhow in the dissertation schedule, and was anyhow ridden and anxious with my wrongdoing in regards to the proposal, it didn't take much to tame my creative enthusiasm. Secondly, I must admit there was also an apprehension on *my part*, stemming from the fact that I was going to introduce my ideas, in their entirety, still unbounded and "unsigned," to colleagues working in the exact same field. I wasn't too sure about that—would they reciprocate? Would they show openness to my initiative? Would they not call these ideas their own? I was ashamed by some of my thoughts, which reiterated some of the aforementioned ideas of "intellectual ownership" rather then resisted them. And shame, to be sure, did not revitalize my enthusiasm and creativity.

So finally I relapsed and confined myself again to a more traditional format and compromised for a detailed dialogical review of my colleagues' work,[6] which took the shape of a sub-chapter. Indeed, I was its sole author, yet the writing style was not the custom theory-oriented literature review, but more a close and detailed—and personal or dialogical—discussion *with* their voices and works. I felt it gave my fellow researchers more light and space than they would have received if I were to review their work conventionally.

Forms of Presenting Writing: Norms of Transcribing and Editing

The move from the *pro*posal to the dissertation was also a move from the pragmatic or instrumental to the expressive and artful. While the former was a document indicating what the researcher should attain, the latter was the materialized conclusion of the work. However, when writing it, it was clear that the work could not be conveyed in the genre suggested by the proposal. So it was more of a bottom-up kind of process where I tried to fit the right lid on the pot the interviewees—the backpackers—and I had crafted, rather than making a conscious decision that I should write in a different way (engaging, as Denzin [1999] put it, in a "guerilla warfare against the repressive structures of everyday lives" [p. 572]). I thought that if writing is a "mode of thought" (Richardson,

1997), then I should search for the most appropriate mode of thought for my work.

Trying to give voice to personal experience is quite impossible when it comes to positivist language, which addresses a presumed "universal, passive, unengendered reader" (Frank, 1995). In this case—where I found myself researching bodily experiences that were narrated by women backpackers, I faced the need to compose a new terminology where traditional or conventional terms either did not exist or carried irrelevant associations. I was exploring a language of research and representation, and this creating of language, which was at the onset *only instrumental*, gradually became *a goal* in and of itself. Struggling with how to write the experiences of a "lived body in motion," I could not resort to using a traditional type of supposedly neutral writing. The need to give a vivid and tangible feel to the bodily experiences backpackers were narrating was a scholarly responsibility, and an intellectual endeavor and challenge. I have grappled with it in two separate levels: The *visual representation* of the different voices presented in the work, mainly through forms of transcription, and *structural or editorial decisions*, pertaining to the adequate presentation of the experience of bodies immersed in adventurous narratives.

The first issue dealt, then, with finding the appropriate visual format for the transcriptions. This was a relatively easy task, as I had whom to learn from: ethnographers and linguists have long grappled with this question, and have pointed to myriad ways in which transcribed text can be graphically represented in an evocative and poetic form. The presentational convention according to which the informants'/interviewees' words are represented in a block marked and separated from the text by double space was problematized. Tedlock (1983), to mention but one voice, has suggested that the visual formatting of the text represents in fact its *interpretation*. There is no "neutral" formatting, and the boxed and justified representation of the oral excerpts carries an array of implications, among which are moral ones. The presentation of transcription had to do not only with the interpretation of the transcribed vignette, but also with *conceptualizing its genre*; is it poetry, prose, and so on? The different genres are presented in different graphic and spatial forms.

Quite paradoxically, it was only in the "methodological chapter," in which usually the limits are set rather than challenged, that I allowed myself to experiment with such representations. These presentations suggested reading/listening to some parts of the backpackers' stories as rhythmed narration, as poetry. This was of particular interest, and nearly vital, when it came to embodied narratives of movement. The texts describing the body in motion had to *move* their readers in a way that conveys the trance like feelings the women backpackers were narrating. The rhythm of the oral narration was transformed into a poetic written transcription, mimetically conveying the embodied and enspaced experience, reflecting and evoking the ways in which body and space were experienced and performed. When the backpackers narrated the strenuous experience of climbing the high mountain, their words were delivered in a way conveying their heavy breathing; when they narrated the hurried "falling down" of their bodies from the peaks and passes of the mountains they trekked, so were their texts presented in hurried words, stumbling down the page, leaping lines and wordly distances.

In other cases it was my own words that needed different, less traditional graphic representation. So was the case when I recalled my own memories as a backpacker a decade earlier in the form of personal vignettes. In that case I wrote memories from and reflections on the travel, depicting my experiences in a more poetic and style-conscious manner.

The second aspect I grappled with concerned not the more visible graphics of transcription and printed word, but the structure of the work and the editorial decisions having to do with the divisions and contents of chapters. I found myself at odds with some basic tenets of scientific-positivist scholarly writing. I found the structuring of the relationship between chapters and sub-chapters quite difficult: While scientific writing forms are linear and entail hierarchical distinctions and categories, I felt that my work was not a linear or ordered development of concepts and could not be represented well in orderly forms of writing.

Some subchapters had the quality of what William Labov (1972) termed "floating phrases," that is, they could fit just about anywhere as they were "nonnarrative." Other parts could hardly fit under any title and would require new labeling and new chapters. While some of the writing could have resorted to more traditional forms, the "lived experience" component of the work, the embodied quality of the narratives, and the way in which I read the texts simply *had* to be expressed through a different kind of less rigid, ordered, and hierarchal writing (Handelman, 1993). The work I wrote seemed—I regret having to say it—in fact was marginally organized. It was quite "messy" (Denzin, 1997); only "near" the spot.[7] It hardly had any overarching conceptual hypothesis that was studied systematically throughout the dissertation, and if there was a governing point to the dissertation, it was not explicitly spelled out within it. I was not able or not successful in crystallizing a clear "vertical structure" of knowledge, and, needless to say, in laying it out linearly and progressively.

My (last) hope was that while engaging the work, readers would transform from commentators or critics, reading an account of the development of a hypothesis, into readers who moved along "with" the work (Frank, 1995). This would mean following how I was trying to create meaning and meaningfulness, however idiosyncratic and fragile the path. Through that process I produced a kind of writing different than any I had previously known and a kind of writing different than any I had written before. I wished that my readers, and especially the anonymous judges, would be able to bear its "messiness," not to mention to enjoy it and benefit from it.

* * *

When he hands me back a few chapters he read I hear my advisor quietly muttering:
Good work, good work,
but
Who should be its judges?

* * *

Dialogical thinkers: Mainstream academic writing makes it tough for dialogically or relationally oriented thinkers. As mentioned above, academia is a modernist post where individuality is vehemently pursued and repeatedly constituted. Myself, not only do I share ideas with colleagues, or borrow them, "steel" them and so on, but when reading others' works, I strongly feel that the *conversation* created between us is the primary mode of knowledge creation. Works have their way of "touching" and "moving" me into emotions and actions with an intensity that surprises me time and again. And so the "literature review" sections in my publications are usually in the form of a dialogue (open ended), rather than a monologue (conclusive). I am constantly commented in this regard. I am asked by reviewers to address unmediated "knowledge" directly, rather than from within the relationship or connection I "feel" towards it voicers. But I love conversing with fellow thinkers through their writing. The fact is that when I receive a new publication (usually after having read thoroughly the copy in the library), I look through the pages quickly and think I have a wonderful new space/place in and on which *to write*, that is, to comment and converse (Jackson, 2001).

Mirroring Reflections: Backpacking in Academia

As the research journey progressed the similarities between the backpackers' narratives and my own doctorate research crystallized. In both cases, a mixture of romantic and modern images and archetypes of travel and self-transformation were at the core, allowing the construction of the explorer's or the scientist's progress (Green, 1993). Both endeavors, backpacking as hiking-and-narrating, and the dissertation as research-and-writing, seemed to be discursively constructed and structured as a rite of passage.

This is evident in my colleagues' experiences as well. Doctoral students typically mention the "journey" they have gone through, the "way" they have traveled and progressed from the beginning of their work to their current state. The metaphor of the journey—at times Romantic (a propos nature) and at times modern (a propos science)—means that the experience of becoming a scholar is that of the individual arriving at *new destinations* or colonies of knowledge, previously unknown. This is one of the foundational metaphors of modern science, its progression unto *terra incognita* (Green, 1993). Of course, the institutional metaphor is embodied in the scholar personally, in his or her vectored career: through and throughout their careers scholars are expected to perform a rites of passage and to reiterate it.

The similarities between the backpackers' and my endeavor, that is, between the discursive construction of both the dissertation exploration voyage and the backpacking journey, stood out most clearly in the realm of *narrative*. They are both stories of a rite of passage by which the individual enters in and accesses a cultural capital. More importantly, both socially constructed stories of rites-of-passage are ritualistic in that the meaning they carry is mostly symbolic. Regarding the backpackers, I soon realized that it could be said that they travel *for the stories*. They travel after they have heard numerous stories, which pre-shape the itinerary of the travel and the experiences it bestows. And they progress and "mature" during the trip—they all declare they do—in correlation with the achievements that such (predominantly Romantic) journey and adventure narratives entail (Elsrud, 2001; Green, 1993; Noy, 2002a, 2002b, 2003). Both the personal stories and the larger social and institutional narratives are those of a rite of passage, that is, of a meaningful self-transformation. And this sought after personal change is achieved through owning a story, which the particular events of one's actual journey validate. Veteran backpackers own stories, and are entitled to tell them (Shuman, 1986). They gain the right for audience.

The parallels with the doctoral dissertation, as a symbolic (w)rite of passage, are telling. Consider this: How many people read dissertations? Or, why do disciplinary conferences within the larger social sciences regularly devote sessions to "How to make a book of your dissertation?" Part of the initiation of the "young scholar" is to go through an institutionally constructed "basic training" in order to test her/his worth and to grant her/his formal and social seals allowing entrance into the academic arena. For by no means is there an "inherent" need to pursue research in the monograph fashion of the dissertation.

In any case "young scholars" are expected to publish papers and books based on their work, and these publications are the ones that carry weight when career decisions are made. Similar to travelers, young scholars are expected to "travel," and, at least as important, to compose and write a narrative of their successful (predominantly modern) journey. Although backpackers mostly tell stories, and scholars mostly write them, the narrative dimension of their journeys is constitutive. In his discussion of the "adventurous white male mind" Green (1993) writes that "modernity starts with the adventure tale" (p. 148), which, in our case, refers to the journey narrative. Central to modernity is the scientific endeavor wherein emphasis is put on experimentation. Citing Merchant, Green writes, "experiment expresses the spirit of action, of a 'doing' devoted to '*finding out*'" (p. 144, my emphases).

A final note concerning modern versus post-modern morality is required here. The structure of a self-transforming journey, of a rite and right of passage, is pregnant with value; it is a form of cultural capital, and it endows the successful practitioner with certain esteemed merits. In the modern version, carrying the dissertation about "successfully," that is, completing it within the designated time frame, and within the theoretical and methodological frames *pro*posed at the outset of this modern quest, denotes a complete narrative of a rite of passage. The ensuing and sought after moral revolve around the virtues of commitment, dedication, obligation and fortitude. To the contrary, post-modern and post-structural dissertation endeavors—where the research's structure is negotiable and is at least as much a process as it is a form, and where reflexivity is central—a different morale is bestowed. Here, improvisation, intuition, candidness, and personal as well as social and cultural sensitivities, are sought after and valued. The different narratives of rites of passage educate the young scholar along different avenues and endow him or her with a different moral code: One more conservative and one more liberal, one more "serious" (Gurevitch, 2000), and the other more playful, one more abstract, the other more embodied. Neutrality is exchanged for involvement, passivity for agency.

As with backpackers, I also acquired the right to a story through "going out there" and "going through the motions," that is, through the empirical-experimental paradigm. As with backpackers, I too could have not confined myself to my room when researching. There would have to be a "field," which would be constructed, and then "journeys," which are movements to and from; as with backpackers there is a single, clear model of a successful story, which has to do with coherence, unity, linearity and progressiveness. Stories that are "messy" are considered both troubled and troubling, and more than representing an alternative, they represent a disappointment. And lastly, since these are stories of passage and initiation, i.e. of belonging, messiness and disappointment are faults that lead to non-admission or non-entrance.

* * *

As I finish writing the first chapter, a large essay on voices in the performances of narratives of personal experiences,
and hand it to Amia and Yorm to read, I burst into tears.
I know now that the dissertation will be; that it is.
I am overwhelmed.
I am crying. My mother. I am feeling my mother. From whom I inherited my writing; my writing disability.
And then back into the everyday frustration of writing the next chapter, and the rewriting of the next chapter, and the next . . .

Twice a day she was spared. Momentarily. Before falling asleep and at dawn ideas flowed through her, complete, ideal, worded perfectly. She said to me, "These ideas, I *had* them . . . I held them . . ." But with any move she made, any embodied move to seize them or record them, they would dissolve. This was the curse. I know it well (I'm *writing* it). She took comfort in my father's fluent writing and in my own (which she perceived as fluent). She hoped *I* could help her write. The irony.

I'm thinking writing and/in/as living. Connect all the lines of the letters you wrote, the ballpoint-pen ink, fountain-pen ink, and printer ink to a long (seismographic) line of life. When it ceases—so do you. Writing like biting on something sharper than your teeth. Like scratching your skin too deep. Chasing phantoms. I, even I, could not comfort her/myself. And I cannot hope for or help her anymore. I myself am not "hoped." Writing like blowing air gently, writing like rekindling.

How many times have I decided that I will not *write* any more? How many times have I written these doubts and hesitations, such as now?

* * *

In the beginning of the essay I suggested a different view of narrative—and of lingual communication in general—than the conventional one. Narratives of lives and of lived experiences—such as backpackers' romantic stories and young scholars' modern dissertations—entail enactment and not only present a discernable "reality" (Shotter, 1993). I have tried to show here, using an auto/ethnography, how personal narrative enacts, performs and evokes, rather than conveys. I suggest that in addition to "unity" and "direction" we should regard as central experience and relationships in forming meaning in narrative.

Epilogue

My aunt asked me Where did I travel to for such a long time. I told her To Japan. My aunt asked me That Japan you traveled to what is it and how is it and what did you find there. And I didn't know the answers.
—Ya'akov Raz, *Tokyo and Back*

The above dialogue is taken from the epilogue of a poetic journal of a journey. In one section, Raz describes the way an old Japanese stone-gardener talks about the rocks and stones he "grows" and nurtures in his garden, with more affection and warmth than most people talk about their siblings. The journey, on which Raz embarked, across the southern parts of Japan, followed the footsteps of another journey and another journeyer—the famous Haiku writer Basho—precisely three centuries earlier (1689–90).

Following Raz's awe and bewilderment at his extended journey, I, too, am puzzled: What was it I wrote in the dissertation? What was it I wrote about? Swarthmore (where my post-doc is presently taking place), Jerusalem, the hissing screen, and my mothers' departure—One.

* * *

To publish or perish? If you think of it enough, if you quote it from one context to another, the saying sounds eerie. Some people published *and* perished. Others perished *because* they published.

I am here because I know I *have* to publish, that is, write (I don't want to perish). I am not sure what it is exactly that I am writing about, nor whether this is the central question at stake, nor whether I understand the relationship between ethnography, research, narrative, myself (researcher) and writing. I just know that here, in this occupation, I *have* to write. Not a privilege but a necessity. Deadlines for lifelines.

A write of passage.

Notes

I deeply thank Kenneth Gergen and Matt Kutolowski for their comments on earlier versions of this paper. I would like to thank the Rothschild Foundation (Yad-Hanadiv) for a wonderful postdoctoral research year in the University of Pennsylvania and Swarthmore College, during which this paper was written. Parts of this chapter were presented at the QUIG Conference on Interdisciplinary Qualitative Studies, The University of Georgia, Athens, January 4, 2002; and at the Second Annual Interdisciplinary Qualitative Approaches to Research Colloquium, Texas A&M University, College Station, February 28, 2002. An earlier version of this chapter was published in *FQS: Forum Qualitative Sozialforschung/Forum Qualitative Social Research, 4*(2). Available at URL: http://www.qualitative-research.net/fqs-texte/2-03/2-03noy-e.htm.

[1] Though I am referring to the dissertation, all that is said holds equally for theses writing and perhaps for additional forms of writing in academia.

[2] Following Gurevitch's (2000) search of his "fatherly" sources of writing.

[3] See also Tyler (1986); specifically concerning qualitative dissertation and thesis writing see Garret (2000), and Meloy (2002).

[4] Some contractual aspects of the proposal might come as very useful to the doctoral student, since a contract is, after all, a two-way commitment. Just as it commits the researcher it also commits the institution, in the form of a dissertation committee. In cases of misunderstandings, some clear description of the scope of the work is well advised.
[5] Vicissitudes, including downright reversals in such "conventions of attribution," date back, as Stewart points, at least to the early Middle Ages in an interplay between two dichotomized meta-genres: "scholarly work," on the one hand, and "literary work," on the other. It is clear that the problematization of what these "genres" are, or of what "attribution" means, would require a revisiting of writing and inscription from its beginnings.
[6] Such as Avrahami, 2002; Bloch-Tzemach, 1998; Maoz, 1999; Mevorach, 1997; Salmon, 1998; and Simchai, 1998. For a review of the works see Noy (2002c).
[7] Frank (1991) emphatically uses the term "messy" when he refers to embodied experience and text, as opposed to disembodied, neutral and all-knowing genres (pp. 53, 61).

References

Avrahami, E. (2001). *The Israeli back-packers: A study in the context of tourism and post-modern conditions.* Unpublished doctoral dissertation, City University of New York, New York.

Bloch-Tzemach, D. (1998). *Tourist, dwelling tourist and all the rest.* Unpublished master's thesis, The Hebrew University of Jerusalem, Jerusalem. (Hebrew)

Bochner, A. P., & Ellis, C. (Eds.). (2002). *Ethnographically speaking: Auto/ethnography, literature, and aesthetics.* Walnut Creek, CA: AltaMira Press.

Dent, B. (2002). Border crossings: A story of sexual identity transformation. In A. P. Bochner & Carolyn E. (Eds.), *Ethnographically speaking: Auto/ethnography, literature, and aesthetics* (pp. 191–200). Walnut Creek, CA: AltaMira Press.

Denzin, N. K. (1997). *Interpretive ethnography: Ethnographic practices for the 21st century.* Thousand Oaks, CA: Sage.

Denzin, N. K. (1999). Two-stepping in the 90's. *Qualitative Inquiry, 5,* 568–572.

Denzin, N. K., & Lincoln, Y. S. (1994). Preface. In N. K. Denzin & Y. S. Lincoln (Eds.), *Handbook of qualitative research* (pp. ix–xii). London: Sage.

Derrida, J. (1988). *Limited inc.* Evanston, IL: Northwestern University Press.

Derrida, J. (1990). Force of law: The mystical foundations of authority. *Cardozo Law Review, 11,* 921–1045.

Eco, U. (1989). *The open work.* Cambridge, MA: Harvard University Press. (Org. pub. 1962)

Ellis, C. (1999). Heartful auto/ethnography. *Qualitative Health Research, 9,* 669–683.

Ellis, C., & Bochner, A. P. (Eds.). (1996). *Composing ethnography: Alternative ways of qualitative writing.* Walnut Creek, CA: AltaMira Press.

Elsrud, T. (2001). Risk creation in traveling: Backpacker adventure narration. *Annals of Tourism Research, 28*, 597–617.

Frank, A. W. (1991). *At the will of the body: Reflections on illness.* Boston: Houghton Mifflin.

Frank, A. W. (1995). *The wounded storyteller: Body, illness, and ethics.* Chicago: University of Chicago Press.

Garratt, D. (2002). *My qualitative dissertation journey: Researching the rules.* Creskill, NJ: Hampton Press.

Gergen, K. J. (1999). *An invitation to social construction.* London: Sage.

Green, M. B. (1993). *The adventurous male: Chapters in the history of the white male mind.* University Park: Pennsylvania State University Press.

Gurevitch, Z. (2000). The serious play of writing. *Qualitative Inquiry, 6*, 3–8.

Handelman, D. (1993). The absence of others, the presence of texts. In S. Lavie, K. Narayan, & R. Rosaldo (Eds.), *Creativity/anthropology* (pp. 133–152). Ithaca, NY: Cornell University Press.

Harshav, B., & Harshav, B. (Eds.). (1994). *Yehuda Amichai: A life of poetry (1948–1994).* New York: HarperCollins.

Jackson, H. J. (2001). *Marginalia: Readers writing in books.* New Haven, CT: Yale University Press.

Jones, S. H. (1998). *Kaleidoscope notes: Writing women's music and organizational culture.* Walnut Creek, CA: AltaMira Press.

Josselson, R., & Lieblich, A. (2002). A framework for narrative research proposals in psychology. In R. Josselson, A. Lieblich, & D. P. McAdams (Eds.), *Up close and personal: The teaching and learning of narrative research–The narrative study of lives* (pp. 259–274). Washington, DC: American Psychological Association.

Labov, B. W. (1972). *Language in the inner city: Study in the Black English vernacular.* Philadelphia: University of Pennsylvania Press.

Maoz, D. (1999). *Libi bamizrach (My Heart is in the East): The journey of Israeli young adults to India.* Unpublished master's thesis, The Hebrew University of Jerusalem, Jerusalem. (Hebrew)

McAdams, D. P. (1997). *The stories we live by: Personal myths and the making of the self.* New York: Guilford Press.

Meloy, J. M. (2002). *Writing the qualitative dissertation: Understanding by doing* (2nd edition). Mahwah, NJ: Lawrence Erlbaum Associates.

Mevorach, O. (1997). *The long trip after the military service: Characteristics of the travelers, the effects of the trip and its meaning.* Unpublished doctoral dissertation, The Hebrew University of Jerusalem, Jerusalem. (Hebrew)

Noy, C. (2002a). 'You MUST go Trek there'—The persuasive genre of narration among Israeli tarmila'im (backpackers). *Narrative Inquiry, 12*, 261–290.

Noy, C. (2002b). *The great journey: Narrative analysis of Israeli trekking stories.* Unpublished doctoral dissertation, The Hebrew University of Jerusalem, Jerusalem. (Hebrew)

Noy, C. (2003). Narratives of hegemonic masculinity: Representations of body and space in Israeli backpackers' trekking narratives. *Israeli Sociology, 5*(1). (Hebrew)

Pirsig, R. M. (1974). *Zen and the art of motorcycle maintenance: An inquiry into values.* New York: William Morrow.

Raz, Y. (2000). *Tokyo and back.* Tel-Aviv: Modan Publishing House. (Hebrew)

Richardson, L. (1997). *Fields of play: Constructing an academic life.* New Brunswick, NJ: Rutgers University Press.

Salmon, R. (1998). *"A distant place, a worryless place": Motivations for participation in the backpacking trip, and gender influence.* Unpublished Masters' thesis. Ramat-Gan, Bar-Ilan University.

Shotter, J. (1993). Becoming someone: Identity and belonging. In N. Coupland & J. F. Nussbaum (Eds.), *Discourse and lifespan identity* (pp. 5–27). London: Sage.

Shuman, A. (1986). *Storytelling rights: The uses of oral and written texts by urban adolescents.* Cambridge, MA: Cambridge University Press.

Simchai, D. (1998). *"Untrodden, not always marked, this trail starts here. . .": Israeli backpackers in the Far East.* Unpublished master's thesis, Haifa, Haifa University. (Hebrew)

Stewart, S. (1991). *Crimes of writing: Problems in the containment of representation.* Oxford: Oxford University Press.

Stewart, S. (1993). *On longing: narratives of the miniature, the gigantic, the souvenir, the collection.* Durham, NC: Duke University Press.

Tedlock, D. (1983). *The spoken word and the work of interpretation.* Philadelphia: University of Pennsylvania Press.

Tyler, S. A. (1986). A post-modern ethnography: From document of the occult to occult document. In J. Clifford & G. E. Marcus (Eds.), *Writing culture: The poetics and politics of ethnography* (pp. 98–122). Berkeley: University of California Press.

19 Becoming and Belonging: Learning to Do Qualitative Research

Stuart Lee and Wolff-Michael Roth

In this chapter, we link *legitimate peripheral participation*, a concept designed to describe how we become and belong to communities, and *auto/biography*, a form of accounting of our experiences. We use *legitimate peripheral participation* as a double normative frame for defining (a) a doctoral program and the struggles that ensued as the two authors produced and reproduced their identities as graduate student and supervisor and (b) a methodology for doing research among environmental activists. Auto/biography provides us with a referent for understanding this dual trajectory of becoming and belonging. Our chapter is fundamentally about the contradiction in the production|reproduction of identity while a graduate student is becoming a member in two communities, that of (qualitative) researchers and that of the researched (environmentalists).[1] We conceptualize struggle as transformative rather than destructive. We argue that this involved personal style of graduate training on research is part of methodologically sound and valid research training. We use individual and collective voices to create a literary structure that is reflexive of its content.

Learning as Becoming and Increasing Belonging

The concept of legitimate peripheral participation had been introduced to theorize how a community of practice reproduces itself by accepting individuals as newcomers who, in the process of changing levels and intensity of participation, become recognized as core practitioners (Lave & Wenger, 1991). In some discussions, the assumption is made that a community of practice is more or less stable so that the trajectory from the outside to core practice is describable in terms of changing practices while an individual becomes enculturated. Such a

379

view, however, is inconsistent with cultural-historical activity theory (Leont'ev, 1978) in which legitimate peripheral participation is grounded. Thus, the relationship between individual (subject) and collective is always dialectical, meaning that (a) they are contradictory yet mutually constitutive and (b) they cannot be theorized independently. Legitimate peripheral participation therefore always also involves transformation of the community, including transformation of its practitioners. Legitimate peripheral participation constitutes a constant process of becoming in and belonging to a community that is itself becoming and belonging to the practitioners.

A central aspect of subjectivity is identity, a concept based on the dialectical relation of sameness and selfhood. Selfhood itself is dialectical such that who we are in any one situation (or something) is an emergent feature of transactional praxis and therefore changes from situation to situation and over time (Roth, 2005). In the work presented here, we conceptualize doctoral studies and research method in terms of legitimate peripheral participation in two communities, those constituted by qualitative research and an environmental group, respectively. This situation gives rise to multiple reflexive and dialectical relations: (a) the graduate student (Stuart) has been subject both in the activity systems of research and researched, involving two trajectories of legitimate peripheral participation; (b) the individual researcher (Stuart) has aspired to be recognized by the academic collective (represented by Michael) but also has wanted his graduate studies to qualify him for a career outside academia; and (c) the graduate student has been researcher and researched. Contradictions are embedded within these dialectical relations, relations that often led to struggle. This article is about the struggles in the production and reproduction of identity in multiple (marginal) communities.

In our research and graduate training, we had used the concepts of community of practice and legitimate peripheral participation to conceptualize graduate training (Roth & McGinn, 1998). We had not, however, substantively considered the productive changes that accompany reproduction of the community. We started by conceptualizing our relationship as one of legitimate peripheral participation and core practice. It was through the struggles that we experienced in our roles as graduate student and supervisor, respectively, that we came to better understand the praxis and theory of graduate student training. The struggles we write about in this article were an outcome of the dialectic nature of legitimate peripheral participation. Heeding Marshall McLuhan's suggestion that the medium is the message, we use first- and third-person voices to create a literary structure reflexive of its content.

Legitimate Peripheral Participation: In Praxis

Learning means to become, that is, to belong somewhere or differently than we do at the moment. We conceived of Stuart's doctoral studies in terms of a trajectory of legitimate peripheral participation in the practices of qualitative research as performed by Michael, his supervisor, and other individuals already in Michael's research group when Stuart joined. After two months Michael asked Stuart to write his first paper for publication, followed by further requests for writing conference presentations and articles; at no time was Stuart required to do something that had an end in itself, such as writing a course paper. Nothing Stuart did ended up in the dead-end of a course instructor's pile of marking for the term. Instead, he presented at conferences, wrote articles for publication and worked in the community. His training plunged him into participation in academic qualitative research.

But that was not the only world in which Stuart was becoming and belonging. His research project involved participating in a local grassroots environmental group, a project for which Michael had received funding from a national funding agency. Stuart conducted his research by becoming a useful member of the group. He volunteered in almost all activities and acted as personal assistant to the group's leader. Near the end of his term in the group, Stuart had developed sufficient competence to be interim leader while the coordinator was absent.

In this way, Stuart was engaged in a double world of learning, of becoming. He was activist, researcher, and a researcher while being an activist. Participating and therefore being and becoming as activist, researcher, and researcher-activist does not come easily. Participating involves struggles as Stuart attempts to find and continuously construct an identity, which inherently involves the dialectic of difference—different Self–Other relations in different communities—and sameness—a sense of sameness carried across situations (Ricœur, 1990). In this article, we explore the struggles arising from this double learning-to-be as it was played out through the course of Stuart's graduate studies. Throughout, the notions of learning, researching, and identity are interwoven to explicate a form of research and research training that is personal, engaging and productive in a way recognized by the research community.

* * *

Stuart: From the beginning of my program, there was an emphasis on participating in ways that contributed to discourse, research, and inscriptions that were meaningful to an ongoing research project. I, as a graduate student, was always expected to be participating in the community of scholars who

would ultimately judge my scholarship, presented as conference presentations and papers for publication. Six features of this approach stood out for
me: immediate engagement, scaffolding of activity, an emergent, negotiated
research project, theoretical discourse linked to participation with other
scholars in the field, involvement in practical details such as equipment
purchase and grant crafting, and finally, participation in the reproduction of
the culture of researchers among novices. Although these activities are often
part of other graduate students' training, in my case they were the basis for
the training and were not supplemented with simulations (such as courses or
seminars about grant writing) prior to my engagement. The other strong focus of this activity is that there was always an emphasis on the graduate
student's activity to be part of and important to the research unit as a whole.
I was constantly aware of the importance of my relations with others on the
research team. Through scaffolding, negotiations and struggles, an experience that could be looked back on as an *education* emerged. And I emerged,
feeling confident in many of the standard practices of academia.

Legitimate Peripheral Participation: In Theory

Legitimate peripheral participation (LPP) is a particular articulation of learning
within a broader tradition of research and theorizing in education representing a
social- and cultural-historical view of learning (Lave & Wenger, 1991). The
term "legitimate peripheral participation" refers to a way of understanding learning that explicitly acknowledges the dialectical relation of individual subjects
and the collective in which they are a part; learning can be best regarded as
changing participation in these settings rather than passively absorbing and
processing information presented to them. The LPP approach unites two major
strands of scholarship: practice theory (e.g., Bourdieu & Wacquant, 1992) and
situated cognition theory (e.g., Lave, 1988). What unites these two strands of
authors is the insistence that learning must be theorized in terms of the relations
between individuals and their material and social environments. Four points
about this analytical framework—pertaining to learning, legitimate participation,
peripherality, and community of practice—are salient to our chapter.

    First, learning is always embedded in the social—this does not imply that
all learning is group activity, but acknowledges that we can never escape being
embedded in material and social relations. Even activities such as reading,
which may appear to be solitary are deeply social—the means of production and
distribution of the book, the ability to read script, the house and chair are all socially determined entities, depending on resources available, money (socially
agreed exchange), taste, and so on. The implication of this argument is that we

must always take into account where learning is taking place, and its role in the ongoing means of social production|reproduction in that particular time and place. It also implies that learning of knowledgeable skills is subsumed by the learner's experience of participating in a community of practice.

Second, legitimate participation suggests that the learner's participation is a legitimate contribution to the respective community of practice. This contrasts educators' traditional claims that they prepare potential participants in some community of practice by having them participate in activities (such as doing lab experiments whose results have been known for years) that have little relationship to the workplace and communities for which the student prepares. From the perspective of LPP, the fake activities are legitimate practices in reproducing the culture of educational institutions, and work must then be done to make the practices in which they engage at school relevant to workplaces for which they are ostensibly being prepared. Through an LPP perspective, people learn what they do, in relation to the socially and materially mediated situation they find themselves in.

Third, *peripheral* is intended to convey that the learner's participation is part of a network or community of practitioners and thus is a part of a collective effort. Peripheral is not meant to indicate that a newcomer has a more peripheral position relative to an old-timer who is more central. Rather, it points us toward a unit of analysis where all members' participation is legitimate and peripheral to (or always a just part of) the ongoing functioning of the whole. As they become more "expert" (recognized as such by other practitioners), individuals become more fully engaged in the community-defining events, become more entangled in the relations that constitute its activity—in fact, becoming more fully engaged and becoming an expert are two sides of the same coin. The direction of learning in an LPP model is always toward full participation. This implies not just mastery of a set of skills, but a belonging in a community, an ability to participate in more and more of its practices (which includes knowing what is appropriate to talk about in the hallway, and what is more relevant to the coffee room). This way of articulating learning seeks to de-center mastery and domination of others or situations in favor of a description that focuses on an increasing entanglement in the relations that constitute the community of practice.

Fourth, the concept *community of practice* articulates those human and non-human entities that are part of the activity in which the learner seeks to participate. A novice's trajectory is an emergent feature arising from the dialectic of the collective subject (community) and the individual subject (Holzkamp, 1983); it is a continued production of the individual subject and the collective in which it is a constitutive part. The community of practice also includes the settings, such as buildings and locations, as these are often socially meaningful aspects of the practice.

Bridging the Worlds—Identity through Activity

In this section we introduce our perspective on activity and struggles, and articulate some of the types of struggles that emerged for Stuart as we attempted to enact our graduate student-supervisor relationship. We consciously conceptualized our relationship in terms of legitimate peripheral participation in qualitative research and conceptualized this research *itself* as a form of legitimate peripheral participation (and sometimes as apprenticeship) in a particular community (here an environmental activist group shaping the politics in the community where Michael lives).

Struggles

Becoming and belonging are not necessarily easy. Social reproduction, the co-determined fitting of one individual into a new community, is a process that may be fraught with struggle. In our present understanding, it involves the mutual transformation of both the community and the individual. The novice, wanting to belong, must learn the practices and discourses of the community, but the community, needing to reproduce itself, also must find a place for the novice. By bringing their own uniqueness to a community, the novice also always has the power to transform it even as they are being transformed.

   This work of belonging is also the work of becoming. Identity is something emerging from the struggle between the individual and the community of practice into which they are entering. Identity, socially negotiated, involves different activities in different environments. From this perspective, the individual is seen as the nexus, or site of mixing, of the various activities that they engage in throughout their network of communities. Identity is not stable, but is a constant work in progress, which allows our auto/biographies to continuously unfold and change.

   From this perspective we acknowledge that identity is work, and that this work is often highly personal. The very moment individuals enter some field (professional or for playing), they subscribe to playing by the rules because they "have an *investment in the game, illusio* (from *ludus*, game)" (Bourdieu & Wacquant, 1992, p. 98). *Illusio* implies that the participants in a community are interested because of their stakes in both community and their own place in it. It implies that the participation can sometimes overtake the participants, who can then risk their lives, to continue in the activity or maintain the status they want to have in the community. Our activity matters to us, we are invested in it, it becomes a passionate undertaking. A felt tension ensues, and conflicts arise as the novice attempts to balance his interest with the demands of the community. Identity is not experienced by an individual as a detached entity, but as a suite of emotions, passions, and interests that play themselves out in the field of their body and experienced community.

In Stuart's graduate training, this work of becoming/belonging, and the stakes involved on both sides were often enacted as struggles with Michael. However, our self-conscious awareness that these struggles were part of the process of identity formation allowed us to experience and enact them as transformations. In the following excerpts, three thematic struggles are detailed: expression, balancing multiple identities, and doing explicit identity work to fine-tune the student supervisor relations. Through our narrative, we both explicate the rich entanglement between personal and institutional interests, and how through these struggles, new or transformed bodies of work, or ways of being emerge.

Importantly, we do not consider this to be a story about "power over," that is, a supervisor squelching a graduate student's desire to "write what must be written." This is, rather, a story about the tensions and struggles as both people, each in their own way peripheral participants, seek to produce something in a way they consider acceptable to the community. It is a story about two people attempting to come to terms with what they must say to their community amidst concerns of being accepted.

Expression—How to Write, Who We Are

Concerned for Stuart's learning and enacting culturally appropriate practices of writing and research, Michael attempted to ensure that Stuart's work was compliance with those expectations. Stuart, on the other hand, came into the degree program with his own historically constructed desires and practices. As noted previously, Stuart's graduate program was oriented towards production of publishable material that bore the names of both mentor and student. What was written would be public material and would place both Michael and Stuart in the community of academic researchers. We both had something at stake, and what was written needed to be appropriate to both individual's sense of good writing and research. This arrangement set the stage for many struggles over expression. In the following, we present our different ways of experiencing our relation while we worked on our first co-authored article, which was a contribution to a special issue on auto/biography in science education that Michael edited (Lee & Roth, 2000). The two-column format allows us to rally our different ways of writing and accounting for experience without having to filter what we want to say through the collective author's voice. The two-column format structurally represents the simultaneity of our original experience better than a sequential format.

Writing Research: The Doctoral Student's Perspective

We co-authored a piece on auto/biography as a research tool in science education. It was meant to be a conversational piece. We would both write auto/biographical sections, and then follow-up by having a theoretical conversation over and about the respective pieces. Michael had initially responded to my auto/biographical section as too "flowery". After I had edited it once to remove superfluous language, he repeated the claim and suggested that I re-write my auto/biographical section to be like his.

Stuart, I had a look at it. I find that your language is a bit too flowery. For example, take a look at the following paragraph: I won't be able to sell this. Would you mind going back through your part and write it in such away that it is passionate, yet reads a bit more like the other parts, a bit on the hermeneutic side. It is not even clear whether you experienced it as this, or whether this is your post hoc objectification. (April 16, 1999)

I received this e-mail just before Michael left for a ten-day trip. During this time e-mail contact would be very limited. Through my conversation with another grad student about the

Writing Research: The Supervisor's Perspective

When Stuart and I had our first meetings about becoming a graduate student in my research team, it appeared natural that I described my conceptualization of graduate studies not as a rite of passage riddled with tests of manhood (in his case) but as a guided and supported, changing participation in a field where I was already a core participant. I foresaw him learning to do research by doing it with me. To me, this implied also applied a certain level of trust. On Stuart's part, I expected trust that I would protect him from harm, which could come, for example, in the form of rejection of his ideas, and that I would increasingly facilitate his ideas to be published in various professional venues. On my part, I expected Stuart to trust me in as far as I was a benevolent mentor rather than a malevolent tyrant attempting to undermine his growth. This trust also implied that I would be able to speak as it came to me without having to censor the way I talked or wrote. With Michael Bowen, another graduate student of mine, this form of relationship had worked extremely well. It would be very different in this relationship.

When Stuart began to write, I felt that he was not sufficiently close in

situation, a solution to the problem of having to write an auto/biography just like your supervisor's emerged. I would use his e-mail as the first comment in our conversation! Because Michael was away and not able to readily communicate, I had time to research my resistance and articulate in terms of feminist theory and "liberation" pedagogy. I responded to his e-mail in a scholarly fashion, pointing out what I thought the problems in his comment were through a critical analysis.

Take a look at your memo to the first draft of my auto/biographical account (Figure 1). These are strong comments and a suggestion for action that I think has rich implications. The term "flowery" with its pejorative and dismissive connotations could have been substituted with "emotive" or "descriptive." I see the adjective you chose as an expression of domination. It is also a very macho put-down—calling another man's work feminine and superfluous (Spender, 1980, p. 78–81). It reflects the masculine, competitive nature of science (Connell, 1993, p. 200–201), which is something we work against in creating an inclusive "science for all" (Roth & McGinn, 1998)." (Lee & Roth, 2000, p. 63)

This exchange set the tone for the whole paper, which emerged as a discussion about power relations in the academic community and these relations' effect on language and expression, the masculine, heroic language tendencies of scientific narratives and style and content to what the community for which we were writing would be willing to accept. On one occasion, I wrote to him that I would "not be able to sell" our co-authored piece, "too flowery in style," which would appear in a special issue that I edited, to the main editor of the journal. I took the familiar expression to be consistent with the trust that I thought existed between Stuart and me. When I wrote the comment, I was certain that Stuart trusted me—had I not created the opportunity for him to publish his first first-authored piece? My intention had been to protect him from rejection. Yet his response was that of someone who had been attacked, someone who had experienced an attempt of subjugation, and who fought against it. Thus, something that was to me an act of friendly advice given in a relationship of trust, Stuart experienced very differently. Of course, now I understand that ideology would have prevented me to see how I reproduced inequality in a hegemonic relation (Gramsci, 1977).

More than anything, this episode taught me that the levels of trust that existed with Michael Bowen did not exist here, at least on the part of Stuart. Although I was as supervisor and special editor in the position to stop the eventual publication of the piece, we turned the article into an account of the struggle over the piece itself (Lee & Roth, 2000). That is, the article was not just about our own auto/biography but reflexively, an ac-

the question as to whether science could ever be truly libertarian.

As I think about teaching in terms of cultural reproduction, and reflect on your discipline comments, I now consider an important part of the curriculum its "repressive" aspect. We need to be cautious in our rhetoric, not to promise a utopian vision that does not include the means of social reproduction that have been discussed in this article. If we can't escape them within the constraints of an article, how do we expect to escape them when society confronts a radically different notion of science? (Lee & Roth, 2000, p. 71)

From an education perspective, it was through these times of conflict that I did the most theoretical work. Whether attempting to respond to editor's comments, discovering ways of articulating the emotions or impressions I had about what I was writing, or responding to an intellectual challenge by Michael, I turned intensely to books and to other scholars for help. These conflicts required deep answers to ameliorate. I felt an urgency, a drive, *illusio*, to "win" the game, to be able to express myself in a way that was both intellectually and emotionally satisfying and to be able to withstand the critical eye of the "gatekeeper" of the first "obligatory passage point" to the community I encountered.

This struggle over expression, evident from an Email from Michael during the early period in my graduate studies, would continue to manifest it-

count our subjectivities in the struggle to write an auto/biographical piece. I took this episode as a learning experience that other science educators might find interesting to read about and did what I could to see this rather unusual piece through to publication.

Our next collaboration was a paper given at the annual meeting of the Society for Social Studies of Science subsequently submitted to the journal Social Studies of Science about the role of inscriptions in how an environmental group represented a creek and redesigned some aspects of it. Through the early drafts, I again felt that Stuart was not writing for the audience but used a style that the readers of the journal would be unfamiliar with. I struggled with my feedback, sensing that Stuart would experience emotions similar to the ones during the writing of the earlier article. At the same time, I "saw disaster coming," a fear that seemed to be reified when the reviews asked for major revisions. However, during the revisions, I felt that Stuart was moving even farther away from the cultural patterns represented in the journal rather than coming closer.

At home in my study, I threw my hands up in despair but made a resolve that I would attempt to assist Stuart in the best way I could to publish the piece in his style by articulating and addressing any potential problematic issue that became salient to me. The product of our struggles eventually

self in later efforts.

I read the manuscript and was a bit discouraged, a bit a lot. . . . There is so much that is changed, and the coherence we put in does not exist anymore. . . . There is no more theory, you say that we theorize something but we don't. . . . You have written in the informal style you use when you are talking . . . I was sweating, being embarrassed. (October 18, 2000)

My more personal, informal style, a deliberate political and aesthetic choice on my part, often clashed with Michael's preferred "objective" or removed style. In our auto/biographical piece, though it was difficult to experience, the way we "played out" the struggle allowed it to surface, to take over from our preconceived notions about what the article was to be and transform the work. Our words, as Bakhtin (1981, p. 340) might say, reacted in a "chemical union," creating something entirely different from what we had planned. All our conflicts over expression have ended in reconciliation, in my finally being able to craft something acceptable to both of us. Michael wrote to me, almost with a sigh of relief:

Finally, this is a very fine piece. Congratulations. (January 16, 2001)

This example also plainly shows how membership in a community crucially affects the creative activities of its members. As he articulated in his

was accepted and I regard it as an exceptional piece in its own right, not just because of the first rank that the journal takes in its domain based on the citation impact rating scale (Lee & Roth, 2001).

In subsequent collaborations, Stuart took an increasingly central role in the writing. At the same time, I saw my role increasingly as one of doing everything that I could to bring an article into the form that by the reviewers of the journal to which it would be submitted could accept it. More so, looking back over the my writing that I have done independently of the collaboration with Stuart, I can see how it too changed away from the more formal style that I used to employ having been trained as a physicist and subsequently as a statistician.

Looking back at the three years with Stuart, I see that my understanding of graduate student training as continuously changing. While I used to understand graduate student training in terms of a more or less linear trajectory of increasing participation in the practices of a field, the tensions and contradictions between the production|reproduction of a field are now the most salient aspects. It is true that my realization was not simply brought about by the interactions with Stuart. Rather, I had become increasingly familiar with activity theory and materialist dialectic philosophy that it is based on and the role it attributes to contradictions (Marx & Engels, 1970).

criticism of my auto/biographical contribution, Michael experienced a felt need to "sell" the special edition due to the typical practices and standards of acceptability of the rather conservative community of science educators for whom the issue was targeted. My struggle with Michael, then, was not my struggle with just Michael, but also with the scientific community and its way of articulating experience. And it was also an outcome of his struggle with the same community for similar purposes. A "community of practice" perspective allows us to appreciate the complexity of interactions which become manifest through our daily actions.

From a supervisor position, then, I experience the tensions arising from the intent to support the doctoral student in his or her process of becoming a member without having to experience rejection of work and application to membership status. The tension exists between insisting on a certain level of reproducing the cultural patterns of the field while at the same time supporting the production of new cultural patterns. A second level of tension may arise from the different assessments that the student and I make about what may be acceptable by the field as an innovation and therefore production and to what extent the cultural patterns have to be reproduced to make the work acceptable.

Selfs in Qualitative Research and Environmentalism: Multiple Marginality

Stuart: Because of the research methodology that I enacted, my graduate studies plunged me into a situation where I was simultaneously an apprentice in two different worlds. I was becoming an increasingly full participant in environmental activism and in academic qualitative research. How was I able to manage my identity while being an activist when I was simultaneously being a researcher of activists?

* * *

Collectively: Star (1991) writes of the experience of "multiple marginality," where membership in multiple communities leaves one "at once heterogeneous, split apart, multiple . . . we have experience of a self unified only through action, work and the patchwork of collective biography" (p. 29). She writes of the "high tension zone" of living between accepted communities, of negotiating rival allegiances, of unifying some sort of identity among the many identities we enact in our different communities. This is *reconciliation work* (Wenger, 1998), the ongoing effort to bring coherence to a self that has multiple, sometimes conflicting roles due to its participation and belonging in many different communities of practice. They both emphasize that self is unified in the moment, through activity. Perhaps it is better to say that self becomes singular in each moment of praxis, even though analysis puts all of these singular, diachronic Selfs into the same plane and thereby synchronically juxtaposes them. Stuart also experienced the effects of this multiplicity but during reflection synchronic. But what seemed more salient to him throughout his studies was the unity experienced, as Star puts it, through action.

* * *

Stuart: While I was with the environmental group, I was an activist working with them on whatever problem they had assigned me. When I left the site and began writing field notes at home or talking to Michael, I was a researcher. This seamless activity across the "two worlds" is shown through different documentation I produced in response to a fish kill. One afternoon, as I began doing some routine in-stream volunteer work with another volunteer, I discovered that there had been a kill-off of trout, the fish the activists were working so hard to create viable habitat for. Meagan (the group's coordinator) was away, so I helped to organize an investigation into the incident. As I was helping with the fish kill, I was also doing participant observer research. My actions, though, were seamless across the two different communities because I was familiar enough with each to know what type of action was appropriate. In e-mail correspondence, I write about the "same" incident to two different people. To Michael, my academic supervisor, I wrote:

We found a fish kill in the creek today. Bad news for the fish, very bad news, but good news for a 'construction of event' piece. I've written about our work in the attached field notes. The case is so small yet so nice that I think there's potential to do some good work with it. What do you think? . . . I've got the video camera. (June 24, 2000)

The same event was described differently in an Email message to Meagan, the coordinator of the activist group, who has very different concerns.

I've attached the water data. Jane has the stuff from Friday afternoon. If she calls me today, I'll add to the table and send it off to you. Here's some more numbers: As of yesterday, we'd pulled twenty-three trout, between about thirteen and twenty-three centimeter from the stream over the course of Friday evening and Saturday. On Saturday, I put on hip waders and used a dip net to collect an extensive count. I waded the stream from the culvert at Sprite road until the logjam just past the two felled trees farther up the trail (just before the private property). I was pretty careful in my search and checked under the surface of duckweed etc. that was on the water, so I'm pretty confident that I got everything that was there until that time. I also pulled out a (dead) stickleback and a crawfish. There were fry (or small fish at least)

a (dead) stickleback and a crawfish. There were fry (or small fish at least) throughout the reach. There was a thick scum on the surface of much of the water, it was not
iridescent—this makes me think it's not an oil scum. (June 25, 2000)

Together with Michael, we also wrote up the incident as a paper submitted to an academic journal. These different writings underlie the fact that
a text is always part of some community's discourse. Though I appear to be
writing different identities for myself: that of scientist, student, researcher,
author, my felt experience was that of being one person communicating to
many others, my identity "unified through action" (Star, 1991, p. 29).

I rarely experienced a conflict of allegiances or identities while involved in my research. Since I was involved in a practice that involved multiplicity, this felt congruency is a phenomenon that requires an explanation.
My feelings of congruence were helped by three salient aspects of the research situation: a common discourse of activism in both communities, a
prior relationship of trust with the coordinator which allowed me to be "just
another" volunteer, and the lack of relations between the two groups.

Both Michael and I consider ourselves activists and both of us identify
with the goals of the environmental group. Thus I did not experience the
conflict of doing things while an activist that were at variance with the philosophies and goals of our research team. The method of participant observer research legitimized my deep involvement in the activists' activities,
thus my direct participation with the activists was congruent with my role as
a researcher. As is apparent from the links above, the text I wrote as an academic author also depended on my engagement with the activists.

My prior relationship with Meagan, coordinator of the environmental
group, made for a non-problematic entry in the group. Because I was "just
Stuart" and not "the researcher from the university," I could form relationships of trust quite quickly with others. I also chose a "non-invasive" research style, which was based much more on recording what I did and what
I overheard rather than querying participants with specific research questions. Although my role as a researcher was never completely erased, I behaved as if, and was treated as if I was just another volunteer. For example,
in my letter reporting the fish-kill incident to Meagan, I did not speculate on
the "construction of a fish kill," nor did she wonder how I would use the incident in my theoretical work. Because I did not attempt to bring social science discourse into the activist community, I did not need to make choices
about "who" I would be at a research site at any given moment.

The other important factor in the ease of my identity experience was
that the two communities of practice were relatively isolated from each

other. Thus, I did not need to perform mediation or translation work between others—who may have been similarly involved and may have had stakes in certain interpretations or consequences of what I did—and myself. This is also apparent from the correspondence shown above, as there is little overlap between what I write about to the different parties. The environmental group did not take much interest in the results of my research, as it did not become applicable to their undertakings. Thus I did not have to account for my research activities to those on whom I based my research. Similarly, the outcome of my activities with the activists relative to the activists' goals was of little relevance to Michael. Because of the isolation between the activities of the two communities, it was easy to maintain a separation of activities while also maintaining a congruent identity. I could use one voice and doings while helping the activists, and another while helping Michael, and because I could experience both voices as part of my overall career trajectory, I did not experience identity conflict as I carried out my research.

I experienced the high-tension zone much more as I attempted to balance the relevant activities of the two communities into my life. Thus, I recorded in one field-note entry:

Arrrrgghhhh! What a stupid day. I am having difficulties at the moment. Tired, pouring stimulants—coffee, sugar, into my tired body to keep it going, keep it going. Feeling the strain of having a life where every day, it's a different project. Feel the stress of being passionate about part of my work and wanting to pour more time and energy into it, but being held back by other parts, by my commitments to others."

And am being divorced from the smug self-satisfaction of "working hard to get things done" by the words of Sasha urging me to "take time to connect." I am also noticing more and more what gets lost as my life speeds up and to me, what gets lost is the time I have to just chat with people. As an ethnographer, this could be a grave methodological error. Not just "just chat" it means that much of my talk is about all the stuff I am doing, how I am suffering, what else I have to do etc. this must be so Boring to people—I feel boring. So now I'm in a double bind: I feel guilty if I relax and take things more slowly, I feel guilty (somewhat) if I don't. (February 22, 2000)

The field note quoted in the previous sentence shows I experienced tension through limits on my time, and how this spilled over into how I enacted my identity and led me to question my research practices. I was worried that my harried state, brought about by trying to balance the demands of multiple communities of practice—"Feeling the strain of having a life where every day, it 's a different project"—would prevent me from having insight-ful conversations or deep relationships with others whom I was working with. Besides feeling guilty about not being a valuable friend, I was also concerned that such shallow interaction would then reduce the quality of my research "data."

Identity—Constructed, Emerging

Stuart: The issue of what I spent my time doing went beyond the issue of what was good research practice, however. This was a high tension zone because I was not participating in graduate studies to belong to a community of aca-demic researchers, but to enter into a different, hybrid community, one I hadn't defined yet, but one that involved writing, analysis, science and soci-ety in a way that affected the practice of those whom I researched and wrote about. As someone on a career trajectory, I felt the need to explore, to ex-pand my understanding of opportunities, and to define myself within soci-ety. I could not just follow Michael around to conferences and meet his friends. This was the third major struggle I faced during graduate school: what community was I attempting to enter? Who was I to become? Thus the question of how this graduate program of study/research fit into my bio-graphical trajectory and how I would fit myself into some community's his-torical trajectory became central. It felt like, and still feels like, a basic sur-vival issue.

Through my relationship with Michael, I felt forced to create myself in writing. I was dependent on funding from Michael for my survival while a grad student. I was not only his graduate student, a novice in social science research and writing, but also the person Michael was depending on to run a legitimate research project and write publications to ensure that he receive continued funding. Thus he had a stake in the style and substance of my writing. He had a stake in how I spent my time, and what my interests were. We were related through both employer–employee relationship and that of student–supervisor; there are different and conflicting aspects to these rela-tionships, especially with respect to how the student–employee spends their time and what they produce. These aspects were not worked out in seminars of self-discovery but rather forged in the heat of ongoing practice, always in the context of participating in research. In the heat of one conflict, Michael wrote to me that he felt duped, deceived and hurt by my proposition not to work on writing and thought we might have confused and conflated differ-ent kinds of issues and relations.

It may well be that we can work something out that involves partially collecting further data. But in any case, I would expect that we are clear about our roles. Primarily, I see your role as employee in the construction of a physical database (boundary object). If you do not want to be a co-author (to a certain extent your interest and your time in these activities), then so be it, though I would find that regrettable. As a grad student, if you want to peruse data that you have collected qua employee on my research project, you are expected to make an appropriate request and appropriate acknowledgment of the SSHRC grant under which you have been employed. (November 9, 1999)

He suggested that we meet and further discuss the issues. It was through this pressurized real-life situation that I was compelled to create myself in text. At another time, Michael asked me to help him understand or describe our relations in my own terms so that we could come to an agreement on a mutually satisfying working relationship. I wrote back:

I frame my primary responsibility as "what do I need to do to enter the community of practice for which I am preparing myself, and for which the federal government, and you, are supporting me?" I do not wish to enter the community of practice of full-time university-employed academics (as you know), but rather participate in translation of science in the public sphere. Right now, that involves two domains for me: community development or liaison, and secondly NGO work, which would be more oriented toward writing and policy. Perhaps some contracting or consulting work with government would also be a potential. Taking that into consideration, I focus my activities in a number of areas:

(i) writing and working towards publishing papers. My goal in this is to present myself as a credible thinker, and emerge from the Ph.D. process with discursive repertoire which will help me in contributing to the talk and practices around "sustainability."

(ii) researching literature in order to have a credible background to be able to speak about that which i am speaking.

(iii) Creating a network of colleagues and associates who support me in this work, and provide a "community of practice" starting point for when I graduate.

This third point is especially important to me in this situation because I feel that your ability act as a "God father" and tie me into well-positioned contacts is limited because my potential desired community is different from the ones you traverse. Thus I spend some time researching and connecting with others who are in the community into which I would like to fit.

I consider this part of my training, and I think you would agree that it is LPP for academics. (And as an afterthought is part of fulfilling the obligations of the SSHRC research grant that pays my wages.) (November 1, 2000)

* * *

Stuart: The struggles of which these emails were a part were experienced also as lack of sleep, panic, anxiety, probably on both sides. What is important here is that both of us worked to move toward clarity. Michael did not label or censure me, but requested my definitions, my terms of our agreement. I continually attempted to define myself in relation to our shared research project. This is not easy, as I have been exploring my role with respect to the research, the role of research with respect to my own life, present and future. But I could embrace these struggles as not something standing in the way of the development of my career trajectory or an indication of a pathological relationship, but events that were instead crucial to it, and indeed, to be expected, if the theory on which my research is based holds up in practice. This reduced the anxiety-provoking aspects of those experiences. Over time, I realized that I was able to write myself into a community in a way consistent with how I had envisioned it. Through this struggle, I gained competence at declaring who I was and where I wanted to go with my future. I experienced greater security and confidence through this practice.

I was also given support to travel to whatever conferences I chose; this was very important in my exploring what community of practice I was to enter. I have traveled to many different locales, some not typical places for

Michael: As a supervisor, I experience the tensions arising from the intent to support the doctoral student in his or her process of becoming a member without having to experience rejection of work and application to membership status. The tension exists between insisting on a certain level of reproducing the cultural patterns of the field while at the same time supporting the production of new cultural patterns. A second level of tension may arise from the different assessments that the student and I make about what may be acceptable by the field as an innovation and therefore production and to what extent the cultural patterns have to be reproduced to make the work acceptable.

I see the individual identity of members of a group and their collective identity as inherently linked. Based on my understanding of the relation between individual and collective subjectivity and the notion of *concrete universals*—which are the genetic precursors of concrete particulars—I view individual identity as a concrete realization of the generalized identity of the group. With each doctoral student who participates increasingly in the practices of a field the collective identity of the group changes alongside the identity of the individual. Tensions arise from the struggle between continuity of group identity all the while allowing the group to reproduce itself by accepting new members, which inherently adds new individual

West-Coast students of science education. I was able to travel to Vienna, to attend the social studies of science conference, to Seattle, to attend the "teach-ins" prior to the now infamous protests, to the interior of British Columbia on an "Indian Reserve" to attend a conference on bringing indigenous and scientific knowledge together sponsored by a provincial forestry extension and research agency. Thus not only was I encouraged to imagine and express through writing my career trajectory and potential communities, but I was given means to experience these communities in an embodied sense by attending conferences. This typically self-determined aspect of my graduate studies has been instrumental in facilitating the type of transformation that I had hoped it would do.

identities and therefore changes the collective identity.

This dialectical perspective gives me a different understanding of auto/biography: Our lives are but concrete realizations of generally available ways of living within a particular culture. Our auto/biographies always also are biographies, which continuously move along the fine line between the singularity of lived experience and the generality of lived experience within the culture.

Looking back, I now see how Stuart's doctoral work changed our field in more than one way. It changed because his work has become part of its literature; it also changed because his participation changed the range of concrete subjectivities present in the field; and it changed because I have changed through our interactions.

* * *

Collectively: Through this process a specific typical mix of activities, a style of writing, a type of theory and a way of articulating and researching questions emerged a research identity. By embracing struggle and negotiation as part of the entry into a community of practice, both of us have seen ourselves transform the community and noticed ourselves becoming transformed. It helps us to surrender our notion of control, of exclusive identification with a certain identity and instead focus on the process of becoming, of negotiating our participation across the many communities that we traverse. By acknowledging *illusio*, the passion, the interest, the deep role participation has with identity, conflicts yield to new creations, identities, and possibilities.

Learning Researching—Becoming Objective Subjectively

Scientific research is usually constructed as obeying rational norms. The opposite is the case, that there is no rational or general answer of how fictions become true. However, this does not mean that anything goes. It simply means that such questions are too important that we leave them to norms. But we have the choice between approaches, and therefore also the choice to take an approach to the singularity not only of the individual but also that of the sciences—in both, interests, truth, and history cannot be dissociated. Thus,

[w]henever the question "Is this scientific?" resounds with regard to an innovative proposition, that question does not oppose scientific truth to opinion. It is a question asked by very interested people who wonder what they may take into account in their own investigation. . . . The reliability of a scientific result thus depends on the heavy demands of scientists for whom it makes a difference. (Stengers, 2000, p. 48)

Stengers underscores the importance of an interested, involved community of practice in determining what counts as objective research. Thus, "what persuades the other scientists is not this particular human, it is their own incapacity to offer another interpretation" (Stengers, 2000, p. 47). Thus the artifact produced by the scholar must hold up to the practices of verification of the community, which can be as many as there are interested researchers. This definition of what passes as good, valid or reliable science allows us to build a space where passion, interest and emotion can co-exist with good, reliable scholarship. Researchers as subjects do not need to erase themselves from the pursuit of research but rather need to strive to generate data and articles that are worthy of acceptance by those researchers whose community that they seek to join.

The auto/biography of Stuart's graduate studies, integrally tied to his auto/-biography in qualitative research community (here represented by Michael) is one being caught up in choices, in conflicts, in activities rather than of dispassionately going about collecting objective data. Stuart has developed friendships with those that he researched. He has butted heads with his supervisor, Michael. Stuart has tried to impose his point of view on the data and has had it altered. His journey and experience have been far from dispassionate. He achieved objectivity through the process of writing about his experiences, of analyzing the data that he retrieved in a certain way that is recognized as objective, and by writing with Michael, who is a community member well-versed in the construction of "objective" data. Even though Stuart may be passionate about what his activists do, he approached his data in a way characteristic of the community of qualitative researchers. He continuously asked questions, "Can my evidence support my claims?" "Do my claims make sense given my embodied experience and continued participation with this particular group?" or "Do my claims make sense given my participation with other similar groups?" Such questions remained, uncontaminated by the enthusiasm or passion Stuart had for his work. In fact, they required a deep passion to be persistent and effective.

As Stuart was becoming a researcher and an activist, as he was coming to belong in a community of practice, he also was becoming competent in their practices. This chapter presents reflexively the double auto/biography of both trajectories. These two forms of becoming are two complementary and mutually constitutive sides of the same coin. And if these practices involve "objective" reporting, then he was also becoming competent in these practices to fit in with the community. The ability to write objectively was becoming an object of passion in and of itself. There is no reason to separate the two. The activity of producing text that is considered reliable, valid or objective is another practice within the community of researchers and writers into whom Stuart wished to be included. Therefore, it is something that he is interested in, it holds for him, *illusio*. Stuart has stakes in being recognized as becoming skilled at this challenging practice. Where there are interests and stakes, emotions and tension will follow.

We cannot discuss the experience of becoming someone new, belonging to a new group of people without involving emotions. They are part of our human physiological experience of being in the world. Through the style of training Stuart received, he had a chance to belong somewhere, somewhere he had worked hard to make explicit. Belonging was signified by more than simply being in the presence of others or merely of doing work together; to Stuart, belonging was achieved through explicit acknowledgement of his competence.

* * *

Stuart: Sometimes I realized that I was doing what I had always dreamt of. This type of recognition is a familiar sign of success to those who study "flow" or optimal experiences (Csikszentmihalyi, 2000). Through my experience of belonging, I was becoming—a researcher, an activist, someone who was able to participate articulately. I realized that my interest was bearing fruit.

My research ability increases as I am recognized by Michael as a competent researcher and travel with him to new places and begin new ethnographies. I learn from doing ethnography alongside someone I definitely have a relationship with. I feel happy when I am able to 'capture' a good scene on video, or recognize an aspect of the environment that becomes salient to his thought about it.

I learned many life lessons from watching Michael do ethnography. Most important is his "aggressiveness" that I would shy away from doing—but how people connect with his direct questions and requests to participate and they all seem really excited to teach and talk to him. Often the talk generates great data. But also the people seem happy and not offended. Very interesting. My feeling is one of expansion. (May 24, 2001)

My learning continues. That *feels* good. I am becoming a better researcher, more skilled at telling an objective story. Along with the passion,
the competence emerges. I find myself in a place that I have worked hard to
articulate and become present within.

Conclusion

In this chapter we chose an auto/biographic approach and the concept of legitimate peripheral participation to examine three aspects of a graduate-student
training and research project that were particular sites for struggle throughout
their duration. The first, concerning struggles about expression, examines an example of how the activity of writing for publication provides a focal point for
many other struggles about power and identity within a community. We outline
how an activity approach to identity allows us to articulate the dual nature of the
LPP in multiple, reflexively related ways: (a) in his research, Stuart was becoming a member in an activist and a research community, the first trajectory being
part of the data that became an object in the second trajectory; and (b) from the
interactions with Stuart over his data (trajectory in the environmental group) and
his identity as a researcher, Michael, representing the pre-existing community of
research, also began to change. That is, through our struggles, the community
changed twice, both by accepting Stuart as a member and thereby expanding and
accepting new ways of doing qualitative research and by transforming itself as
an existing member (Michael) was changing in the way he looked at and understood research and at graduate student training. Here, we particularly detail how
choosing and articulating the reasons for the balance of activities in which Stuart
took part played a crucial role in forming his identity as a graduate student embarked on a historically constructed career trajectory. We frame this style of
education as a dialectic of *belonging|becoming*, emphasizing the temporally and
socially situated nature of the learner. By acknowledging the creative potential
involved in the struggle, we were both able to learn, that is, change our ways of
participating in the community.

    We embody multiple perspectives in the structure of our writing, using in-
dividual—in stand-alone and parallel contrasting columns—and collective
voices. We thereby not only acknowledge the presence of tensions and contradictions when two individuals with different social positions and worldviews attempt to articulate their inherently contradiction-laden relationship without giving more voice to one or the other. Thus in a language where transcendental
identity is not an issue, we find emotions, activities, struggles, longing, expression becoming through belonging. We thereby confront how the inclusion of

these embodied experiences of learning and doing research problematize the writing of research. By including struggles, contingency and emotions into the discourse about research, we challenge the traditional discourse of validity (and much of information processing-based learning) that assumes an objective, unaffected researcher.

Ultimately, to be able to learn from conflicts requires openness to *cogenerative dialoguing* as a way of dealing with contradictions. Cogenerative dialoguing is a practice that allows us to engage in expansive learning, based on the affordances that collective activity brings to the reflexively related understanding and explaining of contradictions. Cogenerative dialoguing is aimed at expanding the range of actions available to each participant, who then can do his/her part in improving the situation. Such a practice could also lead to new forms of learning in doctoral studies but would require that traditional institutional structures be changed to allow more collective forms of studying and supervising. Even if a supervisor is radically open to the needs and ideas of students, and facilitates open dialogue and a praxis of solidarity (Roth, 2000), existing institutional structures still make him responsible for a range of decisions, including the assessment that the thesis submitted conforms to existing institutional standards. In cogenerative dialoguing, the multiple relations arising from many individuals all socially located in different ways, mediates the effects that individual gradients of difference may produce. Groups in which professors, postdoctoral fellows, and doctoral, masters, and undergraduate students participate and make collective decisions in all respects of their learning and assessment might lead to very different forms of changing participation, and ways of understanding ourselves as participants in scholarly activity.

Notes

This chapter was made possible in part by a grant from the Social Sciences and Humanities Research Council of Canada. An earlier, now substantially revised version was published as Lee, S. H., & Roth, W.-M. (2003). Becoming and belonging: Learning qualitative research through legitimate peripheral participation. (64 paragraphs). *Forum Qualitative Sozialforschung / Forum: Qualitative Social Research, 4*(2). Available at URL: http://www.qualitative-research.net/fqs-texte/2-03/2-03leeroth-e.htm

[1] In this chapter, we make use of the sign "|" to create dialectical concepts by uniting and simultaneously separating two mutually exclusive concepts. The sign "|"is called the Sheffer stroke and corresponds to the truth-functional connective equivalent to the operation "NAND." The combined expression is inherently true, because it contains both a term and its opposite and therefore embodies a contradiction.

References

Bourdieu, P., & Wacquant, L.J.D. (1992). *An invitation to reflexive sociology*. Chicago: University of Chicago Press.

Csikszentmihalyi, M. (1999). If we are so rich, why aren't we happy? *American Psychologist, 54*, 821–827.

Gramsci, A. (1971). *Selections from the prison notebooks*. New York: International Publishers.

Holzkamp, K. (1983). *Grundlegung der Psychologie*. Frankfurt: Campus.

Lave, J. (1988). *Cognition in practice*. Cambridge: Cambridge University Press.

Lave, J., & Wenger, E. (1991). *Situated learning: Legitimate peripheral participation*. Cambridge: Cambridge University Press.

Lee, S., & Roth, W.-M. (2000). Auto/biography and the paradox of change: (Dis)locating ourselves in the process. *Research in Science Education, 30*, 57–73.

Lee, S., & Roth, W.-M. (2001). How ditch and drain become a healthy creek: Representations, translations and agency during the re/design of a watershed. *Social Studies of Science, 31*, 315–356.

Leont'ev, A. N. (1978). *Activity, consciousness and personality*. Englewood Cliffs, NJ: Prentice Hall.

Marx, K., & Engels, F. (1970). *The German ideology* (C. J. Arthur, Ed.; W. Lough, C. Dutt, & C. P. Magill, Trans.). New York: International.

Ricœur, P. (1990). *Soi même comme un autre*. Paris: Seuil.

Roth, W.-M. (2000). Learning environments research, lifeworld analysis, and solidarity in practice. *Learning Environments Research, 2*, 225–247.

Roth, W.-M. (2005). Making and remaking self in urban schooling: Identity as dialectic. In J. Kincheloe, P. Anderson, K. Rose, D. Griffith, & K. Hayes (Eds.), *Urban education: An encyclopedia*. Westport, CT: Greenwood.

Roth, W.-M., & McGinn, M. K. (1998). Legitimate peripheral participation in the education of researchers. In J. A. Malone, B. Atweh, & J. R. Northfield (Eds.), *Research and supervision in mathematics and science education* (pp. 215–230). Mahwah, NJ: Lawrence Erlbaum Associates.

Star, S. L. (1991). Power, technology and the phenomenology of conventions: on being allergic to onions. In J. Law (Ed.), *A sociology of monsters: Essays on power, technology and domination* (pp. 26–56). New York: Routledge.

Stengers, I. (2000). Another look: Relearning to laugh. *Hypatia, 15*, 41–54.

Wenger, E. (1998). *Communities of practice: Learning, meaning, and identity*. Cambridge: Cambridge University Press.

20   Home and Away: Self-reflexive Auto/Ethnography

Christiane Kraft Alsop

Practicing ethnography means shifting one's notion of center and periphery and coping with the complexity of multiple centers with multiple peripheries. In this contribution I introduce one attempt at connecting centers and peripheries by interrelating what it means *to be home* and *to be away*. I will do so by referring to different aspects of my identity as teacher and mentor, as ethnographer and writer, and as a German immigrant to the United States. By using these different voices I intend to demonstrate that being home and being away are two very human states of being that are intimately connected. By referring to etymology, cultural psychology, psychoanalysis, and anthropology, I provide a description of those two states to open up various dimensions of their meanings.

In the wake of colonialism anthropologists came up with the term self-reflexivity to understand ethnographic limitations and potentials. The concept and method called auto/ethnography is an attempt at practicing this self-reflexivity by having a closer look at one's own longings and belongings, at the familiar that—when viewed from a distance—can change one's perspective considerably. This change comes about when the auto/ethnographer places the self within a social context by connecting the personal and the cultural (Ellis & Bochner, 2000; Reed-Danahay, 1997). In the latter part of this chapter I will consequently focus *not* on the traditional ethnographic notion of the "other" but on the familiar from the perspective of the person immersed in the life of the "others." What remains is a characterization of auto/ethnography—illustrated by two examples—as an artistic walk along boundaries made up by dialectic connections and paradoxical twists and turns.

Roots of Meanings

One approach to understanding the meaning of terms is to look at the roots of the words themselves, their etymology. As a native German speaker I decided to look at the German roots of *being home* versus *being away* as the facets of their emotional meanings are more familiar to me (Braun et al., 1993; Kluge, 1995).

The German language has two words for home: *Heim* and *Heimat*. The roots of both words are found in Old and Middle High German, Old English, Nordic, Irish, and Russian. These roots point to a meaning that encompasses the material residence (like one's farm, or the village), the material means to make a living such as farmland, as well as the social environment of family and significant people. The word *Heimat* has roots in the Indo-Germanic word for residing but also hints at meanings of wasteland, poverty, and treasure. *Heimat* consequently has at its poles the rather awful prospect of living in a desert of the familiar, the same; at the other extreme it is a jewel, a gem, something special and very dear and precious to you.

Digging for the roots of its antonym "foreign" holds yet another surprise. The German word for foreign or strange is *fremd*, an adjective formed out of the roots of "away from" and "forward." In its current usage *fremd* means "coming from abroad, not from home, not belonging, unknown." However, the roots of the term also hint at meanings of being brave, strong, and competent. There is an aspect to the person coming from far away or leaving for the far away, or the object originating in the foreign, that is considered brave, strong, and competent. However, hostile reactions to the foreign are not to be found at its roots.

The Cultural Psychological Meanings of Home And Away

In his "Skizze zur Psychologie des Heimwehs," Ernst E. Boesch (1991) looks at childhood as the foundation of *Heimat*. It is most obvious in childhood how interrelated being home and being away are. The child who can return to a safe haven after each step forward can explore the unknown. Crawling on the floor of the family room a baby will frequently turn around to make sure her caretaker is still in sight before crawling around the couch, the chair, or even out of the room. The frightened child, however, will cling to her caretaker and stick to the familiar, unable to further her development (Ainsworth, 1979; Boesch, 1991).

What makes *Heimat* so special is that it provides the primary experience. We are exploring for the first time. And it is so special because the processes of exploration happen simultaneously: we are exploring our physical environment, our selves, and our identifications. No other explorations later in life are equally simultaneous and primary.

Heimat provides the original template that allows for orientation and communication in our mother tongue. This template is crucial in a double sense. First, it allows us to anticipate. When we perceive others we can *read* their faces, their gestures, and their tone of voice in a way that allows projections into the future because we can rely on a long history of experiences.

> As an immigrant to the United States I become aware of this most painfully in moments of crisis. The tone of voice, the mimic of a speaker, and the deep emotional meaning and historical roots the words of another language convey are not, or are barely or only partly accessible to those not native. Listening to the news after September 11, 2001, I found myself missing the familiarity of German radio and TV broadcasts. Not that they convey the golden path to wisdom but their native familiarity to me provides a sense of basic orientation in a moment of utter confusion. Shortly after the terror attacks I gave a talk about this very same topic of home and away. Afterwards a woman in her late fifties approached me. She had left her Canadian Heimat thirty-five years ago. She explained to me that she never felt an urge to go back but at the first awareness of the attacks she sensed an immediate longing to be back in her hometown.

Secondly, from childhood on we make use of the original template provided by *Heimat* by conjuring up fictional worlds of a better home using the stories, fairy tales and movies we encounter while growing up.

Heimat therefore provides security by enabling us to develop an *inner compass* (Amery, 1980) that we rely on unconsciously in every second of our life—unconsciously as long as we are at home. *Heimat* becomes significant only when leaving (Rauschenbach, 2001). Consequently, *Heimat* dialectically links our past and our future (Boesch, 1991); being home dialectically refers to being away.

In his sketch of homesickness Ernst E. Boesch (1991) goes on to explain that compared to home the foreign is merely an area of projection because the foreign lacks the inner template home provides. The foreign is amorphous and unstructured. It does not allow for anticipation because we cannot read it, cannot interpret what is possible or impossible, attractive or repulsive. We lack the history of personal and cultural experiences. This lack of transparency holds potential for both euphoria and frustration. By immersing ourselves in another culture, we can expand our selves and our identifications by exploring the foreign just like a child explores its new environment. Discovering the unknown environment and unknown parts of our selves makes us feel empowered, empowered by expanding our potential and reinventing ourselves. We can do all this because away from home we get labeled as outsiders. Outsiders can be eccentric. They are even supposed to be eccentric. That way outsiders can be romanticized by the natives or treated with hostility as foreigners.[1]

> I remember my first time at West Beach up in Beverly where I live. I changed from my bathing suit to my normal clothes after swimming by loosely wrapping a towel around my body. A woman on this beach approached me: You must be from Europe, she said. No one on the beach dares to change clothes your way. She and other teachers in culturally correct behavior were amused at the behavior I displayed here and in other situations. And I felt relaxed about those "mistakes." After all, how could I have known? I felt the freedom granted only to fools.

However, the euphoric phase is followed by frustrations. Gerda Lerner (1997, p. 35, 38), an émigré from Nazi Austria describes: "Living in translation and lacking both an adequate vocabulary and the sense for the rhythm of the language, it was as though my adult knowledge had to be transposed into the vocabulary of a six-year-old. . . . To come . . . to the imbecile stammerings of an immigrant American was a fall." And this is just one of many ways of "falling" when abroad.[2]

In my childhood, girls in Germany, third graders mostly, loved to keep a *Poesiealbum*, a poetry album. You asked your friends to write a favorite poem, quotation, or proverb on a page of your album. I found the following in mine and remember it had been one of the most popular ones (e.g., Rauschenbach, 2001, p. 230):

Never forget home where your cradle stands,
You'll never find a second home in the foreign lands.

This wisdom threatens the one who dares to leave that her inner compass will fail to serve her away from home. The wisdom also hints at something all cultures do: they tend to dichotomize the world into a *here* and *there, we* and *they, the civilized* and *the savage*.

Just like the dialectic of home versus away there is the dialectic of nationalism versus the foreign. Connotations of a nation include the incarnate belonging, to a place and its people, to a heritage, to a community. Nations provide a "quasi-religious text" not only about their historical and geographical landmarks but also about their official enemies and heroes (Said, 2000). Nationalism, again, dialectically refers to imperialism. Ever since humans have written history there has been the effort to conquer the foreign and incorporate it into the familiar on all levels of being. It remains to be seen what the future brings both for the idea of nations as well as for the idea of *Heimat*. Tommy Dahlen (2000) ventured some thoughts on the substitution of nations by corporate identities. Jean Amery (1980) predicts a future of objects without history, foreseeing the replacement of the individual calendar and address book by the universal palm pilot. And Brigitte Rauschenbach (2001) elaborates on borders open only for the inhabitants to leave and return not for the intruders to stay. *Heimat,* she predicts, will be substituted by "non-places."

Between the *here* and *there*, the *we* and *they*, the gap of not belonging opens up to the outsider. There are various ways of reacting to this not-belonging. On an individual level we might try to cope with feelings of resentment at those who are at home. The literary critic Edward Said (2000) points at yet another coping strategy. Immigrants, he finds, often create their own world to rule. They become novelists, chess players, or political activists. On the cultural level one can often observe the first generation of immigrants attempting to create an imitation of *Heimat* with familiar shops, restaurants, houses, and organizations. "In New York City's Washington Heights they created a small Mittel-Europa of familiar shops, coffee houses and organizations. Their cynical stance towards the USA gave them a sense of continuity" (Lerner, 1997, p. 39).

However, leaving not only turns me into an outsider in the new culture, I also become an outsider at home. My leaving disturbs the order of the divide into a *here* and a *there*. Those who stay at home identify me as belonging to their *we*, whereas I offend them by preferring the company of a *they*. The ones staying react with suppressed dissatisfaction and envy that springs from the conscious or subconscious knowledge that home is not perfect, limiting or even existentially threatening (Boesch, 1991). Why is that? I think it is because every person feels the gap between her factual and her fictional home, between the wasteland of the familiar and the treasure of the "promised land." And by leaving I point my finger at that gap for all those who stay behind. Auto/biographical accounts of émigrés, refugees, and expatriates give multiple witness to the difficulties of those left behind (e.g., Fremont, 1999; Reich-Ranicki, 2000). However, cultures are inventive in their ways of coping with this dissatisfaction and envy. They invent farewell rituals like presents and the promises of frequent contact via letters and phone calls.[3]

Fernweh and *Heimweh*

The dialectics of home and away, of nationalism and the foreign, and of insider and outsider become even more apparent when looking at the feelings that emerge when home gets too close and when home is too far away. While hinting in opposite directions of their longing, both feelings are captured in two German words that share the same noun: *Fernweh* and *Heimweh*.

Weh means a cry of pain, of fright, or of surprise at which roots are rage, anger and sadness (Braun, 1993; Kluge, 1995). And while *Heimweh* easily translates into homesickness, I am at a loss when it comes to the term *Fernweh*. The English *wanderlust* expresses the longing to leave but it emphasizes the tourist's longing for a week or two of adventure. The German meaning, however, entails a horizon narrowing down on me to a point where home becomes suffocating and almost wanders off. We leave the desert of the familiar. Consequently, I meet the new environment with enthusiasm, experience the widening of our horizon as empowering, and explore aspects of my identity that were buried at home. I fall in love at first sight. However, stuck in the foreign land for some time, the wasteland I left turns into a jewel in my memory, the treasure of the familiar, the compass of our feeling, thinking and acting. I get struck with homesickness, the cry of pain for what we left at home.

How could this happen to me? How could my euphoria change so rapidly into misery?

In what follows, I will walk along part of the way with Brigitte Rauschenbach's exploration of homesickness (2001) as it leads to the central paradox that will open up questions for auto/ethnographic accounts.

Rauschenbach (2001) explains the meaning of homesickness by referring to Freud's understanding of two phenomena: *mourning* and *melancholia*. The loss of a significant relationship, whether that be a person or an abstraction like homeland, means that all invested energy is now homeless, producing pain in the bereaved person, followed by an intense longing to continue the relationship, prolonging it even if only in fantasy. A major loss of interest in the world and in other people is the consequence.

Reality-testing has shown that the loved object no longer exists, and it proceeds to demand that all libido shall be withdrawn from its attachments to that object. This demand arouses understandable opposition—it is a matter of general observation that people never willingly abandon a libidinal position, not even, indeed when a substitute is already beckoning to them. This opposition can be so intense that turning away from reality takes place and a clinging to the object through [hallucinating it]. Normally, respect for reality gains the day. Nevertheless its orders cannot be obeyed at once. They are carried out bit by bit at great expense of time and psychic energy, and in the meantime the existence of the lost object is psychologically prolonged. . . . When the work of mourning is completed the ego becomes free and uninhibited again. (Freud, 1917, p. 237)[4]

While the mourning person experiences an impoverished and empty world, the melancholic person experiences an impoverished and empty "I," not knowing what makes her sad. Therefore she cannot mourn because the loss is accompanied by a major disappointment that can have anger or even hatred at its roots. The melancholic holds on to parts of her early childhood identifications that she secretly blames. Melancholia turns into self-destructive hate that is meant to target someone or something else.

Rauschenbach (2001) concludes that homesickness is a combination of Freud's understanding of mourning and melancholia. *Heimweh* has at its roots an accusation against home: It does not provide a living be that in the material, social or ideological sense. Consequently, I am forced to search for a future abroad. However, abroad I rely on an inner compass that my home provided me with. Homesickness, then, replaces the original meaning of home with a nostalgic longing which covers up my home's failure to provide the help and security I need in order to explore and find stability in the unknown environment (Amery, 1980).

> When I left Germany I felt frustrated. To me, this Germany seemed narrow-minded and inflexible. They still refuse to use the Internet, I thought, they cling to a job market of professions that have been invented a century ago, and devoutly believe in authority and hierarchy. However, from this distance that Germany had put on a new face. I found myself glossing over the cracks. I found myself praising the Germans' skepticism towards each and every technological invention, praising their recycling of each and every bottle, plastic or tin can, every shred of paper. Looking back, Germany's ways seemed glorious to me.

At the center of homesickness lies a paradox (Rauschenbach, 2001): *Homesickness is the nostalgic longing for a home that symbolizes the happiness that home could no longer provide.* The underlying anxiety and rage become apparent when the homesick person blames the hosting culture for the various ways in which it does not provide the security the inner compass guaranteed at home.

> When bound by anxiety and confusion at my inner compass not working for me in the United States, I would tear apart what I found was wrong with "the others." I would rant: Americans are stupid. They don't manage

to look beyond the rim of their dinner plates and have no idea what deep friendship really means.

Paradoxes, I believe, are the most fruitful states of mind. The paradox of homesickness leads me to the central question relevant to every person who crosses borders, relevant to every person engaging in ethnography:

- What causes my *Fernweh*? What causes my *Heimweh*?
- What were the hopes with which I left? What were the disappointments with home that made me leave?
- And where does my inner compass fail to guide me in my new environment?

I can give a glimpse at my disappointments that I became aware of long after the fact of their occurrence.

First, there were my disappointments with my career. In Germany the academic system demands that—after finishing your Ph.D.—you have to work on another thesis called *Habilitation* that takes another five to seven years to complete. Germany is one of very few countries in the world that clings to this ritual of obedience and control. It led me to blame not only the German academic system but also social science in general for my feelings of being stuck in my career. Away, in the United States, the horizon seemed open and wide. The land of possibilities would be mine. I would reinvent myself. However, when my euphoria evaporated in the distance of my ever so widened horizon in my second home country, after having played with the idea of starting various other careers I realized that what I had hated in Germany was the system of academia, not social science itself, which indeed had become so much part of my identity that I decided to practice it the way I believe is reasonable.

Second, as the daughter of the World War II generation there were the numb, amorphous and undefined feelings of shame and guilt about my country. I wanted to leave those behind, at home, tucked away in the basements and attics of friends who politely offered their storage room for the things I did not want to bring to the US right away. But instead of succeeding in running away from my numb, amorphous and undefined guilt and shame, I found it vibrant, tangible and very conceivable here in the United States. I saw Americans proudly presenting their national flag at the entrance to their houses—back in Germany I had observed right wing nationalists or Neo-Nazis using the German flag (see Proud German?, 2001). I saw at the bottom of my mother-in-law's eyes the pain that was still alive at the loss of her brother who flew a bomber over North Africa and was shot down by Germans. And I marveled at the fact that my brother-in-law proudly displayed his father's WWII-military medals in the hallway of his house. My late father-in-law had fought for the winners.

Suddenly stories popped up in my mind I had had no access to while living at home (see Alsop, 2005).[5] I will give an example of one of those stories later on. Let me put it into the words one of my students used: "I became Japanese, she said, after I left my country to relocate in the US."

What I wish to convey with these examples: No matter how strong my *Fernweh*, *Heimat* is in my storage. I cannot leave it back home. No matter how far I venture out, my inner compass travels with me and I experience its constant change. Every person who leaves undergoes these processes. Ethnographers involved in exploring and relating cultures can make use of them systematically.

Central Auto/Ethnographic Questions and Journeys Back Home

My first example of how ethnographers can make use of these processes is the analogy of training a psychotherapist. To the best of my knowledge all approved and scientifically respected methods of psychotherapy demand that a therapist explore every angle of her own mind by undergoing a therapy herself (The Boston Psychoanalytic Bulletin, n.d.). The idea is that the therapist has to explore her own secret wishes and fantasies, her anxieties and angers, her joys and delights to support others in exploring theirs. After all, how can she help her clients to make peace with themselves, and with their strengths and shortcomings, if she herself does not take a close look at her own? In this case it seems so obvious that therapists need to engage in self-reflexivity. Transferring this self-reflexivity to the level of culture, we—who study other cultures—should explore our home, the wishes and fantasies it provides us with, the anxieties and angers it causes, the joys and delights of our everyday lives, the gaps between our factual and our fictional homes.

Another reason to engage in self-reflexivity becomes obvious when looking at the history of anthropology. Anthropology started as a colonial undertaking. We Euro-Americans examined people in the world to determine their place in the hierarchy of *our* value systems. There is much evidence that when we colonialists went away without reflecting on what we left, we measured the unknown against our own inner compass. And when that inner compass did work the others failed, not we. When the Aborigines of Australia failed the psychologists' so called culture-free intelligence test, we thought we had proof that they were just not as smart as we were (Cole, 1996). And when we found the Ilongots of the Philippines clinging to their ritual of head hunting when one of their loved ones died, we thought we had proof of their savage state of mind (Rosaldo, 1989/1993). It was the atrocities and mass migrations of two world wars that made it difficult for us to simply blame the others. We had to look inward. It was also the critical voices of feminists who pointed at the power hierarchies in our own homes that caused abuse, alienation and exploitation between and among the sexes (see Behar & Gordon, 1995; Nash, 1997). And, there were the voices of those we judged. They suddenly faced us as experts of their own in-digenous cultures, the ones we had put at the bottom of the totem pole (Behar, 1996; Smith, 1999).

All this and more caused a major crisis in anthropology and the social sci-ences in general. One way out is the striving for self-reflexivity. That self-reflexivity can take various forms and shapes such as asking ourselves about our frame of mind, about our power position in the network of cultures, about the ways in which we produce knowledge, and about our notion of center and pe-riphery (Alsop, 2001; Bourdieu, 1990; Staeuble, 1996). One possible way to practice self-reflexivity is auto/ethnography.

Auto/ethnography can be defined as:

an auto/biographical genre of writing and research that displays multiple layers of con-sciousness, connecting the personal to the cultural. Back and forth auto/ethnographic gaze, first through an ethnographic wide-angle lens, focusing outward on social and cul-tural aspects of their personal experience; then, they look inward, exposing a vulnerable self that is moved by and may move through, refract and resist cultural interpretations. . . . As they zoom backward and forward, inward and outward, distinctions between the per-sonal and cultural become blurred, sometimes beyond distinct recognition. (Ellis & Bochner, 2000, p. 739)

But instead of further defining this genre in the abstract I will give two ex-amples of auto/ethnographic works.[6]

My first example of what can be found looking back home, is the work of the literary critic Svetlana Boym (1996). She left Russia, her home country, some ten years ago as a political émigré and returned to better understand the home she left. In her article on *Unsettling Homecoming* she describes a particu-lar event that took place when she was a child and her parents hosted foreigners for the first time. The family lived in a so-called communal apartment. Their neighbors, to whom she refers as *Aunt Vera* and *Uncle Fedia*, were home.

"Uncle Fedia," she remembers, "usually came home drunk, and, if Aunt Vera refused to let him in, he would crash right in the middle of the long corridor . . . obstructing the entrance to" her family's apartment. On this particular night "we were all in the living room listening to music, to tone down the communal noises, and my mother was telling our foreign guests about the beauties of Leningrad. . . . As the conversation rolled along, and the foreign guest was commenting on the riches of the Russian Museum, a little yellow stream slowly made its way through the door of the room. Smelly, embarrassing, intrusive, it formed a little puddle right in front of the dinner table. This scene, with the precarious coziness of a family gathering, both intimate and public, with a mixture of ease and fear in the presence of foreigners and neighbors, remained in my mind as memory of home. (Boym, 1996, p. 264)

She then goes on to work with that memory by transferring it to a metaphor. That metaphor captures a feature of the Soviet's culture unconscious *inner compass*. "If a Soviet cultural unconscious ever existed, it must have been structured as a communal apartment—with flimsy partitions between public and private, control and intoxication" (p. 265). This example shows how taking a look back home helps to understand *Heimat* by having memories crystallize in form of a cultural metaphor.

In my second example I quote a short part of a story I wrote for a book I am working on. This book deals with the relationship between German World War II participants and the Second Generation, and in this case, the relationship between my father and me.

It is one of those days when mother is out singing in the choir—a winter afternoon. Again, I have to sit with my father in the living room and listen. He drinks beer, canned beer. He loves it whenever Mother is out, because she hates cans and only buys him bottled beer. With relish he gathers the empty cans on grandma's embroidered tablecloth until they form a semi-circle around him, his fortress against invading memories. Each time he opens one, he rips off the lid and carefully aims it at the trash can under grandfather's oak desk.

Today it's wartime stories. It is war every time he made me sit and listen. Every beer can, another story. After a while he gets up.

"Shouldn't we go on a walk around the block?" he asks.

This request in disguise means wrapping ourselves in thick winter coats, getting the boots out and, armed with hats and mittens, stepping out into the cold of a snowless, late, dim, almost dark, winter afternoon. A walk around the block means turning right at the Weber's house, going up Magdalenenstrasse, and on to the main street alongside the shops. First, we will have a glance into the jeweler's window, then the post office and, right after that, the pharmacy. Between its window and entrance door hangs the thermometer and the barometer. My father needs these tools to validate his state of health.

"I knew it was way below freezing."

He knocks at the barometer glass.

"No wonder I feel so queasy," my father says.

And on to the hairdresser's shop and past the village pub. Always his hesitation, here. His longing to dare enter. With a slight touch of his elbow, as if it were my temptation from which he had to dissuade me, we move on to the window of the drugstore. We pause. Always his questions.

"Do you need a hair dryer? Or should we get a new heating pad?"

But these questions come later when I am a student in Hamburg visiting my parents. Here I am eleven, young enough to sit through his stories and accompany him on his walk without opposition, curious to learn about my father and ennobled by his demand for my presence, confused, though, by expectations and meanings that exceed my capacity.

About here, as we leave the drugstore behind, the story begins.

Father is a radio operator. He has been drafted into the war right after his third semester at medical school. It is his first war year. He is in Greece with his unit. Compared to his stories about Russia these times seem golden. Enough to eat, alcohol and cigarettes always at hand. And it is warm. I see the chamber under the narrow corrugated iron roof. Military desks, the simple kind, made from steel. It is night. He is on duty, reading the incoming Morse-coded messages, and passing them on to his lieutenant, the urgent ones; he makes a note of the others in the book for incoming messages and hands them over in the morning to the next officer on duty. I see him stepping out into the night to catch a cool breeze and have a cigarette, leaving the office clerk inside. A woman. Is she Greek? I imagine a dark-haired woman in her late twenties with slightly careworn features. At other times I cannot see her at all, or perhaps just her back. The radio equipment chatters. My father steps back inside to find the nameless woman at the radio reading a message, her back turned towards him. She rips the tape off and holds it in her hands. She lets it disappear. Does she burn it? Throw it in the trashcan? How does he tell? I cannot remember. The words weigh heavily; his story is told so hastily and driven by forces over which he is about to lose control. He doesn't want to, but he has to finish the story. It demands its well-deserved ending. Suspicious he is, here, but not yet alarmed. But I must have been. Otherwise I would remember, wouldn't I?

He fishes the tape out of the trashcan, the ashtray, the drawer, in to which she has pushed it in panic. He realizes it is a strategically important order. He raises his eyes, meets hers and immediately recognizes the enemy. The enemy of the German Reich, the war criminal, la femme de resistance. He feels torn. He could finally win respect from the authorities by demonstrating faithfulness. He could become the eternal hero in this woman's life by showing mercy. Both ends seem immensely rewarding. He trembles for seconds. And alerts his lieutenant. I hear the pride in his voice, the pride of the righteous one. And now also and painfully perceptible the alarm, the fear. He is afraid of me, his daughter, the involuntary witness, who, tangled up in shame, longs to make herself invisible, turn the clock back and start all over again so that he does not need to be afraid of me.

We are far beyond Sperlings Pond and onto the alley between the orderly houses of the Schmidts', the Beckers', and the Schneiders', where father and I used to secretly steal each fall, with our plotted gangster glances, some asters off the stems that protrude from between the wired fences. Here, it blurts out of me.

"What happened to the woman?'

"No idea. Probably death sentence. They showed no mercy back then."

They.

Back then.

Silence.

His averted body, the head slightly bent forward under his felt hat. The hat Anne Beyer, my classmate, used to joke about, because he lifts it whenever he encounters one of those well respected members of the community. Those a decade younger than he, the lucky ones, who had been too young to get involved in the bloody business of war. His body posture commands that I forget. And I will forget as eagerly as I will listen at school tomorrow when Miss Polinski will feed us more of the gruesome deeds of those Nazi thugs. My fear of losing his closeness turns me into his willing accomplice in our joint mission to widen the gap between him and history. History is something that happens to others. And, walking through the silence emerging from that gap, we turn back onto Birkenstrasse.

What becomes obvious in Boym's as well as in my memory is yet another dialectic that auto/ethnographers have to tackle. It is the dialectic between the personal and the cultural. That dialectic is the purpose as well as the challenge of our work, a challenge as a language is lacking that captures both levels, the personal and the cultural. Auto/ethnographers who set themselves the task of relating cultures are boundary walkers: they crisscross between the boundaries of being home and away, of being insider and outsider, of being personal and cultural selves. There is nothing more difficult than this back and forth between ways of living, speaking, thinking and feeling. There is nothing more risky than switching between various identities and practices of estrangement. We expose ourselves, we make ourselves vulnerable and we are constantly in danger of remaining on one side of the border:

- Getting personal for the sake of getting personal;
- Sticking to the aloof criteria of being objective; and
- Circling our ego or, at the other extreme, circling the "other" without getting any further.

However, it is at those crossroads, at the bottom of these difficult paradoxes, I believe, that we have a chance at understanding.

Conclusion

Having outlined both the necessity as well as the risks of becoming personal when relating cultures, the question remains: How can this particular form of self-reflexivity—the auto/ethnographic account—be practiced? To answer this question I first have to re-define what it means to practice ethnography. According to Emerson, Fretz, and Shaw (1995) the ethnographer in the field gets to know people and participates in their daily routines while regularly excluding herself to reflect by creating written records of others' lives. This immersion leads to some degree of re-socialization. The ethnographer tries to connect the personal life of the observed with their social context and their culture without ever becoming an insider herself. In a way the ethnographer learns a new language but speaks it with an accent. No matter how fluent she feels, she will never blend in completely (e.g., Roth & Harama, 2000). The others will always hear the accent both in the literal sense of the word and in the metaphorical sense of remaining an outsider, because the connection between the personal and the cultural is constructed and re-constructed. Daily interactions happen against the background of a horizon that only partially overlap with the new one.

The same can be said for the auto/ethnographer, be that the anthropologist who goes native (see Kenny, 2000), the social scientist of any provenance (see the historian Eksteins, 1999), or the auto/biographer (i.e. Chernin, 1983). Presenting our own culture and ourselves with a redefined version of itself changes our language, widens our horizon and makes us an outsider to those we re-visit. We find ourselves re-socialized.

The auto/ethnographer's self-reflexivity comes into play at various levels of complexity:

- on the level of the actual ethnographic fieldwork, be that away or at home;

- in the process of writing, both in order to transform the multi-channeled experience to the linear mode of the written language, as well as to translate from one experiential world to the other; and
- in the process of discovery, in the state of creative uncertainty that is present throughout all phases of the research process.

Emerson et al. (1995) recommend that in the process of ethnographic fieldwork we should take notes, particularly when events run counter to our expectations, when events excite, shock, anger us, or cause feelings of isolation and alienation. It is in those events that our inner compass fails and we are inclined to refer to our original template for meaning and explanation. Consequently it is in those moments that auto/ethnographic work is needed.

> When I first moved to the US, I was not only shocked by the fact that the death penalty is still a legally practiced form of judicial punishment but also by the approval this form of punishment meets at all levels of society. I felt threatened by this cultural practice to a degree that surprised me. It was my look back home, my connecting my personal background with the cultural framework in which I grew up that allowed me to understand the roots of those feelings.

All ethnographic writing transforms the multi-channeled real life experience into the linear form of the written record. Many things happen in the course of this transformation that lend themselves to auto/ethnographic reflection. I focus on the inner censorship and the envisioned audience here. This inner censorship can relate to our real or imagined ideal of the proper scientist incarnate, the one who knows it all and has it all. The categories of the good and the bad, the objective and the subjective, the fact and the fiction—all the categories we acquired over the course of our academic training—come along in various impersonations. And we are engaged in an inner dialogue with them while deleting sentences and denying ourselves certain thoughts while others are celebrated and underlined (see Alsop, 2001). And last but not least there is the invisible audience, a person or a group of people we love and we unconsciously or consciously dedicate our work to. We write for them, we converse with them while writing. Richardson (2001) refers to this form of reflexivity as writing-stories or microprocess writing-stories.

Reflecting on his work as a member of a study panel Shweder (1997) concludes that the central criteria for funding research should be the process of discovery and the creative uncertainty. It is the dormant, the unknown emotional and cognitive structures that are activated in ethnographic fieldwork because of our lack of anticipation, because our inner compass fails us. To unveil these structures is what the auto/ethnographer is striving for. Post-modernism taught us that when researching we are engaging in a continual co-creation of self and social sciences. "Knowing the self and knowing about the subject are inter-twined, partial, historical, local knowledges" (Richardson, 2000, p. 929).

In this chapter I show one way of being self-reflexive: the look back home. The Turkish psychologist Aydan Gulerce (2001, p. 4) puts it this way: Once "the West has gained sufficient self-reflexivity to prevent further patronizing and the rest of the world has gained sufficient self-assertion for emancipation, we can hope for a genuine intercultural interchange."

Notes

An earlier version of this manuscript was published as part of a special issue on subjectivity and reflexivity of *FQS: Forum Qualitative Sozialforschung/ Forum Qualitative Social Research, 3*(3). Available at URL: http://www.qualitative-research.net/fqs-texte/3-02/3-02alsop-e.htm. I am grateful for the constructive criticism of Susanne M. Fest and Cassandra S. Goldwater.
[1] American hotel chains abroad ease the pain this lack of anticipation causes in the tourist or the business person; they take away the feeling of being an outsider by creating an environment identical to the one at home (Heller, 1995).
[2] I am not talking about the temporal challenge of being a tourist but the long-term immersion in other ways of life. Tourism is in fact something dear to Germans—they have the highest rate of tourism in the Western world. The "itch to get away" is something the material prosperity of modern industrialized countries brought along (Rieff, 1994).
[3] There are various reasons to leave home. Said (2000) distinguishes between exiles and refugees on the one hand versus expatriates and émigrés on the other—the latter category having a touch of deliberate choice to it. I exclude the tourist who goes on an adventurous trip for a week or month. This is not what I consider immersion in another culture.
[4] The changes Freud later made to his theory are not relevant in this exploration.
[5] This is a daring hypothesis to pose because who knows, I might have eventually gotten access to those feelings at home as well. After all, it often takes two generations to face the trauma a country has undergone (see the various memoirs by members of the second generation. However, there are also the frequent tales ethnographers tell that when gone, with the distance of borders, countries and oceans between themselves and their home, they see what they had been blind to before (see for example Arts in America, 1998).
[6] For a good overview on the history of auto/ethnography see Reed-Danahay (1997). Another example for an auto/ethnographic approach is Kenny (2000). In a recent article entitled "Power, Anxiety and the Research Process" (Alsop, 2001) I open up yet another way of practicing self-reflexivity. There I describe the various phases of my experience with the research process, concluding that it is crucial to write an auto/ethnography of the research process. You can engage in self-reflexivity by interrelating struggles for power as

academics with struggles with anxiety about not meeting the standards this academic system sets. Approaching the research process in that way one gets a chance at renegotiating the boundaries between the researcher's subjectivity, the academic field and the framework of the society in which one's research takes place.

References

Ainsworth, M.D.S. (1979). Infant-mother attachment. *American Psychologist, 34*, 932–937.

Alsop, C. K. (2001). Power, anxiety and the research process. Reflections on my research experiences in midstream and where to go from here. In C. K. Alsop (Ed.), *Grenzgängerin. Bridges between disciplines. Festschrift für Irmingard Staeuble* (pp. 173–192). Kröningen: Asanger.

Alsop, C. K. (n.d.). *Freight stations.* Unpublished manuscript.

Amery, J. (1980). *At the mind's limits. Contemplations by a survivor on Auschwitz and its realities.* Bloomington: Indiana University Press.

Arts in America (1998, September 8). Bilingual author finds something gained in translation. *The New York Times*, p. B2.

Behar, R. (1996). *The vulnerable observer: Anthropology that breaks your heart.* Boston: Beacon Press.

Behar, R., & Gordon, D. (1995). Out of exile. In R. Behar & D. Gordon (Eds.), *Women writing culture* (pp. 1– 32). Berkeley: University of California Press.

Boesch, E. E. (1991). Skizze zur Psychologie des Heimwehs [Sketch of a psychology of homesickness]. In P. Rueck (Ed.), *Grenzerfahrungen. Schweizer Wissenschaftler, Journalisten und Künstler in Deutschland* (pp. 17–36). Marburg: Basilisken Presse.

Bourdieu, P. (1990). *The logic of practice.* Stanford, CA: Stanford University Press.

Boym, S. (1996). Unsettling homecoming. In M. Garber, R. L. Walkowitz, P. B. Franklin (Eds.), *Fieldwork: Sites in literary and cultural studies* (pp. 262–267). New York: Routledge.

Chernin, K. (1983). *In my mother's house. A daughter's story.* New York: HarperCollins.

Cole, M. (1996). *Cultural psychology: A once and future discipline.* Cambridge, MA: Harvard University Press.

Dahlen, T. (2000, September). *The future of nations.* Talk for the Program for Intercultural Relations at Lesley University.

Eksteins, M. (1999). *Walking since daybreak. A story of Eastern Europe, World War II, and the heart of our century.* Boston: Houghton Miflin.

Ellis, C., & Bochner, A. P. (2000). Auto/ethnography, personal narrative, reflexivity: researcher as subject. In N. K. Denzin & Y. S. Lincoln (Eds.), *Handbook of qualitative research* 2nd ed. (pp. 733–768). Thousand Oaks: Sage.

Emerson, R. M., Fretz, R. I., & Shaw, L. L. (1995). *Writing ethnographic fieldnotes*. Chicago: University of Chicago Press.

Fremont, H. (1999). *After long silence. A memoir*. New York: Delacorte Press.

Freud, S. (1917). *Mourning and melancholia. Vol. 14. The standard edition of the complete psychological works of Sigmund Freud*. London: Hogarth.

Heller, A. (1995). Where are we at home? *Thesis Eleven, 41*, 1–18.

Kenny, L. D. (2000). *Daughters of suburbia. Growing up white, middle class, and female*. New Brunswick, NJ: Rutgers University Press.

Kluge, F. (1995). *Etymologisches Wörterbuch der deutschen Sprache* [Etymological dictionary of the German language]. 23. Erw. Auflage. Berlin: Walter de Gruyter.

Lerner, G. (1997). *Why history matters. Life and thought*. New York: Oxford University Press.

Nash, J. (1997). When Isms become Wasms. Structural functionalism, Marxism, feminism and postmodernism. *Critique of Anthropology, 17*, 11–32.

Proud German? (2001, March 24). *The Economist*, p. 62

Rauschenbach, B. (2001). Heimat im Übergang [Home in transition]. In C. K. Alsop (Ed.), *Grenzgängerin. Bridges between disciplines. Eine Festschrift fuer Irmingard Staeuble* (pp. 229–251). Kröning: Asanger.

Reed-Danahay, D. E. (1997). Introduction. In D. E. Reed-Danahay (Ed.), *Auto/ethnography: Rewriting the self and the social* (pp. 1–17). New York: Berg.

Reich-Ranicki, M. (2000). *Mein Leben*. München: Deutscher Taschenbuch Verlag.

Richardson, L. (2001). Writing. A method of inquiry. In N. K. Denzin & Y.S. Lincoln (Eds.), *Handbook of qualitative research* 2nd ed. (pp. 923–948). Thousand Oaks: Sage.

Rieff, D. (1994). German hatred (of Germans). *Harper's Magazine, 288*, 30–34.

Rosaldo, R. (1989/1993). *Culture and truth. The remaking of social analysis*. Boston, MA: Beacon Press.

Roth, W.-M., & Harama, H. (2000). (Standard) English as second language: tribulations of self. *Journal Curriculum Studies, 6*, 757–775.

Said, E. (2000). *Reflections on exile and other essays*. Cambridge, MA: Harvard University Press.

Shweder, R. A. (1997). The surprise of ethnography. *Ethos, 25*, 152–163.

Smith, L. T. (1999). *Decolonizing methodologies. Research and indigenous peoples*. Dunedin: University of Otago Press.

Staeuble, I. (1996). Emancipation—a failed project? Remarks on the discourse of radical critique. In K. Gergen & C. F. Graumann (Eds.), *Historical dimensions of psychological discourse* (pp. 243–262). New York: Cambridge University Press.

The Boston Psychoanalytic Society and Institute (n.d.). *Bulletin*, p. 12.

VI

Epilogue

21   What Bang for the Buck? Usefulness of Auto/Biography and Auto/Ethnography to Collective Knowledge

Franz Breuer and Wolff-Michael Roth

In this contribution we establish a framework for understanding the contributions to this volume and articulate some of the salient issues concerning auto/-biography and auto/ethnography that arise from the volume as a whole. We are concerned with questions such as "What kinds of experiences come to be articulated in auto/biographical and auto/ethnographical descriptions?" "What relationship do such descriptions have to other social science 'data'?" and "In which way can auto/biographical and auto/ethnographical text become relevant and interesting to social sciences in general?"

History and Philosophy of Science

There is a long tradition in the philosophy of science and scientific methodology of discussing—for the purpose of self-assurance—the acceptability and legitimacy of sense data and their verbal articulation, "elementary descriptions," "primary statements," or "protocol sentences." In the case of verification or falsification, these serve as starting points for or test criteria of scientific hypotheses and theories. For example, the discussion led—in the logical empiricist and critical rationalist discussion of the twentieth century—to the ban of introspectionistic data as the basis of or test for (synthetic) scientific statements.[1] According to Karl Popper, descriptions useful for scientific argumentation take the form of *basic statements*, which are articulations of elementary facts, singular existential statements that describe observable events that do not refer to personal experiences or the perception of individual epistemological subjects. The validity of these basic statements has been ascertained through consensus among critical testers. In the context of this methodological approach, it is acknowledged that the objectivity of descriptions of empirical facts and truth of scientific conjectures cannot ever be achieved. Instead, scientists have to use supplemental criteria. Doubts about the proof power of basic sentences therefore can never be eliminated with any finality. On the other hand, objectivity and truth continue to function as regulative end goals to be achieved.

Behaviorism was seen as the social scientific approach that most corresponded to the criteria of "good" research as exemplified by the natural sciences; behaviorism therefore constituted an ideal type. Although the close and strict behaviorist conception in the social sciences has long been eroded and has had its day—even in mainstream psychology—an understanding of science and scientific method fundamentally marked by traditional conceptions of objectivity and truth continues to exist.

This volume concerned with auto/biography and auto/ethnography presents a radically different approach: fundamental epistemological and methodological convictions about traditional science are violated. Do auto/biographers and auto/ethnographers share anything with *Popperian social scientists*?[2] The differences and gulfs between the two ways of doing (social and behavioral) science appear to be so large that it would take considerable rhetorical power to group the two lines of work into the same category of cognitive/cultural endeavors. Are we dealing with two planets, metaphorically speaking, revolving around the same star but at different distances, inclinations, and so on? Or have auto/biography and auto/ethnography left the gravitational center "science" and are headed for a different planetary system?

In respect to the relationship between the two ways of doing research, one might want to argue that we are dealing with two very different, opposing cognitive genres or types of texts—e.g., science versus humanities, science versus feuilleton, science versus journalism, and science versus poetry/belles-lettres. The associated border politics conducted by the members of the two ways of doing and writing research has a tradition in the newer history of the social sciences, especially concerning qualitative research methods focusing on everyday phenomena.[3] One might also see in the two directions variants of mutually interesting and relevant *ways of worldmaking* in the institutional context of (social) science.[4] In this case, we would be in a position to reflect on the mutual blind spots, sharpness of perception, truth claims and their justifications, or strengths and weaknesses.

The language philosopher Gilbert Ryle (1971) articulated the problem of the behaviorist description of comportment in terms of an analogy of eyelid movements that can be interpreted in widely different ways—involuntary twitching and purposeful winking. He contrasted the behavioristic conception with *thick description*, which became the basis of and reference for Clifford Geertz's (1973) well-known maxim for doing ethnographic research. Behaviorist descriptions of actions miss members' perspectives of meaningful personal and sociocultural contexts in which they act. To the members of a culture, behaviorist descriptions appear as underdetermined, empty, estranged, and foreign.

The idea of a *thick description* takes as its starting point the principle of sense in meaningful actions. It thereby does not make the assumption that there is only one right interpretation of observed behavior.[5] In their use of *thick description*, Ryle and Geertz presuppose manifold and numerous ways of understanding, interpreting, or reading that arise from the different positioning of the same and different observers, all of which may be internally coherent and intelligible. Thick description therefore results in a multiplicity of meanings and interpretations that are or can be interrelated. There is a problem of method: The orientation of social scientific description and analysis in the wake of Ryle and Geertz are convincing to a great number of scientists—but a consistent method about how to construct such a description cannot be extracted from Geertz's text. The creative component of description thereby takes on particular importance. A foundational, heuristic principle exists in the analogy of binocular vision (Bateson, 1980)—different perspectives contain different versions of the world. In this way, a metalevel is constituted, which gives rise to information about differences and therefore information of a different logical type. Metaphorically speaking, this is *depth* information. Some contributions to this volume create depth information by contrasting and sometimes textually juxtaposing different points of view involving different individuals (e.g., Barton/Darkside [Chapter 2], Pereira et al. [Chapter 3], Lee/Roth [Chapter 19]), involving the same individuals who take different lenses to elucidate some phenomenon (e.g., Kraft Alsop [Chapter 20], McGonigal [Chapter 12], Noy [Chapter xx], Osborne [Chapter 10], Roth [Chapters 4, 15], Tobin [Chapter 9]), or mixing impressionistic tales with other forms of data including interviews and surveys (Geelan [Chapter 11]).

Auto/biography and Auto/ethnography as Specific Intellectual Endeavors

There are two characteristics of auto/biography and auto/ethnography that make them both interesting and difficult in the context of the (social) sciences. First, epistemic subject and epistemic object are identical. Scientists take themselves (their experiences, actions, biographies) objects of their research. Their object is not *out there*, but consists decidedly *in* and *of* their own, situated bodies. Research pertains to the personalized, social, cultural, and historical context. Sec-

ond, the modes of thought and representation typical of auto/biography and
auto/ethnography do not correspond to those traditionally used in the sciences.
One can find a rejection with respect to some core ideas of traditional ways of
knowing. In auto/biographic and auto/ethnographic writing, there often are no
attempts to explicitly theorize the epistemic object for the purpose of reaching
generalizable results. Frequently, the interpretive flexibility of texts itself is exploited with the possibility and intent to make a transfer to the readers' lifeworlds possible. The contents and ways in which these are represented frequently violate accepted and dominant forms. Self-disclosure of the researcher,
frequently with respect to private aspects of life and taboos, are taken in the
mainstream scientific community as embarrassing, alarming, revolting, and so
on. Thus, writing about intellectual and personal struggles in school teaching
(e.g., Tobin [Chapter 9] or academic pursuits (e.g., Eisenhart [Chapter 14],
Scantlebury [Chapter 16], Noy [Chapter 18], Lee/Roth [Chapter 19]) rather than
writing narratives of scientific heroism still means exposing oneself as weak. In
the following, we address two main issues—the subject–object relation and the
types of observational language and texts used.

On the Subject–Object Relation

In the social and behavioral sciences, the epistemic subject (researcher) is normally regarded as a source of error and noise, which has to be eliminated or at
least controlled as much as possible. The inclusion of the embodied person—
characterized by emotions, intentions, desires, believes, and so on—in the epistemic act is a taboo in the scientific community. Science has to be a-personal
and transpersonal; researchers have to be invisible, carrying a magic hood, so
that knowledge can be depicted as existing in itself, outside of human bodies.
There are few attempts to recognize the embodied person as an epistemically
fruitful condition for the production of knowledge and even fewer attempts in
realizing this approach in and as research method. Besides systemic approaches
in the context of family, communication, and organizational counseling, the
psychoanalytic tradition has offered an alternative approach to understanding the
subject–object relation (e.g., Breuer [Chapter 5]). The systemic approaches take
into account the interventionist role and function of the person (e.g., therapist,
counselor, or researcher) who approaches a social system (e.g., family) consisting of different actors, interests, and perspectives. The approach is premised on
the notion that information about the system and its structures can be gauged
from the reactions of those who approach. The psychoanalytic and depth-
psychological approach (e.g., Devereux, 1967) focuses on two issues: (a) the effects brought about by the researcher's presence in the field and (b) the effects

that the field and participants bring about at the body of the researcher. The researcher who has learned to read in this sense can use these effects in the same way that psychoanalysts use themselves as sources for understanding the client (object). Auto/biography and auto/ethnography can be considered additional methods for the construction of knowledge through a reflexive and reflective focus on Self.

Auto/biography and auto/ethnography raise the question of the special competencies and qualities that are required for self-observation and self-description. In the training of systemic family therapists, the development of an observational sensibility is emphasized concerning the processes and effects during approaches by, and entanglement in family affairs through, the different protagonists. The training of psychoanalysts generally requires years of analytic experience under supervision; this training focuses on and emphasizes the training of attention and interpretive competence with respect to transference and countertransference. What are, we ask, the competencies required of an auto/-biographically or auto/ethnographically working social scientist? Such researchers cannot merely live, experience, and suffer their mundane, everyday, sociocultural and cultural-historical contexts but must have the competence and willingness to represent, depict, and reflect social life by appropriate (linguistic, pictorial, etc.) means. They have to engage the utter concreteness of mundane everyday life—get their hands dirty, so to speak—and have to fix their experiences on paper (or some other medium) after metaphorically cleaning their hands. This requires (a) a receptive sensibility in the context of psychological, interactive, sociocultural, and cultural-historical determinants of meaning and (b) a specific literary (or other artistic) competence and ambition for the detailed, multileveled, and poignant description and depiction of personally relevant phenomena such as teaching (Osborme [Chapter 10], McGonical [Chapter 12]), writing a dissertation (Noy [Chapter 18]), going to the cemetery (Ellis [Chapter 17], and emigrating (Kraft Alsop [Chapter 20]). It also requires the willingness and ambition to expose oneself (biography, personal experiences, thoughts) to an—in principle—unlimited public and to represent and even reveal oneself. This willingness and ambition is in some respects a precarious characteristic of this form of research, which is worthy of some reflections regarding the personal motivations of, effects on, and consequences for authors in their social contexts.

Auto/biographers and auto/ethnographers are members of two sociocultural lifeworlds or discourses (explicitly articulated in Lee and Roth [Chapter 19]). On the one hand, they are members of everyday contexts, which they describe and reflect in their studies. On the other hand, they are also members in a social

science or community of practice; their reports are primarily written and addressed to this second community. In the context of the auto/ethnography of science (e.g., Eisenhart [Chapter 14], Roth [Chapter 15], Scantlebury [Chapter 16],
Noy [Chapter 18], Lee/Roth [Chapter 19]) the two worlds/contexts coincide:
Their lives *as* researchers and academics are described *for* other researchers and
academics.

This double membership to the domains of epistemic subject and epistemic
object is the really interesting characteristic of auto/biography and auto/ethno-
graphy. It includes personal competencies of the protagonists in two fields and
requires the ability to do two things at once: speaking the languages of the mundane setting and of the scientific discipline. These languages are different even
if the experiences reported are those of research and academia, for the languages
of doing research and going about academe are different from those of talking
and writing *about* these pursuits.[6] Researchers have to be familiar with the ways
of making sense in both mundane setting and scientific discipline, they have developed the different forms of habitus characteristic of the field and that of the
discipline. This double competency opens up opportunities and perspectives be-
cause the auto/ethnographical subject|object is in a better place to understand
and navigate both cultures, is recognized as insider, and less likely is threatened
by the intellectual dominance of science. This double competency also enables
researchers to better understand the limitations and one-sided nature of perceptions and conceptualizations of each, field and discipline. Auto/ethnographers
capitalize on this competence in their writing, for they write from their membership positions in the field, but they make thematic topics, phenomena, approaches, and foci relevant to the targeted audience of scholars. This audience
can be provoked and new ideas may be introduced because the writer can draw
on the multiple discourse worlds productively to criticize, uncover, and counter
received ways of understanding. It is here that we see the heuristic potential of
auto/biography and auto/ethnography as methods for the construction of knowledge in the social and behavioral sciences.

How we deal with multiple membership (also *multiple marginality* [Star,
1991]) and the associated competencies in multiple interpretation and relevance
frameworks is a critical aspect of doing auto/biography or auto/ethnography.
The auto/biographical and auto/ethnographic contributions to this volume tend
toward the social science audience. The general model for the intended reader is
another social scientist. But we need to keep in mind that auto/biography and
auto/ethnography have a critical potential—possibly not yet realized in the presented works. On the one hand, there is the form of auto/biography and auto/-
ethnography, a decidedly subjectivist, centered, and positioned way of represent-

ing and writing—very much implementing the call of critical sociologists, feminists, and Marxist scholars for subject-centered sciences (e.g., Harding, 1987; Smith, 1990). Critical psychologists aim at bringing about a *Subjektwissenschaft*, science from the perspective of the subject (Holzkamp, 1991). This way of proceeding constitutes an intended disruption of the habitual practices of mainstream science. Sometimes this leads to social problems for authors with respect to acceptance, recognition, and career opportunities in their respective scientific communities.[7]

On the other hand, auto/biographical and auto/ethnographical texts foreground particular topics, aspects, and characteristics of social life—for example, when authors articulate that they are not or insufficiently recognized in the attendant scholarly debates. Consequently, the authors of auto/biographical and auto/ethnographical texts frequently are decidedly critical with respect to their discipline or the issue at hand (e.g., contributions to Section IV, *Writing Institutional Critique*). The authors frequently pursue a strategy of *critical heuristics*, eye opening, and bringing to light of new, interesting, and unusual perspectives. Simultaneously, such presentations foreground not core (central) membership but marginality in the scientific community. Neither margin nor center ought to be privileged, but a new position may combine the two into a dialectical approach where central and marginal participation are in continuous interplay and inherently inseparable (Roth, Hwang, Lee, & Goulart, 2005).

Of Observation Sentences and Types of Text

Epistemologists and historians of sciences frequently distinguish empirical languages consisting of observation sentences, on the one hand, and observation categoricals or theoretical languages, on the other (e.g., Quine, 1995). In this respect, auto/biography and auto/ethnography normally use the former language, though researchers drawing on these genres rarely discuss the problem of theory-laden character of observation. Such texts mostly strive to document events and experiences. Characteristically, the texts therefore constitute observation sentences close to the actual events, that is, as seen by the members of the culture. A second type of sentence construction concerns the justification of method and self-assurance. In fact, the opposition to auto/biography and auto/ethnography appears to precipitate the need for justification and self-assurance. Questions such as "Is this still science?" and "What else could it be?" are repeatedly articulated and discussed. This is especially the case when authors address themselves to audiences that have allegiances to more traditional forms of scholarship and are unfamiliar with their different ways of writing and thinking.

Observation categoricals constitute a third sentence type. These are object-related statements that classify and explicate claiming generalizability and articulating theoretical frameworks said to be supported by the narratives. This sentence type is constitutive of conventional scientific texts, where specific phenomena are subsumed under general constructs and theories. Such sentences are the ideal product of scientific research. In auto/biographic and auto/ethnographic texts, such sentences are found with varied frequency. There are texts devoid of such sentences (e.g., Ellis [Chapter 17]). In other texts, this domain is more articulated, elaborated, and explicated—for example, juxtaposing different types of sentences and texts (see Roth [Chapter 4, 7, 15]). Observation categoricals obviously are not the necessary and inevitable goal for the authors of auto/biographical and auto/ethnographical works. We have to ask, however, on which grounds any generalizations can be made in such works. In this respect, we consider the following aspects as interesting, relevant, and worthy to be problematized.

First, auto/biography and auto/ethnography differ from other empirical social sciences in the way they configure the idea of generalizability. In most sciences, efforts are made to construct synthetic statements that are valid not merely for a particular case but in fact for a range of cases. Auto/biographical and auto/ethnographical authors generally are little interested in such statements. They are more interested in empathy and solidarity, which allow the reader to re-live or vicariously experience perceptions, sensations, or feelings. It is in the act of *recognizing* perceptions, sensations, and feelings that the reader accomplishes an act of generalization—the original experience has been reproduced in another person so that the description is valid for more than the original case. This form of generalization has to be distinguished from attempts to elicit the reproduction of explanatory schemes offered in the text on the part of the reader.

Second, in conventional (social) science texts about research, observed phenomena (data) are related to specific theoretical constructs often claiming to be independent of and unequivocal in this ordering. Authors are required to specify the sense in which constructs and statements are used—disregarding that rigorously pursued, such an agenda leads to an infinite regress. The control over the interpretation of the text always lies with the author; the reader has no interpretive room to maneuver. The claim is constitutive of the conventional idea of science, but is ridden with theoretical and methodological problems. In auto/biographical and auto/ethnographical texts, little effort is devoted to the explicit ordering of events in terms of categories and concepts. The depicted phenomena remain semantically underdetermined and interpretively flexible; readers are asked to make sense on their own by relating the descriptions to their personal experiences and lifeworlds.

Third, auto/biographical and auto/ethnographical texts offer possibilities to identify or empathize. This places researchers in the vicinity of literary authors. The texts are characterized by interpretive flexibility, which allows different readers in different eras to (legitimately) read them in different ways—in fact, interpretive richness is sometimes considered to constitute the relevant quality criterion. Here, then, scholars in literary studies may feel at home. However, hermeneutics, the foundational practice in literary studies, also suggests that there are limits to the possibility of reaching an endpoint in the determination of a definitive interpretation for a work—it can never be reached.

Fourth, the idea of interpretive flexibility is foreign to the forms of conventionally practiced scholarship. Auto/biographical and auto/ethnographical texts constitute outsider or outlaw genres (e.g., Nichols/Tippins [Chapter 13]). From a pragmatic point of view, one has to ask where such texts can be published. On the one hand, there are ever-new outlets created for the purpose of building new communities of scholarly practice, thereby becoming a critical element within the social sciences. On the other hand, these new outlets open up the possibilities for reaching beyond the scholarly disciplines toward new audiences that exceed any discipline and even academe.

Let us, for the moment, pursue this idea as a thought experiment. Written productions that have an open structure similar to auto/biographical and auto/-ethnographical texts already exist. We mentioned the belletrist variants (literary autobiographies, memoirs, studies of the social milieu). These are cultural forms that academics like to be associated with. However, to be successful in these genres, one has to submit to the quality measures of literary esthetic productions. Does current scholarship in auto/biography and auto/ethnography stand up to these measures? Or, in other words, are publishers interested in taking on such works to make them available to wider audiences?

What other forms of text are suitable? We may think, for example, about journalistic productions. This idea is familiar to social scientists especially in the works from the Chicago School. There also exist many variants from confessions to exhibitionist displays in the print and audiovisual media. Such junk productions are also intended to engage others emotionally; and there are other forms of self-therapeutic texts that range from self-reflexive diaries (including blogs) to "bibliotherapy." Where do we draw the boundaries between auto/biography and auto/ethnography as scholarly pursuits and such other genres? Should we draw such boundaries at all? These are open questions that have yet to be made thematic, discussed, and advanced.

Characteristic topics of auto/ethnographic texts include personal experiences with unfamiliar countries and living abroad (Kraft Alsop [Chapter 20]), death and its aftermath (Ellis [Chapter 17], dying, illness, and difficult situations (Pereira et al. [Chapter 3]; Tobin [Chapter 7]; Eisenhart [Chapter 14]; Roth [Chapter 15]; Scantlebury [Chapter 16])—all of which deal in some way with loss, suffering, pain, and hurt. In the mainstream, such topics normally are dealt with cautiously; they are literally kept at a distance, and therefore receive very little consideration, treatment, and explication. What if, for example, auto/ethnographic texts dealt with sexual experiences not only with respect to the negative aspects that one may already find in accounts of abuse and incest but also in its positive forms and practices? Where would be draw the boundaries to pornography? Or would auto/biography and auto/ethnography shy away from these and other topics? To push the issue a little further, what should we think about reports in this genre concerning violence, torture, sadism, or murder? Where do we draw the boundaries that establish some areas as taboo? How do we justify such boundaries?

To summarize, our reflections bring out that besides constituting a positive heuristic for research in the social and behavioral sciences, there are potential problems and dangers that come with auto/biography and auto/ethnography as methods and genres. Engaging in these forms of scholarship means walking the tightrope between intellectual textual genres, forms of argument, self-presentations, and ethicomoral considerations—an experimental praxis that some scholars will find inappropriate and that are unsuited for some topics.

Positioned (Situated) Writing: From the Margins?

Michael: In drafting our email conversations preceding the writing of this final chapter, you pointed out that the authors of auto/biographies and auto/-ethnographies coming from social sciences frequently took a marginal position in their community. In a sense, they were writing from the margins. From my perspective, however, margin and center are dialectically related. Even the writing done from the margins has its center (authors, readers). The real question appears to be one of whose narratives and depictions of social life not only make it into the scholarly literature but also have repercussions in and to social life more generally. As soon as politicians, business people, and others pick up these narratives, their actions, conform to the narratives, and then reify the existence of the phenomena described.

Franz: The sentences "I am in the center" or "I am on the periphery" always are ways of worldmaking; they only constitute descriptions within a frame of reference, which I contribute to constituting. This frame may change as human agents change their foci and enact new constructions. This idea is especially liberating in those instances when I feel to be near the margins of the social—whatever context this might be. This is true also for the social sciences and its disciplinary communities of practice, where there are changes in points of view, margin and center. When I change, for example, the frame from social science to the politics of research, a gap may rapidly develop within these relations. In this sense, I agree with you. Nevertheless, I believe that the discourse of margin and center makes sense in our context. Thus, the actors in the margins are better positioned to question the unquestioningly accepted and unreflected aspects within the worldviews of the central actors and to show their constructed nature or how these worldviews can be reconstructed.

Michael: I therefore think that if a person like Ken Tobin (Chapter 9) writes about his failures to enact successful teaching despite his extensive career as a teacher and teacher educator, there is a lot of potential for mainstream members to become aware of the precariousness of their own points of view.

Franz: The marginal nature of auto/biographical and auto/ethnographical scholars inherently contains possibilities for taking a critical and innovative gaze at the ghosts and practices that characterize the various centers of the social sciences. In this sense—viewed epistemologically—there is an advantage to be situated in the margins.

Michael: At the same time, margins have their own centers—I am thinking about how auto/ethnographers rally around and ground themselves in Carolyn Ellis' work—with their own politics of inclusion and exclusion. It is for this reason that we recently conceptualized of a margin|center dialectic, so that all advantages of a particular positioning also come with disadvantages and constraints that characterize all other positions.

Franz: So this positioning has aspects and consequences for the researcher, including material, social, and psychological.

Michael: It may also have consequences for the institutions within which researchers operate. I am thinking, for example, about the repercussions the initial publication of my critique of the processes at work in the main Canadian funding agency for social scientists (Chapter 15). Someone within the agency found and circulated it, which led to a lot of upset managers and directors. However, my informants told me that once the initial emotional upheaval had settled, the agency as a whole, in and through the action of individual managers and program directors, began to organize discussions ultimately leading to changes in the program. Here, then, my writing, though some may judge it to be whining and marginal, became a mediating element in the changes of the agency.

Franz: In this situation, everything turned out well and you have had a nice effect in this move, which was not without risk for you. Tentatively I would describe it like this. You have a certain level of self-reflexive ability and courageous personal willingness to step outside the centered perspective of the Canadian research world, outside the perceptual schema of the review committee and into a decentered position and to make salient the schema and practices of the actors involved. You were able to go back and forth between the different position of the observer and participant; and finally, you have had the opportunity to make all of this available to the community of social scientists. You did this from your social position in the center (as important, central member of the scientific community, the peer review system, etc.): only in this way did you have access to the information that you used in your description and analysis.

Michael: And in this way, your own analysis is consistent with my earlier point about the margin|center dialectic: One has to be positioned central and marginal at the same time to have access to relevant information and to be able to critique it and the system from which it issues. It is out of such experiences that I have come to think of participation in terms of a margin|center dialectic.

Franz: I agree, but want to add that in a certain sense you risked *writing* to *the margins*: Your community of peer reviewers and the disciplinary hard core could have banned you, because you violated and laid bare a behavioral code—and there possibly were some individuals in the system who might have aspired to such a ban. You violated the rules in a both courageous and very calculated way. You were able to do this, because you are a core member in the context that you describe in the auto/ethnography of the incident. That there was a positive resonance or outcome in the Canadian research community has to be attributed to the fact that you are from the center of the community. If you truly had written *from* the margins, few probably would have cared. Center and margin, inside and outside—your text is a nice example—can be set into play to a certain extent as the voluntary (intellectual) movement of a person. The contribution by Christiane Kraft Alsop (Chapter 20) also is a nice example of the movement between center and margin, which provides us access to a theoretical depth about *Heimat* (where you feel at home) and *Fremde* (abroad).

Michael: Positioned/situated writing constitutes a resource for others to take notice of forms of experience that they inherently find intelligible and even can empathize with, but that they had been unaware of. In this, however, lies the very nature of positioned writing—it can be heard as accusing and being critical. It not only accuses and is critical of the fact that other forms of experience are not taken into account but also blames the other for not knowing about the possibility of experiences different from their own. It is in this way that I read much of the feminist critique—it alerted us not only of the fact that women's forms of experience did not enter science, political life, or business, but also that male-centered language did not have the conceptual tools for the acknowledgement of women's forms of experiences. The contributions by Angie Barton and Darkside [Chapter 2], Alberto Rodriguez [Chapter 6], and Kate Scantlebury [Chapter 16] all speak to this dimension.

Franz: I fully agree with you. This is what we earlier called the critical and innovative potential of auto/biography and auto/ethnography in the context of the standard science (in the center): they constitute ways of uncovering, seeing, and articulating phenomena that are normally excluded in the tunnel vision of social science in its center. The enrichment and diversification of ways of seeing and perspectives leads to depth information in the way Bateson described it.

Michael: Reading stereoscopically rather than with double vision is an art that few of us have yet to culture. Therefore, multiple perspectives often irritate both in their multiplicity and in the particulars of one or the other part.

Franz: I agree, and I want to add that there are in fact a number of means and processes to irritate and challenge standard ways of seeing and to bring about new ways: something between art and social science. Bertolt Brecht, for example, once developed the effect of estrangement, which helps looking at social and societal conditions in new ways through the (unpsychological) art of drama. I find it interesting, too, the idea of the dialectical subject|object orientation of knowing. With an enrichment and diversification of ways of seeing I obtain a more profound understanding of the object, on the one hand, and more knowledge about the person/position/situation of the subject(s), on the other hand. Knowledge then is advanced by a contrast of perspectives because there is always the possibility to read the act of knowing in two directions: information about non only the known object but also the knowing subject.

Forms and Limits of Representation

Michael: The contributors to this volume not only have written from the positioned perspective of the auto/biographer or auto/ethnographer, but also engage in new and different ways of *writing the social*.[8] There are possibilities
and opportunities that come with writing differently—w/ri(gh)ting as I
called it elsewhere[9]—but, as I experience every time I finish a piece, there
is also a sense of frustration that I have not truly transgressed the possibilities of expression.

Franz: I also think that the traditional and conventional forms and principles of
re/presenting, the writing of texts (prototypically the genre of the scientific
report) deserve and even merit being violated. In anthropology and ethnology there have been many attempts to innovate, generally discussed under
the heading of the *crisis of representation*.[10] I think that it is necessary and
useful in the qualitative social sciences to creatively experiment with forms
and media of representation. I consider it interesting and meaningful to
learn and borrow from other cultural domains that do not belong to the social sciences in the classical sense, such as literature and (fine) arts. I also
believe that we can learn from literature theory and its discussions of
auto/biography as genre[11] or in historiographic studies concerning the characteristics of personal documents.[12]

Michael: We also have to consider here that the book and journal formats limit
how we can express ourselves, and therefore what aspects of our life experiences can be expressed. To me, this is a one-sided approach just as it
would be one-sided (and even foolish) for a physicist to claim that "everything is wave" or "everything is particle" while talking about light or other
electromagnetic phenomena. In a dialectical approach, the unity of mutually
exclusive forms of expression is presupposed—attempts to reduce a gesture
or photographic image to words will lose exactly the special contributions
to knowing and understanding these other expressive forms contribute.
Traduttore, traditore!

Franz: The institutional pressure on social scientists with career ambitions to
publish in research journals that have high rejection rates does not necessarily encourage new forms of writing and representing. Such mechanisms
lead to conformity rather than to thinking outside the box.

Michael: Nevertheless, perhaps some of us who are more central in the field,
again capitalizing on the margin|center dialectic, ought to lead the way in
experimenting. Much like with any other trend in culture, there will be an
increasing number of individuals who follow, until the new forms of repre-

sentation are as much part of the mainstream as other forms. In this volume, a number of contributions make use of photographs (Ellis [Chapter 17], McGonigal [Chapter 12], Roth [Chapters 1, 4, 7]) in their writing or as a tool in their educational practice (Nichols/Tippins [Chapter 13]). These should be seen neither as additions to the text, nor as more economical forms of representation for things that could have been said with text. We need to learn to see and understand them in the dialectical relation to the surrounding text and caption. This may initially be difficult, because of our (Western) ideology, which Jacques Derrida evocatively—but not iconically—denoted by *phallogocentrism*.[13]

Subjectivity and Intersubjectivity

Michael: In our introduction, we hinted at the fact that introspection was outlawed by mainstream psychology as a legitimate form of inquiry. Sociology, too, took a turn to methods in which the researcher and author was evacuated from the accounts of new knowledge. The particular fear this ousting was to address is the role of the human subject as knower, and the inherent possibility to end up with knowledge that does not generalize across epistemic subjects and epistemic objects. In other words, the fear was that scientists would end up with subjective perspective selling out on the necessarily agreed upon understandings—representations of transcendental knowledge Kant wrote about. In the limit, we would end up with parallel, solipsist views of what the world is like.

Franz: For me, it is an important problem to find a meaningful (middle) way between the different epistemological and methodological extremes. This preference is due both to epistemology and to my "personal psychology." (On a personal level, we can only generalize empathically; unfortunately, I cannot provide more contingent rational arguments.) On the one hand, I consider myself a constructivist and therefore presuppose the foundational importance of the subject-centered conditions for the processes and products of knowing. Neuronal, linguistic, social, cultural, societal, and historical conditions influence, select, and mediate what and how something becomes visible and representable. But I also want to maintain the realistic idea: All of this may well have some correspondence with the world out there. . . .

Michael: Which is what I think materialist dialectics already incorporates. Thus, any object exists twice, according to A. N. Leont'ev, once in material form, once in the way the material is available to consciousness. I cannot but agree with you on this point.

Franz: . . . The other balancing act to be accomplished is this: Even if each act of perception and each experience is highly idiosyncratic, I want to retain the idea of an intersubjective world of knowing that can be shared by people, subjects, and researchers. . . .

Michael: Which I think is the very presupposition of every interaction. The very moment we use language, it presupposes not only a shared tool of communication, but also a shared world aspects of which we make salient to the other person.

Franz: . . . Articulating and rendering more precise the particularities, specifics (and therefore also the accentuation of the differences) appears to me an interesting possibility from the perspective of method and methodology.[14] The central idea of auto/biography and auto/ethnography to get as close as possible to the most personal and individual forms of perceiving and experiencing ultimately is linked to the conviction that other human beings can find themselves in the author's subjective idiosyncratic world.

Michael: A different way of approaching the problem lies in presupposing a subjectivity|intersubjectivity dialectic in the way both Marxist and critical hermeneutic philosophers do it.[15] Those of us critically thinking about everyday conversation come to face this dialectic as a pervasive feature of collective life. Every time a person speaks, he or she presupposes that the (generalized) other not only hears sounds but also that the said is inherently intelligible both in terms of process (how it is said) and content (what is said). All contributions to this volume are grounded in this presupposition— however singular the experienced talked about, however personal the issue, the other would not understand *unless* the said is already grounded in mutual understanding. However varied the different contributions, they all reflect possibilities of experience that exist at a general, cultural-historical level. Even if an individual has not had a particular experience, its possibility is already prefigured in understanding.[16] We may therefore speak of the "*sense* of a given singular work" or the "*singularity* of a given meaningful work"; in either case, we presuppose the self|other and subjectivity|intersubjectivity dialectics. At the very moment I employ my pen to write for the benefit of another, I transgress subjectivity in direction of intersubjectivity, not in the least because I have to use a language that is not mine.[17] Thus, although many authors write about experiences that I have not had, I am able not only understand but also to empathize, inherently re-realizing the generalized possibilities of such experiences at the cultural-historical level. Thus, the experiences of tending graves (Ellis [Chapter 17]), learning to

the experiences of tending graves (Ellis [Chapter 17]), learning to write a narrative dissertation (Noy [Chapter 18]), or teaching first graders (McGonigal [Chapter 12]) and African Americans (Tobin [Chapter 9]) articulated in this volume are expressions of general forms of experience.

Potential Pitfalls

Michael: I remember that as part of your first reaction to some of the contributions your articulated a complaint—you felt that some authors, perhaps me included, sounded too much like (inappropriate) whining about being marginalized.

Franz: I do believe that exactly there lies a problem with some auto/biographical and auto/ethnographical texts. Frequently they are written from the perspective of suffering an unpleasant, unjust, or difficult fate or of becoming a sacrificial lamb. I find this very important, potentially revealing, and innovatively perspectival, with respect to the phenomenology of the experiences and the public articulation of particular forms of experiences. However, especially when the power, interests, secrecy, or maliciousness of others are involved and blamed, I am much more skeptical. In this case, authors may only be involved in the reification of presuppositions regarding good and evil. Such forms of explication appear to be more phenomena *at the author*, which are interesting and relevant in relation to the experiencing fate rather than as relevant and valid scientific proof.

Michael: This is what I address in my own attempts to play the accounts of pain and suffering involved in coping with the rejection, for example, of a grant proposal (e.g., Chapter 15) against a more classical social analysis in terms of a theoretical analysis of the institutional relations in the context I suffer.[18]

Franz: But this does not always remove the problem. Here again we are dealing with the aforementioned issue of the different types and categories of sentences in auto/biography and auto/ethnography: some of these texts do without any (explicit) generalization of the theorized object. When generalization exists, that is, when there are claims about how to explain or explicate a personally experienced and described phenomenon, I find the justifications often weak. Here, we can often find emotional, empathic, personal, and solidary partiality for the described experience and therefore also for the subjectively articulated explanations. In this respect, I think we have to draw the line. And I have the impression that one can still learn a lot in this respect from the method of doing methodological self-critique from the center of the respective social sciences.

Michael: Some of the authors in Part II point out other potential pitfalls that come with auto/biographic and auto/ethnographic writing. Alberto Rodriguez (Chapter 6) articulates the possibilities of reifying ideologies, Joe Kincheloe (Chapter 8) highlights the role auto/biography and auto/ethnography may play in establishing a teacher persona, and my own contribution (Chapter 7) points out the false sense of self that may come to be embodied in the text. In the limit, all contributions point to the potentially deleterious effects of auto/biography to reify a narcissistic, exhibitionistic, schizophrenic, and therefore pathological sense of self—though a lot of boundary work is involved on all sides and by all participants in a group to distinguish the pathological from non-pathological ways of experiencing.

Notes

[1] We are thinking here particularly about the discussion between the Würzburg School of psychology, which used introspection as a way of generating data to access consciousness, and Wilhelm Wundt, who rejected the method as unscientific.

[2] We take this term as a gloss, the content of which would have to be articulated, explicated, and differentiated upon closer inspection of a broad range of social scientists included.

[3] Sociology of the Chicago school and qualitative methods in psychology are but two examples of research approaches that have been subject to the exclusionary politics of the reigning mainstream in the field.

[4] We take *ways of worldmaking* in the sense Nelson Goodman (1978) articulated it in his book of the same name.

[5] The ego- and culturally centered anthropologist in the early years of Western ethnology understood their interpretation in this way (cf. Geertz, 1988).

[6] This difference has been articulated in terms of language as a primary—language as tool *for* doing something—and secondary tool—language as tool to talk *about* doing something (e.g., Wartofsky, 1979).

[7] Such problems were quite evident in the stories new members to a recently established mailing list on auto/ethnography provided as part of their introduction.

[8] Referenced is made to the book of the same name authored by the feminist sociologist Dorothy E. Smith (1999), who, interestingly enough, does not make use of auto/biography or auto/ethnography as a genre in and of itself.

[9] We originally coined the term in an article concerned with the representation of multiple voices, lifeworlds, and perspectives on learning and teaching physics (Roth & McRobbie, 1999).

[10] See, for example, the review of the state of the art by Clifford and Marcus (1986).

[11] See, for example, Marcus (1994).

[12] See, for example, White (1987).

[13] For non-initiates: the term phallogocentrism includes reference to phallus, the male organ, to allude to the male-centered forms of scientific knowledge, and logos, Greek for word. The term, therefore, denotes both the male- and word-centered epistemology of the Western culture.

[14] See also our introduction to the special issue on subjectivity and reflexivity in social science research (Breuer & Roth, 2003).

[15] Among the Marxist philosophers, we note Evald Il'enkov (1977) and Felix Mikhailov (1980); a typical hermeneutic philosopher is Paul Ricœur (1991).

[16] An important part of Heidegger's (1996) *Being and Time* is devoted to this inherent and presupposed intersubjectivity.

[17] This is the central point of *Monolingualism of the Other* (Derrida, 1998). At the very moment that we articulate our innermost being and most personal experience, we already have transgressed subjectivity and use the language of the other.

[18] Other works, for example, deal with the peer review system (Roth, 2002).

References

Bateson, G. (1980). *Mind and nature: A necessary unity.* Toronto: Bantam Books.

Breuer, F. & Roth, W.-M. (2003). Subjectivity and reflexivity in the social sciences: Epistemic windows and methodical consequences. *Forum Qualitative Sozialforschung/Forum: Qualitative Social Research,* 4(2). Available at: http://www.qualitative-research.net/fqs-texte/2-03/2-03intro-3-e.htm

Clifford, J., & Marcus, G. E. (Eds.). (1986). *Writing culture: The poetics and politics of ethnography.* Berkeley: University of California Press.

Derrida, J. (1998). *Monolingualism of the other; or, The prosthesis of origin.* Stanford, CA: Stanford University Press.

Devereux, G. (1967). *From anxiety to method in the behavioral sciences.* The Hague: Mouton.

Geertz, C. (1973). *The interpretation of cultures: Selected essays.* New York: Basic Books.

Geertz, C. (1988). *Works and lives: The anthropologist as author.* Stanford: Stanford University Press.

Goodman, N. (1978). *Ways of worldmaking.* Indianapolis, IN: Hackett.

Harding, S. (Ed.). (1987). *Feminism and methodology: Social science issues.* Bloomington: Indiana University Press.

Heidegger, M. (1996). *Being and time* (J. Stambaugh, Trans.). Albany: State University of New York Press.

Holzkamp, K. (1991). Experience of self and scientific objectivity. In C. W. Tolman & W. Maiers (Eds.), *Critical psychology: Contributions to an historical science of the subject* (pp. 65–80). Cambridge: Cambridge University Press.

Il'enkov, E. (1977). *Dialectical logic: Essays in its history and theory* (H. Campbell Creighton, Trans.). Moscow: Progress.

Marcus, L. (1994). *Auto/biographical discourses: Theory, criticism, practice*. New York: Manchester University Press.

Mikhailov, F. (1980). *The riddle of self*. Moscow: Progress.

Quine, W. V. (1995). *From stimulus to science*. Cambridge, MA: Harvard University Press.

Ricœur, P. (1991). *From text to action: Essays in hermeneutics, II*. Evanston, IL: Northwestern University Press.

Roth, W.-M. (2002). Editorial power/authorial suffering. *Research in Science Education, 32*, 215–240.

Roth, W.-M., Hwang, S., Lee, Y-J., & Goulart, M.I.M. (2005). *Participation, learning, and identity: Dialectical perspectives*. Berlin: Lehmanns Media.

Roth, W.-M., & McRobbie, C. (1999). Lifeworlds and the 'w/ri(gh)ting' of classroom research. *Journal of Curriculum Studies, 31*, 501–522.

Ryle, G. (1971). *Collected papers*. New York: Barnes and Noble.

Smith, D. E. (1990). *Conceptual practices of power: A feminist sociology of knowledge*. Toronto: University of Toronto Press.

Smith, D. E. (1999). *Writing the social: Critique, theory, and investigations*. Toronto: University of Toronto Press.

Star, S. L. (1991). Power, technology and the phenomenology of conventions: on being allergic to onions. In J. Law (Ed.), *A sociology of monsters: Essays on power, technology and domination* (pp. 26–56). London: Routledge.

Wartofsky, M. (1979). *Models: Representations and scientific understanding*. Dordrecht, The Netherlands: Reidel.

White, H. (1987). *The content of the form: Narrative discourse and historical representation*. Baltimore: Johns Hopkins University Press.

Index